Cinemasaurus

Russian Film in Contemporary Context

Film and Media Studies

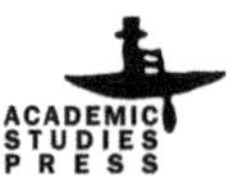

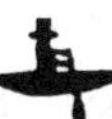

CINEMASAURUS

RUSSIAN FILM IN CONTEMPORARY CONTEXT

EDITED BY
NANCY CONDEE,
ALEXANDER PROKHOROV,
AND ELENA PROKHOROVA

BOSTON / 2020

Library of Congress Cataloging-in-Publication Data

Names: Condee, Nancy, editor. | Prokhorov, Alexander, 1965—editor. | Prokhorova, Elena, editor.
Title: Cinemasaurus : Russian film in contemporary context / edited by Nancy Condee, Alexander Prokhorov, and Elena Prokhorova.
Description: Boston : Academic Studies Press, 2020. | Series: Film and media studies | Includes bibliographical references, filmography, and index.
Identifiers: LCCN 2019044665 (print) | LCCN 2019044666 (ebook) | ISBN 9781644692707 (hardback) | ISBN 9781644692714 (paperback) | ISBN 9781644692721 (adobe pdf)
Subjects: LCSH: Motion pictures—Russia (Federation)—History and criticism. | Motion picture industry--Russia (Federation)
Classification: LCC PN1993.5.R9 C56 2020 (print) | LCC PN1993.5.R9 (ebook) | DDC 791.430947--dc23
LC record available at https://lccn.loc.gov/2019044665
LC ebook record available at https://lccn.loc.gov/2019044666

ISBN 9781644692707 (hardcover)

ISBN 9781644692714 (paperback)

ISBN 9781644692721 (Adobe PDF)

Book design by Tatiana Vernikov
Cover art by Joseph Parker (selfsamegames.com)
Cover design by Ivan Grave

Published by Academic Studies Press
1577 Beacon St.
Brookline, MA 02446, USA

press@academicstudiespress.com
www.academicstudiespress.com

CONTENTS

Part Three. Evropsk or Russia?

Part Four. The Ideological Occult

Part Five. Interviews

LIST OF ILLUSTRATIONS

FOREWORD

Stephen M. Norris

Cinemasaurus is a treasure chest of a book, a compilation that assesses the state of Russian cinema today while helping to classify it usefully. Featuring the work of twelve young scholars—who will no doubt guide the field of Russian cinema for years to come—this volume allows us to learn about the ways recent Russian cinema has embraced new genres, dealt with the flotsam cast aside with the Soviet collapse, and attempted to redefine imperial and national ideas. These features alone make this volume stand out.

Yet the book offers even more. The incubator that hatched these essays—and one that continues to maintain exciting new growth in Russian cinema—is the Kinotavr Film Festival. Created in 1989, Kinotavr is the world's largest regional festival. More importantly, it has played a major part both in the revival of the Russian film industry after 1991 and in fostering a truly creative environment within this film world. The essays in *Cinemasaurus* therefore analyze what Kinotavr has done for contemporary Russian cinema. The films discussed in these chapters were also all reviewed in the online journal *KinoKultura*, which debuted in 2003 and has served as the most important English-language source for regular, insightful reviews of recent Russian films (all the scholars involved in the volume have contributed to it). *KinoKultura* has covered the Kinotavr festival in recent years, helping those of us who cannot make the annual trip to Sochi receive reports of what is happening within the Russian film industry. The remarkable Pittsburgh Russian Film Symposium, now more than two decades old, has also acted as an important venue where scholars, students, critics, and journalists engage in intense dialogue about Russian films (the contributors to this volume have all participated in this symposium too). These three entities—film festival, online journal, and film symposium—in a way have loosely categorized Russian cinema over the last thirty years, so it makes sense that *Cinemasaurus* also includes interviews with the festival organizer, the journal's editor, and the symposium's founder.

Cinemasaurus is a storehouse that will be used for years to come, both as a reminder of what defined Russian cinema at this moment in time and as a means to track future changes in Russian film.

ACKNOWLEDGMENTS

First among the debts we wish to acknowledge for this volume is our gratitude to three extraordinary figures who brought about, sustained, and fostered Kinotavr: Sitora Alieva, Alexander Rodnyansky, and Mark Rudinstein. Their inspiration, determination, and patience offer a model of how to make a lasting contribution to one's home culture and to its place in the world.

Closer to home, we would like to thank our own institutions, the College of William and Mary and the University of Pittsburgh, for their financial and logistical support. At the College of William and Mary, we would like to thank Joseph J. Plumeri for his generous support of faculty research, the College of Arts and Sciences (in particular Kate Conley), the Reves Center for International Studies, the Department of Modern Languages and Literatures (in particular Silvia Tandeciarz), and the Film and Media Studies Program for their continuous support. At the University of Pittsburgh, we would like to thank the Dean's Office of the Kenneth P. Dietrich School of Arts and Sciences (in particular, N. John Cooper and Kathleen Blee), the Department of Slavic Languages and Literatures, the Film and Media Studies Program, the University Center for International Studies (in particular, Larry Feick and Ariel Armony), as well as the staff at the Russian, East European, and Eurasian Studies Center for their patience and generosity. We are grateful, too, for support from the Richard D. and Mary Jane Edwards Endowed Publication Fund (University of Pittsburgh), which provided key assistance in bringing this volume into shape at its final stages.

We would also like to thank our colleagues—more than 150 scholars, journalists, film critics, and programmers in both Russia and elsewhere (many of whose names appear in this volume)—with whom we have been in dialogue for several decades. In particular, we are grateful to colleagues who welcomed us in the halls of the late NII kinoiskusstva, an invaluable research hub that is sorely missed.

This volume has also greatly benefited from conversations with colleagues from the United States, United Kingdom, Austria, the Czech Republic, and Australia who attended the Russian Film Symposium over the course of the past twenty years. Without their ideas and insights, this volume would not have been possible. This list, of course, includes Birgit Beumers, Vladimir

Padunov, and the twelve contributors to this volume, as well as a dozen other younger scholars on whom we did not impose the burden of this work.

Our great thanks, too, to Carolyn Pouncy for her patience and flawless judgment, as well as to the staff of Academic Studies Press, in particular to Igor Nemirovsky. Finally, we thank our families: our absence and distraction are hardly compensated for by this volume, but we offer it as evidence of our commitment to hard work and to an utterly absorbing cultural terrain.

NOTE ON TRANSLITERATION AND TRANSLATIONS

We transliterate Russian-language materials using the Library of Congress system, except when an alternate spelling is either commonly used—for example, Sergei Eisenstein (instead of Sergei Eizenshtein)—or preferred—for example, Alexander Rodnyansky (instead of Aleksandr Rodnianskii). All translations from Russian into English are those of the contributors, unless otherwise noted.

CINEMASAURUS: INTRODUCTION

Nancy Condee, Alexander Prokhorov, and Elena Prokhorova

> There is one integral indicator of the state of Russian cinema after 1988: its absence from the screens of its own country.
>
> —*Daniil Dondurei, "Kinodelo," 1995*

During his curtailed lifetime (1947–2017), film sociologist Daniil Dondurei wrote some of the most trenchant analyses of Russian film in the contemporary period—"contemporary" to him, to us, and to the first readers of this volume. Dondurei's flat expository style—apparently lacking in affect—was designed to goad its reader, who might finally therefore react to the unbearable nature of the situation that he describes. Dondurei's (apparently) chilly tone was a key aspect of his analytic signature: in a voice so recognizably matter-of-fact, relentlessly descriptive, and drained of concern, he reveals no trace of the human who was in fact deeply tormented by the situation he was describing.

Imagine, by analogy, a United States in which—after 1988—we ourselves gradually disappeared from the screen: a year-by-year fading away of Hollywood melo-pageantry, Disney Studio cartoons, arthouse films, documentary, to a point where there were virtually no self-representations on the screens of our home country. By 1995—the year of Dondurei's essay—cinema production had already plummeted and its very existence was uncertain. And while such extreme conditions were in no way evident (yet) in Russia's 1988,[1] that year was nevertheless the moment at which (in retrospect) we can first notice the signs of water in the bulkheads, so to speak.

1 Indeed, at the time, 1988 had seemed to be a promising year for cinema. Soveksportfil'm had left Cannes in 1987 with two million dollars in foreign sales (Fisher). Over the course of 1988, Soviet cinema received sixty major international awards ("State Group"). As of January 1988, the major studios' creative associations were permitted to retain profits (a function of the new self-financing system [*khozraschet*]); to lobby the government for direct support; to hire and fire workers; and to enjoy more creative independence from the studio (Faraday, 131). By 1988, for example, Mosfil'm Studio came to comprise eleven creative associations, led by such key figures as Iurii Arabov, Rolan Bykov, Karen Shakhnazarov, and Sergei Solov'ev. See brief descriptions of these creative associations in *Soviet Film*, no. 5 (1988): 8–9 and 12–17; for Lenfil'm, see *Soviet Film*, no. 8 (1988): 16–17. Later in the same year, the Law on Cooperatives (July 1988) permitted independent production companies, such as Andrei Razumovskii's Fora-Fil'm.

In a culture where exaggerated pathos can often be an everyday affair, Dondurei's cool analysis could not help but make the reader of 1995 respond in protest to such an impending cinematic death. Reading his work became in fact a kind of mithridatism—the voluntary ingestion of life's poison—incrementally, so as not to die from a sudden exposure to its lethal truths. One came to read Dondurei as a precautionary practice of survival. We begin this volume with a tribute to his memory.

Cinemasaurus: Structure and Historical Limits

Our story of contemporary Russian cinema begins in 1991, three years after Dondurei's 1988 alarm, with Vadim Abdrashitov's *Armavir* (Armavir, 1991), a film about a shipwreck. By 1991, cinema had taken on peculiar, even monstrous dimensions. Like an ocean liner raising its huge hull far above the water line just before it reaches the final stage of sinking, the film industry appeared to be growing when in fact it was collapsing: the normally steady late Soviet production rate of roughly 150 full-length feature films a year suddenly rose to 300 films in 1990, then fell to 213 films in 1991 (Segida, 76). By 1994, production had plummeted to sixty-eight full-length feature films, then further still, placing film production for the largest country in the world behind Sweden and Poland.

Then things got worse: in 1996, the nadir of post-Soviet Russian cinema, only thirty-four films reached completion (Segida and Zemlianukhin, *Fil'my Rossii* 2004, 245),[2] and a mere 28–30 percent of promised government production funding was actually provided (Franklin, 13). Yet 1996 was—ironically—the same year that the Law on Cinema was finally signed (after five years) by Boris Yeltsin,[3] providing among other things tax incentives and a daunting set of aspirational responsibilities—heritage conservation, database maintenance, education,

2 Production figures vary from source to source, depending on how the parameters are defined (co-production contribution, release date, etc.). This figure from Segida's and Zemlianukhin's 2004 *Fil'my Rossii: Igrovoe kino/TV/video (1992–2003)* is updated from their earlier (2001) *Fil'my Rossii: Igrovoe kino (1995–2000)*. While this is the nadir of post-Soviet Russian cinema production, it is surpassed by the year 1951, when only nine completed films were released, the smallest number since 1918. Compare Segida and Zemlianukhin, comp., *Domashniaia sinemateka*, 6 (the compilers do not list Vera Stroeva's musical *Grand Concert* [Bol'shoi kontsert, 1951] or Sergei Gerasimov's *Country Doctor* [Sel'skii vrach, 1951]) and Kinoteatr.ru, https://www.kino-teatr.ru/kino/movie/sov/y1951/.

3 See Federal Law. The bill was signed 22 August 1996.

infrastructure development, registration, licensing, promotion (Beumers, "Cinemarket," 976)—for implementation by the state cinema agency Roskomkino.[4]

It is at this historical moment—as the waters finished settling over *Armavir*—that our story seeks coherence around four key themes. Two of these themes—most evident in parts one and three—are geographically inflected. Part one concerns cinema that returns to, among other projects, the irresolvable challenges of empire and periphery, in particular the eastern periphery. In chapters by Olga Kim, Justin Wilmes, and Ellina Sattarova, existing geographic determinacies (or so they would seem to be) and the imaginative resistance to those empirical constraints are rendered more complex by the spectacular resurgence of a new, archaic empire in a blockbuster era.

Skipping ahead to part three, this shared geographic orientation takes a different turn, away from the metropole and eastern periphery to other sites. These include the problematic category of "heartland," that region within the empire where the discursive "folk" (*narod*) resides. This folk matters for reasons that extend far beyond the remit of this volume (or cinema, for that matter). Let us limit ourselves to the assertion—polemical for some, self-evident for others—that the substantial differences between "folk" and "nation" (as a post-1789 aspiration) sustain complex contradictions between Russia's overland empire and the discursive nation-state as a recent, constructed myth founded on the principles of liberty, equality, and fraternity. This distinction between "folk" and "nation"—a stubborn cultural failure of synonymity—highlights the debates between an imperial genesis story rooted, on the one hand, in birth, earth, and mother (to which Herderian tradition bears affinities); and a genesis story rooted in self-determination, revolt, and populist autonomy, on the other. While these debates are reducible neither to this rude dichotomy (the presumption, for example, that the imperial folk cannot enact the aspirations of nationhood) nor to a set of expressive homologies (e.g., "heartland" = "true Russia"), the difference between "folk" and "nation" animates many of the arguments contained in part three.

Related to this geographical preoccupation with heartland are two related questions that circulate in part three. Both concern the nature of marginality and a gaze turned westward. The first question (a painful contemporary question: "who is marginal to whom?") stages

4 In 1996, Roskomkino was renamed—once again—Goskino, as it had been known from 1978 to its initial elimination in November 1991. See, for example, Razlogov, "Gosudarstvennyi," 100–101; and Beumers, "Cinemarket," 872–73.

a polemical inversion: what if Russia's western periphery demarcated that place where Russia became peripheral to a European Ukraine? This second question concerns the transformation of marginality from a geographic category to one grounded in identity debates, including those to which the hegemonic culture (both on the screen and in the offices of the Ministry of Culture) is averse. In chapters by Zhanna Budenkova, Tetyana Shlikhar, and Trevor Wilson, these three incompatible engagements with marginality—the heartland, the western periphery, and identity otherness—form the core concern of part three.

If geography has been the underlying preoccupation of parts one and three, then parts two and four concern the actors—literal and metaphorical—who inhabit this vast geography in time. These two parts offer a different cluster of arguments about agency, both government-sponsored and privatized. Agency brings a host of other considerations: generic visions of identity, body politics, legitimacy of violence, authorship, and entrepreneurial models of film production.

Part two participates in a debate that has enlivened both journalism and academic writing for all three of the decades under examination here. That debate concerns the point at which we become horrified not only at the bedlam that is laid out in hilarious proportions on the screen before us, but also at ourselves for having taken perverse delight in the fatal inevitability of bedlam. When does hilarity become horror? When does the fêted eccentricity of Russian screen behavior become an exercise in the Grotesque, a category with its own trans-European cultural traditions? The violence of contemporary Russian cinema is legendary, dominating discussions equally at Western film festivals, domestic press conferences, and the columns of an outraged nationalist press. Russian cinema's violence is sometimes understood to be the legacy of genocide and (by this logic) even a healthy search for equilibrium. As the topic of contemporary state violence becomes increasingly foreclosed, and violence accordingly becomes framed as a practice of private entrepreneurship, how do we understand each other as viewers—at times, mutually accusatory of complicity or political correctness? Chapters by Daria Ezerova, Robert Crane, and Denis Saltykov examine the elusive and protean limits of acceptable laughter, the utopian space of eccentricity, and the function of privatized violence in the social order.

Part four—to which we have assigned the enigmatic title of "The Ideological Occult"—looks to the figure of the revenant, the familiar element that returns to the screen, initially unrecognized or disavowed but deeply familiar and even comforting. This pattern is by no means a matter of the return of Soviet times—as Olga Mukhortova argues, the re-visitor may be a reconfigured *auteur*, legendary from Soviet times but in fact a more ancient ancestor from Western film theory. Theodora Trimble poses important questions about visual representations of patrimony and celebrity culture. Unavoidably these visions of patriarchy raise questions of heteronormative masculinity and modes of its visual sustainability. Beach Gray explores the magic solution to all problems at once: the cinematic franchise, in which the benevolent state and its aspirational geography become one on New Year's television screens. The horrific revenant—just for one magic New Year's night—turns into its avuncular double in Timur Bekmambetov's *Elki* franchise. But the unsettling and—we would argue—occult question remains: when the 2018 viewers of Anton Megerdichev's *Going Vertical* (also known as *Three Seconds*) (Dvizhenie vverkh, 2017) rise and applaud a 1973 victory over the United States, what time and space does this audience inhabit?

Our volume concludes with two additional contributions. The first of these is a series of short interviews with key figures in the Russian cinema industry and with its Western interlocutors: Russia's most prominent media executive Alexander Rodnyansky; its leading festival programmer, Sitora Alieva; a key US entrepreneur, Paul Heth, who has been instrumental in Russia's transition to a post-Soviet exhibition system; and the two Western colleagues whose work (the journal *KinoKultura* and the Russian Film Symposium) has provided invaluable scaffolding for our ongoing engagement with contemporary Russian cinema.

A second closing contribution, Kino-Grafik, is an idiosyncratic timeline. To be sure, other, more comprehensive timelines exist and deserve scholarly attention.[5] Our Kino-Grafik combines an informational resource with an invitation to a conversation: for each year (without commentary), it provides five "unrelated" facts: the year's prizewinners in three distinct competitions (the Kinotavr Grand Prize, the Nika, and the nationalist Golden Eagle Awards);[6] a Word of the Year that appeared in mass circulation; and a significant political event. More a puzzle than a historian's aid, our Kino-Grafik is intended to open a portal: Why were such

5 See Arkus, *Noveishaia*; Beumers, *History*, 260–91; Beumers, ed., *Companion*, 585–613; Dziewańska et al., 11–85; Fomin's four volumes of *Letopis'*; and Kudriavtsev, 467–92.

6 The Nika Award, conferred by the Russian Academy of Motion Picture Arts and Sciences, was established in 1987 by actor-director Iulii Gusman. As Russia's most prestigious national film award, it is often contrasted with the Oscars (conferred by the Academy of Motion Picture Arts and Sciences). At the domestic level, the Nika is contrasted with the Golden Eagle Award (National Academy of Motion Picture Arts and Sciences of Russia), established in 2002 by Nikita Mikhalkov and awarded in both cinema and television.

different cinemas recognized by Kinotavr, Nika, and Golden Eagle? Why did a particular word capture the public imagination? Where do politics figure in this (at times) rarefied world of cinema production? In the spirit of Daniil Dondurei, we aim to provoke the reader into providing the other half of our (as yet, intentionally incomplete) dialogue.

What Is a Cinemasaurus?

It is difficult to define a word that does not exist. Let us start instead by suggesting that the thesaurus is a text that groups words together in a very specific way, not by *fixed meaning*, but by *similarities of meaning*, in a cluster, constellation, or environment of sense. Unlike a dictionary, a thesaurus never tells us what something means; instead, it situates a given word in a spectrum, alongside kindred ideas, their juxtapositions serving as contrast as well as common filiation. In contrast to a dictionary, the thesaurus—to quote Peter Mark Roget (1779–1869), compiler of the best-known "thesaurary," as he sometimes called it—seeks to "find the word, or words, by which [an] idea may be most fitly and aptly expressed" (Kendall, 266). It is fitting that the archaic Scottish "thesaurary" (from Middle English) is closely related to "treasury," offering the reader a collection of things one values, and for which one holds oneself responsible to account.[7]

If the thesaurus is a treasury of words, constellated so as to highlight their similarities and differences, so this cinemasaurus is a constellation of film tendencies. If the word-based thesaurus is concerned with natural language, the cinemasaurus provides a secondary modeling system,[8] juxtaposing artistic texts so as to point up their shared and divergent habits

7 See http://www.dsl.ac.uk/entry/dost/thesaurary. For background information, see Skretcowicz et al., comp., *Dictionary of the Scots Language* [Dictionar o the Scots Leid], an intercompilation of two historical dictionaries, *A Dictionary of the Older Scottish Tongue* (twelve volumes: twelfth century to 1700) and *The Scottish National Dictionary* (ten volumes: 1700–2005).

8 The reference here is to cyberneticist Vladimir Uspenskii, associated with the early years of semiotics, later developed by Juri Lotman (95–98). Here, we use the term with an awareness of Uspenskii's wry comment that "secondary modeling" (*vtorichnoe modelirovanie*) served primarily to hide the more contentious term "semiotics" at a time when the latter word met official opprobrium (e.g., the 19–26 December 1962 Symposium on the Structural Studies of Sign Systems at Moscow's Institute of Slavic and Balkan Studies). As Uspenskii (Grishakova and Salupere, 176) explained to Lotman, the term "secondary modeling systems" had several advantages: "(1) it sounded very scientific [*zvuchit ochen' nauchno*]; (2) was completely incomprehensible; (3) if really needed, it could be explained: primary modeling systems that model reality are natural languages,

of thought. It does not aspire to provide the meaning of Russia's contemporary films, but rather to cluster them around shared preoccupations: a cinemasaurus of similarities and contrasts.

There is, however, another association at least as relevant to the volume's title. Kinotavr is Russia's most successful film festival—and indeed the largest regional festival worldwide. "Kinotavr" is an odd word in any language, perhaps an extrapolation from the Minotaur (half human, half bull), who dwelt at the center of the Labyrinth;[9] or "centaur" (half human, half horse), who carried off Hippodamia on her wedding day; or bucentaur (half ox), onocentaur (half donkey), and on through the imaginary wildlife park. If this is correct, then "kinotavr" is "cinetaur": half human, half cinema, as if part of our bodies were transformed into a cinema object. Elusive as the mythical animal itself, Kinotavr has been the totem being around which Russian cinema of the late twentieth and early twenty-first centuries has taken on enhanced cultural meaning.

Cinemasaurus, therefore, borrows from each of these—the thesaurus, the minotaur, and Kinotavr—all three sharing creative juxtaposition, unforeseen revelation, and the shock of the new.

What Is on Offer Here?

This volume has three aspirations. First, it offers a view of contemporary Russian cinema of the three decades as a collection of loosely related visual practices. The twelve chapters presented here aspire, on the one hand, to accept those practices on their own (individual and incompatible) terms—as a credible set of pageantries, anxieties, preoccupations, celebrations, self-parodies, panoramas, nightmares, reveries, carnivals, and other ranging concerns. On the other hand, the volume seeks to look for recurrences, patterns, or—to use a sacred term—

and all the rest that build upon them are secondary." See also Vladimir Uspenskii, 99–127; and Vladimir A. Uspenskii. Uspenskii recommended to Lotman that the latter adopt the term (see relevant documents in *Simpozium*; Vladimir Uspenskii, 99–127; and Zalizniak et al.).

9 A more local association bringing "Minotaur" into renewed circulation was Arkadii and Georgii Vainer's detective-adventure novel *Visit to the Minotaur* [Vizit k Minotavru, 1971], which first appeared in the journal *Searcher* [Iskatel'] in July 1971 (part 1) and January 1972 (part 2), in the Vainers' series "Investigator Tikhonov." The complete novel was published by Molodaia Gvardiia in 1972. In 1987—two years before the start of Mark Rudinshtein's 1989 effort to launch what would become Kinotavr—the novel was filmed as a television series with the same title, directed by El'dor Urazbaev (1940–2012).

observances that might resonate with each other across the thirty years of this historical tranche in which we have lived. When possible, the contributors situate their observations in the social context of the period, in hopes of teasing out additional moments of significance outside the cinematic text, while at the same time making no claim to writing a cultural history.

A second aspiration is the registering of work by young scholars who—with luck—will outlast us and for whom this volume is an introduction into a profession in rapid transition. This younger generation of scholars must work with rapidly changing regimes of production and consumption in transmedia storytelling, all of which call for fresh methodological approaches. Our younger colleagues also conduct their research across a minefield: have Cold War binaries returned to the analysis of cultural production, or are the similarities merely spectral, a familiar and comforting pattern that conceals radically changed rules of engagement?

Third, the volume is an in-kind contribution to work done over several decades by three key institutions that—with no intentional effort to work in synchrony—nevertheless are at the very center of cinema analysis. The three institutions—a major regional festival, a journal, an academic symposium—are vastly different in scale, economic heft, media visibility, and influence, but each has played a definitional role for US and UK scholars of Russian cinema. The three institutions have unintentionally become interdeterminative of how we understand Russian cinema of the present moment.

We would like to sketch each briefly in order to map out the ways in which—from Russia to the United Kingdom to the United States—this infrastructural triad has had a profound impact on how Anglophone (and not only Anglophone) scholars conceive of the cinema of Russia and its near neighbors.

Kino . . . tavr . . . *Kul'tura* . . . Sympozium

Whether in feudal pledge, academic analysis, or artistic style, "homage" signals a dedication to an earlier source that has had a profound and sustained effect on those who offer the homage. Ranging from arcane allusion to rank imitation, the homage may be explicit or may be barely visible, deeply embedded in the cultural expression itself. At the center of this triad is the Kinotavr Film Festival. And while Kinotavr's date of birth might be a topic of legalistic debate, the cinema community chooses 1989, four years before it was officially registered as "Kinotavr" (1993).

Twenty-five miles south of Moscow, Mark Rudinshtein lived in Podol'sk and ran Moscow Outskirts (Podmoskov'e), a modest show-business firm that booked concerts, film screenings, video rentals, and rock festivals. In 1989, Moscow Outskirts organized the Festival of Unbought Cinema (Festival' nekuplennogo kino), the beginnings of what came to be unofficially known (1990) as Kinotavr. This 1990 First Open Festival attracted some twenty "unbought" films, including Vitalii Kanevskii's (now classic) drama *Freeze, Die, Come to Life* (Zamri—umri—voskresni, 1989), with a jury headed by film journalist and scholar Elena Bokshitskaia.[10] By 1991, Kinotavr had moved to Sochi, where Mark Rudinshtein was soon joined in 1993 by actor Oleg Iankovskii as the festival's president.

A worthy history of Kinotavr would be a volume unto itself. Because our focus is closer to the present, we will skip ahead to 2005, when Kinotavr was transferred to Alexander Rodnyansky (chair, Board of Trustees) and Igor' Tolstunov (general producer), with a board that signaled it had come of age.[11] The festival survived the economic crisis of 2008, but the effects of that shock were considerable and may have contributed to Igor' Tolstunov's sale of his partnership to Alexander Rodnyansky in 2010 (Tolstunov). By that time, Alexander Rodnyansky had founded A.R. Films, which housed Non-Stop Production, the independent film distribution company Cinema without Frontiers (Kino bez granits), as well as Kinotavr, by then the world's largest and most successful regional festival.

Of the many strengths of the festival, perhaps the most remarkable has been the guiding hand of Sitora Alieva, the festival's program director who has demonstrated by example what it means to shape the contemporary film environment through a diversity of films in vertiginous juxtaposition.[12] Together with a dedicated Selection Committee keenly attuned to

10 Elena Bokshitskaia, founder and editor-in-chief of the newspaper *House of Cinema* (Dom kino), went on to work as artistic director of Kinotavr during its first years in Sochi (1991–92). She was elected co-president (1992–94) of the Guild of Film Scholars and Film Critics, serving together with Miron Chernenko (1992–2004).

11 The Kinotavr Board initially included Petr Aven (Alfa Bank), Oleg Deripaska (Russian Aluminum), Konstantin Ernst (Channel One Russia), Vitalii Ignatenko (ITAR-TASS), Mikhail Shvydkoi (Federal Agency for Culture and Cinematography), and Aleksandr Tkachev (governor, Krasnodar Region). This is the moment when the festival's mascot of the three-legged "cinetaur" was replaced by the yellow and blue "sun-and-sea" logo. See Maslova.

12 Let us take, for example, the year 2007, in which the fiercest competitors for the Grand Prize were Aleksei Popogrebskii's sunny *Simple Things* (Prostye veshchi, 2007) and Aleksei Balabanov's neo-noir *Cargo 200* (Gruz 200). Without adjudicating their artistic merits, one could safely say that these two films inhabit incompatible cinematic universes; the fact that the jury chose to award Popogrebskii the Grand Prize is a sociological fact

the differences among domestic, international, and festival exhibition practices,[13] Sitora Alieva has provided a fearless model of how to challenge the utterly incompatible expectations of the public, elite journal critics, and fickle juries, while providing viewers with remarkable films they would otherwise be unlikely to see.[14] In the words of one well-known colleague (Razlogov, "Kinotavr"),[15] whose professional loyalties cannot easily be reduced to the Kinotavr community:

> Kinotavr also confirms that a creative environment has emerged, not a homogenous one but a heterogeneous one. The festival's program of films clearly demonstrates the variety of directions in which the television company that organizes it is currently working. Honor and praise to Aleksandr Rodnianskii [*sic*], who screens films at his festival that are deeply alien to him as a media magnate. . . . In principle, Kinotavr has the potential . . . to close the gap between television magnates and film industry figures as they continue to participate in it.

A second addressee of the volume is the quarterly cinema journal *KinoKultura* and its founding editor, Birgit Beumers, who is an international scholar in her own right.[16] Here, though, she is framed as an initiator of two key cinema journals.[17] Launched in 2003, *KinoKultura* is the profession's leading periodical in new Russian cinema. It has been an international crossroads

worthy of sustained analysis (for which, see Razlogov, "Kinotavr," for example).

13 The frequent team for the Selection Committee includes Viktoriia Belopol'skaia (Kul'tura [Culture] television channel), Evgenii Gusiatinskii (critic, *Russian Reporter* [Russkii reporter]), Sergei Lavrent'ev (cinema historian), Irina Liubarskaia (critic, *Sources* [Itogi]), and Alena Solntseva (critic, *Moscow News* [Moskovskie novosti]).

14 Among the best Grand Prize films unlikely otherwise to reach viewers, for example, is Uzman Saparov's *Little Angel, Make Me Happy* (Angelochek, sdelai radost', 1994).

15 Kirill Razlogov has also been host of the television program *Cult Cinema* (Kul't kino) on the Russia-Kul'tura television channel; he is currently president of the Guild of Film Scholars and Critics of the Russian Federation. From 1989 to 2013, he was director of the Russian Institute for Cultural Research.

16 See the many citations and bibliographic references to Birgit Beumers's work in this volume.

17 Birgit Beumers's other major periodical initiative, *Studies in Russian and Soviet Cinema*, was launched in 2007, first at Intellect Books and then (from 2014 onward) at Taylor & Francis. The journal tends to focus on a broader historical range—prerevolutionary, Soviet, and post-Soviet Russian cinema—as well as the cinema industry, aesthetics, and ideology.

for scholars, journalists, and critics from at least three generations—including first-year PhD students, whose first publication is often in this venue.

The journal's collaborative ties to colleagues in the Russian Federation are close: in 2006, the Guild of Film Scholars and Critics of the Russian Federation, the country's leading professional organization, awarded *KinoKultura* a diploma for providing a publication venue where cinema scholars from a broad range of countries, languages, specialties, and expertise have found an audience. Together with the journal's deputy editors and guest editors,[18] Birgit Beumers has also produced nearly twenty special issues devoted to the cinemas of East Central Europe, Central Asia (2004), and the other post-Soviet states.[19] These issues are invaluable to the field: outside their own communities, the cinemas of smaller cultures would otherwise never have found a larger environment of cinema scholars with whom to debate, compare notes, and collaborate.

The third addressee is the Pittsburgh Russian Film Symposium, the longest-running US forum for contemporary and historical Russian cinema.[20] Since its May 1999 founding by Vladimir Padunov, the weeklong symposium has screened more than three hundred films (feature films, documentaries, and shorts); it has brought in five Russian directors,[21] as well as Pittsburgh's own director George Romero (*Night of the Living Dead*; *Dawn of the Dead*, etc.). Other professionals have included Russia's leading scriptwriter (Aleksandr Mindadze, now also a director), film actor (Sergei Makovetskii), conceptualist performance artist (Dmitrii Prigov), and two film producers (Sergei Chliants and Evgenii Gindilis). Nearly fifty of Russia's most prominent film critics, historians, and theorists have engaged in debate and dialogue

18 The deputy editors have been US scholar Vladimir Padunov (2003–8) and UK scholar Julian Graffy (2008–).

19 These include special issues on the cinemas of Armenia (2016), Azerbaijan (2018), Estonia (2010), Georgia (2011), Latvia (2012), and Ukraine (2009). Its scholarly reach into East Central Europe has included special issues on the cinemas of Albania (2016), Bosnia (2012), Bulgaria (2006), Croatia (2011), the Czech Republic (2006), Hungary (2008), Macedonia (2015), Poland (2005), Romania (2007), Serbia (2009), and Slovakia (2005).

20 Over its two decades, the Russian Film Symposium has attracted media attention in such fora as the émigré daily *Novoe russkoe slovo*, the Voice of America, Russian elite journals (*Iskusstvo kino* [Art of the Cinema] and *Kinovedcheskie zapiski* [Cinema Studies Notes]), and the popular press (*Novye izvestiia* [New News] and *Novaia gazeta* [New Paper]).

21 These are Vadim Abdrashitov, Aleksandr Bashirov, Khusein Erkenov, Rustam Ibragimbekov, and Larisa Sadilova.

with international film faculty and PhD students from Australia, the Czech Republic, Hungary, Germany, the United Kingdom, and across the United States.[22]

In the current geopolitical climate, the sustained interaction and collaboration among these three actors—utterly incomparable in scale though they may be to each other—is a source of intellectual sustenance at a time of highly contaminated global debate. If one can speak of Russian culture's contribution to transnational civil society, it would include the example set by these colleagues, institutions, and activities.

Postscript

An odd set of circumstances brings together two elements of this introduction. First, it turns out that Roget himself has a serendipitous relation to cinema, even before there was such a thing. In 1824, he presented his "Explanation of an Optical Deception in the Appearance of the Spokes of a Wheel Seen through Vertical Apertures." History came to show—sadly enough—that Roget's explanation was factually wrong; it nevertheless contributed to a history of animation based on the misperception of continuous motion, a precursor to the "wonder turner" (thaumatrope) and, more familiarly, the zoetrope that shows us repeated sequences of motion. It would be overstatement to claim a connection between Roget's "Explanation of an Optical Deception" and the cinemasaurus introduced here, but we will suggest there is a thin link all the same.

A second connection—again, more rhetorical than empirical—is the historical fact that our effort—like Roget's—is multigenerational. Following its inception in 1805, Roget's *Thesaurus*

22 Other Russian Federation and regional guests as of the time of this writing include Gulnara Abikeyeva, Liubov' Arkus, Oleg Aronson, Anzhelika Artiukh, Petr Bagrov, Ekaterina Barabash, Viktoriia Belopol'skaia, Miron Chernenko, Aleksandr Deriabin, Anton Dolin, Marina Drozdova, Iurii Gladil'shchikov, Denis Gorelov, Valeriia Gorelova, Svetlana Ishevskaia, Nikolai Izvolov, Sergei Kapterev, Andrei Khrenov, Aleksandr Kiselev, Svetlana Khokhriakova, Aleksandr Kolbovskii, Dmitrii Komm, Vsevolod Korshunov, Pavel Kuznetsov, Kseniia Leont'eva, Larisa Maliukova, Igor' Mantsov, Evgenii Margolit, Viktor Matizen, Elena Petrovskaia, Andrei Plakhov, Elena Plakhova, Kirill Razlogov, Irina Rubanova, Dmitrii Savel'ev, Ol'ga Shervud, Irina Shilova, Aleksandr Shpagin, Natal'ia Sirivlia, Alena Solntseva, Elena Stishova, Igor' Sukhmanov, Oleg Sul'kin, Sergei Sychev, Diliara Tasbulatova, Mikhail Trofimenkov, Nina Tsyrkun, Maya Turovskaya, and Neia Zorkaia. The symposium's film introductions, responses, discussions, and roundtables are digitally recorded and are available at the symposium's webpage (http://www.rusfilm.pitt.edu). During their visits, cinema professionals and scholars have donated publications and media copies to the university's library, contributing to what has become one of the largest collections of materials on Russian and Commonwealth of Independent States (CIS) cinema in the Western hemisphere.

was taken up in turn by his son, John Lewis Roget (1828–1908) and then by his grandson Samuel Romilly Roget (1875–1952), six years after the lexicographer's death at the age of ninety. We think of this book as an analogous multigenerational commitment, tying our own past to the future of younger scholars who have already become as entranced by the "wonder turner" of Russian cinema as we ourselves have been.

Filmography

Abdrashitov, Vadim, dir. *Armavir* (Armavir, 1991).

Balabanov, Aleksei, dir. *Cargo 200* (Gruz 200, 2007).

Gerasimov, Sergei, dir. *Country Doctor* (Sel'skii vrach, 1951).

Kanevskii, Vitalii, dir. *Freeze, Die, Come to Life* (Zamri—umri—voskresni, 1989).

Megerdichev, Anton. *Going Vertical* (also known as *Three Seconds*) (Dvizhenie vverkh, 2017).

Popogrebskii, Aleksei, dir. *Simple Things* (Prostye veshchi, 2007).

Romero, George, dir. *Dawn of the Dead*. 1978.

———. *Night of the Living Dead*. 1968.

Saparov, Uzman, dir. *Little Angel, Make Me Happy* (Angelochek, sdelai radost', 1994).

Stroeva, Vera, dir. *Grand Concert* (Bol'shoi kontsert, 1951).

Urazbaev, El'dor, dir. *Visit to the Minotaur* (Vizit k Minotavru, 1987). Television series.

Part One

BORDERS OF IMPERIAL DESIRE

Framing Essay

Nancy Condee

Our section title—borders of imperial desire—invites the reader's speculation about several understandings of "borders." For us, the first is historical: the border of 1991, when the Soviet Union encountered a decisive temporal limit beyond which the world's first socialist empire ceased to exist. A second border that informs the chapters in this section is a geographic one: new spatial limits, set as a result of successive independence declarations by the Soviet republics, profoundly reconfigured the Russian territory of 1991. These border changes were not a mere substitution of solid lines where dotted ones had earlier been: when the USSR collapsed, "Russia"—if we take this as a shorthand for both the Soviet Union and its successor state—lost more than two million square miles, territory considerably larger than that of India.[1]

A third set of borders examined in this section are demographic: the ascribed border, for example, between the titular ethnicity and Russia's many minorities, including migrants into post-Soviet Russia from Central Asia, the Caucasus, and elsewhere. A fourth border is juridical: the boundary between legal and shadow economic systems (as well as cross-border remittances), between normative and antisocial models of behavior. Finally, the period witnesses successive violations of ideological borders—the end to state jamming of radio broadcasting (1988); to the Communist Party's monopoly on political power (1990); and to the bipolar world itself (the 1997 Russo-Chinese declaration of a multipolar world order), reconfiguring, as we used to say, the "imaginary relationship of individuals to their real conditions of existence" (Althusser, *Lenin*, 109).

In the same historical context, military engagement at Russia's southern peripheries served as a backdrop to northern metropolitan life: the First Chechen War (1994–96); the military conflicts in Dagestan (1999); the protracted Second Chechen War (1999–2009); the war in

1 The loss of approximately 2,047,870 square miles is in fact considerably larger than the size of India (1.24 million square miles in 2013). Reduced by 24 percent of its late Soviet size (8,649,538 square miles in 1991), the Russian Federation today occupies 6,601,668 square miles. Both polities (the USSR and the Russian Federation) are, of course, smaller than the Russian Empire at its largest (approximately 8.8 million square miles during the period of 1815–67). See Central Intelligence Agency, *The World Factbook*; *Nationmaster*; and *World Bank: Data (Land Area)*.

Georgia and surrounding territories (2009); the separatist insurgencies in the North Caucasus, including Ingushetia (2009–17); and military incursions in Eastern Ukraine and the seizure of Crimea (from 2014 to the current day). Mars and Minerva—the sword and the pen, violence and wisdom, southern military action and its (largely) northern artistic representation—intertwined in a shifting choreography of slaughter and culture. A perpetual administrative renegotiation of permissible representation—culture's boundaries to what may be visually and narratively authorized—has been very much at the heart of how Russia's newly configured socialities are staged for its own citizenry. Contemporary Russian cinema found itself at the very center of an effort by "those who live in the aftermath of calamity," as Olga Kim puts it in her chapter, to forge new matrices of attachment.

It is a recurring truism about empire that its borders are unstable, permeable, and fluid; its territorial limits are marked by a tolerance for "both/and," rather than the "either/or" of the idealized nation-state. The empire's expansionist assertions of sovereignty are—paradoxically—executed in a fashion than perpetually militates *against* sustainable sovereignty, if we understand "sovereignty" to mean the ability to defend authority over territory. I will refer to this pattern as a recurrent spatial contradiction of empire.

A second contradiction, also relevant to the three chapters that follow, might correspondingly be framed as a temporal contradiction; it concerns the trajectory of Soviet collapse. We are accustomed to believe that the life of empire follows a linear path, for which the emblematic Western example is the British Empire—a country on which, as the pseudonymous Christopher Norris said of George IV's dominion, "the sun never set" (North, 527).[2] Or at least it did not set for 350 years, until it set altogether in 1931 (the Statute of Westminster) or in the post-1945 period (the 1947 partition of India, the 1948 abandonment of Palestine) or in 1997 (the transfer of Hong Kong). This myth of an empire's linear trajectory is neither true nor false but merely compelling—culturally familiar to our lived experience.

But "empire life" for Russia, by contrast—whether or not contiguous empires are themselves a consistent set—embodies a different myth: the Russian "sun" did not set forever in 1917 or in 1991 (or—more controversially—back in 1610). Its empire life has turned out to be relentlessly

2 "Not a more abstemious man than old Kit North in his Majesty's dominions, on which the sun never sets." The pseudonym "Christopher Norris" was used by John Wilson (1785–1854). On the complex authorship of "Noctes Ambrosianae," see Wardle.

cyclical, a recurrent story of expansion and collapse. And while Russia's cultural artifacts may sometimes craft the Russian collapse as a linear apocalypse—as in Pskov monk Filofei's 1510 prognosis (Toumanoff, 438) to Grand Duke Vasili III ("two Romes have fallen; the third stands; a fourth shall never be")—this millennialist streak in Russia's cultural mentality is infused all the same with a latent certainty that the empire will return, since there is no other choice. "Britain's oceans"—if that is what they were once envisioned as being—turned out to have more fleeting claims to dominion than the stubborn expanse of Russia's contiguous lands. It is this apparent temporal contradiction—anxiety of "permanent disappearance" coupled with the conviction of "eternal return"—that informs several moments in the chapters that follow.

One might consider that these two contradictions—the spatial expansionism that conditions its own collapse; the temporal apocalypse that promises return—share a cyclical pattern, an agriculturally inflected emphasis on a consoling rise and fall; a wax and wane that would confirm its innate self-sufficiency and affinity to the natural world (hence "natively" immune to scrutiny).

Olga Kim begins chapter 1 with Walter Benjamin's (*Origin*, 194) emblem of the rose "simultaneously half in bloom and half faded, and the sun rising and setting in the same landscape." To these two emblems, she adds the example of the building site, in a state of simultaneous construction and decay. The sleepwalkers and revenants invoked in her chapter title ("Somnambulants, Ghosts") retain some kind of knowledge, but it is a knowledge unavailable to those same creatures in their earlier state—as the woken subject or as the living being. They operate instead by some kind of "aftermath knowledge" with its own logic and laws.

A different "eternal return" can be found in chapter 2, in several films examined by Justin Wilmes ("Empire Reloaded: Sacred Power in a Postmodern Era"). Here the return is not seasonal but regulatory, even convenantal. The cycle is enacted by the subject's—typically, the male subject's—recurrent suturing of his will to state power. The young financier Maks (Roman Prygunov's *Dukhless 2* [Dukhless 2, 2015]) must return to Putin's Moscow in order to help confront the larger Western threat. The young Viking prince Vladimir (Andrei Kravchuk, *Viking* [Viking, 2016]) must return to Novgorod to assume power after the death of his father Sviatoslav I, first defeating Iaropolk and then taking up the larger challenge of Byzantium. In Fedor Bondarchuk's *Stalingrad* (2013), the soldier Sergei—last surviving member of the doomed "five fathers"—dies, calling in an air strike against his fireteam's own building (later memorialized as Pavlov's House), a symbolic bulwark of resistance against the vastly superior German army. Yet his unborn child (also Sergei), once grown, returns at the film's end to close the framing narrative: as a post-Soviet rescue worker, the young Sergei also serves humanity in extremis, young German victims of the 2011 Japanese tsunami. The younger Sergei's heroic aid as a state rescue worker resurrects and honors his father's wartime heroism.

The patriotic-militarist tenor of this last example is grounded in a repetition that extends even to the conditions of its production: both the director, Fedor Bondarchuk, and his actor Andrei Smoliakov had earlier also participated in Iurii Ozerov's 1990 *Stalingrad*; actor Thomas Kretschmann had acted in Joseph Vilsmaier's 1993 *Stalingrad*—as if (by some apotropaic logic) such cinematic repetition would pass the war knowledge along and thereby ward off its reenactment in real life.

An analogous knowledge-beyond-knowledge informs the films examined by Ellina Sattarova in "Russia's Quiet Other"). Dmitrii Mamuliia's *Another Sky* (Drugoe nebo, 2010) and Aleksandr Kott's *The Test* (Ispytanie, 2014), despite their apparent differences, share the act of remaining silent as a precondition for accessing a different kind of knowledge. Kott's "silent" film—with ambient sound, but virtually stripped of human speech—and Mamuliia's film, in which key episodes pass without dialogue, share a stubborn commitment to gesture over speech. The cultural text's "gesture of silence" (*signum harpocraticum*)—traditionally portrayed in the visual arts as a figure who holds a finger over his or her lips—has a history that is both long and broad across the arts (Zhizhina).[3] The figure classically serves as both the subject matter and the artist (in our case, the film and the film director), cautioning the viewer on how to be in the presence of the text. The *signum harpocraticum*, an allegorical call for restraint in the presence of a higher truth that is "more interior than the lips and the tongue" (Bitton-Ashkelony, 303–31), has survived into the secular era, even during the Soviet years through a well-known series of Soviet posters and statuary, most often as a call to patriotism.[4] The post-Soviet

3 See also Bitton-Ashkelony, Muers; Panou; Russell; Thunø; and Tikkanen.

4 The most familiar Soviet legatees of *signum harpocraticum* include Nina Vatolina's and Nikolai Denisov's 1941 poster *Do Not Blab!* (Ne boltai!), which enjoins the viewer to refrain from loose speech in an awareness of the higher commitment to the Motherland. Vatolina's and Denisov's peasant heroine was later mass-produced as a 1959 bronze statuette (artist unknown). I thank Sean Guillory and Tricia McGough for directing my attention to this example. Other instances of Soviet *signum harpocraticum* include Viktor Dobrovol'skii's 1941 poster and Iurii Chudov's 1958 poster of the same title, with male figures adjuring us to silence for the sake of a higher purpose.

invocation to silence, in the films examined here by Sattarova, eschews patriotism for a return to the tradition's more metaphysical knowledge-beyond-knowledge.

"When we are tired," Friedrich Nietzsche was supposed to have said, "we are attacked by ideas we had conquered long ago."[5] Many of Russia's governing limits—historical, territorial, demographic, juridical, ideological—have been abandoned, reinstated, exceeded, and recontained during the thirty years under consideration here. The 1990 ban, for example, on one-party monopoly was a hard fact; today, it is less of a fact. Indeed, it is increasingly evident that a strong, one-party system may be an integral and enduring element of Russian political life. Cinema's capacity to capture the contradictions described above—without premature resolution of their tensions—renders film one of the most productive cultural practices of Russian social life today.

5 It is doubtful that this quotation is from Friedrich Nietzsche's work, although it has been customary for the last sixty years to attribute it to him. For its first documented attribution, see Flesch, 124. For a history of the quotation's (mis-)attribution, see Quote Investigator. I am grateful to Kira Condee-Padunova and Peter Price for their efforts to track down this "mis-genealogy."

1. Imperial Fatigue: Somnambulants, Ghosts, and Monsters

Olga Kim

If one were to represent the thesis of this chapter in a single image, it might paradoxically look like the ruins of a building that has yet to be constructed. Along the lines of Walter Benjamin's reading (*Origin*, 194) of the baroque emblem, where "a rose [is] simultaneously half in bloom and half faded, and the sun rising and setting in the same landscape," I imagine a construction site of a not-yet-built but already decaying building, not an uncommon sight across post-Soviet space. This oxymoronic ruinous site of simultaneous de- and reconstruction is perhaps one of the chief characteristics of the post-Soviet condition that persists to this day.[1] This is perhaps the condition of indeterminate suspension of any historical teleology or unifying project, be it the project of nation-state building, imperial renovation, or something else. Cracks, fragments, and ruins—in both literal and figurative senses—are the hieroglyphs of this uncertain and ambiguous site. How some post-Soviet films figure various aspects of this ruinous site and reflect upon this condition is the primary inquiry of this chapter.

My interpretation of this cinematic ruinous site draws on Benjamin's rethinking of historical periods of decline and melancholy through the figures of ruins and allegories. The aim here is not so much to provide a coherent and unified picture of the post-Soviet chronotope captured in cinema, but rather to attend to the imperfections, fragments, and heavy-handedness evident in the cinematic body. To undertake this task, I take a close look at the recurrent figures of the

1 The argument here is also in dialogue with Sergei Prozorov (*Ethics of Postcommunism*), which in its turn (through Giorgio Agamben), is in dialogue with Benjamin's ideas on history. Explaining a photograph of a half-ruined site, Prozorov (xiii) writes: "This image of an old country house simultaneously in the process of construction and decomposition resonates strikingly with my approach to the ethos of postcommunism as a dwelling place that has no other substance than the ruins of the previous order that may nonetheless be re-appropriated for free and innovative use that transforms this desolate site into home." The chapter here shares the premise that "the ruins of the previous order" constitute the substance of the contemporary "dwelling place." Prozorov's further suggestion to reappropriate and transform this desolate site along the lines of Agamben's political philosophy is, however, not the concern of this chapter.

debris of state construction and ruination, often accompanied by the uncanny of the imperial legacy and the anxiety of individuals facing state and divine justice. The body of post-Soviet films in which these themes reoccur can be significantly extended or reduced depending on the text's intent. In this chapter, I attend to the three most representative and chronologically diverse cases: Vadim Abdrashitov's *Time of the Dancer* (Vremia tantsora, 1997), Aleksandr Veledinskii's *Alive* (Zhivoi, 2006), and Andrei Zviagintsev's *Leviathan* (Leviafan, 2014).

Debris 1: Somnambulant Dancers

It is hard to find a better entry point to my analysis of *Time of the Dancer* than the following critique by a contemporary critic: "The break, fracture, and rupture that we and our history have experienced stretch through the body of this film. Pieces do not fit harmoniously and perfectly, and we are dissatisfied. But the flaws of this film tell us a hundred times more about the mid-nineties than anything else" (Arkus, "Seansu"). The film is indeed compiled from fragments of cultural memory, present-day contradictions, and vague dreams of the future, which together form a strange mosaic of the post-Soviet Russia of the 1990s. The film is about three friends, originally from a village in the Urals, now new settlers in the area that was recently won, presumably in a Chechen war. Two of the friends (Valerka and Fidel') are war veterans; the third one (Andreika) was supposed to join the army, but arrived at the conflict zone when the war was already over. The narrative revolves around their futile attempts to normalize their lives in their new homes on the southern borders of the country. Out of Abdrashitov and Mindadze's three post-Soviet films set in southern peripheries, *Time of the Dancer* is the one that treats the complexity of the Russian imperial legacy most explicitly.[2]

Central to *Time of the Dancer* is the trope of the house. When Valerka's family arrives at the recently acquired house, the camera—roughly overlapping with his wife Larka's scrutinizing gaze but not identical to it— in great detail tracks the interior of a typical Soviet household, lingering over kitchenware and neatly hanging onions, toy machine guns and soldiers among other play things, an empty aquarium and a school bag, a collection of Soviet-era badges and a carpet hanging on the wall. This sequence strikes the viewers with an ambiguous sense of the extreme familiarity of the inhabited space and at the same time of a strange nonbelonging

2 The other two films are *Armavir* (Armavir, 1991) and *Play for a Passenger* (P'esa dlia passazhira, 1995).

and abandonment. The slight mismatch between Larka's point of view and that of the camera contributes to this eerie feeling. The eeriness of this sequence intensifies when we learn that all the everyday objects shown in the sequence belong to the former owners of this house, who disappeared after the war. This dual sense of uncanny familiarity and alienation will be mirrored later when Timur and Tamara—local intelligentsia ousted from their home during the war—walk around in their own house under the guise of guests. Although it is tempting to interpret this mirrored situation as a colonial one, a simple binary opposition between the colonizer and the colonized is hardly applicable here. Each couple (Larka/Valerka and Tamara/Timur) in its own way turns out to be strangers in their own houses. The house, which might also be read as a stand-in for homeland, becomes the source of the *unheimlich* (unhomely) for both the local people and the new settlers.

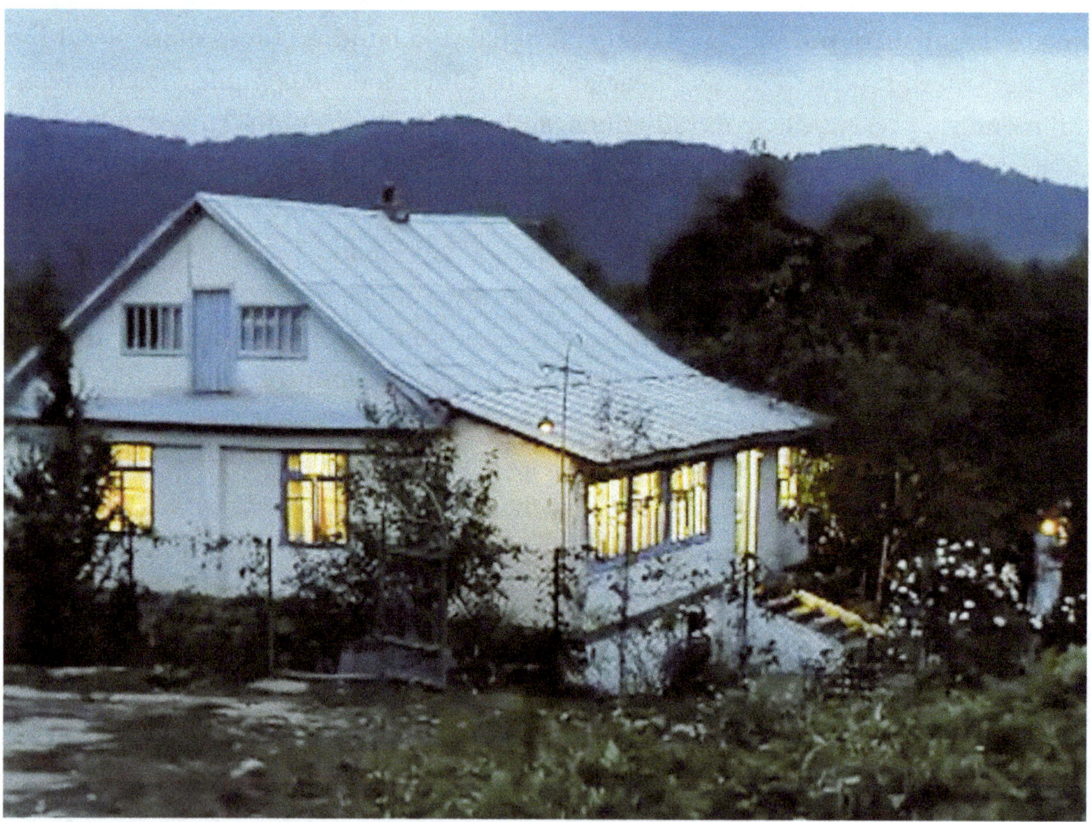

Fig. 1.1. Abdrashitov, *Time of the Dancer*. Valerka and Larka's new house.

The *unheimlich*, according to Sigmund Freud (241), is "nothing new or alien, but something which is familiar and old-established in the mind and which has become alienated from it only through the process of repression." Following Friedrich Schelling, Freud (241) defines the *unheimlich* "as something which ought to have remained hidden but came to light." What then does come to light through the "unhomely" moments in these house sequences? As Homi Bhabha (*Location of Culture*, 13) reminds us, "the 'unhomely' is a paradigmatic colonial and post-colonial condition" that "relates the traumatic ambivalences of personal, psychic history to the wider disjunctions of political existence" (15). Along these lines, it is possible to suggest that the "unhomely" house sequences in this film make visible the absence or ghostly presence of displaced local people. In addition to this implied critique of imperial violence through the unhomely, these house sequences bring to light yet another layer of the repressed, more familiar to Russian cultural texts. What returns is not only the repressed displacement of the local people but also the decrepitude and alienation of the alleged victors of the war, and by extension of post-Soviet Russia as an integrated whole.

As the camera continues to scrutinize the new household, we see Larka's eerie estrangement while she tries on a dress that she finds in the closet of her new house. Similar alienation is enacted by the war veterans in their new home(land). They appear as doubly estranged from the triumphalist rhetoric of the state and by the tacit antagonism of the local people. First, the celebratory mood of the state is particularly strained in the scene when the veterans appear as awkward spectators of the Cossack dance, performed on stage at the Palace of Culture, a relic of Soviet cultural production. Similar alienation infuses the military parade, reminiscent of a circus performance rather than a solemn victory celebration. The staged celebration of military power underscores the discrepancy between the surface triumphalism and the inner fragility and decrepitude of the veterans. A second dimension of alienation becomes visible, for example, during the tense interaction with the local restaurant co-owner and in Tamara's and Timur's hostile reception of the new settlers, an attitude that eventually leads to tragic consequences for both sides.

In this dual alienation of the war veterans and their families, Abdrashitov and Mindadze partly draw on a well-established Russian literary tradition regarding the Caucasus,[3] which,

3 Abdrashitov and Mindadze's strong indebtedness to Russian literary tradition is a significant feature of their films and was pointed out by the filmmakers themselves, as well as by several critics (Abdrashitov, 144; Condee, *Imperial Trace*, 141–58; Sul'kin, 20).

as Harsha Ram ("Prisoners," n.p.) points out, often portrayed "the Russian nation as 'captive,' that is, victim both of the imperial state and of anti-imperialist resistance." This classical literary tradition is not radically anti-imperialist but rather prefers "to 'domesticate' the crisis of empire by focusing primarily on the abuses of power perpetrated by the state against Russians themselves" (Ram, "Prisoners," 26). While staying within this tradition that portrays "the self" as "captive," the film complicates this familiar narrative by offering a more elaborate and radical image of "the other." The filmmakers do not simply reproduce the romantic myth of a "savage man" but, more importantly, show how this myth is deconstructed by the "savages" themselves. In a conversation with her husband Timur, Tamara, who happens to be a teacher of Russian literature, ironically refers to herself as Lermontov's Bela and reveals her secret plan to assume this role in order to return to her own house. She fulfills this plan by enticing Andreika to become her master. In contrast to Bela-Tamara's self-awareness and conscious construction of her role, her Pechorin-Andreika appears as a naïve and ignorant romantic, well-meaning but full of orientalist stereotypes. Not only does the film bring the displaced local people back home, if surreptitiously; it also grants them greater access to cultural memory and knowledge, compared to the partial amnesia and confusion allotted to the new settlers. The new settler Fidel', for example, confesses to his future wife that, while remembering every single moment of the war, he has only fragmented memories of his past. Another new settler, Valerka, keeps repeating that everything is confusing and entangled, that he does not understand a thing (*ni cherta ne poniatno*). This hybridization of traits, which renders indistinguishable the colonizer and the colonized, does not necessarily express an anti- or neo-imperialist message; rather this blurring of the boundary is indicative of the political and moral ambiguity of the imperial legacy in the context of post-Soviet de- and reconstruction.

Yet another instance of borrowing that complicates the traditional Caucasian narrative in *Time of the Dancer* derives from the trope of blood feud, which more broadly concerns the discourse on the relationship of violence to the law. As in many Russian nineteenth-century literary texts on the Caucasus, the law of vendetta serves as a crucial plot-generating device in the film. Set in a contemporary context, however, the mythology of blood feud is less clear in its function, insofar as the blood feud becomes caught in a spiral, engaging other forms of violence.

In its historical context, the local customary law of blood feud engendered an ambivalent attitude that could vacillate between its demonization and valorization. On the one hand, it could be framed negatively as an elemental sense of vengeance; on the other hand, it was contrasted to the coercive norms of the state and European civilization at large.[4] This attitude crystallizes in the figure of the "noble savage," who exists in the liminal zone between lawlessness and freedom and serves, in the words of Hayden White (31), as an "instrument of intracultural critique." While partly drawing on this tradition, Abdrashitov's film utilizes the mythology of blood feud not so much to reinforce the romantic myth as to elaborate the indistinctness between legal and illegal violence, which became particularly prominent in the post-Soviet condition known as *bespredel*.[5]

In Abdrashitov's film, Timur, driven by a sense of vengeance, attempts to kill Andreika, whom Timur mistakenly identifies as the person who killed his friend. This mixed-up shooting scene, both visually and narratively, is strikingly reminiscent of the final shoot-out in *The Man Who Shot Liberty Valence* (1961), John Ford's late Western, which also revolves around the relationship between violence and the law at the foundation of the state order.[6] In contrast to the US Western, however, the outcome of the shoot-out in *Time of the Dancer* does not help to establish (however problematically) law and order. Rather, it proves the impossibility of any kind of secular justice: the law of vendetta entwines itself with the incident of mistaken identity; wartime action is entangled with peacetime morality; as a result, a freedom fighter *cum* organized crime figure is detained by a dysfunctional and punitive state apparatus.

The only way the filmmakers could resolve the impossibility of secular justice in the midst of this violent spiral is by hinting at a higher justice: partly blinded, Timur accidentally shoots Fidel', the actual killer of his friend, while mistaking him for Andreika. Such higher justice

4 See, for example, Souleimanov and Aliyev.

5 Prozorov ("Management of *Anomie*, 38) describes *bespredel* as a "term to describe the socioeconomic disorder and rampant criminality that characterised the later years of perestroika and particularly the 'market reforms' of the Yeltsin presidency. In various enunciative contexts, *bespredel* may refer to the utter disrespect for traditional authorities, the acceptability of physical violence in the resolution of conflicts, the politicians' disregard for public opinion, the radical reversal of moral values, the disappearance of ethical standards in professional practices, the domination of private entrepreneurship by criminal protection rackets, and so forth." Scholars of the post-Soviet period offer various interpretations of this phenomenon. See, for example, Beumers and Lipovetsky; Borenstein; Prozorov, *Ethics of Postcommunism*; and Prozorov, "Management of *Anomie*." My use of the term is closest to Prozorov's interpretation of *bespredel* as "meta-illegality," or a Russian equivalent of what Agamben terms the "state of exception," where no rules apply. See Saltykov (Chapter 6).

6 For discussion of the ambivalent relation of violence to establishment law and political order in *The Man Who Shot Liberty Valence*, see Pippin, 61–101.

seems to work, at least diegetically: Andreika, who survives as the only male character without blood on his hands, embarks together with his long-awaited fiancé, Katia, toward the unknown future at the film's end. The possibility of higher justice recurs with important alternations in the next two films analyzed in this chapter.

Debris 2: Wandering Ghosts

Aleksandr Veledinskii's *Alive* was shot almost a decade after *Time of the Dancer,* during the Second Chechen War (1999–2009). Unlike *Time of the Dancer,* Veledinskii's film is far from arthouse cinema, in both its style and narrative. The director defines his film as a "blockbuster about the life of a spirit." Despite these (and many other) differences, a set of themes that interests us in this chapter persistently occurs in both films. Like *Time of the Dancer*, *Alive* stays within the Russian literary tradition on the Caucasus that "domesticates" imperial violence by refocusing on the alienation of a Russian soldier. Unlike *Time of the Dancer* and other films from this tradition—Sergei Bodrov's *Prisoner of the Mountain* (Kavkazskii plennik, 1997), Aleksei Balabanov's *War* (Voina, 2002), or Aleksei Uchitel''s *Captive* (Plennyi, 2008), among others—*Alive* brings this problem geographically back home from the southern borders.[7] Through this literal "domestication" of the problem, the film refocuses social concerns to examine instead the fissure between the state and those citizens who contributed to the war effort.

The opening sequence in *Alive* literally shows us cracks on the wall of what turns out to be a hospital building, where crippled Chechen war veterans receive their medical treatment. The camera lingers over these cracks, while off screen a soldier's voice accompanies the image with a playful *ekphrasis*: he imagines it as the disfigured body of a naked woman. This opening sequence prefigures several major themes that crisscross in this film: the fracture between the reconstituting state and the ruination of its people; the bodily and spiritual alienation of phantom-like figures; and—stemming from these two themes—the problem of secular and divine justice.

Following this opening sequence, the camera shows the bodies of the injured soldiers in all their physicality. They are dismembered, in plaster, with pus seeping through the bandages,

7 Another film that also literally domesticates the problem of imperial violence is Valerii Todorovskii's *My Stepbrother Frankenstein* (Moi svodnyi brat Frankenshtein, 2004).

but are cheerful and singing nonetheless. The lyrics of the song serve as a pithy refrain to the theme of the fissure between the state and its people: "For the integrity of the state, / For the oil supplies / A hapless soldier of fortune / Sleeps with a cut throat." Not only does the song explicitly condemn the alleged integrity of the state, but it also foreshadows the destiny of the protagonist, who will eventually become a dreaming corpse.

The first shot we see after the film's title is the amputated leg of the main character, Sergei. This feature positions him within the long-standing genealogy of dismembered Soviet war heroes.[8] Unlike them, however, Sergei's character lacks the triumphalist spirit of those Soviet heroes. It is clear from the film that his dismembered body is the price paid for the integrity of the state. After his unsuccessful walk with a new prosthetic leg, and in answer to the nurse's question as to whether he is "intact" (*tsel*)—this question itself echoes the lyrics on "the integrity" (*tselostnost'*) of the state—he answers in a caustic verse: "Hello Mom, I'm back home, but not entirely; here is my leg, hang it on the nail." Further ruination of the soldier's body and life happens after he leaves the hospital and becomes a civilian. First, Sergei encounters a corrupt state official who extorts bribes from him and from other returning soldiers. Later he stabs this state official to death. Finally, he is hit by a car and left on the roadside. From this point on, the main part of the film begins; as we learn toward the end, it is framed as Sergei's last dream while his body lies on the roadside.

This looping story as the last dream of a dying soldier is reminiscent of Lermontov's celebrated poem "Dream" (Son, 1841). In Lermontov's poem, the wounded soldier is lying in the valley of Dagestan and dreams of the evening feasting back in the homeland where "maids with flowers in their hair / spoke of [him] gaily amongst themselves." In Veledinskii's film, the body of a wounded soldier is relocated from the imperial periphery to the roadside of the homeland, while similarly dreaming of evening feasting back at home and of maids gaily speaking of him (they discuss his sexual ability since his leg is amputated). In the poem, the soldier's death is confirmed by the mirrored dream of his beloved; in the film, the priest, who appears as his double (also named Sergei), confirms his death by praying in front of his grave.

8 In his analysis of *Alive*, Vlad Strukov (190) also points out this genealogy. For broader psychoanalytic discussion of dismembered Soviet heroes, see Kaganovsky.

Ram interprets Lermontov's tension between matter (corpse) and consciousness (dream-life) in the poem as an equivalent of "the persistent gap between empire and nation":

> Nationhood, for the poet, is the dream of homecoming, a return to origins that contrasts service to the state with the authentic rhythms and human collectivity of rural Russia. Empire is precisely what frustrates the dream of repatriation: killed for and yet abandoned by the imperial cause, the poet's body remains unburied, destined to decompose into the land he fought to occupy.
>
> Here the unburied body of the poet-soldier abandoned in a conquered foreign land can be read simultaneously as a "figure of imperial expansion" and a symbol of "the social and psychic cost imposed on the Russian nation." (Ram, "Prisoners," 14)

If one accepts this interpretation of the poem and its parallel with the film, then the film's relocation of the corpse to the heartland of Russia can be interpreted as the nation's dream, frustrated from within. While the imperial cause on the southern borders initiated the decomposition of the soldier's body, its repatriation further continues and completes the process of ruination. In this regard, the difference between Sergei's dream life and that of the poet-soldier is meaningful. Compared to the poem, Sergei's dream-life journey back to the homeland is hardly marked by nostalgia for organic national community. Rather his phantom-like presence exposes his alienation from the community at home. He is portrayed as awkward and lost not only in front of the symbols of the state's stability and wealth—be it the cemetery-like Kremlin walls or the commercial billboards[9]—but he is also alienated from his own mother, his beloved, and his friend, who compliantly adjust to the seeming stability of the official status quo. The company of his two ghost-friends, who died while saving his life at war, is the only ideal community available to him. Of course, diegetically his alienation can be explained by his different ontological status: he is a spirit (*dukh*), as the director calls him. But if we read this situation allegorically, his alienation is indicative, too, of his "otherness"

9 Another ditty, recited by one of the phantoms in front of the Kremlin walls, while the camera pans over the busts of the former Soviet leaders, reinforces this comparison: "The cemetery's peaceful, / No friends or foes in sight. / So cultured and so decorous/ Such sweetness, grace, and light." Note the irony of the billboard signs: "Seize the moment" (Lovi moment), "Destiny has chosen us" (Sud'ba vybrala nas).

at home.[10] In Alexander Etkind's (*Internal Colonization*, 2) interpretation, being an alien at home is a symptom of a paradigmatic condition of internal colonization, "in which the state colonizes its people." If we take this interpretation into account, it is possible to suggest that in the figure of Sergei's dreaming corpse, the predicament of imperial expansion and of internal colonization fold into each other, leaving little hope for a proper homecoming from a welcoming homeland.

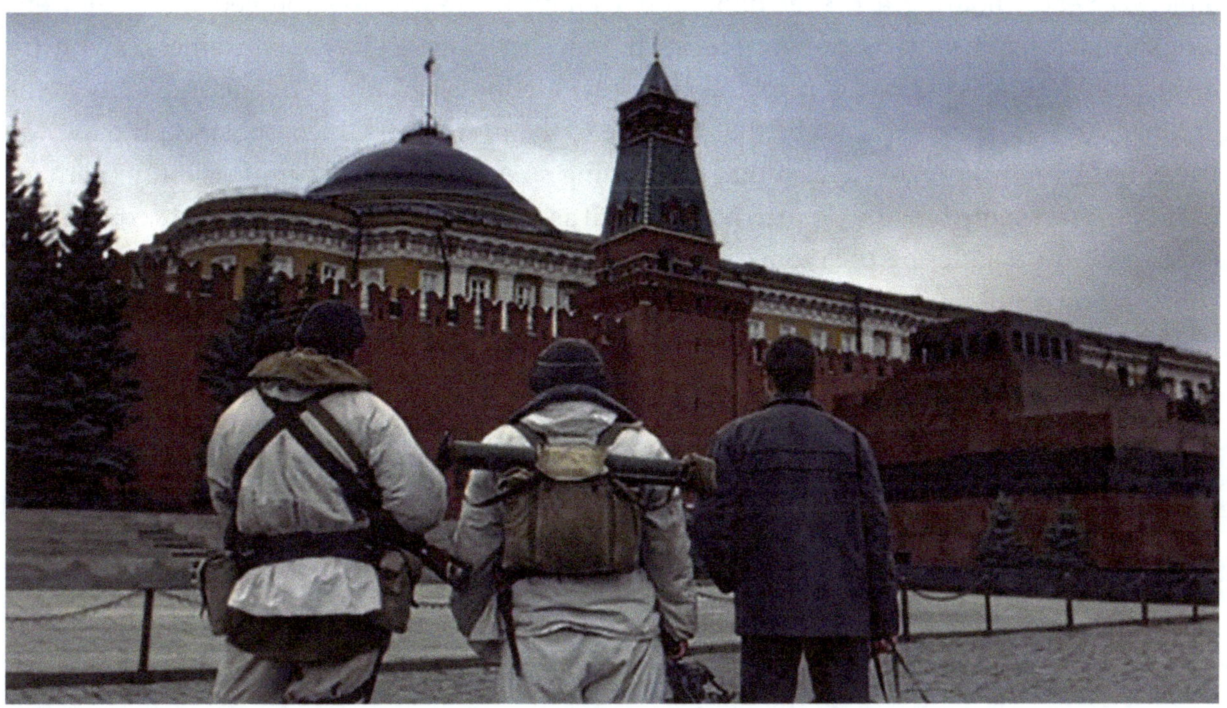

Fig. 1.2. Veledinskii, *Alive*. Ghosts in front of the Kremlin wall.

The only reconciliation with the homeland offered to the abandoned corpse and his alienated spirit in *Alive* comes through the invocation of divine justice. This invocation is akin to the resolution in Abdrashitov's *Time of the Dancer* but raises more doubts than conviction. The protagonist screams toward the sky, calling on God; the protagonist's double, an Orthodox

10 A similar theme of alienation of returning from Chechen war soldiers is prominent in *My Stepbrother Frankenstein*. For an exploration of alienation in *My Stepbrother Frankenstein* through the concept of "uncanny," see Lipovetsky, "War as the Family Value."

priest with the same appearance and name, appears to him. This encounter, rather hastily, leads Sergei's spirit to repent his sins and allows the belated rite of burial and mourning. The sudden seriousness and pathos appear at odds with the overall carnivalesque mode of the film.

The artificiality of this ending has been pointed out by several contemporary critics. Evgenii Gusiatinskii ("Ni svoi") writes: "The scene with a priest—wearing a cassock and poorly attached beard, holding a prayer book and reciting it off-screen—troubled many viewers. Not so much because of its presence as such, but rather due to its unnaturalness, awkward artificiality." How is one to interpret this heavy-handedness and unintended artificiality of the ending? An easy answer would be that it is due to the filmmakers' incompetence. It may well be so, but I am inclined to suggest that this ending speaks more to the impossibility (perhaps for filmmakers more broadly) to provide—as well as for the viewers to accept—any compelling closure for the wandering phantoms of the Chechen war in the context of contemporary state construction. In the absence of faith in secular or state justice, a recurrent reliance on divine justice is both understandable and predictable, given the cultural precedents: the canonical text in this regard would be Dostoevsky's *Crime and Punishment*. The invocation of higher justice becomes progressively less convincing as a resolution, however, in the contemporary situation of the state-supported religious revival.

Debris 3: Hybrid Monsters

The encounter between secular and higher justice in contemporary Russia is perhaps most boldly brought to the fore in Andrei Zviagintsev's *Leviathan*. The double entendre of the biblical and Hobbesian monsters in the title of the film is important. On the one hand, as in the Book of Job, it is a story about the suffering of an innocent man; on the other hand, it is a story about an individual submitting to the power of the state. Both stories, however, are significantly altered in the film. In Zviagintsev's *Leviathan*, neither biblical restoration nor the Hobbesian rationality of the social contract is suggested as a probable closure. Rather, the biblical monster closely intertwines with that of the state, giving birth to a hybrid monster that dwells in post-Soviet state formation.

Like both Abdrashitov's *Time of the Dancer* and Veledinskii's more mainstream *Alive*, *Leviathan* is a hybrid: an arthouse film rendered in a distinct *auteur* style but compatible with a broad distribution strategy. And, unlike *Time of the Dancer* and *Alive*, which engage with colonial borderlands and predominantly question the horizontal—both external and internal—expansion of state power, *Leviathan*, unambiguously set in the hinterland of Russia, problematizes the vertical expansion of state power. For all their differences, the repetition and alternation of the persistently recurring themes—the ruination of the individual caught in a dysfunctional state apparatus and its arbitrary power, as well as the invocation of higher justice—is what draws our attention in this chapter. Compared to the two other films, Zviagintsev's *Leviathan* frames the twin problems of the individual's ruination and the state's expansion of power with greater urgency and angst. Furthermore, if in Abdrashitov's *Time of the Dancer* and in Veledinskii's *Alive* higher justice is offered as a final resort (however implausible), then in Zviagintsev's *Leviathan* higher justice is invoked, but no easy answer is offered.

In *Leviathan*, the inverse proportion between the power of the state and that of the individual is most visibly captured through the fate of the house. At the center of the drama lies a dispute over the land on which the house is built. While the corrupt mayor of the town, with the "blessing" of the bishop, undertakes an (il)legal plot to expropriate the land, the owner of this house, Kolia, together with his friend, the Moscow lawyer Dima, vainly attempts to protect his property rights. As the story unfolds, we witness the gradual ruination of Kolia's life. He loses first his house in court, then his wife, friends, and family, and finally his own freedom. Although the process of ruination of the individual in the film is not simply reducible to the dysfunctional juridical and executive power of the state, the profound corruption and arbitrary violence of the state mechanism is revealed through this process in all its might. This process is visually captured in the final sequence, when the excavator slowly and indifferently tears down the house. The monstrosity of the enterprise is amplified as we learn toward the very end of the film that a new lavishly decorated church has been built on the expropriated land where the ruined house once stood.

The revelation of a corrupt local authority and, by extension, of the state is a familiar topic in Russian culture. Examples range historically from at least Nikolai Gogol's classic play *The Government Inspector* (Revizor, 1836) to Iurii Bykov's film *The Fool* (Durak, 2014). What renders the local authority in *Leviathan* particularly monstrous and resonant with the contemporary political situation is that this corrupt authority seeks and finds its support and legitimacy in the very institution of higher justice, the Russian Orthodox Church. In response to the mayor's concern about the upcoming elections, the bishop repeatedly reassures him,

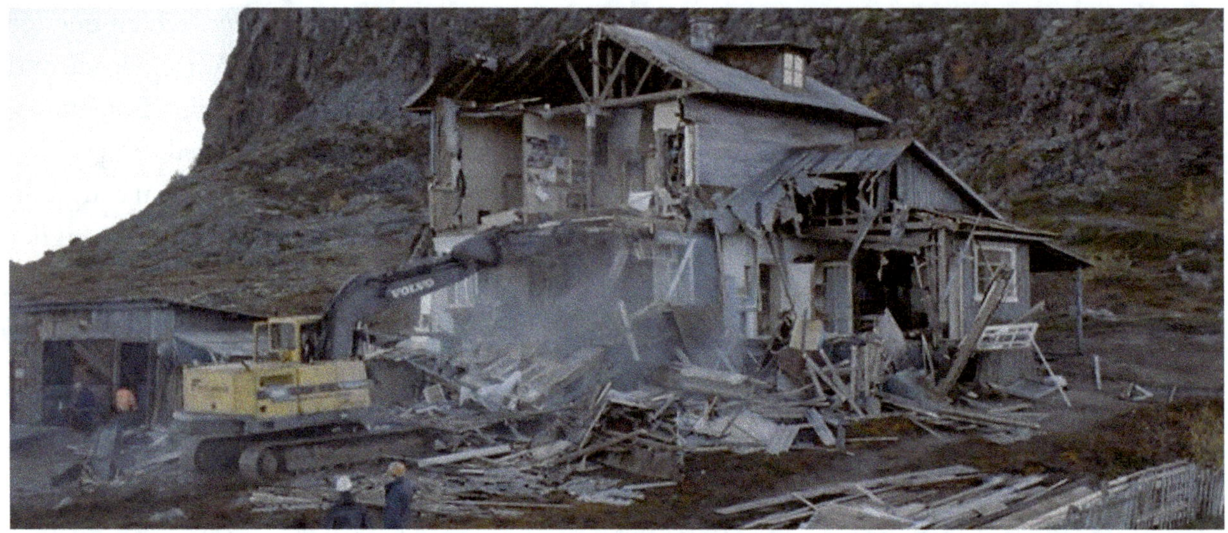

Fig. 1.3. Zviagintsev, *Leviathan*. Destruction of Kolia's house.

"Any power comes from God" (*vsiakaia vlast' ot Boga*), undermining the basic principle that the state's power originates in its people. Reassured, the drunken mayor confidently shouts to Kolia, "You people never had, still do not have, and will never have any rights." During one of his meetings with the mayor, the bishop openly states, "We are collaborators [*sorabotniki*], working for the same cause." The bishop's "blessing" gives the mayor not only legitimacy but also "moral" permission to commit *bespredel*. As if encouraged by the bishop's advice "to resolve local problems using his own power" (since "any power comes from God"), the mayor does not hesitate to organize and participate in kidnapping, beating, and threatening Kolia's lawyer.

The dubious alliance (and ultimate indiscernibility) between the criminalized state justice system and the institution of higher justice are effectively conveyed in the film through bizarre cinematographic repetition. While the film is replete with visual and narrative doubles, the graphic repetition of the two crucial sequences is particularly striking. The courtroom sequence at the beginning of the film and the sequence of the church service at the end of the film are identical in terms of shot composition and camera movement. Both sequences are constructed as frontal three-shots: in the first case, of three judges indifferently announcing the verdict that deprives Kolia of his property; in the second, of the preaching bishop with the icons of Jesus and Mary on either side. The repetition of slow track-ins toward these daringly matched three-shot compositions underscores the eeriness and monstrosity of the rites being performed. This visual overlap not only renders the verbal gibberish of the judge and the sermon of the bishop equally grotesque and nonsensical, but most importantly it boldly declares the identical lawlessness of both secular and higher justice. The function of this steady and unflinching track-in that daringly exposes the identity between the courtroom and church sequences is analogous, I suggest, to the bold and unflinching function of the film itself in the context of contemporary Russia.

Uncharacteristically for Zviagintsev, the film is blunt and overt in its social critique. If in his previous works, the director was more elliptical, allusive, and mysterious at times, in this film the allegories are uncomfortably straightforward, the morals are directly preached, and social ills are uncompromisingly exposed.[11] Of course, Zviagintsev's transcendentalist signature does not disappear entirely,[12] but it is barely recognizable underneath the blunt civic critique of the rampant lawlessness of the state allied with the church. The harshness of the film's critique of the mutual support between the state authority and the Russian Orthodox Church is often compared to that made by Pussy Riot, which is referenced twice in the film. It is not my aim here to fully explain Zviagintsev's stylistic shift to a manifesto-like frankness. Rather, I want to draw attention to the rhetoric of civic urgency that characterizes this stylistic shift and to take this shift as an opportunity to think about the social and political context that makes this blunt style not only compelling but perhaps also inevitable. The ending of the film underscores this unflinching bluntness and makes his rhetoric even more disturbing and urgent.

The aggravation of the protagonist's unjust suffering, along with the impunity and prosperity of the perpetrators, builds up spectatorial expectation for some kind of culminating revenge or rebellion. But the rebellion never happens, at least within the diegetic world. The film rejects a cathartic closure, be it a biblical reward for suffering or a civic revolt against corrupt authority. In that sense, *Leviathan* belongs to a constellation of what one scholar has

11 Although his previous film, *Elena* (2011) is also prone to socially oriented interpretations, it is not as straightforward as *Leviathan*. Moreover, the filmmaker himself repudiates the social message ("They saw socio-class struggle in the film! What class struggle!" [Matizen, "'Iskhodit',"' 671]).

12 Perhaps the death of Kolia's wife, Lilia, is the most mysterious and unknowable element in the film. For a discussion of Zviagintsev's oeuvre as a part of Russia's "transcendental cinema," see Condee, "Knowledge (Imperfective)."

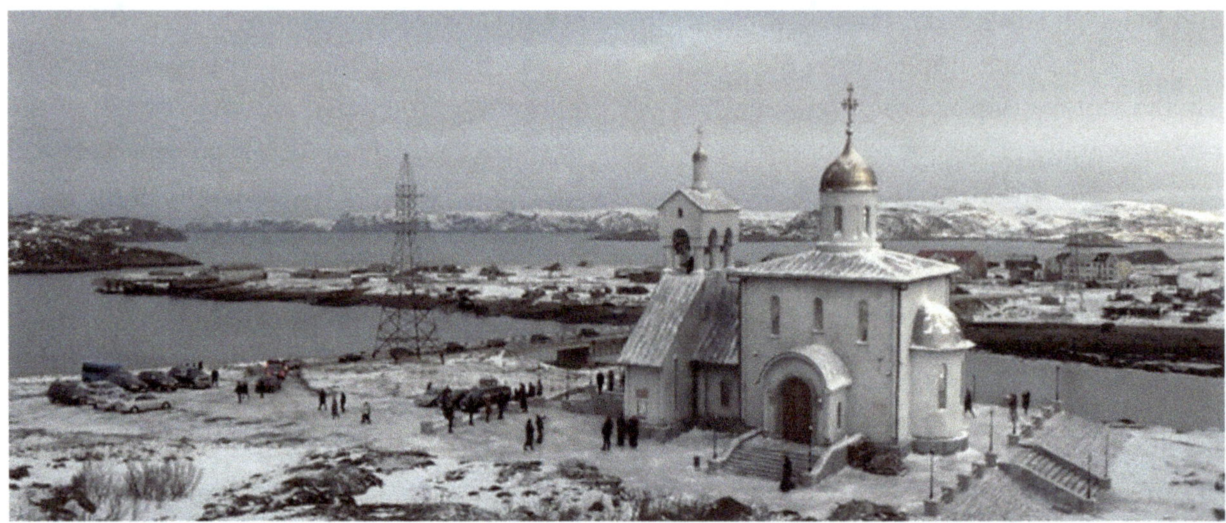

Fig. 1.4. Zviagintsev, *Leviathan*. New church.

described as "feel-bad" films. A feel-bad film, according to Nikolaj Lübeker (2), "produces a spectatorial desire, but then blocks its satisfaction." Lübeker (3) adds, "This is how the [feel-bad] films raise political and ethical questions." In *Leviathan*, as one critic has pointed out, a gun is loaded several times but never fired.[13] The viewers are doomed to leave the theater with no sense of relief, but rather with a renewed sense of angst and urgency.[14]

* * *

The debris and fissures are interpreted here in terms of the ideological ambiguity and historical complexity of the post-Soviet condition—which, to return to Benjamin's Baroque period, is characterized by the suspension of any teleological project and by the piling up of fragments from the country's past, present, and future. I started the chapter with an effort to read the cracks, fragments, and imperfections as signs of the state's de- and reconstruction. *Leviathan*'s new church building, constructed on the site of the expropriated house, seems to point to a worrisome completion of this construction.

13 See Dolin, "Tri kita."

14 The conclusion's urgency is further reinforced through Phillip Glass's music.

Filmography

Abdrashitov, Vadim, dir. *Armavir* (Armavir, 1991).

———. *Play for a Passenger* (P'esa dlia passazhira, 1995).

———. *Time of the Dancer* (Vremia tantsora, 1997).

Balabanov, Aleksei, dir. *War* (Voina, 2002).

Bodrov, Sergei, dir. *Prisoner of the Mountain* (Kavkazskii plennik, 1997).

Bykov, Iurii, dir. *The Fool* (Durak, 2014).

Ford, John, dir. *The Man Who Shot Liberty Valence* (1961).

Todorovskii, Valerii, dir. *My Stepbrother Frankenstein* (Moi svodnyi brat Frankenshtein, 2004).

Uchitel', Aleksei, dir. *Captive* (Plennyi, 2008).

Veledinskii, Aleksandr, dir. *Alive* (Zhivoi, 2006).

Zviagintsev, Andrei, dir. *Elena* (2011)

———. *Leviathan* (Leviafan, 2014).

2. Empire Reloaded: Sacred Power in a Postmodern Era

Justin Wilmes

> Can the current government really formulate Russia's purpose today? These are empty, disingenuous conversations in pursuit of narrow political goals.
>
> —*Iurii Arabov*[1]

Coming to power in 2000 after a decade marked by political and cultural collapse, Russian President Vladimir Putin has placed geopolitical strength and imperial ambition at the center of his administration. Military incursions in the 2008 Russo-Georgian War, the 2014 annexation of Crimea, and involvement in Ukraine's Donbass region have expanded Russia's territorial claims and reasserted its aspirations to former Soviet spheres of influence. Great-power displays in both the military arena, such as the intervention in Syria, and in the cultural arena, as during the 2014 Sochi Winter Olympics and 2018 FIFA World Cup, have also played a role in cultivating Russia's image of geopolitical prominence.[2] In light of these events, Russian public intellectuals and political scientists have frequently remarked in recent years on a reawakening of Russian "imperial consciousness," comparing it variously to a "Weimar syndrome," following the humiliations and traumas of the 1990s; a mobilization strategy of the Putin administration; or compensation and distraction from domestic stagnation.[3] Regardless, imperialist rhetoric and action have proven effective tools of political consolidation. This is clearly borne out by

1 See Matizen, "Iurii Arabov."

2 For an insightful discussion of the imperial significance of the Sochi Olympics, see Anisimova, "'E' Is for Empire."

3 Numerous Russian intellectuals have criticized a re-emergent "imperial consciousness": Svetlana Alexievich, Grigorii Iavlinskii, the late Boris Nemtsov, Irina Prokhorova, and Liudmila Ulitskaia (see Gordon; Lukashuk; and Mal'tseva). For diagnoses of Russia's *ressentiment* and Weimar syndrome, see Gaidar; Karaganov; and "Stanislav Belkovskii." For discussions of the reliance on empire for legitimacy in lieu of domestic progress, see Aron; Klyamkin; Medvedev ("Otkuda"); and Snyder.

sociological data, as support for the Putin administration spiked to record levels after each of its incursions into Georgia, Ukraine, and Syria, respectively.[4]

A corresponding revitalization of imperial discourses can be observed in the realm of aesthetics and culture. Several studies have examined manifestations of the imperial imaginary in post-Soviet cultural production, perhaps most notably Nancy Condee's *The Imperial Trace: Recent Russian Cinema* (2009).[5] Condee posits that identity formations throughout Russian and Soviet history were primarily imperial rather than national or civic and analyzes how post-Soviet cinema refracts that imperial legacy in complex ways.[6] The present chapter continues this line of inquiry, analyzing Russian cinema since 2010. It considers how recent cinema revives tropes and aesthetic tendencies of earlier periods—stark depictions of self and Other; besiegement by external enemies; spiritual superiority and messianism; monumentalism and grand spectacle—but also updates them for a contemporary context, refracting anxieties about Russia's place in today's global order. I analyze three key tendencies in Russian neo-imperial cinema: (1) a surfeit of films glorifying Russia's victory in the Great Patriotic War, in particular Fedor Bondarchuk's *Stalingrad* (2013); (2) the rise of the new Orthodox blockbuster, with particular attention to Andrei Kravchuk's *Viking* (2016); and (3) attempts to combine traditional imperialism and neoliberal globalism, evident in Roman Prygunov's *Dukhless* duology (2012/2015). This triangulation of recent themes—war, spiritual messianism, and neoliberal leadership—eloquently reflects Russian cinema's response to shifts in imperial culture since 2010.

4 Polling by both the Levada Center and the Russian Center for Public Opinion Research (VTsIOM) reflects these trends. Most strikingly, Putin's approval rating rose after the annexation of Crimea from around 60 percent in 2013 and early 2014 to a staggering 88 percent by the year's end and has since remained in the 80 percent range. Smaller spikes in approval were also observed following the Russo-Georgian War in 2008 and Russia's intervention in Syria in 2015 (Levada Center; VTsIOM).

5 See also Anisimova, "'E' Is for Empire"; Beumers ("National Identity"); Filimonova; Hashamova; Noordenbos; and Norris (*Blockbuster History*; "Packaging the Past").

6 Among other factors, Condee (*Imperial Trace*, 37) argues that, while the national cultures of Western Europe underwent intense political processes of nation formation, Russia continued to expand and mythologize empire. She suggests, moreover, that official nationalism in Russia, "bears little resemblance to nationalism and is indeed its opposite. . . . The primary function of official 'nationalism' has historically been the retardation and control of those nationalisms that, occupying that space where civic or ethnic autonomy might seek linkages, would otherwise speak publicly back to the state unless sufficiently restricted" (Condee, "Mediation,"189–90).

Stalingrad and the New War Blockbuster

One of the most prominent themes in Russian cinema since 2010 is undoubtedly the Great Patriotic War. The veritable flood of recent films devoted to the Soviet Union's heroic victory in the war is due in no small part to the ideological priorities of the Russian Ministry of Culture,[7] as well as market formulas and the grassroots desires of viewers.[8] Fedor Bondarchuk's *Stalingrad* (2013) is perhaps the quintessential film of the new war canon, its most commercially successful exemplar,[9] and paradigmatic of an array of tropes common to other recent films of the genre. This war epic is heir to such monumental Soviet-era projects as Iurii Ozerov's *Liberation* (Osvobozhdenie, 1968–72) and Sergei Bondarchuk's *War and Peace* (Voina i mir, 1965–67), directed by Fedor Bondarchuk's father. Notably *Stalingrad* is the first Russian film shot in IMAX 3D format.

The opening scene of *Stalingrad* begins in Fukushima in 2011. Russian crews valiantly rescue survivors of the *tsunami* and nuclear disaster there, buried beneath the rubble. A rescue worker, Sergei, locates a group of trapped German tourists. As a woman in the group cries out that she misses her father, Sergei tells her the heartening tale of his "five fathers" who died in the battle of Stalingrad, defending his mother. Here the main narrative begins about a small group of Red Army soldiers who defend a key Stalingrad building—based loosely on the historical account of "Pavlov's House" [Dom Pavlova]—on the bank of the Volga. The ragtag group of soldiers, gathered from scattered units, discovers a sole survivor in the building,

7 Some of the most prominent war films since 2010 include Fedor Bondarchuk's *Stalingrad* (2013); Pavel Chukhrai's *Cold Tango* (Kholodnoe tango, 2017); Renat Davlet'iarov's *The Dawns Here Are Quiet . . .* (A zori zdes' tikhie . . ., 2015); Kim Druzhinin and Andrei Shal'opa's *Panfilov's 28* (28 Panfilovtsev, 2016); Feliks Gerchikov's television series *Lady Spies* (Razvedchitsy, 2013); Mikhail Kabanov's television series *Night Swallows* (Nochnye lastochki, 2012); Aleksandr Kirienko's miniseries *Snow and Ashes* (Sneg i pepel, 2015); Aleksandr Kott's *Fortress of War* (Brestskaia krepost', 2010); Dmitrii Meskhiev's *Battalion* (Batal'ion", 2015); Sergei Mokritskii's *The Battle for Sevastopol* (Bitva za Sevastopol', 2015); Aleksei Muradov's *Fighters* (Istrebiteli, 2013); Nikita Mikhalkov's *Burnt by the Sun 2: Exodus* (Utomlennye solntsem 2: Predstoianie, 2010) and *Burnt by the Sun 2: Citadel* (Utomlennye solntsem 2: Tsitadel', 2011); Karen Shakhnazarov's *White Tiger* (Belyi tigr, 2014); and Sergei Ursuliak's television series *Life and Fate* (Zhizn' i sud'ba, 2012).

8 For an analysis of the ideological controls of the Ministry of Culture, greatly expanded in recent years, see Nekrasova and Wilmes. Stephen Norris (*Blockbuster History*; "Packaging the Past") provides a complementary viewpoint, emphasizing the role of market formulas in packaging nationalism and patriotism.

9 *Stalingrad* broke all box office records prior to 2013 and remains, as of this writing, the third highest-grossing film at the box office in the history of Russian cinema.

a young woman named Katia (Sergei's eventual mother), to whom they become entirely devoted and whom they protect throughout the film. Katia (Maria Smol'nikova), whose first name evokes the iconic Soviet song from the war,[10] becomes a cinematic embodiment of the Motherland (Rodina-mat'), as the men sacrifice their lives so that she may survive and mother future generations. Although the film—with its iconic director, its massive $40 million budget, marketing campaign, and epic historical subject—was arguably Russia's biggest cinematic event of 2013, it was met with an ambivalent reaction from viewers and critics. Praised for dazzling special effects and production values, it was widely criticized for, among other things, a schematic and superficial script and its loose treatment of history.[11]

Stalingrad's most unusual feature is the frame narrative set in 2011 Fukushima, which, as critics pointed out, is only tenuously connected to the main story.[12] But for all its incongruity, the paralleling of these disparate situations conveys a clear message about Russian global significance. As the narrator tells us, "Stalingrad was not only a turning point for my great country, but . . . for all of humanity," reminding both domestic and international viewers "to whom the lives and freedom of millions and millions of people are owed today." Just as Soviet soldiers saved the world in the 1940s from the threat of the Nazis, in 2011 Russia is shown saving the Japanese (as well as Germans and others) in Fukushima.[13] Perhaps not coincidentally, Russia here is ameliorating a nuclear disaster at the site where its chief antagonist, the United States, had inflicted a disaster decades earlier. Like many recent blockbusters, *Stalingrad* taps into domestic desires—and serves a public relations function abroad—for a view of Russia's positive role in the world, both historically and in the global order today, assuaging anxieties at a time of increasing geopolitical isolation and embattled national reputation.[14]

10 The song "Katiusha," composed in 1938 by Matvei Blanter and Mikhail Isakovskii, became the iconic song of the war in the USSR, and allegedly inspired the Red Army's Katyusha BM-13 artillery vehicle.

11 See Plakhov ("V raskopkakh Stalingrada"); Sokolov; and Tsyrkun.

12 See Graham ("Fedor Bondarchuk"); Stishova ("Mne ne bol'no"); and Tsyrkun.

13 Russia did play a role in lending aid and rescue crews during the Fukushima crisis in 2011, totaling around 160 rescue workers. They were one of many countries to lend significant aid during the crisis; the scale of the comparison to the Battle of Stalingrad strikes the viewer as somewhat incongruous.

14 Since Putin's third term in 2012, an array of events has shaped Russia's image as geopolitical aggressor, including the annexation of Crimea; involvement in the War in Donbass; the MH-17 catastrophe; the doping scandal at the 2014 Olympics; alleged meddling in the 2016 US presidential elections; and the Novichok poisonings in Britain in 2018.

In *Stalingrad*, the House of Pavlov reflects another common theme in recent war blockbusters. As in Aleksandr Kott's *Brest Fortress* and Kim Druzhinin and Andrei Shal'opa's *Panfilov's 28*, the House of Pavlov in *Stalingrad* serves as a spatial metaphor, evoking the potential present-day media narrative of a Russia besieged by enemies. In all these films, Red Army soldiers are surrounded and outmatched by foreign invaders, but through valor and self-sacrifice, they defy the odds and turn the tide of the greater war effort.[15] Through *Stalingrad*'s meticulous mise-en-scène—the filmmakers famously employed over four hundred people for six months and a budget of $3.5 million to model the city—it recreates "Dom Pavlova" as a metonymic stand-in for the homeland, replete with quaint personal effects and a nostalgic colorization and stylization of interiors. The film's many "chamber" scenes, such as the hot bath and birthday cake prepared by the soldiers for Katia's birthday, heighten the intimate, affectionate depiction of the family-nation, clearly worth fighting and dying for, against the antagonistic elements beyond the walls. The spatial construction of *Stalingrad* creates a "fortress chronotope," in which time seems to stand still, offering a fairytale reprieve from the incessant fighting beyond. Notably in *Stalingrad*, as in the other war films discussed here, virtually everyone dies, adding an element of martyrdom and quasi-religious reverence for the sacrifice.

Yet, like many recent Russian blockbusters, *Stalingrad* presents uneven and somewhat incoherent ideological messages. Scholars have often observed contradictory ideological notions in Putin-era cultural production, noting the pervasive use of pastiche, combining previously incompatible elements from imperial, Soviet, and post-Soviet culture; and an unexpected "convergence of imperial ideology and postmodernist style . . . devoid of its progressive elements and critical content" (Anisimova, "'E' Is for Empire").[16] In a similar manner, *Stalingrad* attempts to combine highly conservative and imperial notions with global film formulas and nominal gestures to progressive values—human rights, critiques of mass state terror, and so on. In this way, the film straddles its competing goals of international marketing and appeals to domestic patriotic fervor.

15 As will be discussed later in the chapter, the fortress chronotope in recent cinema is not limited to the Great Patriotic War. Spatial and narrative constructions of Russian besiegement can be found in a range of recent films depicting various time periods and topics—particularly the medieval period—such as Vladimir Khotinenko's *1612* (2007); Andrei Proshkin's *The Horde* (Orda, 2012); Dzhanik Faiziev's *Furious* (Legenda o Kolovrate, 2017); and Andrei Kravchuk's *Viking*.

16 For related discussions of pastiche and postmodern imperial discourse, see Norris ("Packaging the Past"), Noordenbos; and Lipovetsky ("Anything Goes").

Like its socialist realist predecessors, *Stalingrad* offers little ambiguity in its construction of self and Other. The Russian soldiers are saintly figures and superhuman fighters, rebuffing an outfit many times their size. In the opening battle sequence, Soviet troops are engulfed in flames by detonated oil tanks, but incredibly they charge forward aflame for hundreds of meters, striking fear into the hearts of the Germans. One notable exception notwithstanding, the Germans are faceless or barbaric. In another hyperbolic scene, the German colonel Henze (Khenze) orders his men to burn alive a mother and daughter—whom he mistakes for Jews—in a bus, a "human sacrifice before battle, as our German ancestors would do." Throughout the film, classical use of mise-en-scène contrasts German decadence with Russian humility and camaraderie. Recalling such Stalin-era works as Mikheil Chiaureli's *The Fall of Berlin* (Padenie Berlina, 1950), the German colonel is framed with a bottle of wine on ice, dishing out cream from a saucer, surrounded by paintings and other luxuries. While the Soviet soldiers are motivated by a solemn duty to the homeland, the German captain exhorts his men before the final battle by promising them "six-armed prostitutes" in India after Stalingrad has fallen. And yet the film makes superficial gestures at humanizing the Germans through the character of Captain Kahn (played by European film actor Thomas Kretschmann). Kahn briefly attempts to defend the Russian mother and daughter who are burned alive. He becomes infatuated with the local Russian beauty Masha, who resembles his late wife—dead of tuberculosis years earlier—and

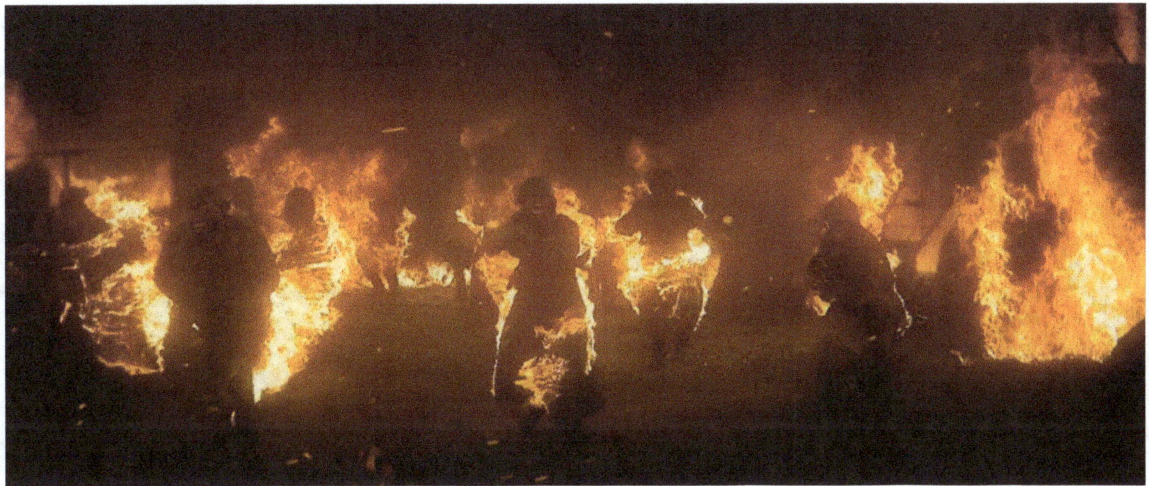

Fig. 2.1. Bondarchuk, *Stalingrad*. Soviet soldiers storm German ramparts in flames, accompanied by dramatic orchestral score.

tries to protect her. This gesture at humanizing the Other and showing the universal suffering of war, however, is an unconvincing aside in a broader depiction of Russian moral superiority.

In another nominal gesture to international film audiences, a key scene points to the shared tragic experience of totalitarianism in Germany and the USSR that fueled the war. As Captain Kahn delivers a pre-battle speech—equating God, Hitler and the nation—his soldiers are framed against a vast mural of Joseph Stalin: they are dwarfed, as it were, by the ideological symbols that entrap them. This brief visual framing, however, is drowned out in the film's broader discourse that— echoing contemporary Russian media narratives—unreflectively celebrates authoritarian measures that were implicitly "necessary" for Soviet victory. In one scene, Captain Gromov (Petr Fedorov), the ultimate military hero of the film, summarily executes a Soviet sailor who had defied orders and attempted to leave to rejoin his unit. The brutal execution inspires awe and obedience from the others and is quickly swept aside in Gromov's broader heroic characterization. Narrative logic that reaffirms authority and obedience—what Nancy Condee ("Cold Snap") refers to as the key to "obey-or-die films"— underpins a range of genres in recent Russian cinema. Elsewhere in this volume, Theodora Trimble analyzes similar tendencies in an array of new "emergency films" about human-made or natural disasters.

Reflecting broader trends in Putin-era memory practices, *Stalingrad* presents a hodgepodge of communist and Orthodox ideas and symbols. Christian iconography appears throughout

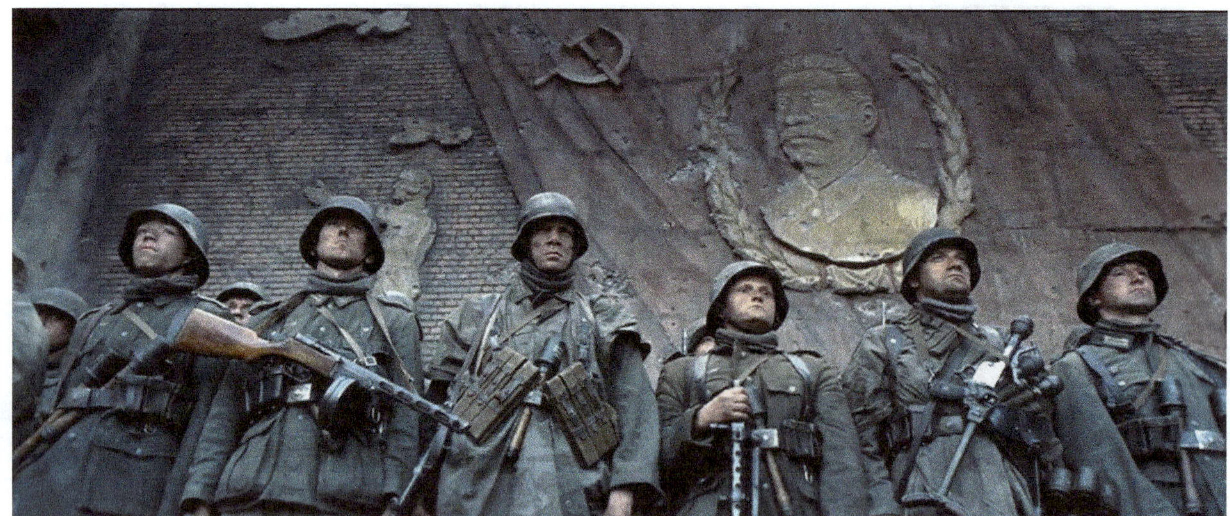

Fig. 2.2. Bondarchuk, *Stalingrad*. German soldiers prepare for battle before a mural of Stalin.

this story about the (nominally atheistic) Soviet Red Army. As Andrei Plakhov observes, the five Russian soldiers recall the apostles, while the portrayal of Katia—innocent, completely desexualized, giving birth as if by immaculate conception—evokes the Madonna. The home itself is a Noah's ark of sorts, preserving Russian (Christian) civilization. Various characters, such as Poliakov (nicknamed "Angel"), are overtly religious and pray throughout the film. The incongruity between its sacred discourse of war and a video-game aesthetic is driven by special effects and comic-book-style action. Nonetheless, while not always satisfying critics and viewers, with the help of its massive advertising campaign *Stalingrad* seems to have achieved its commercial goals. In addition to its record-breaking domestic sales, it made significant profits in targeted international markets (particularly Asia and CIS countries), and was Russia's official nominee for the Oscar.[17]

Several striking parallels could be found in Sergei Mokritskii's blockbuster *The Battle for Sevastopol* (Bitva za Sevastopol', 2015), which similarly underscores Russia's salvatory mission during WWII. The film portrays the suffering and heroism of Liudmila Pavlichenko, a legendary Soviet sniper during the war. Interlaced throughout the film are meetings between Pavlichenko and her friend and admirer Eleanor Roosevelt, again intimating present-day narratives about great-power status and multipolarity. At the film's conclusion, Pavlichenko pleads with a feckless US Congress to join the war effort and "stop hiding behind our backs" and is met with a standing ovation, ostensibly turning US public opinion about the war and again saving the world. Unlike most of her compatriots who die defending Sevastopol, Pavlichenko survives, but her suffering and sacrifice are accentuated throughout the film and messages about Russian messianism are clear.

In *The Battle for Sevastopol*, the ideological incoherence and hybridization we found in Bondarchuk's film are even more pronounced. Capitalizing on global interest in heroines, the film traces the biography of the sniper Pavlichenko, dwelling frequently on the loss of her femininity and individuality during the war. The camera zooms in on her melancholy, wistful expression as for the first time she tries on an expensive party dress, given to her by the US First Lady. When Pavlichenko hesitates to accept the Red Army's "invitation" to leave the university for sniper training, the KGB officer tells her menacingly, "I advise you not to decline." Such

17 In China, *Stalingrad* broke records as the highest grossing non-Hollywood film in history. In total international sales, the film earned approximately $15 million (compared to $51.7 million domestically).

moments throughout the film present facile critiques of Soviet totalitarianism, lending the film a degree of progressive sophistication.[18] Pavlichenko suffers tremendously throughout the narrative, sacrificing her innocence, femininity, and education and enduring endless traumas from the war, but she is compensated by the admiration of her valor and her contribution to national greatness. In the context of what political scientists have called "patriotic mobilization" in Russia today,[19] individual aspirations are subsumed into the national-imperial. In this way, the film's tagline—"War isn't just death. War is a kind of life"—takes on particular significance.

And, as in *Stalingrad*, the film includes a brief, token gesture at humanizing the German enemy. Near the end of the film, when Pavlichenko defeats a rival German sniper in an elaborate duel, she weeps over his body when she discovers his photographs and personal effects. As we will see next, a similar blend of domestic imperial discourse and international blockbuster formulas are also found in films that thematize a legendary Orthodox past, as well as in cinema about Russian leadership in the global neoliberal order.

Orthodoxy Reloaded: Andrei Kravchuk's *Viking*

Orthodox Christianity, another recurrent theme in recent cinema, shares with its war counterpart the drive to construct a heroic, usable past that channels imperial and messianic discourses. A striking number of films in the past decade have centered on Orthodox and spiritual themes.[20] Here a distinction should be made between the Soviet/Russian tradition of

18 Another interesting example is found in the Odessan Jew and doctor Boris. Although he is dismissed early in the film as a "coward" for his pacifist views, he arguably becomes the film's most heroic male character, sacrificing himself to save Pavlichenko at the film's conclusion. As with the female hero Pavlichenko, this nontraditional construction of heroism in a Jewish pacifist sets the film apart from the portrayals of other war films, but *Battle for Sevastopol* nonetheless reinforces the same prevailing concepts—authority, obedience, wartime valor and sacrifice—as the ultimate values.

19 The terms "patriotic mobilization" and "war patriotism" have been used in recent years by Russian political scientists such as Igor Klyamkin and Leon Aron. The terms refer to a range of policies and rhetoric employed by the Putin administration that emphasize patriotism and loyalty in the face of external enemies and draw legitimacy from patriotic and imperial notions, rather than from domestic civic notions (Aron; Klyamkin).

20 Some of the most prominent examples include Nikolai Dostal''s *The Monk and the Demon* (Monakh i bes, 2016), Vladimir Khotinenko's *The Priest* (Pop, 2009), Andrei Kravchuk's *Viking*, Pavel Lungin's *The Island* (Ostrov, 2006) and *Tsar* (2009), and Andrei Proshkin's *The Horde*.

"Orthodox cinema" and what might be called a new "cinema about Orthodoxy."[21] The former tendency can be traced back to Andrei Tarkovskii's high modernist works, which explore spirituality as an alternative to mainstream Soviet genre cinema. This tradition is (arguably) continued today by such practitioners as Pavel Lungin and scriptwriter Iurii Arabov. Distinct from the spiritual striving of these films, more recent "cinema about Orthodoxy," as I call it, instrumentalizes Orthodox themes to advance contemporary ideological and commercial agendas. Andrei Kravchuk's *Viking* is a case in point: like *Stalingrad,* it enjoyed a massive, largely government-funded budget and advertising campaign and was one of the top five highest-grossing films in Russian box office history, despite poor reviews from viewers and critics.[22]

Kravchuk follows his previous work—most notably, *The Admiral* (Admiral'', 2009)—continuing to mine the historical biopic genre and tap into post-Soviet desires for a highly mythologized history. Similar to *Stalingrad, Viking* combines overt ideological appeals to a domestic audience with international commercial formulas, capitalizing on the popularity of the global fantasy genre and borrowing liberally from such models as *Game of Thrones, The Lord of the Rings* trilogy, and the Irish-Canadian serial *Vikings*. As with *Stalingrad,* Kravchuk's film reflects a symbiosis between the government's recent interventions in cinema—soliciting "preferred themes" and selectively awarding funding to favored ideological blockbuster projects—and popular demand for special effects-driven productions (*attraktsiony*).[23] The active promotion of Russian Orthodox heritage, along with the victory cult of World War II, attempts to fill the ideological void and echoes President Putin's 2012 call for the promotion of "spiritual bonds" (*dukhovnye skrepy*) to strengthen national cohesion. Perhaps not coincidentally, as Kravchuk was releasing this cinematic monument to Vladimir the Great in 2016, a massive seventeen-meter-high monument to the same "baptizer of Rus'" was erected in front of the Kremlin on Borovitskii Square.

21 Thanks to Vlad Strukov for originally pointing out this distinction in personal conversation.

22 Tellingly, *Viking* has a user rating of 4.6/10 on the Russian site *KinoPoisk*. For negative critical reviews, see Anastas'ev; Dolin ("Viking"); and Youngblood.

23 In a review of *Viking,* critic Larisa Maliukova eloquently sums up this tendency: "There is a deficit of national history, a void that is then filled in a fairly odd manner with spectacle [*attraktsion*]" ("*Viking* stal").

Viking's plot is loosely based on the account in *The Primary Chronicle* of Prince Vladimir, ruler of Kievan Rus' from 980 to 1015 CE.[24] The narrative begins as the three sons of Sviatoslav I—Iaropolk, Oleg, and Vladimir—vie for control of the territories of Rus' after their father's death. While hunting a giant bison in the forest, the army of Prince Oleg crosses paths with Iaropolk's men, an encounter that escalates into a battle and leads to the accidental death of Oleg. Meanwhile Vladimir, the youngest brother of the Riurik dynasty, returns from exile with a band of Vikings to take revenge on Iaropolk and solidify his position. Notably, as in many recent blockbusters, most of the shooting takes place in present-day Ukraine (Sevastopol, Kiev, and Korsun), evoking the imperial imaginary of Russia today and building "civilizational" claims to former territories.[25]

Rather than attention to historical complexity or accuracy, *Viking* reveals a preoccupation with presentist ideological concerns. The accounts of Vladimir I in historical sources are conveniently incomplete, providing a useful palimpsest on which Kravchuk's film explores contemporary mythologies. In addition to asserting Russia's civilizational claims to Kievan Rus' and Vladimir,[26] the film shares ideological tropes common to other recent blockbusters. As in *Stalingrad*, during much of the film, Vladimir's men are besieged in a fortress, surrounded and outnumbered by encroaching enemies. Pecheneg mercenaries, hired to overthrow Vladimir, comprise the chief Other in the film, but strained relations with Rome and Byzantium are also present. As one character warns Vladimir: "Accept what Byzantium offers, but don't believe them. For them we will always be different [*chuzhie*]. . . . They 'hired' your father and when he disobeyed, they killed him." Vladimir's ascent represents Rus' "rising up of from its knees" into both a formidable world power and a holy empire, chosen by God. Though outnumbered

24 Co-producer Konstantin Ernst quipped that the film's scriptwriter was "Nestor," the alleged author of *The Primary Chronicle* (Anastas'ev).

25 Around the time of the annexation of Crimea in 2014, a striking number of Russian films have been set in this former territory, emphasizing explicitly or implicitly Russian historical claims on the region. These include Kravchuk's *Viking*, Mokritskii's *The Battle for Sevastopol*, Nikita Mikhalkov's *Sunstroke* (Solnechnyi udar, 2014), Aleksei Pimanov's *Crimea* (Krym, 2017), and Oleg Stepchenko's *Forbidden Kingdom* (Vii, 2014).

26 A 2016 Twitter feud erupted in conjunction with the unveiling of Moscow's monument to Vladimir. When Russian state television repeatedly announced the Moscow statue as "the first monument to Vladimir the Great," the official Twitter account of Ukraine posted an acerbic response: "Don't forget what real Prince Volodymyr monument looks like. Kyiv brought Orthodox Christianity to the Rus. Kind reminder to @Russia." See Walker.

and faltering, Vladimir's army is aided throughout the narrative by a series of miracles. When his men are surrounded in a defenseless area by Pecheneg riders, one ally exclaims, "Your luck has struck again!" as the sky darkens and a deluge of rain shifts the advantage to Vladimir's men. Divine intercession and a "baptismal" water motif recur throughout the film, culminating in a dazzling scene of Vladimir leading the nation in a mass baptism in the Dnieper River.

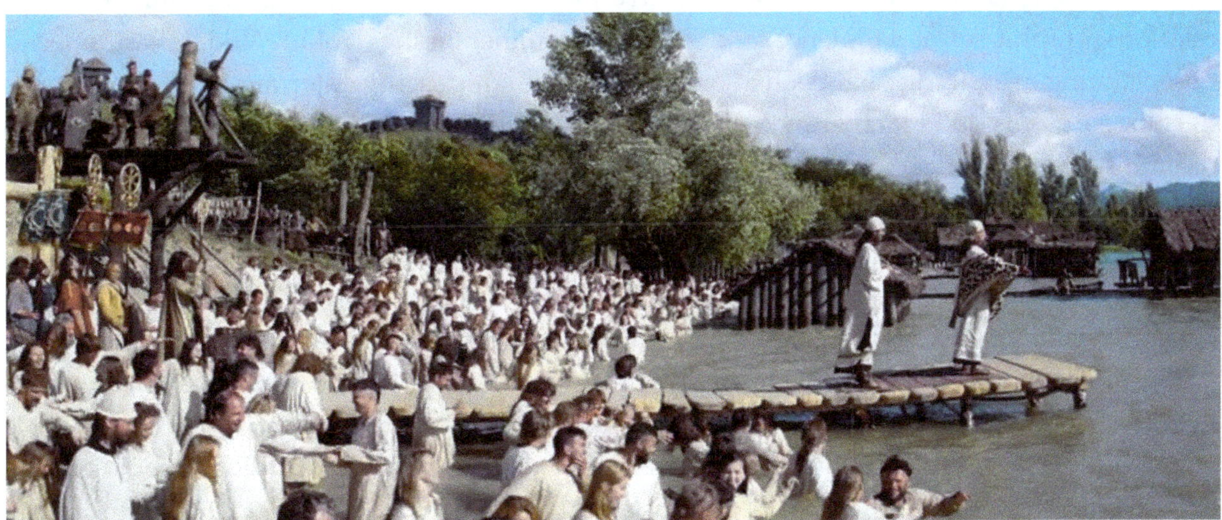

Fig. 2.3. Kravchuk, *Viking*. Grandiose scene of the baptism of Kievan Rus'.

Russia's exceptional status and spiritual mission in the world—mythologized throughout Russian history by the Slavophiles, Eurasianists, Soviets, and in a new iteration today in Putin's Russia—is personified by Vladimir himself. Having defeated and captured his enemy Variazhko, Vladimir spares his life rather than executing him. After wrestling with guilt and confessing his sins of rape and murder to the Byzantine priest Anastas, Vladimir is purified in a scene dramatizing the Orthodox rite of confession. In the film's finale, Vladimir declares, "I will no longer kill," lowering his sword, thereby converting the brutal warrior through his example of Christian love. Despite obvious affection for his brother's widow Irina, Vladimir resists temptation and remains loyal to his pagan wife Rogneda. This hagiographical depiction of Vladimir, of course, conflicts with historical accounts that reference large-scale bloodshed and hundreds of concubines. And while Vladimir's kingdom is clearly inferior in wealth and military might to the Western powers, spiritual vitality and divine favor remain with the weaker

Russian lands. In this way, the film re-encodes for the present the Slavophile and Eurasianist motif of weakness inverted into spiritual superiority, echoing media narratives about Russia's position in the global order today.[27] Furthermore, the idealized portrayal of Vladimir as leader of the nation, anointed by God, bolsters mythologies about the present-day leadership.

As we have seen in *Stalingrad* and many other recent patriotic blockbusters, *Viking* combines global commercial formulas with conservative pieties, at once delighting in primitive power relations, graphic sex and violence, and—as one prominent critic (Dolin, "Viking") quipped—"proclaiming everything sacred, all at once, in a single supposedly entertaining film." A thinly developed plot is tied together by lengthy action scenes, punctuated by moments of spiritual solemnity. Special effects and characters are borrowed whole cloth from the global fantasy genre. Among Vladimir's army of Vikings—itself a pop culture adaptation of the historical Varangians— is "Berserker" (played by Swedish actor Ioakim Natterkvist), a noble giant twice the size of an ordinary man, who single-handedly takes on a band of Pecheneg riders and is curiously similarly to Mag the Mighty from *Game of Thrones*. In another memorable scene, Vladimir's men miraculously ride a ship down a muddy mountainside—overcoming entirely the laws of physics—in order to wipe out a band of Pecheneg riders. Such scenes invoke Hollywood special effects and action devices, appealing to particular audiences but creating a dissonance with the film's spiritual and historical aspirations.

Prygunov's *Dukhless*: Neoliberalism with a Soul

While *Stalingrad* and *Viking* update familiar discourses of war and Orthodoxy recurrent from previous centuries, Roman Prygunov's *Dukhless* and *Dukhless 2* are a fascinating attempt to transpose these and similar notions onto the contemporary global order, rejecting the eponymous "soulless" version of late capitalism to seek Russia's unique path within it. Like

[27] Slavophile and Eurasianist imperial narratives rely foremost on such inversions. Nancy Condee writes: "The Russian imperial intelligentsia of the late nineteenth century could paradoxically resolve the status of the humble commune by rendering it a parallel (i.e., metaphysical and sacred) empire, invisibly magnificent in proportion to its earthly poverty, drawing an internally contradictory equivalency between collective suffering, potentially without content or limit, and a perpetually expanding, transcendent empire at a time when, perhaps not so coincidentally, the process of nation-formation in the West was most intense. This symbolic empire could function as a spiritual and cultural retort to the measure of the Western nation-state and to Russia's own official *narodnost'*" (*Imperial Trace*, 37).

Stalingrad and *Viking*, thanks to its star power and far-reaching marketing campaign, *Dukhless* became one of the biggest box-office successes in the post-Soviet era.[28]

The hero of *Dukhless*, Maksim Andreev (Danila Kozlovskii), is a twenty-nine-year-old top manager of an international Moscow bank. His days are filled with high-stakes business deals, luxury sports cars, night clubs, and a revolving door of beautiful women. As he tells us in a voiceover during the opening montage, "I've made it in life" (*zhizn' udalas'*). We follow as Maks jockeys for position among company executives, enjoying favor at first from the bank's vice-president (Mikhail Efremov) and plotting to overcome his rival, the seedy Frenchman Garrido. For a full thirty minutes, the film revels in the glamour and excesses of the Moscow elite, inviting the viewer to vicariously enjoy its sensual overload, reinforced by the exhilarating pace of the editing. Maks begins to question the meaning of such a life, however, when he meets the beautiful nonconformist Iuliia (Mariia Andreeva), a member of the activist group Colors (Kraski).[29] Lured into a fraudulent business deal with nightclub owner Misha Voodoo and losing his bank job, Maks hits rock bottom—literally dropped into a landfall by a garbage truck in the final scene—and finally begins to reevaluate what is important in life. In this way, *Dukhless* becomes a parable about navigating the treacherous world of global capitalism, rejecting a narrowly materialistic, hedonistic life, often associated with the Moscow elite of the 2000s, for something more "soulful."

In this sense, *Dukhless* is part of a larger cinematic discourse in recent years lamenting the loss of nonmaterial ideals in the post-Soviet era. In the last decade, films as utterly different as Karen Shakhnazarov's *Vanished Empire* (Ischeznuvshaia imperiia, 2008) and Natal'ia Kudriashova's *Pioneer Heroes* (Pionery-geroi, 2015) have explored similar concerns about the loss of professed Soviet values of collective responsibility, equality, and so on in an age governed by individual, material prosperity.[30] Maksim Andreev is Russia's response to today's

28 *Dukhless* was the highest-grossing Russian film in 2012, while *Dukhless 2* was the second-highest-grossing film of 2015, following Konstantin Feoktistov's animation *Three Heroes: Horse Course* (Tri bogatyria: Khod konem, 2014).

29 As many have pointed out, this group is an apparent allusion to the contemporary Russian street-art group War (Voina), famous for pranks and provocative performance art.

30 Nostalgic discourses are truly the domain of Russian television serials, even more than of cinema. Numerous recent serials appeal to notions of an idealized past and lost ideals in the present, reflecting somewhat older target audiences.

global, neoliberal order: a corporate capitalist with a soul. Not surprisingly, the misguided and decadent versions of the new materialism are embodied by characters associated with the West—the unctuous Frenchman Garrido and conman Misha Voodoo, both of whom practice sadomasochism in their spare time. While tracking down Misha Voodoo after having been defrauded by him, Maks exclaims: "I don't get it. Do they put something in your water in America? You all become such faggots [*pidarasy*] over there."

Like Danila Bagrov of Aleksei Balabanov's *Brother* (Brat, 1997) a decade earlier, Maksim Andreev is a composite "hero of our time," who stands up to and defeats the threats of encroaching, foreign culture.[31] In *Dukhless*, Maks ultimately gives away much of his ill-gotten wealth to a boy dying of cancer. In *Dukhless 2*, he has initially left behind his life of external success to move to Bali, where he finds solace in surfing and yoga. Yet he returns to Moscow and ultimately chooses to stay and run for political office when billboards lining the streets remind him "You are needed at home!" As in *Stalingrad* and *Viking*, besiegement by global forces—here, in the form of warring cultural imperialisms and neoliberal values—combine with a traditional inversion of weakness as spiritual strength to constitute the narrative logic of *Dukhless*.

Like several other recent Russian blockbusters, *Dukhless* dabbles paradoxically in a politically liberal critique, creating an ideological dissonance at the heart of this film, similar to what we have already noted above. Its depiction of the Colors group and the street protest in its finale even led some to view *Dukhless* as meaningful political commentary.[32] However, the protests of the activist group are entirely stripped of political content and their spirit of protest is redirected against "office plankton," "consumption," and "materialism." In this way, *Dukhless* in fact appropriates political activism to reinforce its own statist messages. In another memorable scene, Vladimir Putin appears to Maksim during the hero's evening reverie after smoking marijuana. To Maks's disbelief, Putin flies up to his balcony dressed as a superhero and exhorts Maks to realize his potential. On the one hand, this ironic nod to the contemporary

31 For example, in *Dukhless 2* Maksim develops a new cryptocurrency technology to outsmart various groups conspiring against his company. The film's depiction of weaponizing global financial instruments is timely, given the Russian government's active interest in this area.

32 In his review of *Dukhless*, Iurii Saprykin comments on its topical political content, remarking: "This is definitely the first appearance of the 'people of Bolotnaia,' so to speak, in a feature film." For other interpretations of the *Dukhless* films as political critique, see Artiukh and Fridman; and DeBlasio ("Roman Prygunov").

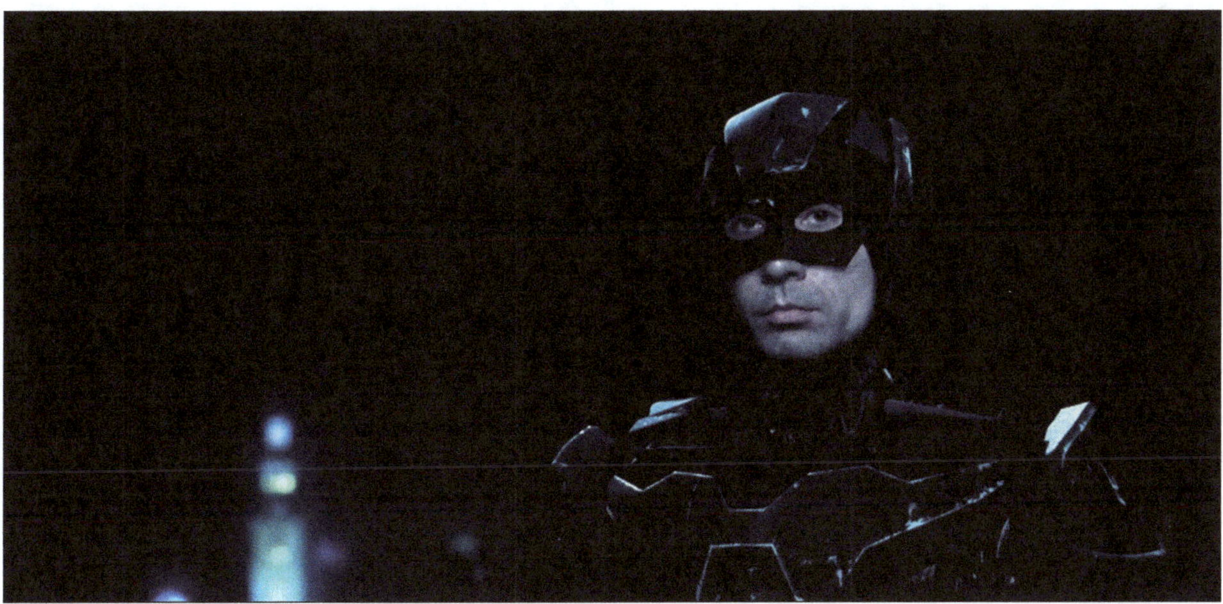

Fig. 2.4. Prygunov, *Dukhless*. Putin's appearance as superhero.

cult of personality around President Putin—and perhaps to the ideological exigencies in which the film was made—acts as a wink to viewers, signaling self-consciousness and campy sophistication. Dispelling any doubt about its position vis-à-vis authority, *Dukhless 2* ends by providing Maksim an opportunity to confer yet again with President Putin in the back of the presidential limousine. Putin urges Maks to remain in Russia and join the current government, which is a reforming and modernizing force. As Maks stutters in awe of the omnipotent leader, the film again gives a subtle wink to viewers about its overt ideological messages—but asserts them nonetheless. Such ironic distancing becomes its own sort of strategy, allowing the filmmakers to distinguish themselves from Soviet-era ideological clichés, and rendering statist messages more palatable. Such faux critiques and ironic gestures reveal the growing sophistication of ideological cultural products in an era of channeled discourses, "release valve" policies, and postmodern authoritarianism. Indeed, *Dukhless*, like *Stalingrad* and *Viking*, raises the core problem common to Russian blockbuster cinema today: how is it possible to depict sacred power in the postmodern era?

Filmography

Balabanov, Aleksei, dir. *Brother* (Brat, 1997).
Bondarchuk, Fedor, dir. *Stalingrad* (2013).
Bondarchuk, Sergei, dir. *War and Peace* (Voina i mir, 1965–67).
Chiaureli, Mikheil, dir. *The Fall of Berlin* (Padenie Berlina, 1950).
Chukhrai, Pavel, dir. *Cold Tango* (Kholodnoe tango, 2017).
Davlet'iarov, Renat, dir. *The Dawns Here Are Quiet . . .* (A zori zdes' tikhie . . . , 2015).
Dostal', Nikolai, dir. *The Monk and the Demon* (Monakh i bes, 2016).
Druzhinin, Kim, and Andrei Shal'opa, dir. *Panfilov's 28* (28 Panfilovtsev, 2016).
Faiziev, Dzhanik, dir. *Furious* (Legenda o Kolovrate, 2017).
Feoktistov, Konstantin, dir. *Three Heroes: Horse Course* (Tri bogatyria: Khod konem, 2014).
Gerchikov, Feliks, dir. *Lady Spies* (Razvedchitsy, 2013) (television serial).
Kabanov, Mikhail, dir. *Night Swallows* (Nochnye lastochki, 2012) (television series).
Khotinenko, Vladimir, dir. *1612* (2007).
———. *The Priest* (Pop, 2009).
Kirienko, Aleksandr, dir. *Snow and Ashes* (Sneg i pepel, 2015) (miniseries).
Kott, Aleksandr, dir. *Fortress of War* (Brestskaia krepost', 2010).
Kravchuk, Andrei, dir. *The Admiral* (Admiral", 2009).
———. *Viking* (2016).
Kudriashova, Natal'ia, dir. *Pioneer-Heroes* (Pionery-geroi, 2015).
Lungin, Pavel, dir. *The Island* (Ostrov, 2006).
———. *Tsar* (2009).
Meskhiev, Dmitrii, dir. *Battalion* (Batal'ion", 2015).
Mikhalkov, Nikita, dir. *Burnt by the Sun 2: Citadel* (Utomlennye solntsem 2: Tsitadel', 2011).
———. *Burnt by the Sun 2: Exodus* (Utomlennye solntsem 2: Predstoianie, 2010).
———. *Sunstroke* (Solnechnyi udar, 2014).
Mokritskii, Sergei, dir. *The Battle for Sevastopol* (Bitva za Sevastopol', 2015).
Muradov, Aleksei, dir. *Fighters* (Istrebiteli, 2013).
Ozerov, Iurii, dir. *Liberation* (Osvobozhdenie, 1968–72).
Pimanov, Aleksei, dir. *Crimea* (Krym, 2017).
Proshkin, Andrei, dir. *The Horde* (Orda, 2012).
Prygunov, Roman, dir. *Dukhless* (2012).
———. *Dukhless 2* (2015).
Shakhnazarov, Karen, dir. *The Vanished Empire* (Ischeznuvshaia imperiia, 2008).
———. *White Tiger* (Belyi tigr, 2014).
Stepchenko, Oleg, dir. *Forbidden Kingdom* (Vii, 2014).
Ursuliak, Sergei, dir. *Life and Fate* (Zhizn' i sud'ba, 2012) (television series).

3. Russia's Quiet Other: Dmitrii Mamuliia's *Another Sky* and Aleksandr Kott's *The Test*

Ellina Sattarova

Dmitrii Mamuliia's 2010 film *Another Sky* (Drugoe nebo) and Aleksandr Kott's 2014 drama *The Test* (Ispytanie) at first glance have little in common. The former is set in contemporary Moscow; the latter in northeastern Kazakhstan in the Stalinist period.[1] While Kott's film with its stunning geometrically accurate shots and interplay of bright colors is empathically formalist, Mamuliia's "restrained" visual style tends toward that of the documentary film. What these two very different films share, however, is their focus on Russia's Others. Kott's film tells the story of a Kazakh girl, Dina, and her father, Tolgat, who fall victims to the first Soviet bomb test, conducted at the Semipalatinsk Nuclear Test Site on 29 August 1949. In *Another Sky*, Mamuliia's protagonists, Ali and his nine-year-old son, are immigrants who come to Moscow from one of the Central Asian republics in hopes of finding Ali's estranged wife. Both Mamuliia's and Kott's characters are, to borrow Giorgio Agamben's term and conceptual universe, *homines sacri*, bearers of bare life who dwell in the zone of indistinction between *bios* (politically qualified life) and *zoē* (natural reproductive life). Included only by virtue of being excluded, they are outside both divine and secular law—they can be killed but not sacrificed (Agamben, *Homo Sacer*, 73). But unlike in Agamben's conceptual universe, which is notoriously resistant to engagement with imperial and colonial histories in a theorization of the state of exception,[2] Mamuliia's and Kott's films, with their focus on Russia's Others, seem to point to the indispensability of the imperial context for understanding both the Soviet and the post-Soviet biopolitical projects.

In what follows, I investigate the convergence of imperial and biopolitical narratives in Mamuliia's and Kott's films, focusing, in particular, on their limited use of dialogue: here,

1 Neither film explicitly states its location. Mamuliia avoids all geographically grounded shots. That we are in Moscow is revealed only to the attentive eye and ear: one may recognize Moscow's Kiev Train Station or catch a muffled station announcement about a train arriving in Moscow. In Kott's film, it is the plot that leads the spectator to believe that the characters are near Semipalatinsk.

2 For a critique of Agamben's controversial lack of interest in the history of imperial and colonial narratives, see Hansen and Stepputat; Nair; and Schueller.

Russia's Others either do not speak at all (*The Test*) or speak very little (*Another Sky*). While Mamuliia's and Kott's silencing strategies may be interpreted as a replication of an imperial logic that deprives its Other of *logos*, I argue that the silencing of characters in the two films is at least attempted as a liberating gesture. Language, after all, as Agamben argues (*What Is an Apparatus?*, 14), is "the most ancient of apparatuses—one in which thousands and thousands of years ago a primate inadvertently let himself be captured, probably without realizing the consequences that he was about to face." At first glance, Mamuliia's strategy seems less ideologically problematic than Kott's; if the former questions language as such, including the language of cinema, the latter is reluctant to do so and inadvertently aligns itself with the empire. Neither film is without its problems, however. The reticence of both films (including although not limited to their refusal to ground events in a specific time and place) subsumes imperial and biopolitical narratives within the pursuit of larger metaphysical questions and discourages attempts to ponder who it is that is more likely to be reduced to bare life and be abandoned by the law.

In his volume *Language and Death*, Agamben takes issue with the inclination of Western metaphysical thought, from Aristotle onward, to define man as a mortal speaking being.[3] What troubles Agamben most about the Aristotelean definition of man as *zōon lógon échon*, man endowed with language, is that it relies on a separation between animal *phonē* and human *logos*.[4] In his most influential text to date, *Homo Sacer*, Agamben incorporates his work on language into his conception of biopolitical power and argues that the metaphysical view of language as an added capacity, as characterized by a split between *phonē* and *logos*, replicates the structural logic of the sovereign practice of isolating bare life: "The question 'In what way does the living being have language?' corresponds exactly to the question 'In what way does

3 For Heidegger, the human has the "faculty" for death precisely because he has the "faculty" for language, because death is a condition that needs to be uttered (or thought) in advance of its arrival: "Die Sterblichen sind jene, die den Tod als Tod erfahren können. Das Tier vermag dies nicht. Das Tier kann aber auch nicht sprechen. Das Wesensverhältnis zwischen Tod und Sprache blitzt auf" (quoted in Agamben, *Language and Death*, xi).

4 Aristotle's passage reads: "Man alone of the animals possesses language [*logos*]. The mere voice [*phonē*], it is true, can indicate pain or pleasure, and therefore it is possessed by the other animals as well . . . but language [*logos*] is designed to indicate the advantageous and the harmful, and therefore also the right and wrong; for it is the special property of man, in distinction from the other animals, that he alone has perception of good and bad and right and wrong and the other moral qualities, and it is partnership in these things that makes a household and a city-state" (quoted in Agamben, *Language and Death*, 87).

bare life dwell in the *polis*?' The living being has *logos* by taking away and conserving its own voice in it, even as it dwells in the *polis* by letting its own bare life be excluded, as an exception, within it" (Agamben, *Homo Sacer*, 8). Sovereign power, according to Agamben, does not only produce *homines sacri* but can also deprive them of what Western thought considers to be human "essence," their capacity to speak. An extreme manifestation of the plight of *Homo sacer* today, according to Agamben, is the figure of a *Muselmann*,[5] separated by political power from his very "essence," the "faculty" for speech: "It would be impossible for a *Muselmann* to say 'I am a *Muselmann*'" (Clemens, 119).

At first glance, Mamuliia's and Kott's decisions to leave their protagonists speechless in the face of imperial violence appear suspect. Are the two films' quiet *homines sacri* separated from their "essence" like *Muselmänner*? The short answer is no. Neither Mamuliia's nor Kott's characters qualify as *Muselmänner*. Mamuliia's reticent protagonist Ali can and does occasionally speak but often chooses to remain silent. The silence in Kott's film, as Elena Stishova ("Melankholiia," 72) suggests, may be interpreted as a metaphor for the informational vacuum (*informatsionnyi vakuum*) imposed on the Semipalatinsk residents by the Soviet empire.[6] Silence here could be seen as an alternative form of communication, rather than a lack of capacity to speak. In pursuit of the longer answer, the remainder of this chapter explores the nuances of the two directors' silencing approaches and their ideological implications.

* * *

Mamuliia's *Another Sky* begins on the steppe: Ali, the film's protagonist, is struggling with the disease and death of his sheep herd. Together with his son, Ali leaves the steppe for Moscow, where they become migrant wage workers. Although the film never returns to the steppe, the

5 The term was used in Nazi concentration camps to describe those inhabitants who, starved and exhausted, could no longer respond to their environment: "the *Muselmänner*, who, though surviving as a biological organism, could no longer be recognized as human—not only by the Nazis, but by fellow camp inmates themselves. What the death camps thereby . . . revealed is that 'man' (the mortal speaking being) can really be separated from his 'essence' (speech)" (Clemens, 118). For a critique of Agamben's use of the term, see Schueller, 243–46.

6 The 1949 atomic test was the most devastating for human exposure of all the tests conducted in Semipalatinsk, in part because the military had neither much experience nor much concern about protecting local populations. The public were not informed of any details associated with the testing and, unlike the test personnel who were sheltered in special rooms, ordinary citizens were asked to stay outside, with no explanation provided as to why they were supposed to leave their households (Werner and Purvis-Roberts, 281–87).

images of sick and dying sheep remain with the spectator throughout the film, connecting the numerous instances of illness and death into a single thread. Almost immediately after their arrival in Moscow, Ali is dragged (like an animal, by the scruff of his jacket) by a police officer to a sanitation shower. No questions are asked. As Edward Said (*Orientalism*, 39) points out, the Oriental is always already guilty: "The crime was that the Oriental was an Oriental." Stripped and disinfected, Ali is reduced to bare life—not natural life per se, but what remains after *bios* is separated from *zoē*. Without clothes, the thin yet strong shield that holds in place the distinction between the private and the public, Ali becomes one body among the numerous others at the sanitation shower, those belonging to other immigrants and homeless people. Mamuliia "rhymes" the sanitation shower scenes (there will be another one toward the end of the film) with the sequence in which the television, playing in the background in Ali's room, broadcasts news about the spread of swine flu and stresses the importance of disinfection procedures. Disinfection is required to protect the "healthy" from the "sick." Mamuliia reminds us, however, that health and disease function in today's world as biopolitical categories. Subtly yet noticeably, Mamuliia suggests that to be an immigrant and to be homeless are equated by the contemporary "anthropological machine" with being "sick" and in need of sanitation measures.

The bodies of the dying sheep on the steppe and the bodies in the sanitation shower resurge in the spectator's memory when Ali goes to a hospital to check if his wife's name has been listed on the hospital intake list. He walks down the long hallways, peeking into the rooms and looking at the patients' grotesque ailing bodies, sprawled across the beds. The patients' doors are open, allowing Ali (and us) to catch a glimpse of what is supposed to remain private. The camera follows Ali from room to room, catching only fragments of the bodies, reminding us of Ali's (and by extension, our) violation of privacy with respect to those to whom the bodies belong. Fragmented and violated by our gaze, the bodies do not amount to a whole; deprived of identity, they are reduced to bare life.

The trip to the hospital yields no results, and Ali continues his search in a brothel where the body (notably, the immigrant body) becomes a commodity *par excellence*. The prostitutes are shot from the neck down, as "headless" anonymous bodies that are "chosen like items off of a menu" (Draskoczy). If the fragmented naked bodies in the brothel episode "rhyme" with those in the sanitation shower and the hospital, the next body that Ali encounters brings back the images of the dying sheep from the film's opening. Driving home late at night, Ali slows down to avoid hitting a drunk man and instead runs over a dog. One life saved, another one ended. Ali gets out of the car for a few seconds to look at the dead dog, then drives away.

The relief, however, is only temporary. Ali soon finds out that his son was killed in a sawmill accident where the boy had been working. Although meaningful for Ali, his son's body is only one corpse among many zipped into black plastic bags at the hospital's morgue. Like the dead dog that Ali left lying on the street, his son's body has been left lying in the morgue by those indifferent to it. Mamuliia insists on this equation of the boy's life with animal life. At the train station in Moscow, Ali had carried his sleeping son over his shoulder just as he carried the dead sheep in the film's opening shots. The contemporary "anthropological machine," in Mamuliia's argument, equates immigrants, animals, the homeless, and the sick. Killed with impunity as *Homo sacer*, Ali's son is abandoned by the law. In one of the film's grimmest moments, the sawmill foreman puts a "price tag" on the body when he pays Ali for the death of his son: "Here's some money. No one is to blame. It just happened." Ali does not say a word in response.

What is at stake in Mamuliia's decision to leave his hero "speechless," even when faced with the death of his own son?

To some degree, Ali's "silence" is motivated diegetically: Ali does not speak Russian. In those rare moments when he does speak, he relies on the help of an interpreter. If *logos* is what distinguishes the human from the animal, then Ali's forced silence may be seen as further evidence that he has been reduced to bare life. Yet unlike Agamben's *Muselmann,* he says his name loud and clear at the police department. While all the other questions and answers require the mediation of an interpreter, Ali's name is self-sufficient.

That Ali is otherwise reliant on interpretation is telling: Mamuliia is suspicious of language as such. Language functions as an apparatus of capture, finalizing, in the Bakhtinian sense of the word, that which it captures—claiming to know its essence without, in fact, being able even to approximate it. The insufficiency and the inadequacy of language are emphasized by Mamuliia early in the film, even before father and son move to Moscow. In a first brief dialogue, Ali's son asks his father in Tajik whether his mother is beautiful. Ali is driving his truck on a highway. Mamuliia emphatically refuses to use conventional shot/reverse-shot technique; the camera is fixed on the road and on the cars in front of the windshield. Ali responds to his son with a single word: "Beautiful." The boy asks about the color of her eyes. Ali's answer is "black." What color is her hair, the off-screen voice wonders. Ali sticks to one-word responses:

"Black." The boy finally asks: "Why did she leave?" After a long pause, Ali says: "I don't know." The screen cuts to black. The conversation is over.

Mamuliia's refusal to rely on traditional continuity editing underscores the insufficiency of language. Words prove ineffective, at least in part because they are not paired with the images of those speaking and listening. By refusing to pair language with affect, Mamuliia destabilizes the link between language and knowledge. Language does not get to the essence of things but emerges here as an apparatus of biopolitical capture, categorizing its referent only by hair and eye color. Mamuliia stresses this point later when Ali goes to the police department in hopes that the police would help him find his wife. Among the questions are those his son had asked: What is the color of her eyes? And what is the color of her hair?

If language is an apparatus of biopolitical capture, then Ali's silence bears the potential to be liberating. His refusal to use language even when there is no language barrier suggests that he is not so much deprived of the ability to speak as wary of language and its limitations. For Agamben, it is "in man's moments of silence . . . that he at once draws close to animality at the same time as he offers the opportunity to think human potentiality, precisely when that potentiality is not actualized" (Colebrook, 23). In other words, to overcome metaphysics and, by extension, the logic of the sovereign ban, it is necessary to rethink the human capacity for language as "potentiality" in its double appearance as "potentiality to and potentiality not to" (Agamben, *Homo Sacer*, 46). Even though human beings, according to Agamben, cannot call into question their entry into language, "the simple acquisition of speech in no way obliges one to speak. The pure pre-existence of language as the instrument of communication—the fact that, for speaking beings, language already exists—in itself contains no obligation to communicate" (*Remnants of Auschwitz*, 65).

Mamuliia's protagonist Ali exercises potentiality in its double appearance as "the potentiality to and the potentiality not to" speak. The connection between silence and potentiality manifests itself with particular clarity at the end of *Another Sky*, when Ali finally finds his wife but, much to the spectator's frustration, does not say a word to her. She asks him to stop the car at one point but otherwise remains silent as well. Mamuliia draws out the closing sequence, making the silence excruciatingly "loud" in the process. When nothing is said, all the things that could have been said remain present as potentialities. Silence is an antidote to the finalizing ambition of language, as it includes simultaneously what could have been said and what could have been left unsaid.

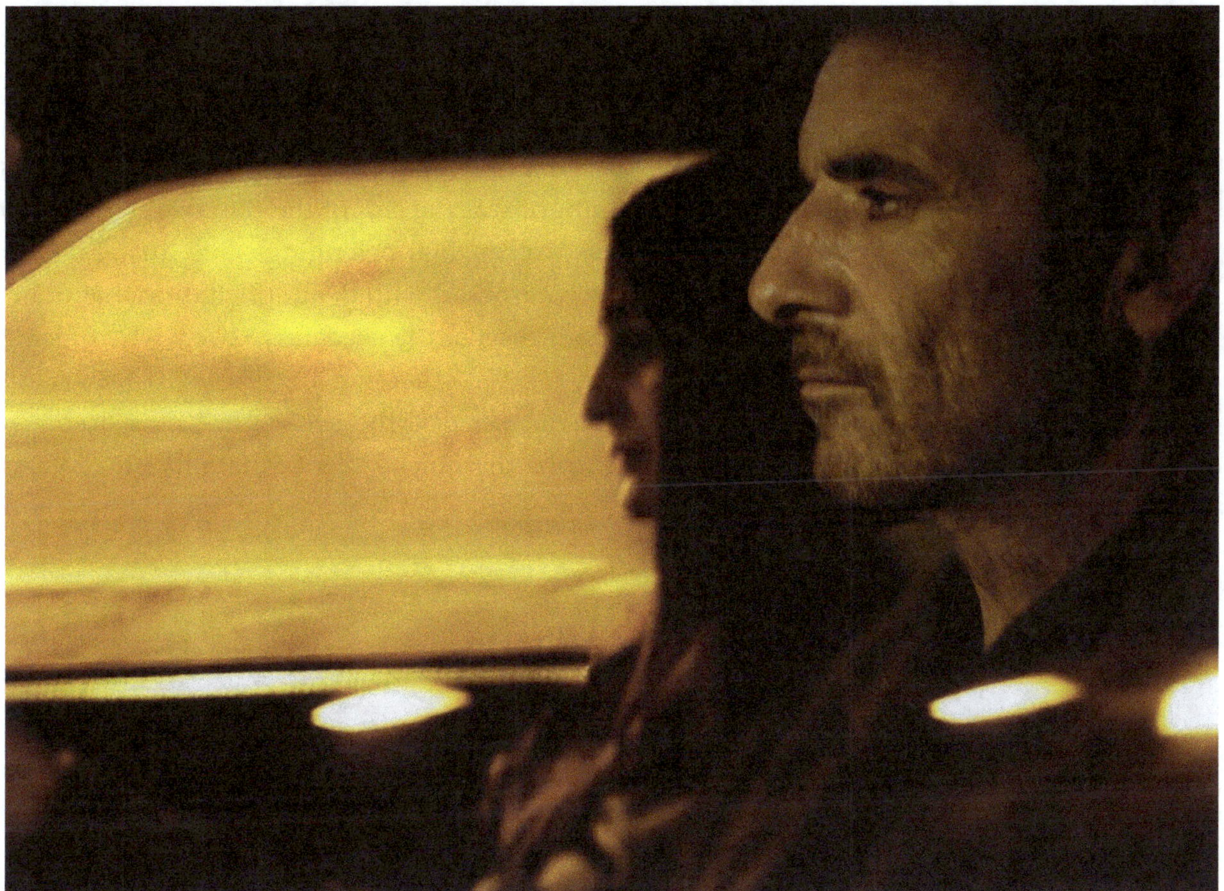

Fig. 3.1. Mamuliia, *Another Sky*. Ali's silent reunion with his wife.

* * *

Unlike Mamuliia, who limits the use of dialogue in his film and motivates this choice by intradiegetic reasons, Aleksandr Kott eliminates dialogue altogether, providing no immediate explanation for the characters' silence. Kott's *Test* at first presents itself to be a coming-of-age drama with a Kazakh girl, Dina, as its protagonist. Living with her father Tolgat, the girl cannot choose between two suitors, a local Kazakh "cowboy" named Kaisyn and a visiting Russian photographer, Maksim. Once her father dies and Dina, as a psychoanalytical reading would suggest, becomes ready to "replace" him with a more appropriate object for her love, the girl opts for the Russian suitor, Maksim.

The love story, however, comes with a twist. The film's characters, it turns out, live near Semipalatinsk, the site of the first Soviet nuclear test bomb; the year, we may surmise, is 1949. Separated from the rest of the empire by a fence, the characters are not simply cut off from the rest of the empire; they are included only by virtue of being excluded. Textbook examples of *homines sacri*, the characters are killed with impunity at the end of the film when the bomb is detonated, turning the bodies on the screen, as well as their belongings, into dust. Like Ali (*Another Sky*), who does not speak a word when confronted with death (including that of his own son), Kott's protagonists—Dina and Maksim—remain "speechless" even when facing their own death.

Unlike the diegetically motivated silence in *Another Sky*, the silence in Kott's drama is a formal device that has led many critics to describe the film as silent. The film, however, is

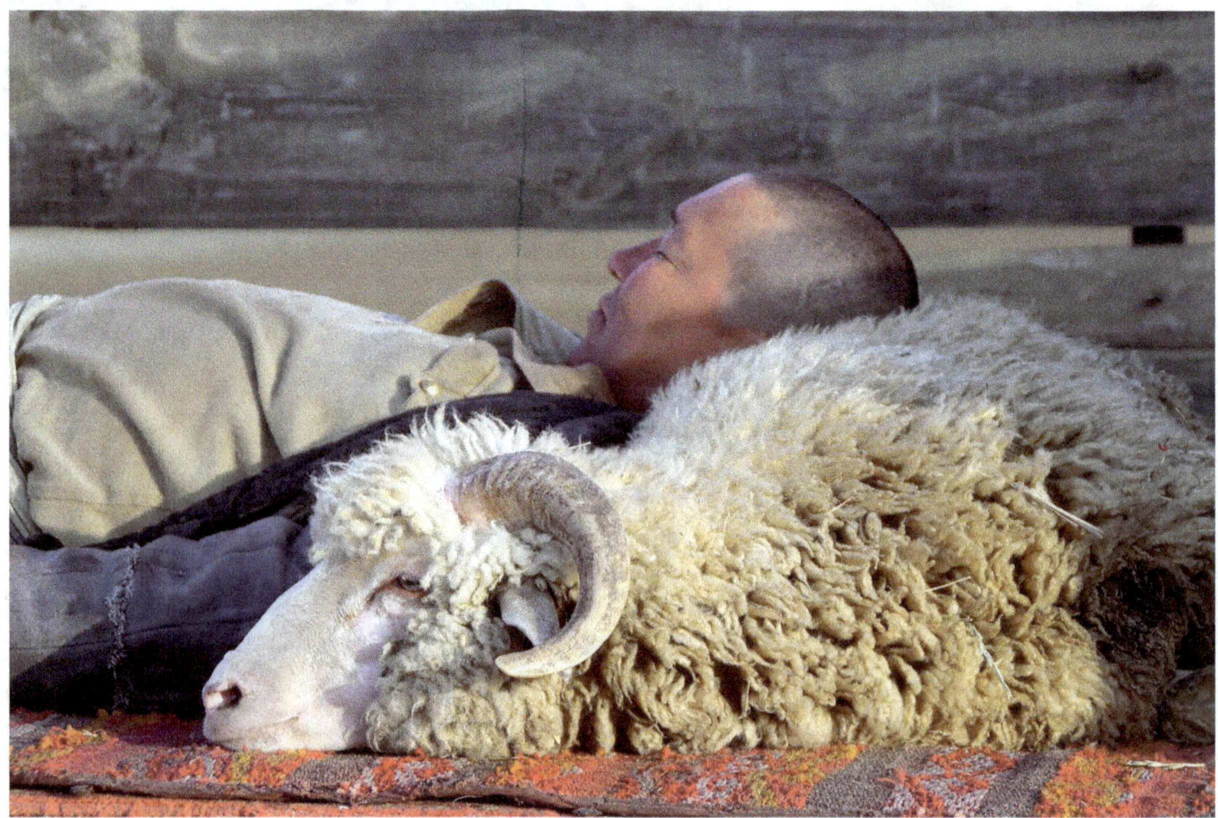

Fig. 3.2. Kott, *The Test*. Tolgat's improvised pillow.

not silent per se: the characters do not speak, but their silence, in many ways, foregrounds the sounds of nature permeating the soundtrack. Occasionally, solemn music fades in and grows louder, only to dissolve into the whisper of wind, the buzz of flies, and the chirping of birds. The film concludes by breaking its own rule—by matching a human body with its voice. Seconds before his death, Kaisyn unleashes a powerful scream. The exception, however, only proves the rule as it maintains the Aristotelean caesura between animal *phonē* that expresses pleasure and pain and human *logos* that is uniquely positioned to articulate the distinction between the just and the unjust. An expression of pain, Kaisyn's scream maintains the characters' separation from *logos* as well as *bios*.

Kott establishes the characters' proximity to the natural world, to *zoē*, early in the film: Tolgat is shot in close-up enjoying an afternoon nap; instead of a pillow, he uses a sleeping sheep. Tolgat and his daughter's lives are confined to the sphere of the *oikos*, "home" (distinct from the *polis*, the locus of *bios politikos*), characterized by "familial relations with the father as head of the household, a subsistence economy, and mere living" (Arnold, 13). Yet despite the characters' "simple" lifestyles and harmonious relationship with nature, their lives are by no means pure *zoē*. After a series of cuts, the serene napping duo in one of the opening sequences is shown lying in a Soviet truck in the middle of the steppe. Kott's characters are bearers of bare life, not natural life per se, but what remains after *zoē* is separated from *bios*.

Throughout the film, the Soviet empire manifests itself almost exclusively through technological means: the truck, the plane, the radio, the Geiger counter.[7] Even Maksim, equipped with a camera and a projector, appears as a "civilizer." He astounds Dina by projecting a black-and-white image of her on the wall. The film arguably reproduces what Madina Tlostanova describes as "the Soviet modernity's grand narrative of the backward people civilized by the Socialist Russians" (8). Kott insists, however, that the Soviet mission to assimilate and accept Russia's Others "into the only correct form of modernity" (Tlostanova, 8) ultimately failed. His characters are included in the *polis* by virtue of being excluded. In one of the film's most eloquent shots, Dina appears as a shadow on a geopolitical map hanging on the wall in her room. She is a figure par excellence of this (inclusive) exclusion of bare life.

7 One of the rare exceptions in the film only proves the rule: the Moscow Kremlin in Dina's herbarium book is made of dry leaves. The imperial center's connection with nature is thus established only through the mediation of its internal Other. It is also notable that it is only in this form that the empire proves vulnerable and perishable.

The empire that has reduced the characters to *homines sacri* has a monopoly on *logos* in the film. The only few instances in which language is used point to the inseparability of the empire from *logos*. In the first, the radio in the background informs its listeners about the beginning of yet another successful harvesting season in the north of the Rostov region. In the second, the newspaper *Izvestiia* is happy to report a surge of inflation levels in capitalist countries. That language is not entirely absent (but is rather restricted to a specific user—political power), then the characters' silence could indeed, as Stishova ("Melankholiia," 72) suggests, be understood as a metaphor for the violence inflicted by the empire on its *homines sacri*, who lived in an informational vacuum and had no say in the matter. If this is indeed Kott's intention, however, then the silence does not allow us to speak about potentiality. As a metaphor, the silence insists on making a point. The point would be Kott's, who incorporates the silence as a device into the *logos* of the film and thus reinforces the distinction between *phonē* and *logos*, *zoē* and *bios*. Notably, the third (the radio news report and the newspaper text being the other two) and the most revealing use of language in the film insists on art's capacity for *logos*. Early in the film, Dina is listening to Colombina's aria from *Pagliacci* on the radio.[8] It is unlikely that Dina understands the Italian words, but that is precisely the point for Kott, who contends that the meaning-making capacity of art (be it music or cinema) has little to do with words per se. Even if the characters' voicelessness may indeed have been intended by Kott as a critique of the imperial biopolitical project, in its attempt to render inoperative the apparatus of language, the film, I argue, inadvertently risks becoming complicit in the same project that it seeks to critique.

If, in Mamuliia's *Another Sky*, silence leaves the spectator with myriad options—none of which is realized—then in Kott's film the options are often limited. Does Kott, in an Orientalizing gesture, suggest that the characters, simple creatures as they are, do not need language to communicate? In a telling scene, for example, Dina summons Kaisyn to fetch a doctor for her sick father. Once Kaisyn arrives, the camera cuts to a shot of Dina. She turns to look and, we assume, sees Kaisyn. The horse makes a noise that ensures continuity between the two shots. Another cut; Kaisyn looks into the hut, at Dina, and immediately rides away: he understood. The camera then cuts to a shot of Dina by the window: she is waiting for the doctor to arrive. The doctor makes an appearance in the following shot. The spectator is left with a clear idea of what it was that was left unsaid ("My father is sick. Go get a doctor").

8 It is noteworthy that Dina's encounter with the opera is mediated through the technology of the empire.

The film's Kazakh characters, however, are not the only ones limited to simple wordless communication. It would be disingenuous to ignore the fact that Dina's Russian suitor, Maksim, does not speak either. In the face of imperial violence, he proves to be just as voiceless and helpless as Dina. The two of them die together, holding hands, silent. Maksim's silence at first glance attenuates the film's Orientalizing impulse; it suggests that he is just as dispensable for the state as Dina, Tolgat, and Kaisyn. They are all *homines sacri*. This narrative choice, however, shifts the focus of what appears to be Kott's argument away from issues of ethnicity and race to issues of class, suggesting that any ordinary citizen (as opposed to a member of the privileged *nomenklatura*), who happened to be in the wrong place at the wrong time, could have become a nuclear test victim, a *Homo sacer* in the Soviet empire. The film thus inadvertently mimics the attitude of the Soviet state, which, as Tlostanova (15) demonstrates, substituted race for class in its official discourse (while practicing racism all along).

Equally problematic is the fact that the film takes it upon itself to "speak" for the characters. That the characters can communicate with each other without language is conveyed by the film's editing choices. Thus, if Mamuliia avoids traditional shot/reverse-shot sequences (as in the example discussed earlier), then Kott relies on such conventional sequences to make legible that which would have remained otherwise unclear. Kott's silencing of the characters frees them from the language of the empire—one particular language—but it does not dismantle the apparatus of language altogether, nor does it at any point question its own cinematic language.

In his review of the film, Robert Bird captures the film's belief in its own capacity for *logos*: "The compositions, like the film's construction, are perfectly centered and relentlessly symmetrical; for all their poignancy, they are almost painfully legible." Further on in the review, Bird aptly describes the film as a "drama of scale." Kott alternates throughout the film between shots of different lengths: "bird's-eye shots . . . render the human world as toy-like or map-like, before zooming in for texture-rich close-ups of sheep's wool, tree bark, or the characters' faces." Kott's cinematic language, in other words, is all-powerful; the camera may replicate the imperial gaze when it surveys the vastness and the greatness of the imperial domain; or it may come close and position us near the characters. The switching itself carries meaning. When Dina discovers the fence separating her home from the rest of the empire, we are at first positioned behind her, discovering it with her as she stops in front of what is revealed to be barbed wire. The back of her head is shot in close-up, and we see only a tiny segment of the wire. The camera cuts, and we find ourselves on the opposite side of the wire; Dina's perplexed face is shot in close-up *en face*. Another cut, and we are behind Dina's back again, now several meters away from the fence, able to "appreciate" for the first time its height—about twice Dina's height. Another cut, and we are now even farther back; the fence, it turns out, spreads for miles; we do not see where it begins or ends. Finally, the camera zooms even farther out and captures Dina and the infinite fence from above: she is just a tiny dot on the screen. She is powerless in her "encounter" with the fence. The camera, on the contrary, can decide on which side of the fence to position itself, finally choosing to stay above the fence, gauging it and visually commenting on it.

Mamuliia's cinematographic choices are strikingly different. The film relies predominantly on medium shots, occasionally zooming in slightly and showing the characters in medium close-ups. It does not assume omniscience, for the most part showing things from one single position and angle. Moreover, it constantly questions its own ability to stabilize meaning. In those rare moments when characters are engaged in dialogue, the camera either shoots the interlocutors from the back or focuses on something else entirely. Even immediate proximity does not guarantee access to knowledge. When Ali, for example, leans against the truck after loading the bodies of dead sheep onto it, we are positioned behind his back and can only guess but not read his affect. On numerous occasions, the camera gets claustrophobically close to Ali, yet we are still left with little information. Dark lighting, an inconvenient angle, as well as Ali's tendency to look down and the general inexpressivity of his face, do not allow the spectator to "read" him, to make him legible (Kott, on the contrary, almost always captures his characters' faces *en face*). The ending of Mamuliia's film is particularly telling in this sense. The spectator's hopes of finally getting some answers are frustrated, in part because Ali remains silent and in part because Mamuliia does not give us access to Ali's emotional world. Shown in profile, Ali stares at the road ahead of him, his expression impenetrable to his wife's and (by extension, our) gaze. In stark contrast to the authorities who strip Ali of his privacy, the film refuses to violate the border between the public and the private or, rather, acknowledges its simultaneous desire and inability to do so.

Kott, by contrast, is more directly editorial in his claims. This is made clear already in the film's opening shots, a prolepsis of the explosion to come—Kott's film knows exactly where things are going. The spectator does not. Like Semipalatinsk nuclear victims, we are supposed to be shocked by the explosion at the end of what first appeared to be a coming-of-age romance.

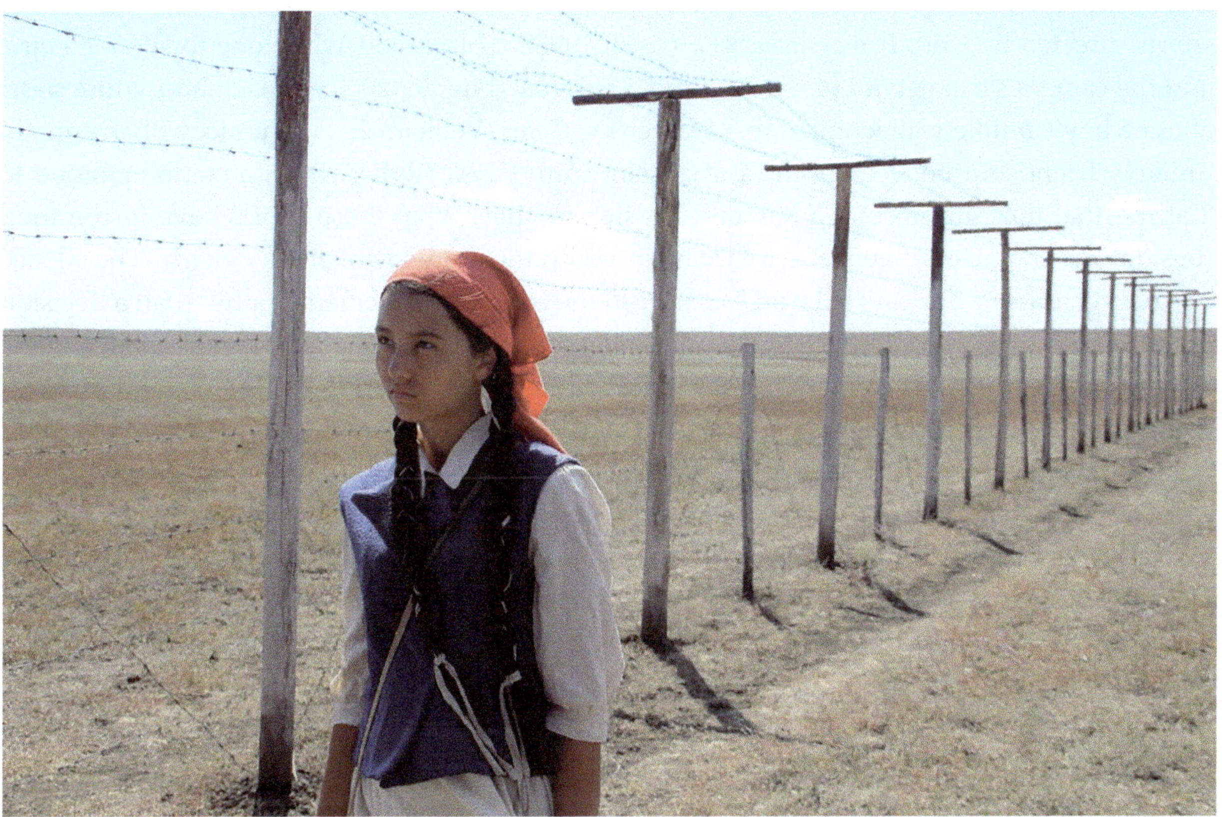

Fig. 3.2. Kott, *The Test*. Dina's encounter with the fence.

If Stishova ("Melankholiia," 72) is right and the silence is to be interpreted as a metaphor for the informational vacuum imposed on the Semipalatinsk residents by the Soviet empire, the film's own surplus of knowledge is, at the very least, suspect.

But is the "silence" indeed meant as a metaphor? Stishova, notably, is wary to commit to this interpretation, suggesting that it might be reading "too much" into it (*perebor*) ("Melankholiia," 72). Kott's passion for silent, or more accurately, wordless cinema justifies the critic's caution. Nancy Condee ("History in a Time") writes: "Since his first arrival in the mid-1990s at VGIK, . . . Kott had been interested in wordless cinema. . . . [H]is wordless script . . . *Zav'ialov and Iula* (2012) was awarded a prize at the 2012 Tekstura Festival on contemporary theatre and cinema. Kott has described the genre of wordless cinema as 'my format . . . where I scramble at the first opportunity; my parallel world.'" Wordless cinema was the "genre" of numerous shorts directed by Kott: *Photographer* (Fotograf, 1998), a black-and-white ode to silent cinema and the camera's capacity to play with time; *Scarecrow* (Pugalo, 2000), a black-and-white short about a boy's unlikely attachment to a scarecrow; *Giant* (Velikan, 2003), the story of an equally unlikely friendship between a girl and a giant mime; *Fish* (Ryba, 2008), a stepping-stone to *The Test* that tells the story of a boy and his sick mother. What these shorts have in common (besides the characters' silence) is a fascination with the aesthetic of silent cinema. The silence of Kott's characters appears to be an *hommage* to the early days of cinema rather than a decision dictated by the film's content. Even though Kott's script *Zav'ialov and Iula* has never been made into a film, the director's remarks about it are telling: "It is a story outside time and space; it could happen now, it could happen today, it could happen tomorrow. And it does not matter where. However banal it may be, it is a story about eternal values, about first feelings."

This sense of timelessness that is characteristic of Kott's earlier work is tangible in *The Test* as well. What can be more universal than a coming-of-age love story? It eliminates, at least in Kott's telling of it, the need for names, words, or any other specifics. That the characters are near Semipalatinsk and the year is 1949 is an educated guess but nonetheless a guess. The nuclear explosion is relegated here almost to an afterthought. The sublime images of the mushroom cloud in the closing sequences bring to mind an earlier scene, in which the lighting strikes and burns down a lonely tree in the steppe. The scene foreshadows the explosion but simultaneously dissociates it from its immediate historical context. The choice of Semipalatinsk as the Soviet nuclear testing site was a political decision that had to do with race, geography, and colonial power.[9] The film, however, chooses to subsume imperial thanatopolitics under the tired message about the transience and beauty of life and love and thus replicates the imperial logic by enacting a double erasure of more than a million Semipalatinsk nuclear victims.

Mamuliia, who refuses to "speak" for the Other and challenges cinema's capacity to finalize, in the ultimate analysis pursues a project similar to Kott's—a metaphysical rather than a political one. We do not know where Ali comes from and can only guess that he relocates to Moscow. We do not know the names of his son and wife. And even though the sudden death of Ali's son comes as a result of his unlawful employment as an immigrant child laborer, the

9 As Gabrielle Hecht argues in *Being Nuclear*, despite the widespread view that "splitting the atom promulgated a new world order that replaced imperialism with 'the bomb,' [i]t was clear that colonialism remained central to the nuclear order's technological and geopolitical success. Even a short list of atomic test sites makes the point: Bikini Atoll, Semipalatinsk, Australian Aboriginal lands, the Sahara, French Polynesia" (ix).

pervasiveness of death in the film makes us wonder whether the sawmill foreman is right and indeed "no one is to blame." Sheep, dogs, people die (today as likely from unnatural as natural causes), and even an all-inclusive law would not be able to change that. Is Agamben (*Homo Sacer*, 114) right to suggest that "what confronts us today is a life that as such is exposed to a violence without precedent precisely in the most profane and banal ways"? Are we "all virtually *homines sacri*" (115)?

Both Kott and Mamuliia—despite the striking differences in their approaches—ultimately fall into the same trap as Agamben himself, who, although perfectly aware of Said's argument, participates in the discourse of orientalism, as Malini Johar Schueller (243) suggests, by refusing to address the "otherness" of bare life: "We might all be 'virtually' *homines sacri*, but only some of us are marked to be in the permanent state of exception."

Filmography

Kott, Aleksandr, dir. *Fish* (Ryba). 2008.
Kott, Aleksandr, dir. *Giant* (Velikan). 2003.
Kott, Aleksandr, dir. *Photographer* (Fotograf). 1998.
Kott, Aleksandr, dir. *Scarecrow* (Pugalo). 2000.
Kott, Aleksandr, dir. *The Test* (Ispytanie). 2014.
Mamuliia, Dmitrii, dir. *Another Sky* (Drugoe nebo). 2010.

Part Two

HILARITY AND HORROR

Framing Essay

Alexander Prokhorov and Elena Prokhorova

The chapters in this section examine filmmakers who deploy genre conventions as analytical tools to explore present-day Russia and its engagement with the past—a past that isn't dead and isn't even past, to paraphrase William Faulkner (73). It is no coincidence that Aleksei Balabanov's *Cargo 200* is inspired by Faulkner's *Sanctuary*. While the hybridity of this exploratory cinema precludes its precise categorization, we would like to argue that it is a peculiar offspring of postmodern neo-noir. Incidentally, American 1990s neo-noir films found a receptive audience in Russia after the fall of communism. Perhaps what post-Soviet filmmakers found congenial in American neo-noir of the 1990s is its irreverent and playful treatment of classical Hollywood tropes and genres along with its faux optimistic social outlook.

Russian neo-noir filmmakers' major contribution is the new cinematic language, which abandons Soviet-era understanding of the nature of the cinematic image as an epitome of truth, whether ideological or aesthetic. This tradition also by necessity suggested that there could be only one truth and that the image is the transcendental passageway to access it. In contrast, such filmmakers as Aleksei Balabanov, Vasilii Sigarev, Valeriia Gai Germanika, Aleksei Fedorchenko, Kirill Serebrennikov, Boris Khlebnikov—and, in their earlier years, Petr Buslov and Aleksei Uchitel'—are among those who explicitly work in what might be described as a post-authentic mode of representation.

One of the prime targets of this new cinema is to denaturalize tropes inherited from Soviet cinema—above all, the performance of togetherness. In Soviet films, such a performance meant the primacy of the collective, a metonym for the loyalty to the Soviet state. Instead, in depicting the relationship between the individual and the state, the filmmakers offer a variety of alternative models: from irony and eccentricity to comedy and horror. This particular trope of loyalty is by no means extinct, as the chapters in other sections of this volume (by Wilmes, Mukhortova, and Gray) show. It is likewise prominent in government-sponsored big budget commercial productions about the Great Patriotic War, Soviet achievements in sports and space, and the spiritual origins of Russia in Crimea.

By contrast, Russian neo-noir films of the post-Soviet era claim that the Soviet collectivity is damaging to the society and the individual. Moreover, the process of this collectivity's disintegration still continues. This collectivity (primarily invested in the state) lurks behind institutions that otherwise seem to exist *outside* the state. The practitioners of this cinema of exploration—such as Balabanov, Fedorchenko, Gai Germanika, Sigarev, Zviagintsev, and Bykov—depict how the state drains life out of the nuclear family, private business, school, male community, or communities built across ethnic borders.

Russian filmmakers also seem to share neo-noir's pessimistic sensibility and philosophy of storytelling. Such films as Jonathan Demme's *Silence of the Lambs* (1991), Quentin Tarantino's *Reservoir Dogs* (1994), or Joel and Ethan Coen's *Fargo* (1996) convey "alienation, pessimism, moral ambivalence, and disorientation" (Conard, 2). In comparison to its classical antecedents, neo-noir films benefited from the absence of Production Code censorship. "Whereas, under the censorship of the Hays Office, for example, no crime could go unpunished, in neo-noir the criminals can, and, indeed, very often do succeed. Good things happen to bad people, and bad things happen to good people (just like in real life!), which seems in line with noir's cynicism and pessimism" (Conard, 2).

The films examined in "Hilarity and Horror" (Section II) by Daria Ezerova, Robert Crane, and Denis Saltykov share a common neo-noir feature—combining comedy with extreme violence and skepticism to the point of nihilism about the power of reason. The most disturbing sequences, such as a torture scene in Balabanov's *Dead Man's Bluff* (Zhmurki, 2005), often border on ludicrous. Life in the absurdly violent world is full of comic possibilities. Thus the cruelty of the society and individual psyche manifests itself in such narratives as pointless journeys revealing the futility of any hope for the affirmation of order at the film's end.

Violence is central for the neo-noir discussed in this section. It emanates from the very fabric of society and is neither valorized nor justified by framing ideological narratives, a familiar storytelling technique from the Soviet past. As a result, released from its narrative bonds, violence has the potential to become a trigger for social commentary.

Because these filmmakers privilege their own idiosyncratic tales over somebody else's vision (be it the state's vision or some admixture), they use genre conventions as heuristic tools to tell their stories as they choose. Genre purity is unabashedly not their strong suit, because they are concerned neither with the task of selling their films to the broadest possible audience nor with the self-imposed constraints of genre compliance. Instead, they practice what we will call hybrid or fusion genres. In the pages that follow, Daria Ezerova examines how comedy and social horror interact in the films of Aleksei Balabanov and Vasilii Sigarev. Robert Crane examines eccentric filmmaking as a practice that consciously blurs the border between documentary and fiction cinema. Denis Saltykov looks at the uses of violence in generic hybrids of male melodrama and social drama.

Comedies and social dramas examined in this section articulate such key tropes of the new Russian cinema as dystopian urban setting as a site of ongoing warfare; a vision of the post-Soviet person as this urban warfare's main combatant; the representation of this post-Soviet subject as a sociopathic monster; and, finally, deep suspicion of any narrative of progress or social justice. As Balabanov summarized his views on history and social progress: "There is no development of humankind at all . . . and never has been" (Condee, *Imperial Trace,* 223). New Russian social drama and comedy depict characters who might be improving their survival skills, but instead follow the regressive path of cruel animals. The rare moments of humanity transpiring through this ongoing savagery provide a moment of comic relief, as in the final scene of Sigarev's *The Land of Oz* (Strana Oz, 2015).

4. Laughing Apocalypse: Horror and/as Comedy

Daria Ezerova

> There's a thin line between horror and hilarity.
>
> —*Robert Bloch, author of Psycho (quoted in Hallenbeck, 3)*

In the early scenes of Jonathan Demme's horror classic *The Silence of the Lambs* (1991), cryptic hints from Doctor Hannibal Lecter (Anthony Hopkins) take Jodie Foster's FBI agent Clarice Starling to an abandoned storage room. After carefully examining the eerie interior, filled with cobwebbed bric-a-brac, Starling uncovers the severed, partially decomposed human head that provides the film's first big shock. During her debriefing with Dr. Lecter, he asks her how she felt when she made this skin-crawling discovery. Hesitant at first, Clarice eventually responds, "Scared at first. Then . . . exhilarated."

Whether Demme planned it or not, Clarice's words aptly describe the experience of watching a horror film. As William Paul remarks in his *Laughing, Screaming: Modern Hollywood Horror and Comedy*, "It is *fun* to indulge in feelings that in the context of the real world would give us a pause, to experience the surge of vitality that comes with the sudden onset of any strong feeling" (422, emphasis in the original). This mixture of fear, excitement, and, according to Paul, fun, attests to the horror film's capacity to manipulate the audience's response to what they see on screen and trigger this odd exhilaration at the sight of corpses, serial killers, evil forces, knives cutting through flesh and sending guts flying, guns blowing brains out, and so on. But what happens when this exhilaration is accompanied by laughter? Is that response not at odds with the other reactions?

What makes humor challenging in the context of horror films may be that it "renders the[ir] most menacing characters impotent" (Miller and Riper, xii), alleviating shock and reducing fear. Yet the different responses elicited by horror and comedy have not prevented filmmakers and scholars from savoring the mix of screaming and laughter. Alfred Hitchcock famously described *Psycho* (1960) as "a fun picture" (Paul, 408). Bruce G. Hallenbeck (4) detects elements of comedy in Stanley Kubrick's *The Shining* (1980). In his 1967 horror-comedy *The Fearless Vampire Killers, or Pardon Me, But Your Teeth Are in My Neck*, Roman Polanski managed to make his viewers laugh and scream, while also allowing himself "to take on the subjects like the deep histories of oppression that beset Central Europe" (Miller and Riper xix). Yet the role of laughter in horror films is not limited to distancing the viewer from the gory goings-on of the film and offering comic relief. As Cynthia J. Miller and A. Bowdoin Van Riper observe in their introduction to *The Laughing Dead: The Horror-Comedy Film from Bride of Frankenstein to Zombieland*: "the varying degrees and configurations of humor present can altogether alter th[e] impact [of the horror genre]. Sometimes, as in the case of family entertainment, humor renders the monstrous familiar and fears are erased; at other times, dark comedy reshapes traditional horror into surreal nightmare; and in both cases, as laughter dulls the supernatural threat . . . , the social commentary the characters deliver becomes correspondingly sharper" (xix).

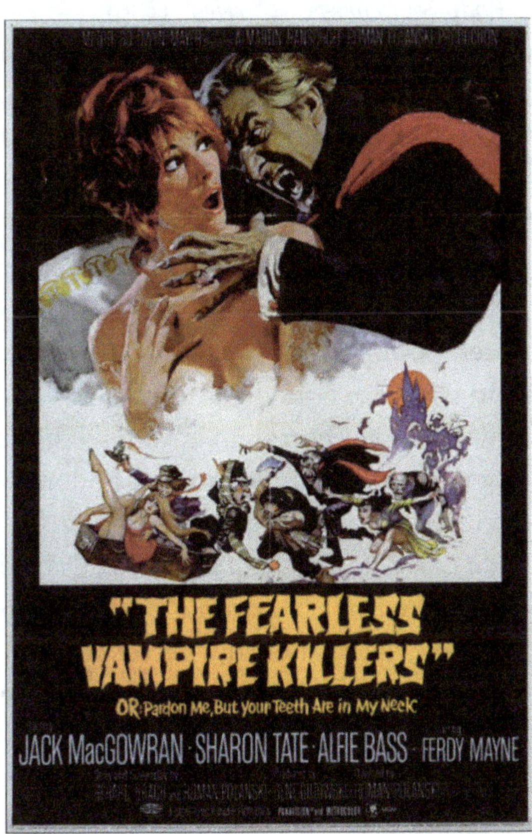

Fig. 4.1. Polanski, *The Fearless Vampire Killers, or Pardon Me, but Your Teeth Are in My Neck.* Comedy horror.

Dating back to early silent film, comedy and horror have always coexisted. The combination of the two comes in a multitude of forms with different social messages determined by the kind of humor introduced into a horror film and the ways in which it is incorporated in it. This chapter is dedicated to a genre in contemporary Russian cinema that channels both comedy and horror.

Russian (So-Called) Horror

Critics have argued that horror in the Russian cinematic tradition has been an underrepresented genre, especially in the Soviet era, when it was viewed as ideologically suspect. In her overview of horror film history in Russia, Josephine Woll writes: "the Russian screen showed horrors in the conventional Western sense . . . in the decade before the establishment of the Soviet Union . . . and in the last decade or so[.] Soviet studios produced many sorts of films, but no *Cabinets of Dr. Caligari*, no *Nosferatus*, no *Psychos*, no *Diaboliques*, *Rosemary's Babys* or *Exorcists*, no *Nights of the Living Dead* or *Invasions of the Body Snatchers* or *Carries*" (336).

A notable exception was Konstantin Ershov and Georgii Kropachev's *Vii* (1967), an eponymous adaptation of Nikolai Gogol's 1835 novella. Even today, decades after communism, few recent Russian films that have been described as "horror" entirely fit with the conventional definition of a horror film. Without trying to fit these works on the Procrustean bed of genre, a broader point can be made that often, rather than observing the generic codes set by classical and postclassical Hollywood cinema,[1] Russian filmmakers have used certain elements of horror to create their own cinematic language in post-Soviet art film.

The "repurposing" of horror is not exclusive to contemporary Russian cinema, of course. Its elements have long appeared in Hollywood cinema in what are not horror films per se (as in several films by Hitchcock and Polanski, for example). Classic horror themes have been lucratively appropriated by recent television series: ghouls and mummies roam London in Showtime's *Penny Dreadful* (2014–16); zombies rise again in AMC's *The Walking Dead* (2010–); vampires fire the viewer's imagination in HBO's *True Blood* (2008–14); and FOX's *Scream Queens* (2015–17) piles up chopped-off limbs. However, I am interested not in horror's proliferation into other genres and media but in how its aesthetics volatilize the relationship between *auteur* and genre cinema when it enters into art film. In the Russian cultural context, where "genre cinema traditionally has a bad reputation" (Seckler, 28), the phenomenon has special import.

I am adapting the term "social thriller" as the basis of a framework to discuss the films in this chapter. Invoked ("Jordan Peele") by the Brooklyn Academy of Music as the title of a film series dedicated to Jordan Peele's directorial debut *Get Out* (2017), a thriller that "wields the tools of the genre to expose racism lurking at the edges of polite, everyday interactions" (Chan). The film series included disparate horror or horror-tinged films such as Wes Craven's *Scream* (1996), Joe Dante's *The 'Burbs* (1989), Stanley Kubrick's *The Shining* (1980), Roman Polanski's *Rosemary's Baby* (1968), and George A. Romero's *Night of the Living Dead* (1968).

1 This does not mean that Russian directors made no attempts to copy from Hollywood. A very few efforts at Western horror films can be found throughout the post-Soviet period, from Nikolai Lebedev's *Snake Spring* (Zmeinyi istochnik, 1997) to Aleksandr Strizhenov's *Iulen'ka* (2009), and more recently. They are not discussed in this chapter.

What defines a "social thriller" then? Adapting the coinage to the Russian context, I propose that post-Soviet "social thrillers" share a number of elements in common. The films I discuss here all use the cinematic language of horror to comment on history and society; the violence and gore they employ are neither purely exploitative nor stylistic. Rather, these elements are meant to serve as allegories for social issues. In Aleksei Balabanov's *Cargo 200* (Gruz 200, 2007) the repeated sexual assault of Angelika becomes an allegory of a hostile and aged Soviet state inflicting violence on its citizens. Fittingly, the film's psychopathic villain, Police Captain Zhurov, is unable to perform sexually, recapitulating the motif of an impotent power of late socialism. In Vasilii Sigarev's dark dramas *Wolfie* (Volchok, 2009) and *Live* (Zhit', 2012), and his "comedy" *The Land of Oz* (Strana Oz, 2015), the ongoing physical abuse and other misfortunes readily translate into what Birgit Beumers and Mark Lipovetsky (153) describe as "a metaphor for cynical violence as a universal language of social communication . . . the post-Soviet war where everybody fights each other."

This allegorical use of horror is what sets social thrillers apart from two related genres: *chernukha* and the "feel-bad film," as elaborated by Nikolaj Lübecker (2). These genres may resemble the social thriller, but they differ in a number of ways. A hallmark of late Soviet cinema, *chernukha* can be broadly defined as "representational art that emphasizes the darkest, bleakest aspects of human life . . . [with] an emphasis on physicality and 'naturalism'" (Graham, "*Chernukha*"). Whatever unseemly side of life it chooses to capture, *chernukha* does so with minimal recourse to allegory. Equally as dreary as *chernukha*, the "feel-bad film" engages in a different way that goes "through the body of the spectator to reach her intellect" (Lübecker, 5) and as a result produces works that are "unpleasant, worrying, and perhaps even manipulative" (5). While social thrillers may elicit a similar affect, creating intense discomfort alone is not what distinguishes them.

Whereas horror films focus on external threats—monsters from the netherworld or outside menaces as Cold War allegories (*Invasion of the Body Snatchers* [1958] or *The Thing from Another World* [1951]), for example—social thrillers situate the threat inside the society itself, creating a sort of "monster within." The threat is neither a thing nor a person but a social issue, a sentiment, or an ideology. The "monster" slain in *Cargo 200* is the Soviet nostalgia that resurfaced in the early 2000s, which Balabanov sees as a symptom of cultural amnesia. In his *Of Freaks and Men* (Pro urodov i liudei, 1998), it is the excessive idealization of prerevolutionary St. Petersburg and early cinema; in Sigarev's *The Land of Oz*, it is the absurd hostility and pitilessness of everyday life in contemporary Russia. In this way, social thrillers hold up a mirror to the spectator: to use the words of the film critic Evgenii Gusiatinskii ("Brat zhil"), "the lead character . . . [is] each person sitting in the movie theater."

Social thrillers tend to be open-ended, speaking to the present and ongoing nature of the problems they address and projecting the anxieties of the current moment into the future. Consequently, even if the film's antagonist eventually dies, the ending still does not offer relief or catharsis. At the end of *Of Freaks and Men*, the antiheroes Johann (Sergei Makovetskii) and Viktor Stepanovich (Viktor Sukhorukov) are eliminated, but this does not preclude the film's dark finale: the twins perish in a tragic and degrading fashion; Liza (Dinara Drukarova) moves to the West and succumbs to her S&M inclinations; and the newly famous photographer Putilov (Vadim Prokhorov)—a memorably nauseating minor character in the mold of Gustave Flaubert's Homais—is chased by a crowed of ecstatic groupies. In *Cargo 200*, the archvillain Zhurov (Aleksei Poluian) is shot dead, but the film does not end there: Angelika (Agniia Kuznetsova) is left chained to the bed, perhaps doomed to die among three corpses; and Valera (Leonid Bichevin), who is ultimately responsible for the tragic turn of events, swaggers into the sunrise with his new friend, the implication being that the rampage will continue and the two young men will likely also perish in the turmoil of the 1990s. In *The Land of Oz*, when Lena Shabadinova's (Iana Troianova) wanderings are finally over, the appearance of a foul-mouthed nurse ("You're all fucked in the head, you fucking singers? Shut the fuck up!") reminds the viewers that the outside world is still not on their side.

Considering that the elements of horror are meant to reflect on post-Soviet Russia and provide social commentary, none of the above characteristics are particularly surprising. However, social thrillers share one feature that seems to demand further explanation—the use of the comic. In classic horror cinema, laughter produces a sort of *Verfremdungseffekt* that paradoxically reassures the viewer that "the characters' worlds . . . will be intact when the credits roll, and nothing similar could happen to *us*" (Miller and Riper, xvi; emphasis in the original). This distancing function of laughter is accounted for in Henri Bergson's "Laughter, an Essay on the Meaning of the Comic": "the comic demands something like a momentary anaesthesia of the heart. Its appeal is to intelligence, pure and simple" (11). Would not laughter then blunt the trenchant critique provided by social thrillers? It does not seem to do so in the films under discussion. As a result, three questions arise: How does horror intertwine with the comic? How do these films prevent laughter from producing a distancing effect? Do they in fact *seek out* laughter to serve and advance their aesthetic project? The remainder of this chapter addresses these three questions in the work of two Russian filmmakers whom I see as the primary producers of social thrillers.

Aleksei Balabanov, *Cargo 200*

Since 2007, when Aleksei Balabanov's *Cargo 200* arrived on the big screen, no other Russian film has polarized critical and public opinion quite as much. From disgust to glowing praise, the film generated starkly divergent reactions among film critics and general audiences. Now a cult film, *Cargo 200* continues to provoke discussion. How do we interpret the film's strange and merciless world, populated with cruel, broken, and flawed characters and an ever-growing number of putrefying cadavers? Is this a form of late Soviet Grand Guignol or, paradoxically, a violent hyperrealism? Can we even trust the intertitle "based on real-life events" that "Balabanov-the-Trickster" (Kuvshinova et al., 242) plants in the opening of the film? Or is the film a complex allegory that extends in its impact far beyond the time of the diegesis (1984)? And why focus on the year 1984 and the Soviet military campaigns in Afghanistan? Is it because this is the year when the term "cargo 200" was first used to designate the air transport of dead soldiers who were killed there? Or is it an Orwellian metaphor, in anticipation of a dystopian narrative? *Cargo 200* is fertile ground for divergent interpretations.

Set in a decaying industrial backwater, the film follows the story of Angelika, a young girl who is kidnapped by the psychopathic policeman Captain Zhurov. After attending a local disco, Angelika goes driving with her love interest, the dissolute Valera, who takes her to the secluded house of a local moonshiner, Aleksei (Aleksei Serebriakov). The intimidating policeman Zhurov, whose relation to Aleksei is not yet clearly established, circles around the house. After Valera drinks himself into oblivion, Aleksei's wife, Antonina (Natal'ia Akimova), hides Angelika in the bathhouse for her own protection. However, Zhurov finds the girl and brutally rapes her with a bottleneck. The next morning, he takes Angelika to his apartment, where he chains her to the bed and leaves her under the supervision of his half-crazy alcoholic mother (Valentina Andriukova). After that, the atrocities multiply and escalate. In what is viewed as perhaps the most harrowing scene in contemporary Russian film, Zhurov takes the corpse of Angelika's fiancé, just transported from Afghanistan, and flings it on the bed next to her. He then releases one of the convicts (Aleksandr Bashirov) from a local prison, brings him to his house to rape Angelika, then executes him. Yet Angelika's torments are not finished: Zhurov sits with her and her corpse fiancé, reading aloud the dead man's love letters. Finally, Antonina breaks in to shoot Zhurov but refuses to set the girl free. Angelika is left chained to the bed, surrounded by three corpses. Her fate is unknown.

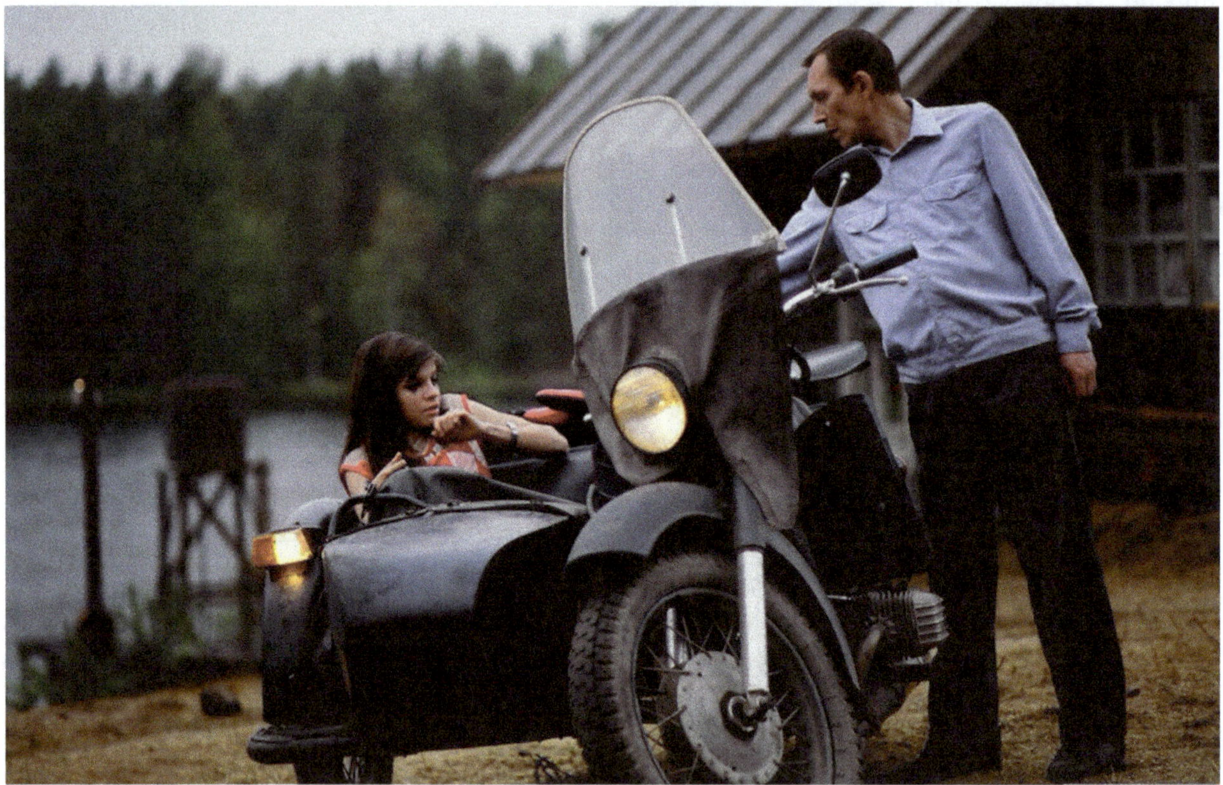

Fig. 4.2. Balabanov, *Cargo 200*. Policeman Zhurov kidnapping Angelika.

Mariia Kuvshinova, a Russian film critic and Balabanov's biographer, recalls her first experience of watching *Cargo 200*: "I don't remember anything in film, literature, or art that would impose itself on man with such inevitable, unbearable heaviness. Balabanov's film knocks the ground from under your feet, deprives you of a point of reference, and once and for all strips you of all personal, religious, or social idealism. . . . *Cargo 200* is incredibly harsh on the viewer; there's not a hint of purification" (Norris, *Blockbuster History*, 203). The first-time screening is described by Daniil Dondurei on the television broadcast *Closed Screening* (Zakrytyi pokaz) as leaving the spectators feeling as if they had been watching something that they should not see, turning the viewing process into "a colossal psychological ordeal." Yet the film is anything but a slasher movie. *Cargo 200* presents the most searing of Balabanov's critiques of late socialism and deals a mortal blow to the popular nostalgia for the Soviet Union.

The power of the film's "shock therapy" comes from the elements of horror in the film,[2] a connection that becomes particularly clear when read through the lens of Julia Kristeva's *Powers of Horror*. On the one hand, Balabanov extensively uses conventional horror-film visuals that are also the most straightforward examples of Kristeva's notion of the abject ("the traitor, the liar, . . . the shameless rapist, the killer who claims he is a savior," and multiple corpses that are "the utmost abjection[,] death infecting life" [4]). On the other hand, as Nancy Condee comments, "most of its [*Cargo*'s] sadomasochism draws on th[e] Stalinist legacy, with which it is intimately, even erotically intertwined" (*Imperial Trace*, 227). The film presents a meticulous debunking of Soviet aesthetics and ideology through inversion (the policeman, a representative of the Soviet state, turns out to be a cold-blooded killer) or juxtaposition (the functioning industrial park, a popular *topos* of socialist realism, is shot in a way similar to that of a Soviet propaganda film—low-angle tracking shots, long takes—but is intended to serve as the backdrop for the harrowing events).

Given the unfinished legacy of Soviet culture, the systematic deconstruction of its symbols becomes a powerful source of the film's shock value. In fact, the deconstruction of the Soviet becomes *Cargo 200*'s own brand of the abject; as Kristeva writes, "the sense of abjection . . . is anchored in the superego. The abject is perverse because it neither gives up nor assumes a prohibition, a rule, or a law; but turns them aside, misleads, corrupts; uses them, takes advantage of them" (15). The visceral response that *Cargo 200* elicits for Russian audiences may be seen as emanating from the post-Soviet superego: it is not the excess of violence per se that frightens and provokes, but precisely its assault on post-Soviet consciousness and its negation of nostalgia for communism.

2 In his chapter on *Cargo 200*, Stephen Norris refers to it as a "shock therapy for those who have failed to remember their history, an electric shot to the brain that wards off the infection of banal commercialized and nostalgic pasts" (*Blockbuster History*, 197).

Once the initial shock subsides, *Cargo 200*'s twisted humor comes into view, posing the inevitable question of why, in a film that sets itself the difficult project of erasing sympathy for the Soviet past, was it necessary for Balabanov to use comedy? Wouldn't laughter, a mechanism that distances the viewers from what they see on screen, undercut critique? We might venture that Balabanov had to find a kind of humor that would not only *not* have the distancing effect on the viewers but would also strengthen the impact of the film's "shock therapy." A closer reading of the humor in *Cargo 200* shows that it is rooted in the same place as its horror: the mode of excess.

The mode of excess in *Cargo 200* is that of *transgression*; as Georges Bataille (*Eroticism*, 63, 65) writes, "transgression does not deny the taboo but transcends it . . . once a limited license has been allowed, unlimited urges towards violence may break forth." But what makes the excesses of *Cargo 200* remarkable is that the escalation of violence tends toward the comedic mode rather than the other way round: "the progressive building up of a gag [or physical and sexual abuse, in Balabanov's case] always seeking its own topper . . . the primary narrative drive comes in the form of an ever-increasing escalation" (Paul, 416–17). Balabanov inverts the classic buildup of comedy, offering us a distorted, funhouse-mirror version: with each subsequent abuse more harrowing and more extended than the previous one, the intensification of gruesome scenes forms the narrative momentum of *Cargo 200*.[3] As in slapstick comedy, the excess does not serve a merely stylistic purpose but becomes the main driving force of the plot, while simultaneously bringing our attention to the ludicrous amount of cruelty that, on second, third, or (most likely) tenth viewing, starts to look comically overdone. This mode of excess goes beyond the amassment of corpses and operates on other levels, inextricably intertwining horror with comedy and fear with neurotic laughter. This excess is what ultimately makes the film generically transgressive.

The disorienting abundance of conflicting generic cues is in force in the very first scene, a dialogue between two brothers, Artem (Leonid Gromov, dubbed by Sergei Makovetskii), a professor of scientific atheism at Leningrad University, and Mikhail (Iurii Stepanov), an army colonel. The two appear to be concerned about current Russian politics ("I feel like something has gone forever, and I don't know what's coming. When Andropov died, they all began to

3 Paul discerns a similar appropriation of this mode of narrative development in Hitchcock's *The Birds* (1963), Romero's *Night of the Living Dead* (1968), and Tobe Hooper's *The Texas Chainsaw Massacre* (1974). Incidentally, like *Cargo 200*, Hooper's film was also (falsely) marketed as "based on real-life events."

fidget") and the war in Afghanistan, perhaps suggesting that these will be the central themes of the film. Despite the seriousness of the topic, the mise-en-scène—from a massive jar of beer and dried fish on the table to Artem's fuzzy mohair sweater—clashes with the subject of the conversation, eliciting smiles rather than foreboding tragedy. Yet once Artem leaves his brother's apartment, the film shifts into a different style and setting, deploying B-movie and horror-film tropes. Artem's car breaks down, leaving him stranded in the middle of nowhere. The full moon and the dark forest provide a fitting, if hackneyed, backdrop. As he stumbles through the woods, Artem runs into a sinister police officer who appears from outside the frame and wordlessly directs Artem to the proverbial cabin in the woods. When Artem enters, the mood changes again: instead of a horror-film turn of events, the viewers find themselves in the home of a local moonshiner, listening to drunken conversation about the existence of God, the future and problems of the Soviet Union, the City of the Sun, Campanella, and the immortal soul. After Angelika and Valera arrive at the site and the first series of tragic events begins to unfold, the film's literary intertext emerges. *Cargo 200* is a transposition of William Faulkner's *Sanctuary* (1931): Angelika is Temple Drake; Zhurov is Popeye; Aleksei is Lee Goodwin; Valera is Gowan Stevens—and a bottleneck is used instead of a corncob as the instrument of rape. By the middle of the film, viewers find themselves caught between a horror movie, a thriller, a comedy, a kind of a period piece,[4] and an adaptation of high modernist literature. Along with the glut of violence that follows, this excess of generic cues contains elements both funny and horrifying.

So, if horror in *Cargo 200* is intermixed with comedy, then what are the elements of Balabanov's humor that negate the distancing effect of laughter and ultimately drive home *Cargo 200*'s commentary? Arguably, if the vehicle for both the comic and the horror is excess, the essence of *Cargo 200*'s humor is located in the untranslatable Russian word *stiob*. Aleksei Yurchak (*Everything Was Forever*, 249–50) defines *stiob* as "a peculiar form of irony that differ[s] from sarcasm, cynicism, derision, or any of the familiar genres of absurd humor. It require[s] such degree of *overidentification* with the object, person, or idea at which this *stiob* [is] directed that it [is] often impossible to tell whether it [is] a form of sincere support, subtle ridicule, or a peculiar mixture of the two" (emphasis mine). *Stiob* thus presents a type of humor in

4 Balabanov's costume and set designers went to great lengths in recreating the atmosphere and fashions of provincial Russia in the mid-1980s.

which the comic effect is achieved not through distancing and alienation but through overidentification and familiarity. The stronger the over-identification, the more powerful the effect of "the displacement of symbolic order" (Yurchak, *Everything Was Forever*, 250) that *stiob* performs. In *Cargo 200*, *stiob* underpins the visual and aural excess, allowing for the necessary overidentification to emerge. As Yurchak remarks elsewhere ("Gagarin," 84), *stiob* humor appeared in the late Soviet period as a result of "the immense incongruity between the messages and cultural forms in the official and non-official spheres." In his own version of *stiob*, Balabanov strives to recreate this incongruity by inundating *Cargo 200* with familiar ideological symbols and pop-culture references, all of which are constantly juxtaposed with abject horrors in the film. On the one hand, *Cargo 200* is filled with communist symbols: stars, busts of Lenin, portraits of Andropov and Chernenko, party speeches, hammers and sickles, and red banners—all of them pointedly deployed. The opening title of the film is already imbued with an eerie premonition of tragedy: the words "CARGO 200" are written across a blood-red map of the Soviet Union, replacing the missing word "USSR." However, the "USSR" can be found elsewhere: on the promotional poster for the film an enormous fist approaches the viewer from a pitch-black background, with "USSR" tattooed across the knuckles—a spot favored by *zona* ex-cons—epitomizing the inversion of symbolic orders. And on the other hand, the film is awash in references to 1980s popular culture, primarily music. It is the film's soundtrack that perhaps most accurately epitomizes the way in which Balabanov's *stiob* fuses horror with laughter and amplifies the effects of the film's "shock therapy."

Balabanov's recourse to hits from the 1980s is one of *Cargo 200*'s strongest points of audience identification: while some details in the film might be somewhat anachronistic, the songs are carefully selected and are allotted significant reel time. Familiar music gives rise to a nostalgia that is cruelly undercut by contrast with harrowing images.[5] These scenes in which the acoustic forms a striking counterpoint to the visual are driven by the same mode of excess as the rest of the film, progressively escalating in intensity. The local disco kicks off with the deafening "Earth in the Porthole" (Zemlia v illiuminatore) by the late Soviet rock band Zemliane. The

5 This clash between the aural and the visual is also a common trope in "feel-bad" films; suffice it to remember, for example, the opening of Lars von Trier's *Antichrist* (2009) with Handel's "Lascia ch'io pianga" (1705) or Brian de Palma's use of "Sarabande" (1703–6) in *Redacted* (2007). However, in *Cargo 200*, the choice of music is much more pointed and sinister, targeted at immediate recognition and a strong association by a specific generation within the specific time period.

party, however, takes place in a dilapidated church that has been turned into a nightclub with an improvised dance floor and half-drunk teenagers, drinking moonshine in grimy toilet stalls. Iurii Loza's mawkish "Raft" (Plot) plays uninterrupted for two minutes when Angelika, who has just been raped, is kidnapped and driven through a sprawling industrial park. Another wistful song, this time about the hardships of loveless military life, plays when the bodies of soldiers killed in Afghanistan are being unloaded from the plane—only to make room for the new platoon of soldiers who are about to be transported to the frontline.

This series of arresting contrasts between image and sound culminates in a jarring audio-visual cacophony as Zhurov and his henchmen bring the coffin of Angelika's fiancé into Zhurov's apartment to the tune of Afric Simone's "Hafanana" (1975), which blares from the television that Zhurov's drunk mother cannot stop watching. The incongruous music continues to play throughout the scene. Like the rest of the soundtrack, "Hafanana" for many Russian viewers would constitute a nostalgic throwback to their late Soviet youth, a sentiment that Balabanov vehemently attacks with this film. It is the pairing of a scene of voyeuristic sadism

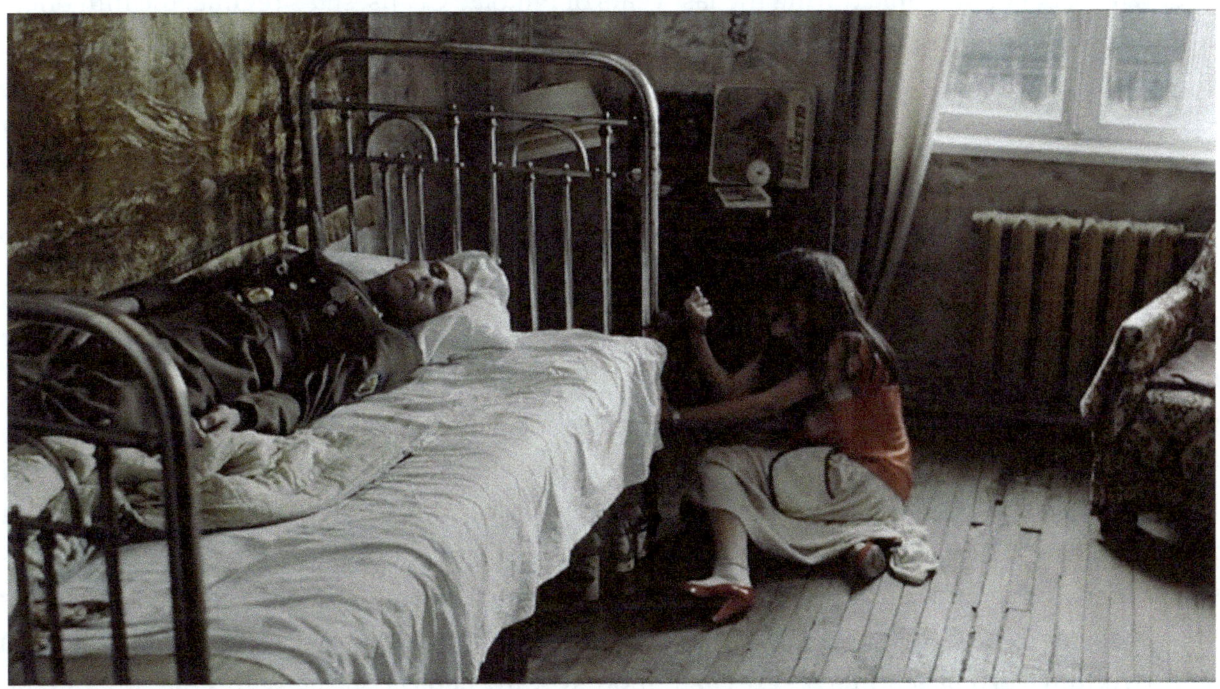

Fig. 4.3. Balabanov, *Cargo 200*. "Your fiancé has arrived!"

with nostalgic pop music that makes the scene so disturbing—and so over-the-top absurd. The contrast between funk-tinged melody and images of sadism culminates in a series of carefully orchestrated cuts between the agile body of Afric Simone whom we see dancing on the TV screen and the corpse of Angelika's fiancé, as Zhurov hauls it out of the coffin and throws it beside her on the bed. It is here that the corpse acquires, to quote Walter Benjamin (218), "the pre-eminent emblematic property": Balabanov creates an acoustic object of nostalgia, a moment of identification—and then hurls a corpse at it, creating the coda for the entire film. Here, at the crossroads of horror and black comedy, of *stiob* and excess, the message is finally driven home.

It may well have been the scene with the soldier's corpse that led Joël Chapron (Vice-President, Unifrance), the permanent selector at Cannes Film Festival for Russian cinema, to hesitate to recommend *Cargo 200* for Cannes. As Mariia Kuvshinova (108) observes, it is ironic that Cristian Mungiu's *4 Months, 3 Weeks and 2 Days* [4 luni, 3 săptămâni și 2 zile], another dark drama about the late 1980s, won both the Palme d'Or and the FIPRESCI Award in that same year (2007). Set in Romania during the last years of Nikolae Ceaușescu's regime, the film offers a similarly bleak portrayal of the period, underscored by the absence of any soundtrack to the film. But as Mungiu's closing credits begin to roll, an upbeat, glaringly inappropriate pop tune starts to play, turning nostalgia on its head to provide a scathing commentary on the legacy of communism.

Vasilii Sigarev, *The Land of Oz*

Vasilii Sigarev might be the most likely successor to Balabanov as a director of social thrillers. A student of Nikolai Koliada, a visionary Ekaterinburg playwright and theater director, Sigarev came into prominence as a playwright associated with the New Drama movement. He began to make films in the mid-2000s and has since been doing both. Critics have pointed to similarities between Sigarev's and Balabanov's styles: the latter's signature technique of "undercutting poignant moments with burlesque register" (Condee, *Imperial Trace*, 231) has surely been adopted by Sigarev. Yet Sigarev's method of mixing comedy with horror differs from Balabanov's combustible combination of the abject with the excesses of *stiob*. Sigarev's first two films—*Wolfie* and *Live*—gravitate more toward neo-*chernukha* with little to laugh at. In *Wolfie*—a film that depicts a daughter's (Polina Pluchek, Veronika Lysakova) unconditional love for her cold and mostly absent mother (Iana Troianova)—the trace elements of humor are primarily confined to the mother's bad language and eccentric hair and makeup. Nevertheless, like the mothers in Sigarev's other works (for example, his play *Black Milk* [Chernoe moloko, 2001] or *Live*), she is a figure of evil in the film, the "two-faced mother" (Kristeva, 157–59) who not only gives life but also brings about the demise of her child. As far as *Live* is concerned, one would be hard-pressed to find anything humorous in its squalid universe: the work offers an example of a "desperation film" that "do[es] not point to a way out of the dead-end, . . . refrain[s] from offering any positive dimension whatsoever" (Lübecker, 125). As Russian film critic Olga Kas'ianova ("Kinotavr-2015: 'Strana Oz'") observes, "after the oppressive magic realism of *Live*, laughter became a medical necessity."

Some much-needed comic relief came in the form of Sigarev's 2015 hit *The Land of Oz*. The film has been viewed as a whimsical holiday comedy, more specifically as an "antiholiday film" or "anti-*Elki*" (Kas'ianova, "Kinotavr-2015: 'Strana Oz'"), intended as an explicit response to Timur Bekmambetov's *Elki* (2010), *Elki 2* (2011), *Elki 3* (2013), *Elki 1914* (2014), and *Elki 5* (2016), a series of highly commercial comedies about New Year's Eve. But while the grotesque characters and situations in Sigarev's film are highly entertaining, the degree of physical violence and inventive, explosive verbal abuse (obscene words, or *mat*, have been outlawed in Russian films since 2014) do not belong—some might argue— in a comedy proper. I would argue that they blur the genre boundaries of *The Land of Oz* and allow us to consider it in the context of horror.

Set around New Year's Eve, *The Land of Oz* is an "odyssey" (Rutkovskii) undertaken by Lena Shabadinova, a provincial young woman who is trying to find the kiosk where she is supposed to start her new job that day. Despite unusual resilience, Lena is a heroine whose quest leaves her beaten, harassed, briefly incarcerated, and eventually with a bullet in her head. From the beginning, her journey is fraught with problems: a driver (Evgenii Tsyganov) who agrees to take Lena to her destination suffers from a barbiturate overdose and crashes the car into a snowdrift. Unscathed, Lena walks along the highway toward the city, where she meets Roman (Gosha Kutsenko), one of the more likable characters in the film, who wrestles with her on an ice slide—playfully, but not without inflicting pain. When Roman knocks himself out with fireworks, launched from the top of his head, Lena is left to look after his lap dog. Playing a grotesque version of Dorothy and Toto from the original *Oz* series, Lena continues on her journey and stumbles upon a self-proclaimed bard (Vladimir Simonov), who takes her to his apartment with the obvious intention of seduction. When the bard's wife (Svetlana Kamynina) arrives in the morning, he pushes Lena from the balcony. She lands on the balcony of a neighbor selling Avon cosmetics (Inna Churikova), who mistakes Lena for a call girl and—out of pity—feeds her dumplings. After further mishaps, Lena ends up in prison, where she is harassed by two prostitutes (Alisa Khazanova, Daria Ekamasova) dressed as New Year's fairytale snow maidens (*Snegurochki*). Released and anticipating that her pilgrimage is nearly over, Lena is accidentally shot in the head by a rowdy group of young men celebrating New Year's Eve. Miraculously, she survives, waking up in hospital with Roman by her side. Lena never finds the kiosk, but her wanderings are interspersed with frequent cuts to two original kiosk workers—Andrei (Andrei Il'enkov, one of the film's scriptwriters) and Duke (Aleksandr Bashirov)—awaiting Lena and whiling away their time discussing a broad range of unpalatable topics, from coprophilia to copulation in various species, further enriching the film's many scatological and sexual jokes.

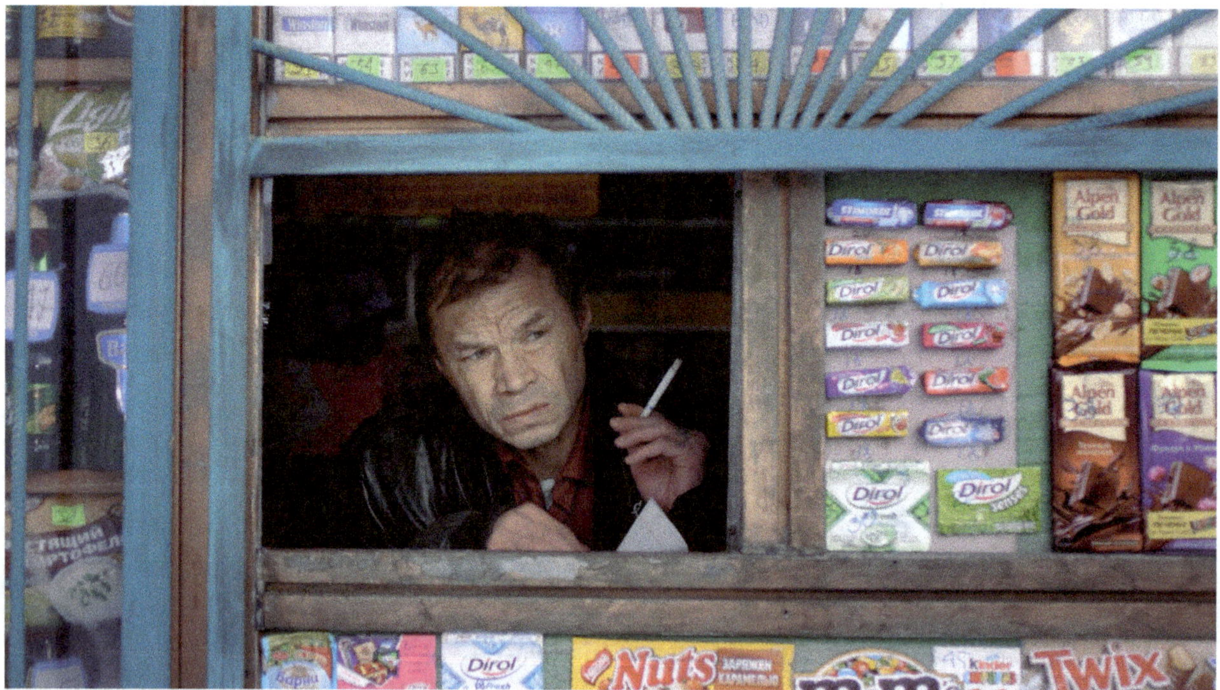

Fig. 4.4. Sigarev, *The Land of Oz*. Aleksandr Bashirov as Duke in Sigarev's New Year "comedy."

With the transgressive Rabelaisian quality of its humor and its sexual language, *The Land of Oz* quickly subverts philistine expectations of a feel-good New Year's film. Punctuated by mindless violence and unprovoked aggression, the film suggests that there is something else behind the veneer of the comedy, however bizarre, and invites the analysis of how and why Sigarev mixes the funny with the scary and the repulsive in his genre-bending work. Among other things, *The Land of Oz* has been called an absurd comedy: Zara Abdullaeva goes as far as to claim that the film's depiction of "spontaneity, dejection, aggression [a]nd . . . exaggerated self-assertion [is] so natural and plausible, that Beckett himself . . . would have laughed at it. Or cried, lying with his face to the wall." Indeed, the film possesses certain characteristics of the theater of the absurd.[6] Lena's wanderings reveal her isolation as a "mere marionette" in a world that is portrayed, to again borrow from Esslin, "as an incomprehensible place" (Esslin, 5). The willful inanity of the film's dialogues has led critics to compare Andrei and Duke to Vladimir and Estragon in Samuel Beckett's *Waiting for Godot* (1949). Akin to the nonarrival of the absent Godot, Lena never arrives at her destination. And most importantly, no matter how absurd the content of what we see or hear, the overall atmosphere remains piercingly familiar, attesting to affinity of *The Land of Oz* with absurd dramas:

> while the happenings on the stage are absurd, they yet remain recognizable as somehow related to real life with *its* absurdity, so that eventually the spectators are brought face to face with the irrational side of their existence. Thus, the absurd and fantastic goings-on of the Theatre of the Absurd will, in the end, be found to reveal the irrationality of the human condition and the illusion of what we thought was its apparent logical structure. (Esslin, 5; emphasis in the original)

Although the analogy to the theater of the absurd has compelling aspects, their unusual combination of comedy and horror has a different modality in these films. Unlike the heroes of Beckett or Eugene Ionesco, who "hardly have any individuality . . . moreover, halfway through the action, they tend to change their nature completely" (Esslin, 3), the protagonists of *The Land of Oz* possess an inherent immutability that turns them into fixed types rather than idiosyncratic characters. In Sigarev's collection of "masks" (the Internet-addicted pervert, the Avon lady, the prostitute), Lena Shabadinova takes up the role of a Bergsonian comic body. Her astonishing

6 My frame of reference here is Martin Esslin's genre-defining essay "The Theater of the Absurd" (1960).

resilience and flat affect render her body almost mechanical. This expertly handled grotesque causes laughter at many points of the film, underscoring Bergson's point that "the more exactly two images, that of a person and that of a machine, fit into each other, the more striking is the comic effect" (21). The puppet-like automatism of her movements and responses effaces Lena's

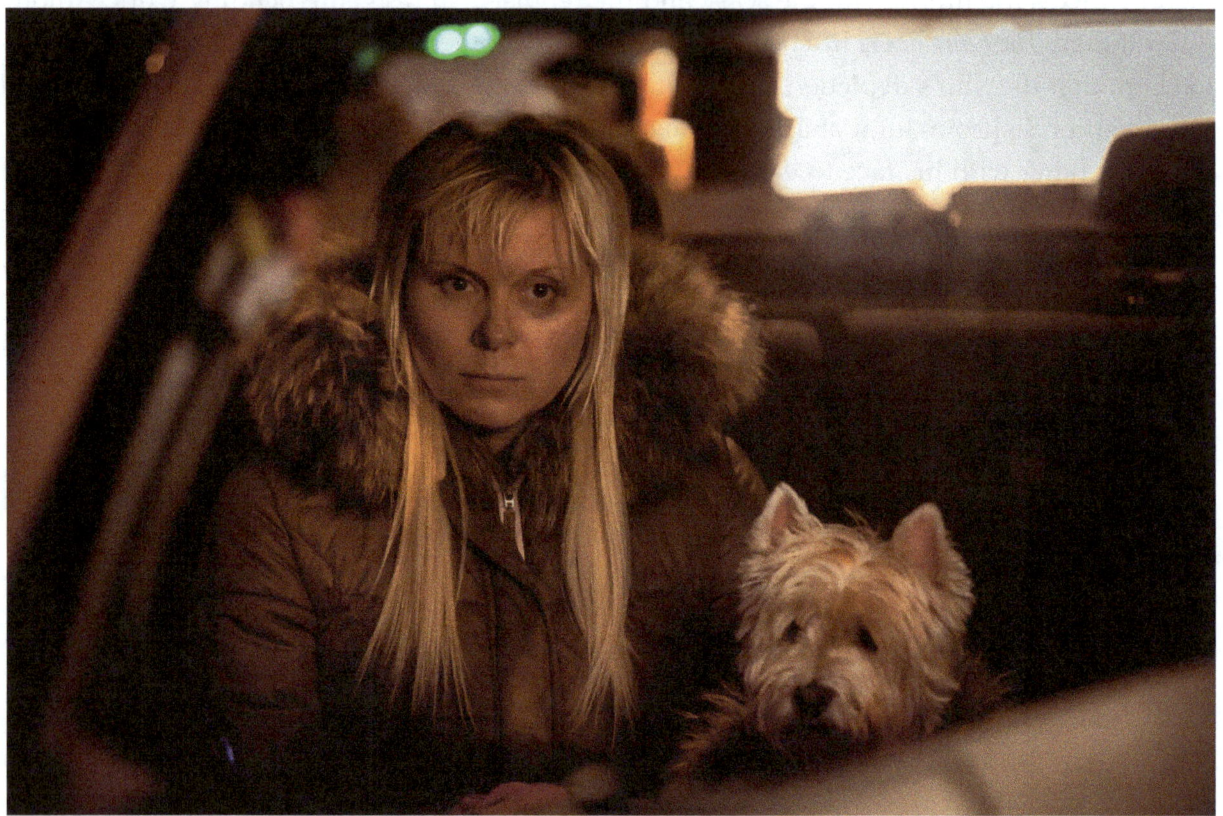

Fig. 4.5. Sigarev, *The Land of Oz*. Lena Shabadinova, already with a black eye, continues her journey.

human qualities, practically turning her into an object:[7] the Avon lady's boxer son uses her as a punching bag; the "bard" as a live pornographic picture. Lena's endearing lack of awareness of her own awkwardness solidifies her as a classic comic character: "the comic [takes] its abode in the person himself . . . comic character is generally comic in proportion to his ignorance

[7] "We laugh every time a person gives us the impression of being a thing" (Bergson, 33).

of himself. The comic person is unconscious" (Bergson, 13, 15). In this way, despite *The Land of Oz*'s ambiguous genre and style, the Bergsonian humor places Lena Shabadinova in the same lineage of misfits as Jacques Tati's Monsieur Hulot, Charlie Chaplin's Tramp, or Rowan Atkinson's Mr. Bean.

Rendering Shabadinova as a comic figure (after the fashion described by Bergson), Sigarev inevitably establishes distance between her and the audience, presenting her as someone whom the audience is not ("the comic demands something like a momentary anesthesia of the heart. Its appeal is to intelligence, pure and simple" [Bergson, 11]). And yet Sigarev's meticulous attention to detail creates a recognizable context, making the milieu of the laughed-at Other (Shabadinova) highly familiar to the audience. Following Koliada Theater traditions, the carefully chosen mise-en-scène of consumer commodities and popular cultural artifacts—cell-phone ringtones, New Year's fireworks, ice sculptures, and dog clothing—and Gogolian precision in the creation of recognizable social types, Sigarev allows the audience to recognize the society in which Lena Shabadinova lives as their own. It is here that any comment on the unseemly side of life in contemporary Russia becomes apparent. Despite the nonidentification with the central comic character, Sigarev's film holds a mirror to the audience itself, and in the mindlessly aggressive, perverted characters who surround Shabadinova, the viewers see the exaggerated caricature of the contemporary Russia they inhabit.

Already we have seen how, in discussing the satire of social types in *The Land of Oz*, one name seems to impose itself: Nikolai Gogol.[8] The elements of Gogolian satire fundamentally inform the aesthetics of *The Land of Oz* through the ways in which Sigarev appropriates the elements of Gogol's poetics of *skaz* and translates them into an audio-visual spectacle. In "How Gogol's Overcoat Is Made" (1919), Boris Eikhenbaum suggested that, for Gogol, the linear development of the plot was secondary in significance to "expressiveness" (*vyrazitel'nost'*) and local color, often taking precedence over logic. This approach results, Eikhenbaum argues, in a "comic incongruity" of tone (*komicheskoe nesootvetstvie*) and grotesque hyperbolizations in Gogol's fiction. The plot is likewise of low importance in *The Land of Oz*, more a shaggy-dog story than a meaningfully structured narrative. The secondary role of the plot is hinted at already in the opening scene: in the Gogolian tradition, Sigarev begins with an anecdote of Lena's sister Irka, thrown over a balcony by her treacherous Greek lover. We then see Irka and

8 Zara Abdullaeva has compared the film in passing to Gogol's *Dead Souls* (1842), but I believe there is more to it.

Lena walking back to the lover's apartment and plotting revenge ("Maybe we should shit on his doorstep. . . . Or let's just do it the Russian way: beat the hell out of him"). Irka is pulled into the apartment, thrown over the balcony again, and breaks her tailbone. Lena then begins her journey. Thus begins Lena's extraneous conversational refrain ("My sister broke her tailbone, you know"), noteworthy for its irrelevance to the plot: her sister does not appear again until the very last scene and has no bearing on the narrative. It is there purely for the "expressivity" of the comic effect.

In a similar manner, Sigarev pays close attention to the speech patterns of his protagonists: Lena Shabadinova's Beckett-like non sequiturs, the amateur bard's lascivious whispering, the prostitutes' foul vernacular, and finally Duke's scatological ramblings—all attest to the importance of an "expressivity" that undercuts logic and emplotment. This Gogolian strain in *The Land of Oz* can even account for the entertaining incongruity of the film's soundtrack: the film oscillates between two main themes: the Italian tarantella song "Mamma La Rondinella" and an equally out-of-place Lluís Llach's "L'estaca," an allegory of Catalan resistance to Spanish fascism. Unlike in Balabanov's film, the songs are not presented in counterpoint to the visuals, nor do they echo them: rather, they are there mostly for what Eikhenbaum would describe as their "harmonic effect" (*garmonicheskii effekt*), for their unique sound.

As Eikhenbaum remarks, "comic *skaz* [quirky oral storytelling] . . . coexists with the declamation of pathos . . . complicating the initial comical style[.] The result is a type of grotesque in which laughter interchanges with sorrow." Sigarev's rendering of Gogolian *skaz* into film informs the duality of *The Land of Oz*—a comedy on the outside; a satire, even a bitter one, on the inside. Even when comically blown out of proportion, the reality of *The Land of Oz* is still recognizable, since for Sigarev the exaggeration is not "an aim, but rather [a] means . . . to make manifest to our eyes the distortions which he sees in embryo" (Bergson, 20). It is here, in the interstices of Gogolian satire, Bergsonian laughter, and absurdist drama, that *The Land of Oz* reveals itself to be a mordant commentary on the absurdity and hostility of life in contemporary Russia, attesting to Sigarev's ability to see "beneath the skin-deep harmony of form . . . the deep-seated recalcitrance of matter" (Bergson, 20). Beneath the laughter is the sadness of recognition; beneath the grinning mask of comedy is the disfigured grimace of suppressed horror.

***

The combination of horror and comedy in contemporary Russian film has created a versatile cinematic idiom for communicating recurrent concerns of the post-Soviet era through a genre that I have loosely defined as the "social thriller." Its capacity for seamlessly incorporating elements of horror, comedy, literary adaptation, and absurdist drama endows it with a unique potential for social critique through allegory, producing works as seemingly dissimilar as *Cargo 200* and *The Land of Oz*.

What can we infer from their differences? On their "journey . . . between apocalypse and carnival" (Kristeva, 141), Balabanov and Sigarev arrive at different destinations. Where Balabanov gives his viewers "tough love" and (finally) moralizing, Sigarev exaggerates and demonstrates. Balabanov gravitates toward an unreliable modernist narrator: the manipulator and trickster, for whom "foremost [is] his mock-serious tone . . . invoking a literary tradition that includes such figures as Gogol, early Dostoevskii, and Kharms" (Condee, *Imperial Trace*, 231–32). Here we would throw Beckett, Kafka, and Faulkner into the mix.

Sigarev, by contrast, is a "diabolical" (Bergson, 20) postmodernist caricaturist who magnifies and amplifies, expounding a motley of punch-drunk characters, transgressive humor, and a variety of disjointed references, all the while luxuriating in consumer culture, "a degraded landscape of schlock and kitsch" (Jameson, "Postmodernism," 55). Yet disparities notwithstanding, the cinematic shock rooted in the combination of horror and comedy in both films becomes not only a "catalyst for the reawakening of experience to history" (Lowenstein, 16), but also a mechanism for reevaluating cultural legacies and for drawing attention to the social reality of the present.

The differences between Balabanov and Sigarev acquire special significance at the turning point where they can be seen as attesting to a watershed moment in post-1991 Russian cinema—and Russian culture of this period in general. As Condee (*Imperial Trace*, 239) observes, many post-Soviet filmmakers, "witnessing their own country's imperial cascade, respond with impulses, manifestly diverse but sharing a common engagement with that process, whether that engagement is expressed as a move toward nostalgic conservation, apocalyptic acceleration, undoing what has been done, transcoding it into a different symbolic register with different valences, or other forms of serotine play." The case is surely true of Balabanov: even his works that are *not* set in the twilight of the Soviet empire focus and comment on this transitional period in Russian history, the lawless turmoil that accompanied the collapse of the old order, and the lives of the ones marginalized by it.

Sigarev's work, in contrast, while often borrowing from Balabanov's aesthetics, shows little interest in these topics. If Balabanov is concerned with driving the last nail into the coffin of the communist *past*, Sigarev, without ever glancing back, focuses on the sufficiently disorienting, hostile, and ultimately unknown *present.* Despite stylistic similarities, the case of Balabanov and Sigarev attest to a breaking point in post-Soviet Russian culture around the turn of the twenty-first century, challenging the hegemony of the very term "post-Soviet" as a referent for everything that came after 1991 and opening the floor to a very different host of questions.

Filmography

Balabanov, Aleksei, dir. *Cargo 200* (Gruz 200, 2007).
———. *Of Freaks and Men* (Pro urodov i liudei, 1998).
Craven, Wes, dir. *Scream* (1996).
Dante, Joe, dir. *The 'Burbs* (1989).
de Palma, Brian, dir. *Redacted* (2007).
Demme, Jonathan, dir. *The Silence of the Lambs* (1991).
Ershov, Konstantin and Georgii Kropachev, dir. *Vii* (1967).
Hitchcock, Alfred, dir. *The Birds* (1963).
Hooper, Tobe, dir. *The Texas Chainsaw Massacre* (1974).
Kubrick, Stanley, dir. *The Shining* (1980).
Lebedev, Nikolai, dir. *Snake Spring* (Zmeinyi istochnik, 1997).
Polanski, Roman, dir. *The Fearless Vampire Killers* (1967).
———. *Rosemary's Baby* (1968).
Romero, George A., dir. *Night of the Living Dead* (1968).
Sigarev, Vasilii, dir. *The Land of Oz* (Strana Oz, 2015).
———. *Live* (Zhit', 2012).
———. *Wolfie* (Volchok, 2009).
Strizhenov, Aleksandr, dir. *Iulen'ka* (2009).
Von Trier, Lars, dir. *Antichrist* (2009).

5. Eccentricity, Theatricality, and the Grotesque

Robert Crane

This chapter focuses on a handful of films that we have labeled "eccentric"—Ivan Vyrypaev's 2010 *Oxygen* (Kislorod), Sergei Loban's 2011 *Chapiteau Show* (Shapito-Shou), and Aleksei Fedorchenko's 2012 *Celestial Wives of the Meadow Mari* (Nebesnye zheny lugovykh mari) and 2014 *Angels of the Revolution* (Angely revoliutsii). Many of the ways in which we usually think about "genre" don't really help to understand the potential relationships among these works. Turning to the vocabulary of film-studies scholar Rick Altman, for example, these films—apart from a proclivity for episodic structures—are not at all alike syntactically. Similarly, there is no shared semantic content—not even at an abstract level, such as "the Soviet Past" or "ethnographic texture," both of which are featured in some but not all of the films. We also cannot reliably turn to audiences or rituals of consumption for the answer—doing this clearly marks these films as arthouse or international festival films. Although true, this line of investigation does not account for their radical differences from the arthouse films of, for example, Andrei Zviagintsev or Aleksei Popogrebskii.

The central genre marker of these films is their shared commitment to foregrounding the junctures between various levels of cinematic and noncinematic reality and nonreality, using a variety of techniques, including four in particular: their narrative structures; their visual strangeness; their appropriation of material from the real world; and the freedom and playfulness with which their filmmakers transform that material.

The opening scene of Aleksei Fedorchenko's *Angels of the Revolution* offers a clear illustration. There is a still shot of a blank chalkboard on a wooden wall. The film's title appears on the board, written in chalk. It disappears and is replaced by the date, 6 April 1934. A man walks in front of the chalkboard and directly facing the camera begins declaiming, "Raccoons! Raccoons! Will someone please get the little raccoons!" Children in raccoon masks file past and (also facing the camera directly) enter into dialogue with him. After their lines are delivered, we cut to a close-up of a harmonium being played, before moving to a wider shot of the scene featuring not just the speaker, children in raccoon costumes, and the musician, but now also other masked characters in what is now clearly a schoolroom's symbolist performance:

hamsters, pigs, a snake. Before long, armed men enter the room and, despite the speaker's protests that they are interrupting a rehearsal, proceed to remove the children, leaving their masks strewn across the floor. The camera cuts to a shot of the doorway just in time to see the last of them leaving the room, after which several reindeer-drawn sleds race by. Against the snowy landscape, framed by the doorway, a new title appears, informing the viewer that "the film is based on actual events."

There is a willful eccentricity to the images and language: the animal masks, reindeer, and largely incomprehensible play-within-a-film all serve to disorient and surprise the spectator. The film jumps rapidly from history to fantasy, from play to violence, insisting to us that what we are seeing actually happened, while simultaneously, through its meticulous composition and visual flamboyance, assuring us that this is merely a work of art carefully crafted by an *auteur*. In many ways, this strategy represents a return to some of the aesthetic interests of Russian theatrical modernists at the beginning of the twentieth century—especially to what avant-garde director Vsevolod Meyerhold termed "The Grotesque." Although the term has accrued a confounding array of meanings to describe, for example, carved stone figures, the monstrous creatures of border decorations, hybrid literary styles (evoking both disgust and empathy), for Meyerhold, the Grotesque is a brutal clash of opposites, "a constant drawing of the spectator from one perceptual plane he has only just comprehended to another he did not expect at all" (Posner, 11). As Dassia Posner has recently argued, this insistence of providing the spectator with an episode that "zigzags between expectation and surprise, appearance and reality, the already expected and the yet-to-be-imagined" (11) stemmed from a modernist conception of art that saw it not as a mirror held up to reality but as a prism through which reality could be refracted according to the idiosyncratic vision of an artist.[1]

1 The best-known example of the Grotesque in Russian modernist theatre was Evgenii Vakhtangov's 1922 production of Carlo Gozzi's *Princess Turandot*. The production barraged its spectators with devices foregrounding the production's existence as both an elaborate theatrical spectacle and an event that was actually happening in the material world from the opening moment of the show, a "parade" of the actors who, in full view of the audience, donned their costumes. The actors then proceeded to play not the characters from Gozzi's fairy tale but actors in an itinerant *commedia dell'arte* troupe performing the characters from Gozzi's fairy tale. The layers of mimesis that this involved did not prevent the actors (in both of their characters) from engaging with the reality being experienced by the audience in the Moscow theater—in between acts, the performers would scold latecomers as they made their way to their seats or engage in debates with critics who might be in the audience. In the words of Vakhtangov's disciple Ruben Simonov (163), he didn't remove the "fourth wall" but moved it "to the last row of the orchestra and gallery."

Mikhail Iampolski (72) has argued that early Russian cinema was conditioned by a culture that understood the film image in premodern, platonic terms as a "pale, degraded copy of reality." Over the course of the 1920s, Iampolski's argument continues, this understanding of the cinematic image was temporarily replaced by an avant-garde aesthetic that emphasized the objectivity of the image itself. The films discussed here use this specific understanding of the Grotesque to jump back and forth between these two representational modes—to play with the multiple layers of reality and performance that are possible within cinema, highlighting tensions between representation and presentation; historical truth and narrative fiction; the authentic existences of the bodies, things, and places captured by the camera's lens and their ghostly reproduction on screen.

Angels of the Revolution oscillates between these levels of reality in a variety of ways, but the one I would like to highlight here is its inclusion of real works of the Soviet avant-garde in its fictional narrative. As a film contemporary to us as viewers, Fedorchenko's selections tend to be extreme examples of the avant-garde's drive to consume reality—Arsenii Avraamov's *Symphony of Steam Whistles* (Gudkovaia simfoniia), Dmitrii Osipov's constructivist First Moscow Crematorium, or Viktor Kalmykov's plans for a city that would circle the earth like the rings of Saturn. In the context of the film, these works serve as ruminations on the power (or powerlessness) of artists to alter reality, while being altered themselves by their attribution to the fictional artists featured in the film.

Ivan Vyrypaev, *Oxygen*

Ivan Vyrypaev's *Oxygen* is a cinematic adaptation of his 2002 play of the same name. Vyrypaev is closely associated with the New Russian Drama movement (*Oxygen*'s Moscow premiere was at teatr.doc), and while his plays are frequently concerned with questions of truth and authenticity, his work displays a skepticism toward the possibility of transferring that authenticity to the stage or screen that distances it from the "verbatim" techniques used by his peers.[2] As Birgit Beumers and Mark Lipovetsky argue, "The constant undermining of one's

2 A good example of this is his play *Illusions* (Illiuzii, 2011), in which four performers tell the story of two couples. The performers play themselves, wearing their own clothes and reporting the story, rather than engaging in any kind of mimesis. But the "authenticity" of this performance is undermined, first, by the fact that they are all very clearly speaking with Vyrypaev's voice, and then by our gradual realization of their fundamental

own 'truth' is a major aspect of the manner of expression deployed in *Oxygen* . . . [as the female performer] constantly challenges her partner [performed on stage by Vyrypaev], sometimes exposing his lies and hypocrisy, and once directly challenging his authority as an author" (248). In bringing the play to the screen, Vyrypaev uses his new medium to bring this textual device to every aspect of the work, constantly signaling the authenticity of what we see and hear, only to undermine it in the next moment.

Oxygen is a "Rap Parable," structured as an album featuring ten "tracks" and two "bonus tracks," which deemphasize the content of its narrative (and which numerous critics have called trite or banal), while emphasizing the nature of the work as a created text. The viewer is repeatedly reminded that the film they are watching is a mere visual accompaniment to this album—the equivalent of a series of music videos—by means of three framing devices. First, the film opens with a DVD menu that displays the titles and order of the tracks; then, the beginning of each track is marked with its title and composer, in the custom of music videos. All this is accompanied by a third frame, the blue shadow of a computer window that remains visible throughout the film, reminding the viewer of the mediated nature of this experience (in case they could forget!).

The film is organized around a double structure in which the performers, Karolina Gruszka and Aleksei Filimonov, play "themselves" sitting in a recording studio, performing a series of rap songs about Sasha and Sasha, whom they also play. The distinction between the real Gruszka/Filimonov and their characters is marked by the presence of microphones in the studio, but also by visual contrast. The "real" Gruszka has black hair, while her character Sasha has red hair. The studio is often shot in black and white, while the world inhabited by the Sashas is oversaturated with color. These juxtapositions between the two on-screen realities are further built on by the inclusion of a huge variety of material ranging from footage of the New York 9-11 attacks to animated Rastafarian mushrooms. As Serguei Oushakine notes, this alienates the narrators from the story they are telling: "The experience described in the songs is distanced and objectified. No emotional attitude is revealed by the narrators . . . the text is presented, not embodied by the narrators."

unreliability as narrators as they contradict each other, recant details, and admit to lying to the audience, just as the characters they are discussing lie to each other.

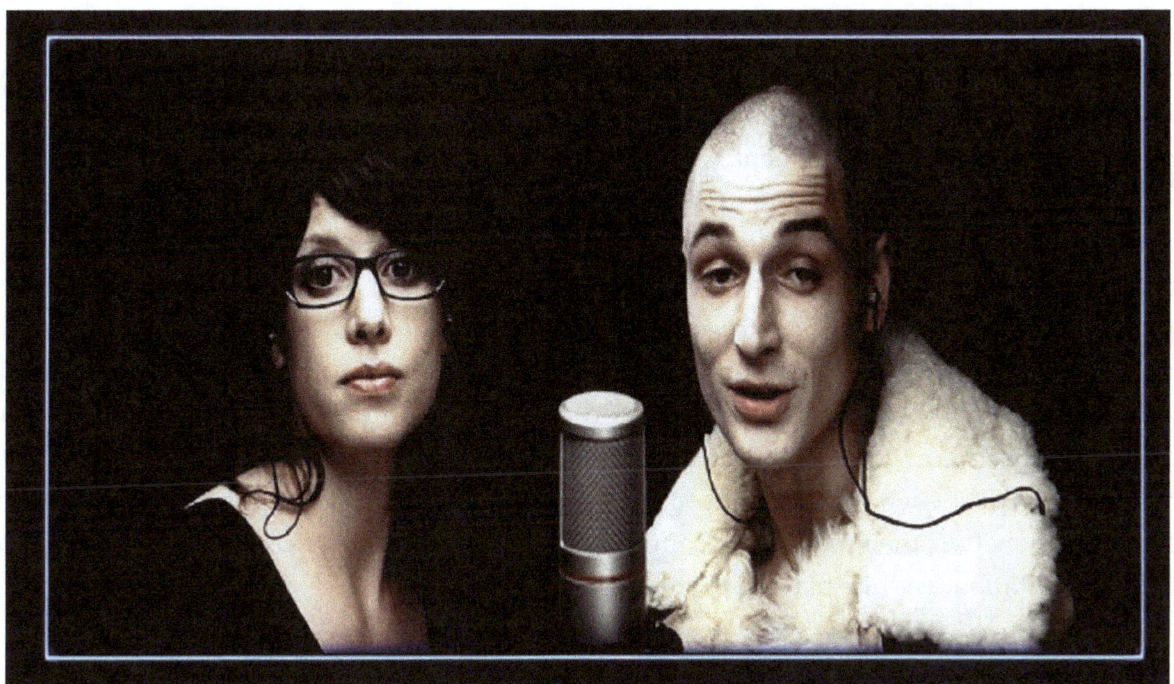

Fig. 5.1. Vyrypaev, *Oxygen*. Gruszka and Filimonov as "themselves."

This double structure and the distance it creates between the narrators and their subjects encourages the viewer to accept the studio scenes as more authentic than the scenes depicting Sasha and Sasha—they could be understood as a documentary of two artists performing number of songs. Occasionally there are scenes interspersed between the songs that could be understood to capture real conversations between the performers. In one such scene, the performers remove their earpieces, hairdressers arrive to touch them up, and while off camera Gruszka asks Filimonov, "What is the main thing for you?" He returns the question, and she eventually replies "Conscience," to which he responds "For me too." Beumers and Lipovetsky (246) have noted the irony of this moment of the text, arguing that "sometimes Vyrypaev tries to provide direct answers to the question of the essence of life, but he understands how plain and unpersuasive such attempts sound." The film furthers the undermining of this seemingly sincere philosophical statement by first showing an "outtake," in which the actors mess up their lines and burst into laughter, and then, after showing the scene again, putting the lines "conscience" and "for me too" into a loop that repeats several times.

The film's engagement with the Grotesque collision between reality and cinema does not, importantly, limit itself to a pattern of setting up a moment of "truth" or "authenticity" and then undermining it. As Beach Gray ("*Oxygen*," n.p.) has noted, the genre of music is not incidental to *Oxygen*'s engagement with the extra-cinematic: "A defining feature of hip-hop music is its penchant for sampling sound bites and music to produce a finished work of art. . . . [by including] unexpected elements such as dialogue, refrains from recognizable songs, startling noises (gunshots, sirens, etc.), lyrical expression, and guest artists who bring their own sampling to the mix." The referential nature of these samples is often as important to the track as the sound that they bring to it.

The final track of the film also relies on a demonstration of the real within a cinematic construct. It replays a scene from the first track, in which the male Sasha smashes all the dishes in his kitchen. The scene is then played in reverse. As the dishes are put back together and return to the shelves, their materiality comes into focus: even in this "fictional" scene, the dishes broken by Filimonov while playing Sasha are *really* broken.

Sergei Loban, *Chapiteau Show*

Theatricality is central to *Chapiteau Show,* in terms of both its themes and its aesthetics. The film is divided into four chapters, each of which is devoted to a different type of relationship: between romantic partners, between friends, between fathers and sons, and between colleagues. Each chapter shows the way in which these relationships—that in principle should be governed by authenticity—are permeated by performances in which participants simulate their roles, knowingly or not. Early on in "Love," for example, when Vera's parents take away her Internet access, she cries uncontrollably and phones her lover—whom she has never met offline or even seen in a photograph, and who goes by the handle "Cyberstranger"—repeating to him clichés ("I can't live without you") out of melodramatic representations of love.

The collision between performance and authenticity—between the representation and the thing itself—are featured heavily in the rest of the film as well—most overtly in the fourth novella, which follows a Viktor Tsoi look-alike, marketed as an "Ersatz Star" by a producer who insists that the copy is more important than the original. But the film also plays with the boundaries between cinematic and noncinematic realities elsewhere—the Producer, Serezha

Popov, is played by the actor Sergei Popov, and the character Petr, a self-centered actor, is played by the actor Petr Mamonov as a parody—maybe—of himself.

While each of Loban's chapters follows a different set of characters, they share a cinematic space and time, overlapping with each other and allowing characters to interact with each other. We see particular moments repeated again and again from the perspective of different characters' narratives. An interview with Serezha Popov plays on a television in the first chapter, and we see him giving that same interview in the fourth chapter. Thematically, this device serves to reinforce the very inability to communicate that frustrates each of the film's characters, as none of them has full access to or understanding of each other's stories. But it also creates a particular sort of pleasure for the viewers as they recognize these moments, combining them with previous information, reevaluating the significance of things that had seemed to be merely a part of the background. And like the Grotesque collisions between cinema and reality, these collisions between one narrative and another also highlight the mastery of the artist who produced them.

The tensions created by the rest of the chapters become even more pronounced during the scenes that take place in the titular Chapiteau—a fairground show tent. The tent is a place located outside of the normal space-time of the film—scenes taking place inside the tent show an interior that is impossibly large for the structure we see in exterior shots. The four chapters are punctuated by performances at the tent in which impersonators perform surreal routines for the characters gathered there. These routines borrow heavily from pop culture but use unexpected juxtapositions to highlight our familiarity with the represented texts so to estrange us from them: we see, for example, Marilyn Monroe seducing a Soviet Cosmonaut Bear. At the end of each of these performances, the tent burns down. Much as in the first scene of *Angels of the Revolution*, the cinematic reality outside the performance intrudes into the performance within the film. The repetition of these fires and the nonrepetition of the performance likewise serve to highlight the artistic control over these collisions—if the overlapping moments in the other parts of each chapter serve to reinforce the sense that each is taking place in the same space, this lack of continuity disrupts it.

Impersonators are not the only ones who perform in the tent. The protagonists of each chapter all present monologues in the mode of pop songs, accompanied by dances. These monologues emphasize the tensions between performance and authenticity as they purport to be a genuine expression of the characters' innermost thoughts and feelings but also are easily

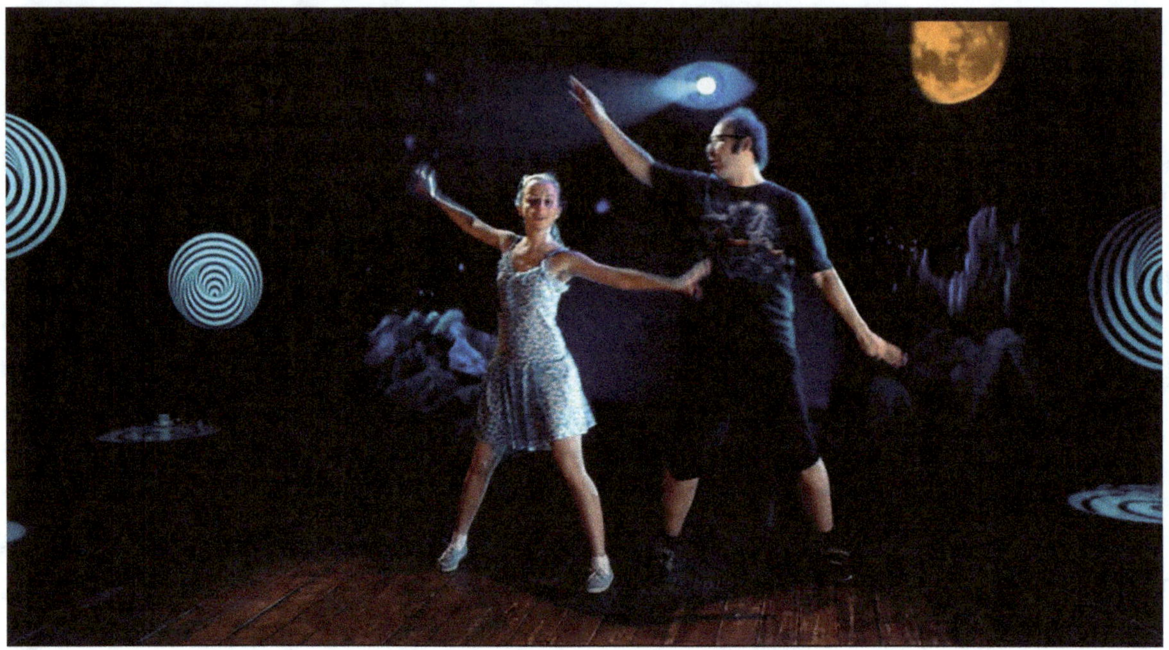

Fig. 5.2. Loban, *Chapiteau Show.* Vera and "Cyberstranger" performing.

contained within the homogenous parameters of pop music. The stage unexpectedly inserts itself into the film again during the credits, as members of the cast—it is not clear if they are still somehow in character or are now playing themselves—dance and sing a song that is, perhaps, the ultimate pastiche of pop music, consisting only of the lyrics "Oh, yeah! Oh, baby, baby!"

These playful transgressions of the boundaries between cinema and reality likewise contrast with the setting of the film: if the action is replete with impersonators, doubles, and the ersatz, the Crimean landscape stands strikingly outside artistic construction, a sublime marker of a noncinematic reality that can be documented but not reproduced.[3] The Crimean Peninsula

3 The value of landscapes as a marker of the "real" in art is significant. As Kenneth Clark notes in his major work on landscape painting, it is a reminder that "we are surrounded by things which we have not made and which have a life and structure different from our own" (x). W. J. T. Mitchell ("Imperial Landscape," 14) complicates this view by remarking not only on the problematic nature of Clark's "we" but also on the ideological value of landscape in art: while we often understand it as "free of human intention," "landscape is itself a physical and multisensory medium . . . in which cultural meanings and values are encoded, whether they are *put* there by physical transformation of a place in landscape gardening and architecture, or *found* in a place formed, as we say, 'by nature'."

offers Loban an ideal opportunity not only to present its striking authenticity—its jagged cliffs and rocky shores seemingly declare themselves to be "not made by human hands"—as a counterpoint to the imitations and simulacra he sets upon it—but also to engage with it as an ideological site that is as strongly implicated with post-Soviet memory as Tsoi or the Pioneers.

Aleksei Fedorchenko, *Celestial Wives of the Meadow Mari*

Aleksei Fedorchenko has built his career on some of the more Grotesque transformations of reality that cinema allows. His *First on the Moon* (Pervye na lune, 2005) is a mockumentary of fictional achievements of the Soviet space program, while *Silent Souls* (Ovsianki, 2010) was a detailed ethnographic depiction of the funeral rites of a (most critics now agree) nonexistent ethnic minority. His description of *The Celestial Wives of the Meadow Mari* as a "documentary fairy tale" aptly evokes this tension. The film, his first with cinematographer Shandor Berkeshi, also marked his transition to a visual style perhaps more appropriate to this subject matter, full of bright colors and unexpected imagery. *Celestial Wives* continues his fascination with the cinematic documentation of ethnicity and the claims to authenticity inherent in this subject matter, even when the filmmaker is engaged in deliberate falsification. Like Sergei Parajanov's *Shadows of Forgotten Ancestors* (Tini zabutykh predkiv, 1965) and Mikhail Kalatozov's *Salt for Svanetia* (Sol' Svanetii, 1930), two other films in the Russo-Soviet ethnographic tradition (however much they are engaged in projects different from this one and from each other's), it relies on the saturation of the film with authentic folk objects (clothes, buildings, talismans, etc.) to create a cinematic texture that offset the director's authorial reimagining of the uses to which these objects are put.

The film is structured around twenty-three episodes, each depicting the events surrounding a different woman of Mari ethnicity (a real ethnicity this time) whose name begins with "O." The use of the names beginning with "O" creates a pattern that playfully emphasizes the film's existence as a construct, while also referencing the world beyond the screen by pointing to the last name of the author of the screenplay, Denis Osokin, who also appears as an author within the film. Each episode is focused on the continuing role of paganism—the traditional religion of the Mari—in the women's lives, presenting us with imagined rituals often centered around a connection between natural fertility and the sexuality of the women. These rituals range from the relatively banal—a girl offering a sacrifice of food to the Mother of Birth when requesting

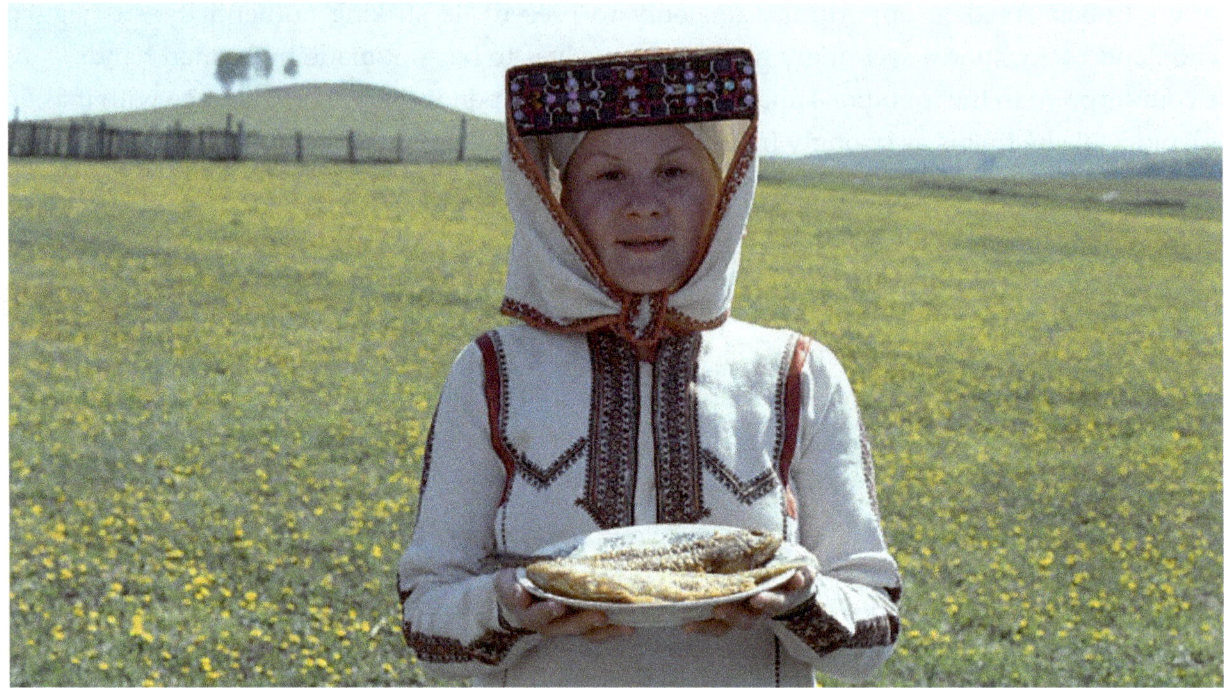

Fig. 5.3. Fedorchenko, *Celestial Wives of the Meadow Mari*. Authentic folk objects on display.

that she make the girl beautiful by removing her freckles—to the surreal—a giant forest spirit placing a curse on a woman's body until her husband impregnates the spirit, who gives birth to a hedgehog.

While many critics have focused on Fedorchenko's transformation of his source material—Andrei Rogatchevski notes, after all, that "the falsification and manipulation of reality is rooted in cinema's very nature,"—it is equally important to note the ways in which Fedorchenko presents elements of that material unchanged. In addition to the authentic objects, the film is performed entirely in the Mari language (by performers who are mostly from Moscow). The episodes also take place over the course of a calendar year—starting with a New Year's celebration—and the changing seasons are marked on the landscape by real snow that characters run through or real carrots that they pick.

In this fashion, the fantastic stories of spells and zombies invented by the filmmakers are set against the real Mari words that form the aural texture of the film, as well as against the real landscape and national costumes that form the visual, jostling the spectator with these juxtapositions.

In her review discussion of the film, Irina Anisimova ("Celestial Wives") has noted that, while women are the protagonists of the film, their representation is problematic because "the women's sexuality is their only defining characteristic." Without debating the accuracy or importance of that criticism, I would argue that the film's significant amount of nudity is a key example of the collisions of cinematic and noncinematic realities that the film engineers as the image on the screen is—in a pronounced way—both the body of the actress and the body of the character she is portraying.

* * *

Taken together, "eccentricity" as a cinematic style is an assertion about the act of filmmaking itself. These films highlight the capricious power of the artist to appropriate realities, to transform realities, to ignore realities, and ultimately to create realities. This approach places these filmmakers at odds with the dominant modes of cinematic production in Russia by positioning them neither as critics or rebels, such as Andrei Zviagintsev, nor as vessels for state ideology, such as Nikita Mikhalkov or Vladimir Bortko, but as agents. This agency is offered to viewers as well, as they are tasked with making sense of the performance they have just witnessed, with relatively little help from the filmmakers, whose constant impositions asserting their authorship of the films simultaneously joyfully undermine their authority over the meaning of the films—a radical departure from the modernist theatricality that they are appropriating and repurposing.

While the exuberance of these films often emphasizes the playfulness of the Grotesque collisions they engineer between the cinematic and real worlds, these transgressions are often profound as well, raising the stakes of the viewer's meaning-making. The final scene of *Angels of the Revolution* offers a coda to the film's exploration of the intersections of revolutionary politics, revolutionary culture, and the attempt to spread both across the Soviet Union. It begins with an establishing shot of two reindeer outside the present-day city of Kazym, complete with a subtitle announcing the location. It then cuts to the interior of a typical Soviet apartment and an old woman supporting herself with a walker, singing a Stalin-era anthem. When her song ends, another title informs the viewer that she is Ekaterina Obatina, the "first girl of Soviet Iugra," a real person, whose birth we had seen reenacted earlier in the film.

In this moment, Obatina serves as a signifier that is simultaneously empty and disturbingly full. On the one hand, her gaze is neutral; she is not challenging the viewer any more than Fedorchenko's unmoving camera purports to be doing anything other than documenting her presence. It is clearly meaningful that she uses her performance of a song—a Soviet song—to mediate her engagement with the spectator, but it is not clear what that meaning is. On the other hand, the interpolation of this documentary footage demands that we confront the relationships between the real history of the Kazym uprising and the carnivalesque fiction that the filmmakers have spun around the event—between those historical realities and unrealities and the present, both as it is depicted on screen and experienced in the auditorium, the distinctions between which are blurred both by Obatina's gaze and Fedorchenko's Grotesque.

Filmography

Fedorchenko, Aleksei, dir. *Angels of the Revolution* (Angely revoliutsii, 2014).

———. *Celestial Wives of the Meadow Mari* (Nebesnye zheny lugovykh mari, 2012).

———. *First on the Moon* (Pervye na lune, 2005).

———. *Silent Souls* (Ovsianki, 2010).

Kalatozov, Mikhail, dir. *Salt for Svanetia* (Sol' Svanetii, 1930).

Loban, Sergei, dir. *Chapiteau Show* (Shapito-Shou, 2011).

Parajanov, Sergei, dir. *Shadows of Forgotten Ancestors* (Tini zabutykh predkiv, 1965).

Vyrypaev, Ivan, dir. *Oxygen* (Kislorod, 2010).

6. Privatized Violence in the New Russian Cinema

Denis Saltykov

How do we approach violence as an object of cultural analysis? I propose here two ways to conceptualize it. The first approach I define as narrow; it understands violence in the simplest way that is close to common sense: violence as a physical action that causes injuries, or a psychological action that makes people do something against their will. The very notion of "common sense," however, was challenged by Michel Foucault with his socio-historical argument that violence is recognized as violence only when it is rhetorically defined as such. Since Foucault, this understanding has led to more refined philosophical attempts to define violence. The broad approach to violence presupposes its ontological dimension that allows us to find its symbolic structure in different institutions. As a precursor to this view, for example, Sergei Eisenstein famously defined art as a form of violence enacted on the viewer (O'Mahony, 9–10), while Jacques Derrida (*Of Grammatology*, 115) described "the originary violence of a language," a concept further developed by Teresa de Lauretis. While acknowledging a complex relationship between these narrow and broad definitions of violence, I deal mostly with the first of them, with representations of empirically recognizable violence, not with philosophical abstractions. In this chapter, the representation of violence in recent Russian cinema is explicit; this choice makes the narrow definition more suitable than the otherwise interesting discussion of discursive dimensions of violence.

In Soviet cinema, violence was largely a state monopoly. Films depicting the October Revolution, the Civil War and, especially, the Great Patriotic War featured legitimate and even sacred violence performed by Russo-Soviet males in service to their state.[1] The monopoly on

1 The term "Great Patriotic War" refers to the war that Soviets fought against Nazi Germany between 22 June 1941 and 9 May 1945. In the USSR and post-Soviet Russia, this term has been preferred to the term "Second World War." One key distinction is the fact that the Great Patriotic War does not cover the period of the Second World War in Europe between 1 September 1939 and 22 June 1941, when the USSR was a de facto ally of Nazi Germany and, alongside the Third Reich, participated in the partition of several Eastern European nations—above all, Poland. In this chapter, I use primarily the term "Great Patriotic War," because this is how Russian cultural producers and audiences refer to the war.

representation of violence changed in the 1980s, when ideological norms collapsed and private individuals—including women and children—acquired agency and started performing acts of violence on screen for reasons other than those sanctioned by the state. Thus individual social violence has been a well-established trope in Russian cinema since the perestroika era. Conservative critics initially responded to this development by applying the derogatory term *chernukha* (black wave) to many films that center on individual acts of violence. The press often blamed the films featuring "pure naturalism, mute pessimism and omnipresent conflict" (Graham, "*Chernukha,*" 13) for social, political, and economic problems. Nancy Condee (*Imperial Trace*, 62) notes that critics acted "as if somehow the thematics of the screen were dictating the social collapse rather than something more interdeterminative." Violence as both a manifestation of individual agency and a symptom of an ongoing crisis of identities remained a central trope in post-Soviet cinema. Since 2000, Vladimir Putin's state claims of a new stable government have moved cultural production in the direction of a reestablished state monopoly on violence, overcoming the violent and chaotic 1990s, a "time of troubles" when individuals and the media could exercise their agency without state interference.

By concentrating on violence depicted on screen, I do not mean that the films I analyze offer a realistic depiction of social processes. As the New Russian Drama director Kirill Serebrennikov (11) puts it, violence is a language rather than an actual depiction of brutality in everyday life. Following this logic, I see onscreen violence as a communicative strategy for portraying contemporary social experience. As Birgit Beumers and Mark Lipovetsky (63–66) have examined in depth, when the communist metanarrative lost its unifying power and legitimacy, violence in the 1990s turned into a decentralized communicative phenomenon. It was privatized by everyone, producing their embrace of *bespredel*—an unstructured use of violence without any purpose or restriction (63).

And yet this phenomenon is by no means unique to Russia: a similar process, described by Zygmunt Bauman (139–62), is endemic of Western societies as well: "The characteristically postmodern stocks of violence are 'privatized'—dispersed, diffused and unfocused" (157). According to Bauman (157–58), "neo-tribes," lacking established institutions, act out of existential fear, escalating violence instead of neutralizing it. Nevertheless, the collapse of the communist master narrative, which legitimated the state monopoly on violence, makes an examination of the transition to neo-tribal cultures and to privatized violence in postcommunist Russian cinema an important case for an inquiry.

Two distinct strategies addressing the shift from the communist to a new social order have emerged in post-Soviet Russian cinema. While federally sponsored epics by directors ranging from Fedor Bondarchuk to Nikita Mikhalkov reinstate, in spectacular and even fan-tastic forms, state-sponsored violence as the hegemonic form of social violence, other Russian filmmakers interrogate the phenomenon of privatized violence as a symptom of unresolved social crises. In this chapter, I examine two recurring themes of such films: first, a comparison of the present Putin-era Russia with the chaotic 1990s; second, explorations of the gendered dimension of social violence. I contend that the vast majority of Putin-era films frame privatized violence by implicitly contrasting it to the Soviet economy of violence, when only state actors had the right to use violence legitimately. Thus the weakening of state monopoly on violence appears in these films as a loss, above all for a stable patriarchal order. Male communities, at the center of many of these films, experience privatized violence as a trauma, even if these men are themselves perpetrating the violence.

I use four films as my case studies: Petr Buslov's *Bimmer* (Bumer, 2003), Aleksei Uchitel''s *Break Loose* (Vos'merka, 2013), Valeriia Gai Germanika's *Everybody Dies but Me* (Vse umrut, a ia ostanus', 2008), and Aleksei Balabanov's *Blind Man's Bluff* (Zhmurki, 2005). Briefly, the first two films portray male communities as captives of unbearable chaos, with the resulting romanticization of these communities as the only refuge from social instability. The third and fourth films problematize these male communities as stand-ins for stable patriarchy. Gai Germanika asks whether women can form a "league of their own" that owns and performs violence in contemporary Russian society. Balabanov, in turn, treats privatized violence and the male community that performs it as cinematic tropes. By decoupling these tropes from any affect, he asks uncomfortable questions not only about the meaning of violence in the 1990s, but also about the so-called transition to stability, aka state monopoly on violence, since Putin's ascent to power.

My main hypothesis is this: even those films that openly deal with unruly social violence as a contemporary phenomenon displace this violence as a feature characteristic of others, tagged by gender or ethnicity. In terms of genre, a useful instrument of the displacement is melodramatization. It permits Russian filmmakers to avoid elements of present-day social life that fall outside genre conventions. Contemporary social drama is a particularly perilous undertaking. Minister of Culture Vladimir Medinskii exemplified this potential danger in a discussion about Andrei Zviagintsev's film *Leviathan* (Leviafan, 2013)—the film that deals with state violence against an individual—when he declared that the ministry would no longer finance films that represent the country as "shitty Russia" (*rashka-govniashka*) (Klochkova). The filmmakers thus are threatened by a very real possibility of being denounced as an internal enemy that seeks to destroy Russia and to pervert its cultural tradition. Kirill Serebrennikov's August 2017 arrest only confirms these fears.[2]

Dead Souls: The Past as the 1990s and the Present of the Twenty-first Century

Buslov: Rebels Without a Cause

Following the collapse of the USSR and the near-death of Russian cinema in the late 1990s and early 2000s, many younger filmmakers turned to the gangster as the new national hero and potential commercial draw. Such films as *Brother* (Brat, 1997) and *Brother 2* (2000),[3] as well as such television series as *The Brigade* (Brigada, 2002), examined privatized violence, the formation of the community shaped by violence, and the transition to the Putin-era status quo. These films and series look backward to ponder the meaning of the changes that occurred in the 1990s and, in one way or another, to pose questions about the present, yet without giving clear answers. One of the most significant films that closely engaged with representations of violence and the new community shaped by it was *Bimmer,* filmed by the twenty-six-year-old director Petr Buslov. Buslov's gangster flick popularized the nickname for a BMW car, which in Russian is "Boomer," rather than "Bimmer" (as in English), the Russian version being a harsher sound that resembles the word "boomerang," according to the director (Savel'ev). This phonetic association reinforces the film's idea that one's fate is recursive: no one can initiate violence and escape its tragic consequences.

2 Serebrennikov is a prominent Russian film and theater director arrested in August 2017. He was charged with the theft of 68 million rubles, allocated by the government to his company Sed'maia studiia. Most Russian oppositional media and intellectuals are convinced that the accusation is fabricated and ideologically biased.

3 Aleksei Balabanov's *Brother* (1997) and *Brother 2* (2000) were among the first commercially and artistically successful treatments of the gangster hero in post-Soviet cinema, and their representations of violence provided a model for younger filmmakers. Because these films received considerable critical and scholarly attention, I choose to focus instead on films that examine the community shaped by violence, rather than the "hero for a new time." For detailed discussion, see Beumers, "Brother," 261–69; Borenstein, 188–94; Condee, *Imperial Trace*, 221–23; and Norris, *Blockbuster History*, 8–11.

The plot of *Bimmer* revolves around four Moscow gangsters who try to run away from the consequences of their violence and hide in Russia's heartland. Each character is individualized by making a specific contribution to their collective demise. First, Dimon, aka "Scalded," gets into a conflict with another gang in a Moscow traffic jam. Then the most violent member of the group, Lyokha, aka "Killa," shoots an apparent gang member who has attacked Dimon. The victim turns out to be an undercover Federal Security Service (FSB) officer; the entire group becomes fugitives. Petia ("Frame") contributes to the foursome's deaths by stealing the bimmer, which one of the characters compares to a hearse.

Finally, the fourth member of the gangster group, Kostia ("Tomcat"), is almost innocent; he is the only one who has a fiancée. The fiancée, Nastia, asks him to quit the gang and move with her to Paris. This narrative turn provides a proverbial folktale element: in the story's violent and male-dominated world, the warrior reaches a crossroads and can go left (and find death) or go right (to Paris) and escape his demise. In the film, the male criminal community is closely associated with Russia itself, which transforms that crossroads after its own fashion: either the homeland destroys you in a spiral of meaningless violence, or you must leave it for good. Within Kostia's understanding of the code of male brotherhood, he is left with only the man's choice. Male friendship is more important than either his heterosexual relationship or, ultimately, his own life.

The film portrays the violent environment as a fact of Russian life. Yet instead of social drama, *Bimmer* offers us a melodrama, where the characters' fate is predetermined and nothing can stop the chain reaction of violent events. To convey this inevitability, Buslov uses flash forwards to prefigure the tragic outcome for secondary characters. Violence is geographically widespread; it may start in Moscow but gradually haunts the whole country. But environmental sources, such as social (dis)order ruled by strong criminals and the police, are also at work. As Frame tells a peasant woman who helps them along the way, "We are not born this way, life makes us this way" (*ne my takie, zhizn' takaia*). This line from the film, which has become a popular saying, provides an explanation for *Bimmer*'s tragic denouement. Within the film's logic, violence indeed is a boomerang and characters lack agency, their fate determined by the times in which they live. Violence is not simply privatized as an autonomous language with different meanings for each individual or small group (the "neo-tribe," in Bauman's terms). Rather, violence here can be derived strictly from an order of things that is almost fatalistic. In that way, *Bimmer* is not a postmodern pastiche but rather a familiar *noir*-style modernist melodrama with an inevitable Russian ending. In the final shot, after all the characters are gone, we see the bimmer-hearse abandoned in the middle of the dark Russian forest. Its headlights gradually dim.

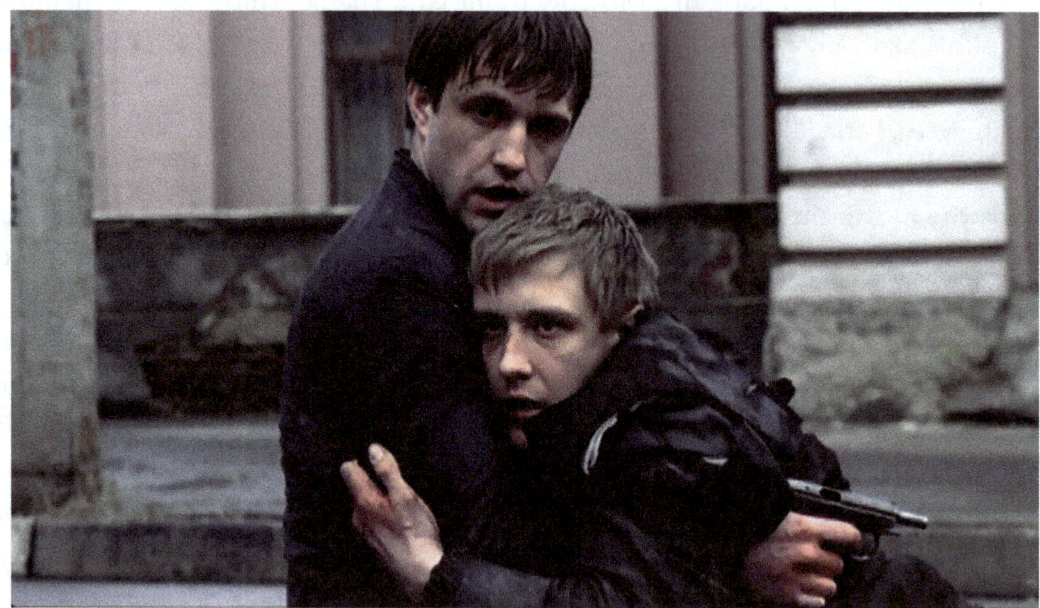

Fig. 6.1. Buslov, *Bimmer*. The man's choice is to die for his male brotherhood.

Bimmer came out just a few years after President Boris Yeltsin's resignation and Putin's ascent to power. In Buslov's words, this was the time when "people were witnessing a new country emerge around them" (Zabaluev). For the filmmaker, it was a confusing time, and this confusion manifests itself in the director's comments about his film. On the one hand, he claims that his story is universal: "This story could have happened anywhere on the globe"[4] (Prokhorova, "'Bumera'"). On the other hand, the film has a meaning of distinctly Russian historical continuity for Buslov: its people are always the same; they are just born into better or worse times; the better times, Buslov seems to think, are those when a lofty cause can justify the violence: "Today they are petty criminals, because they do not have a cause, but during the Great Patriotic War they could throw themselves under [German] tanks" (Savel'ev). The

4 "Moia istoriia mogla by proizoiti v liubom meste zemnogo shara."

mythology of the war would seem to trump all other considerations for Buslov, and the director comes full circle during Putin's third term. In 2016, Buslov was interested in filming a biopic about the young Stalin, whose violence is apparently justified by his pivotal role in the Great Patriotic War: "For me, Stalin is a man who won the war. . . . It is enough to remember the respect with which Churchill spoke of Stalin" (Nigmatullin).

According to Buslov then, in the 1990s the Russian state changed the ontology of Russian culture, allowing individuals to act as independent agents and to create for themselves new fates. Violence without a cause did not produce epic warriors, as in the Great Patriotic War. Of course, it is not war that Buslov explicitly calls for: the director of *Bimmer* blames the 1990s not for violence itself but for the lack of a cause for his collective male hero, the type of normativity that justifies violence as heroic and necessary. In this respect, the film's narrative trajectory provides a fitting metaphor: four violent males, driving through Russian expanses in a stolen German car, know what they are running away from, but have no idea where they are heading.

Uchitel': A Balancing Act between Melodrama and Social Drama

The contrast between the 1990s and the 2000s is similarly a governing concern in Aleksei Uchitel''s *Break Loose*. Here, however, the director withholds any comments as to the meaning of this transition. Social criticism was not Uchitel''s primary concern; instead, the director sought to try out the genre of criminal melodrama (Uchitel'). The film's script is based on the novella by Russian National-Bolshevik writer Zakhar Prilepin, who describes his own experience of working in a riot police unit (OMON) and facing angry criminals every day. In 2007, before the novella was published, Prilepin had made a distinction between Yeltsin's and Putin's Russias: "I didn't like my former country. The system of coordinates was broken; all the concepts of honor and justice were perverted. But there was nevertheless something like freedom" (Prilepin). Initially, Prilepin did not like Putin's politics either until Russia invaded Ukraine, when Prilepin became an ardent supporter of the president's neo-imperialist agenda (Zverev).[5]

5 "I saw a lot of Russian people, full of happiness and energy. Primarily among those fighting in Novorossiia, but not only there. I saw a readiness to make sacrifices, to face destitution. I saw that people were ready to give up their private interests for the sake of their ideals."

The Russian title of the film is literally *Eight,* the model number of a Russian-made car—Lada, Model Eight. As with *Bimmer,* the director chose to name the film after the car, rather than after the humans in the car, to emphasize the importance of a collective identity. One could argue that dates back to Sergei Eisenstein's *Battleship Potemkin* (Bronenosets "Potemkin," 1925) and Vsevolod Ivanov's *Armored Train 14-69* (Bronepoezd 14-69, 1922), but unlike those two Soviet works, where the machine is a fighting vehicle in service of a clear revolutionary cause, here in the two post-Soviet films the car symbolizes a community with no clear goal. The German *Bimmer* turns out to be a death trap, while the Soviet-era Model Eight is a poor match for a Mercedes driven by the city's criminal boss Boots.

Uchitel''s film is set in a provincial Russian town in 1999, right before Yeltsin's resignation. Four army veterans return to their hometown to serve in a riot police unit and, in the line of duty, have to use force against their own citizens and even their own relatives. At night, the protagonists face what they perceive as their real enemies: members of an ethnic gang that controls the local night club. The main character, Gera, falls in love with Aglaia, the girlfriend

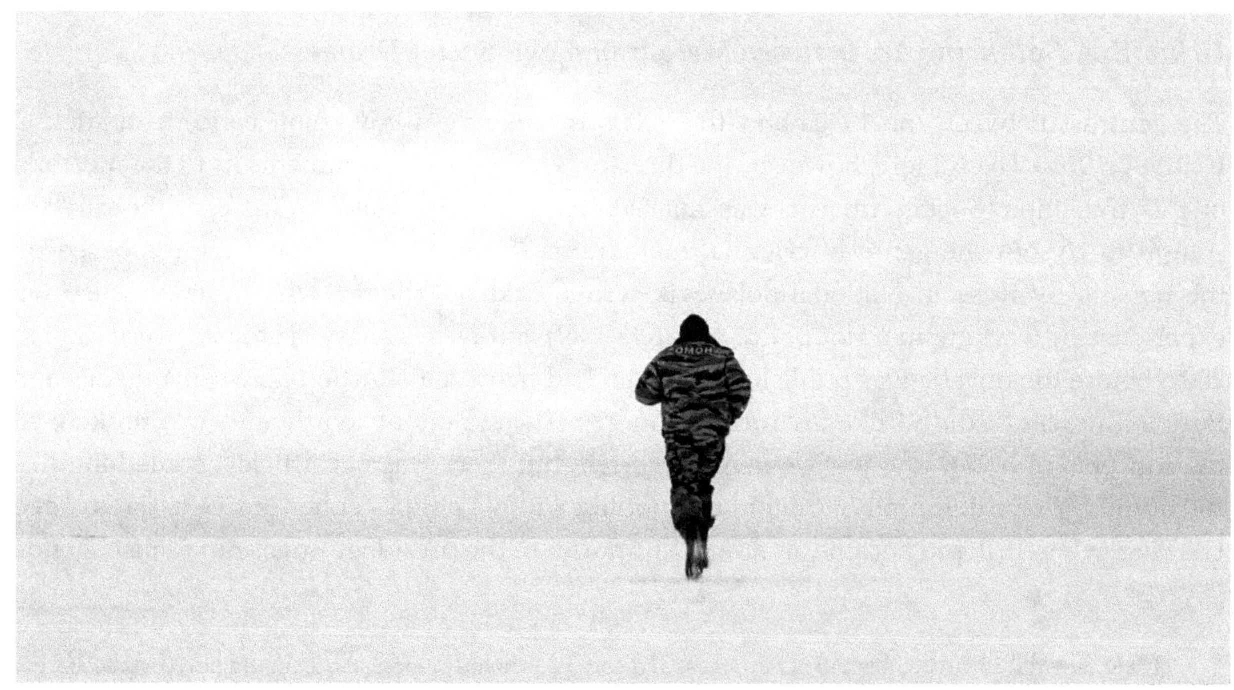

Fig. 6.2. Uchitel', *Break Loose*. Running into the white emptiness.

of Boots, the gang's leader. The nighttime and daytime fighting routines ultimately converge because Boots controls not only the gang (the nighttime foe) but also the mayor and, through him, indirectly the police unit. The resolution of the conflict coincides with the broadcast of Yeltsin's resignation—a crucial moment in recent Russian political history. In the final twist, both Boots and Aglaia perish when their car collides with a train. The last scene shows Gera in police uniform, running into the white emptiness; he is followed by the Model Eight car and picked up by his friends. The end credits roll to the song *Until They Turn the Lights Out* in a performance by the right-wing rap-band 25/17, while the celebrating crowd wave lighters. The change of era, it would seem, is a transition to empty nothingness.

Although the old power structure—locally, Boots; nationally, Yeltsin—is finished, the closing sequence is ambiguous. One might interpret the ending of *Break Loose* in a pessimistic way, as exchanging one violent social structure for another. This view is allegedly shared by Uchitel', Prilepin, and the scriptwriter Aleksandr Mindadze. In this interpretation, the white emptiness denotes the indeterminacy of the future. As the director reminds us, "placed horizontally, the digit 8 represents infinity. The last frame of the film represents precisely this infinity, where the characters set out either toward the bright future or toward the dark past" (Romodanovskaia).

Although some critics saw Uchitel''s film as a social drama commenting on Russia's recent history, Uchitel' offers an alternative reading. He claims that his *Break Loose* is in fact a crime melodrama, rather than a social drama that comments directly on specific issues in contemporary Russia (Uchitel'). By claiming that his film is a commercial genre vehicle, Uchitel' forecloses accusations that he is depicting social ills of Russian life and capitalizing on well-worn clichés of a violent barbaric Russia. The filmmaker downplays both the characters' profession as police officers and the historical moment the film depicts: "I do not make cinema about cops—I film people. I don't care that they wear uniforms . . . It's totally unimportant when the film's action takes place" (Romodanovskaia). Taking "genre" to mean something akin to "discursive claims made by real speakers for particular purposes in specific situations" (Altman, 101),[6] we may respond to Uchitel''s assertions with our own question: What does it mean to designate *Break*

6 Altman uses the notion of pragmatics to take into account the viewer's interpretations as a part of film's generic formation as it is shaped in public sphere. While the public sphere (in the conventional Western sense) in Russia is limited, I treat Uchitel''s claims as an attempt to influence the viewer's interpretation of the film by means of the author's authoritative voice.

Loose a melodrama? Moreover, what would it mean to designate *Break Loose* a social drama? The latter question is also an important one because the director rejects the importance of the very elements that he had decided to include in the narrative. The plot may be read differently in different genre paradigms; its specific use of violence, too, takes on a different significance.

It seems that the logic of melodrama—with its emphasis on binary contrasts and excess—works better in Uchitel''s picture. In contrast, social drama implies a more complex vision of the society and characters as its actors. Discussing post-Soviet visual culture, Eliot Borenstein contends that excessive violence and sexuality work as a compensatory mechanism for the loss of patriarchal authority (43–50). In Uchitel''s film, women and ethnic Others represent an external threat to male community and thus effectively create a polarized world typical of melodrama. The film's logic suggests that privatized violence emanates from ethnic or gender Others. With both gone, the monopoly on violence by the state figures of the riot police is consolingly restored.

In the diegetic world of crime melodrama, Aglaia plays the role of the proverbial *femme fatale.* Mystically appearing in the dark, she seduces Gera, and this puts him in harm's way. In this genre configuration, both Boots (as Aglaia's jealous ethnic boyfriend) and Aglaia herself (as temptress) threaten the entire male brotherhood. Torn between his passion for a woman and his loyalty to his brothers, Gera provides the perfect admixture for male hysteria and more violence. The film's closing image of Gera running into the unknown provides a subtler and more open-ended image than the logic of the narrative had suggested.

At the same time, the film's ending, which eliminates the ethnic and gender disruptions with a car crash, restores the stability of the male community and eliminates the melodramatic threats to homosocial bliss. No matter what the future holds, as long as the militarized homosocial brotherhood stays intact, the future of the nation is safe. While *Bimmer* and *Break Loose* lay claim to a kind of authenticity of the egalitarian male community and its value in standing against a hostile and violent world, the next two films analyzed in this chapter question the very possibility of such a community.

Deconstructing Communities of Violence

Gai Germanika: A Lesson to Learn while Growing Up

Valeriia Gai Germanika's film *Everybody Dies but Me*, set in present-day Russia, examines a community of violent teenage girls. Both the transposition of violence onto a female community and the setting of the film in present-day Russia initially made this film stand out in Russian cinema at the moment of its premiere. The film is set in a lower middle-class neighborhood of a big city and focuses on three female high-school students: Katia, Vika, and Zhanna. We enter the narrative in medias res, as the girls are hanging out on the outskirts of the city, burying a pet cat and discussing the upcoming school dance. Filmed by handheld camera, the scene sets a quasi-documentary tone for the entire film. Soon Katia runs away from her abusive parents and hides in Vika's apartment. Parents and teachers try to blackmail the teenagers into betraying Katia's whereabouts. The bargaining chip—if Katia does not return home—is the cancellation of the school dance. The three girls swear not to go to the dance for the sake of eternal friendship, yet their female community is short-lived.

Upset at the prospect of not having a dance, upper-class girls gang up on the newly formed community and threaten the three protagonists with violence. When the teachers harass Zhanna and Vika into betraying their friend, the pressure works: they explain to Katia that they will go to the dance without her.

Undaunted, Katia decides to go to the dance on her own. She meets a boy, Aleks, whom she likes, and agrees to follow him to the basement, where he rapes her. Even though the experience is humiliating, she responds with the socially appropriate lines, as if for the occasion of transitioning into womanhood: "It was very good for me." She repeats these words like an incantation to alleviate psychological and physical trauma. As she exits the building, Aleks's girlfriend, Nastia, violently attacks her, as other schoolkids cheer on the women's fight.

The director demonstrates women's initiation into adulthood as a process of learning the discourse of violence. And here is the gendered difference: violent discourse, together with institutional violence, dooms the female community, not just the fate of individual members, but as a community as such. On her way home after the fight with Nastia, the bloodied Katya aggressively pushes away a girl who tries to bond with and help her. At home she verbally abuses her parents. The film ends with Katya declaring: "Everyone will die but me," effectively destroying any illusion of possible female allegiances. Violent outbursts are scattered

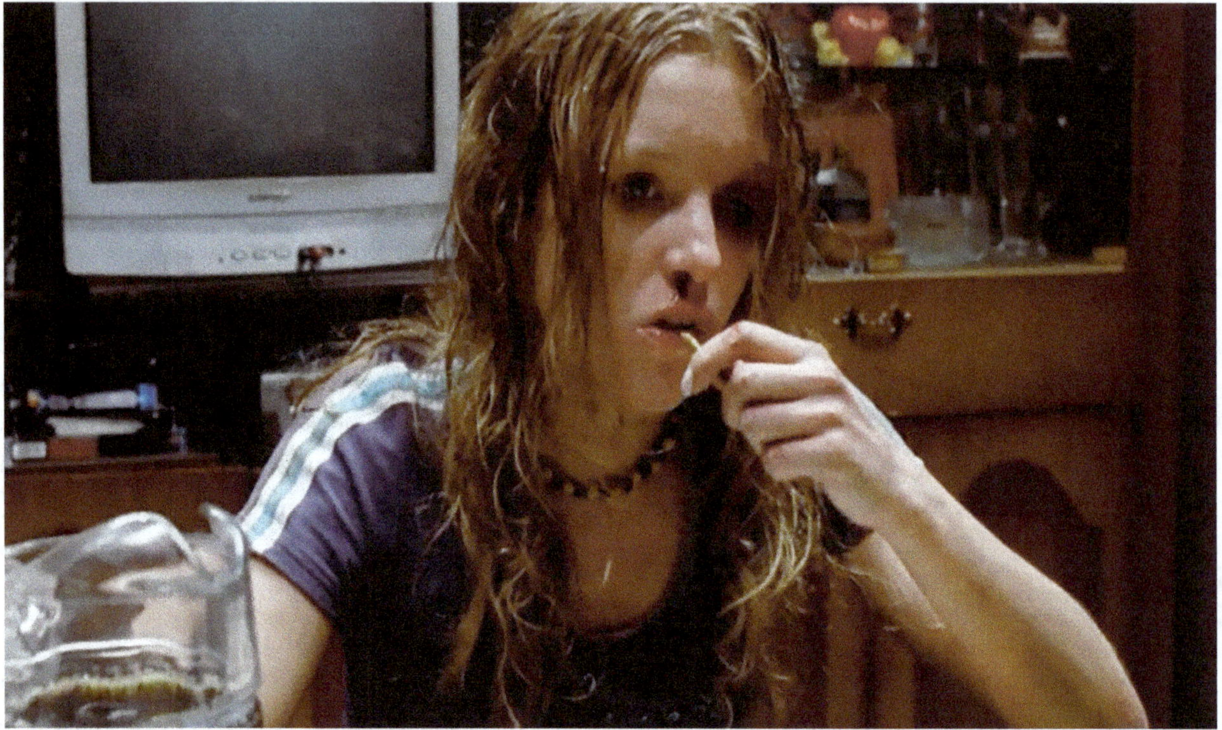

Fig. 6.3. Gai Germanika, *Everybody Dies but Me*. Katia, a schoolgirl—raped, beaten, and deprived of all illusions.

throughout the narrative, yet they endow the women with neither agency nor power. Women may use the language of violence, it would seem, but they do not own it.

On the surface, *Everybody Dies but Me* seems to deal with the topic of violence in an unusually straightforward and progressive way. The film represents Russian women facing violence here and now. However, there is a caveat to this good news. Russian cinema and culture in general tend to honor the tradition of violent male communities as an indispensable part of history. This violence can be legitimate, as in depictions of the Great Patriotic War, or senseless, as in depictions of the 1990s, but the stable fact remains: violence situates men in history. Women, in contrast, are not part of history. In this context, not only does Gai Germanika deny women the ability to form a meaningful and lasting community, but her documentary and slice-of-life aesthetics captures only a snapshot of an essentialized identity that has no specific place in a historical moment. While being unable to group, women interiorize their role of passive objects, owning only the right of using violence in the rules established by others. Women cannot be creative here, so their only option is to give up their agency and to follow the pre-established rituals. In this respect, it is not surprising that Gai Germanika vehemently denies any gender problematics to her film. She sees it as a film not about women but "about people" (Gai Germanika) outside gender hierarchies and thus outside social problematics.[7]

Balabanov: Violent Continuities

If Gai Germanika offers the viewer an aborted attempt at testing violence as a communicative language for women, Aleksei Balabanov's black comedy *Blind Man's Bluff* utterly calls into question the myth of the romanticized 1990s male community held together by violence. In his earlier film *Brother 2*, Balabanov had seemed to suggest the possibility of a serious cause for which a male community could fight; in *Blind Men's Bluff*, such a possibility is ridiculed in the film's narrative structure. The film begins in a university lecture hall, where an economics professor explains to her students the difference between the lawless 1990s and the present of the "aught years" (2000s). She points out that the early stages of capitalism in Russia demanded violent actions to accumulate "seed capital." An abrupt cut then introduces the proverbial excessive violence of the 1990s with the fine edge of a sledgehammer: a series of loosely connected vignettes about two gangsters who attempt to locate a suitcase containing heroin. A parody of a male brotherhood, they work for a mob boss, played by the Russian film industry's own boss, Nikita Mikhalkov. The logic of the film suggests that lawless times are over—now merely a subject of history—and can therefore be treated in a humorous way.

While the viewer expects the flashback to serve as an illustration of the professor's opening claim, Balabanov never returns us to the same classroom, even at the film's end. When the film returns to the present, we are reunited with the 1990s gangsters, who now serve respectively as a member of the Russian Parliament (Duma) and his assistant in the Russian Duma and whose office overlooks the Kremlin. Their former gang boss works as a security man in the office building, where our heroes toil for the prosperity of the fatherland. The change of the characters' fortunes is not directly the subject of the story, although it is also not accidental: they succeeded in their careers while the audience does not understand the circumstances of this transition. What the viewer knows, however, is that they are not changed human beings

7 Gai Germanika is also known for her infamous statements supporting the Russian government and public oppression of the opposition; see "Podderzhivaiu nastoiashchii rezhim. . . . Mne nravitsia, kogda oppozitsionnoe zakryvaiut," in Maliukova, "Pontovaia vyskochka."

now that they are walking the halls of high politics. One of the characters longingly recollects the suitcase of heroin they used to hunt for in the 1990s. In contrast to Buslov or Uchitel', who see a break between the violence of the 1990s and Putin's era, Balabanov sees here nothing but continuities along temporal and gendered lines.

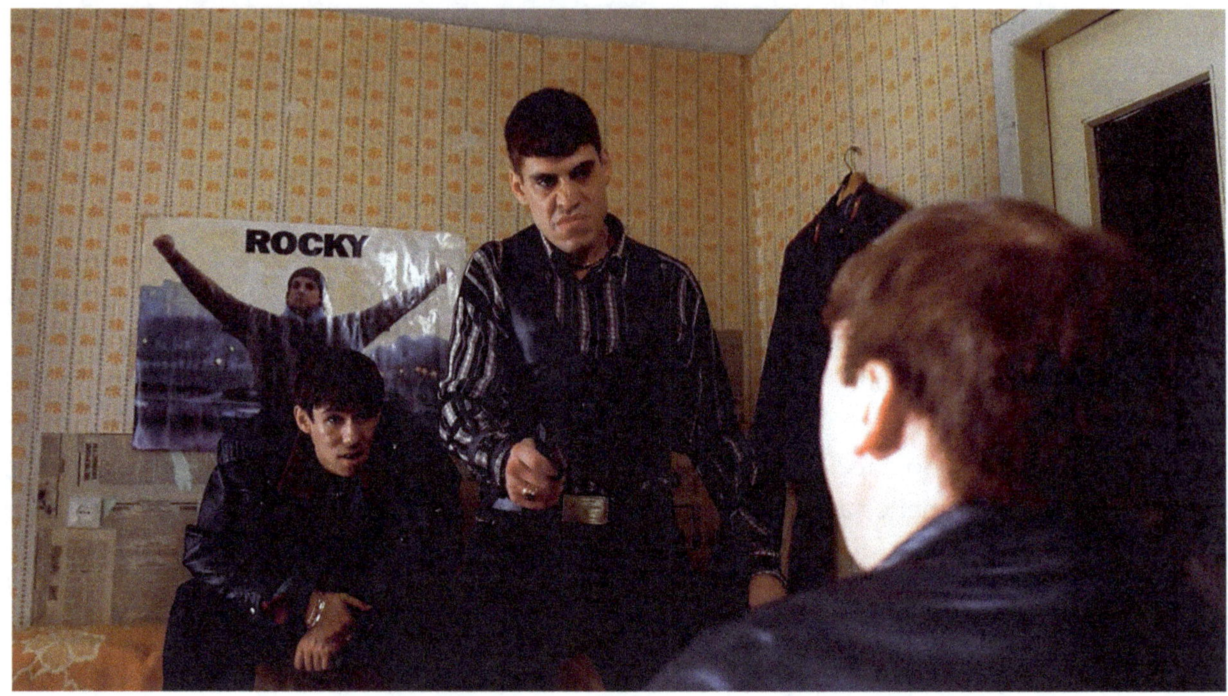

Fig. 6.4. Balabanov, *Blind Man's Bluff*. The accumulation of "seed capital."

Another key difference between the male melodramas of Buslov and Uchitel', in comparison with Balabanov's comedy, is in the treatment of the male community as a collective entity that believes itself to be at war with the world but finds strength in its membership. In Balabanov's version, senseless violence constitutes the very fabric of society; male communities exist only to perform this violence. And while in *Bimmer* and such gangster TV series as Aleksei Sidorov's *Brigade*, the male community is valorized and the gangster is a romanticized figure, in *Blind Men's Bluff* gangsters are dumb thugs and slapstick characters. In Balabanov's film, the male community does not exist to oppose violence; instead, the only reason for males to get together is to look for death in the course of inflicting violence on themselves and on others. The world of violence is exposed as a discourse par excellence, where characters are two-dimensional cartoon figures through whom this language speaks.

A final divergence from the male melodrama of Buslov and Uchitel' concerns Balabanov's source of inspiration, which is profoundly incompatible with melodrama's legacies. Balabanov's "story of the 1990s" follows several groups of criminal males—some cops, some drug dealers, others hitmen for hire—in the fashion of Quentin Tarantino's *Pulp Fiction* (1994). As in Tarantino's film, the narrative excuse is the illusory goal of big money. For Balabanov, Tarantino might be a worthwhile cinematic inspiration, but Balabanov's film cannot be construed as a loving tribute, either to Hollywood cinema or to Western mass culture more broadly. In fact, the film directly links westernization with violence. Of the two protagonists, for example, one carries the Russian name Sergei, the other the anglicized nickname Simon. The difference between the two main characters lies in their intellect. Simon, the dumber of the two, has a particular taste for everything American: he learns English by reading American comic books, enjoys eating at McDonald's, and likes Western music. The most violent scene in the film, full of black humor, resembles the famous torture scene from Tarantino's *Reservoir Dogs* (1992): in Tarantino's film, the sadistic gangster Mr. Pink cuts his victim's ear while listening and dancing to *Stuck in the Middle with You* by Stealers Wheel. In a similar spirit, Balabanov's Simon hits his victim with an axe while listening and dancing to *Look at Me Now* by Electric Light Orchestra. His victim has black skin, and the whole scene is happening in a room with posters of Elvis Presley and 2Pac on the wall. Balabanov links the post-Soviet mode of violence directly with Western influence, above all American culture.

What remains to be said about the uses of violence in *Blind Men's Bluff* concerns the film's treatment of its female characters. In *Bimmer* and *Break Loose,* as in many other gangster films, women are associated with the traditional trope of a nurturing redeemer who intercedes on behalf of male sinners. In *Blind Men's Bluff,* apart from the female professor who tries to provide a didactic moment at the beginning of the film, only one other woman appears in the film, and she redeems no one. Played by Renata Litvinova, she is a nameless waitress, a walking illustration of Laura Mulvey's argument about the male gaze: she has, in the words of Simon, "quite an ass" on her. She too survives into the present diegetic frame of the film, where she serves coffee to Simon, who keeps on playfully slapping her on her butt. While the film definitely fails the Bechdel Test on all fronts, it establishes a not-so-subtle set of continuities between the gangster patriarchy of the 1990s and the glamour-driven patriarchy of Putin's Russia.

The Pragmatics of Genre Violence

The Russian directors chosen for discussion in this chapter deal with a debilitated social life where the most fundamental categories, such as time (perceived as temporal continuity), community, and gender are destabilized. Violence is present here not as a mere language but also as an object indicating a certain condition of state power, its potential appropriation by the private sector, and national anxieties about that appropriation. Violence is performed by corrupt institutions, such as the police, and is taken over by different social groups not just as a way of interaction with reality but as *the only way* of interaction. As a language of social critique, violence is not culturally specific to Russian cinema, but its abundance is telling as an example of communicative violence itself. Staging an assault on their audiences, these Russian filmmakers seek to make hidden violence explicit, bringing an implicit alternative ethical dimension to recent cinematic and political discourse. In a context in which there is no thriving independent or sovereign public sphere, cinema has the potential here to serve as an alternative arena for public debate. Cinematic violence causes shock and triggers painful pleasures of cultural recognition.

Putin-era films tend to show violence as itself "value-neutral power" that can be derived from the state and its police (as in *Break Loose* and, less explicitly, in *Bimmer*), from school (*Everybody Dies but Me*), and from the West (e.g., the United States, as in *Blind Man's Bluff*). The deal for every individual is not to avoid using violence but to learn how to use it in "a proper way." The fact that a proper way exists forms the base for the films discussed here. The heroic violence in male communities is romanticized in *Bimmer* and *Break Loose*. Both films show the moment of transition from the 1990s (with its excesses) to the "aughts," the period in Russian history when violence becomes less apparent and more "civilized," as shown in *Blind Man's Bluff*. While the first way of making violence "proper" is its subjugation to the goal of state and power institutions, the second way is presented to us as male bonding. Male brotherhoods are opposed to individual women, who tend to seduce men, disconnect them from their group, and finally make them vulnerable. Women themselves, as Gai Germanika shows, are incapable of forming cohesive communities, but nevertheless have to learn how to perform violence. The process of learning to perform violence constitutes their coming-of-age experience: women have to learn how to experience, persevere, and even enjoy being violated.

These Russian filmmakers use a specific genre logic in filming violence. They include elements of social drama in their plots, and those elements open the stories up to ethical and political questions. Directors often deny any social discourse in their films and offer alternative, perhaps safer, ways of interpretation using syntactic elements of other genres (the road movie, male melodrama, gangster comedy, and psychological drama). Nevertheless, specific ways of saying something important in public in Russia (and at the same time denying it) tend to form specific pragmatics of visual narration, allowing the author to appear both as a citizen asking difficult questions and as a silent imperial subject.

Acknowledgment

The research for this chapter was funded by the Full-time Advanced Doctoral Program of the National Research University Higher School of Economics (Moscow) and by the Center for Russian and East European Studies of the University of Pittsburgh.

Filmography

Balabanov, Aleksei, dir. *Brother* (Brat, 1997).
———. *Brother 2* (Brat 2, 2000).
———. *Blind Man's Bluff* (Zhmurki, 2005).
Buslov, Petr, dir. *Bimmer* (Bumer, 2003).
Eisenstein, Sergei, dir. *Battleship Potemkin* (Bronenosets Potemkin, 1925).
Gai Germanika, Valeriia, dir. *Everybody Dies but Me* (Vse umrut, a ia ostanus', 2008).
Sidorov, Aleksei, dir. *The Brigade* (Brigada, 2002).
Tarantino, Quentin, dir. *Pulp Fiction* (1994).
———. *Reservoir Dogs* (1992).
Uchitel', Aleksei, dir. *Break Loose* (Vos'merka, 2013).
Zviagintsev, Andrei, dir. *Leviathan* (Leviafan, 2013).

Part Three

EVROPSK OR RUSSIA?

Framing Essay

Seth Graham

Mikhail Bakhtin envisioned his celebrated brainchild, the chronotope, as a tidy concept that "expresses the inseparability of space and time" as represented in fictional narratives (84). But he wasn't pedantic about proportion. Some chronotopes—the provincial town, for instance—rely more on space than time, and some—such as the encounter—the other way round. And it is not only the nature of a specific chronotope itself that determines which, if either, dimension is dominant. The extratextual influences on the form and reception of a particular chronotope (or trope or motif or style, etc.) are also relevant and can tip the scales of customary spatio-temporal perception. Time and space are ubiquitously fused in lived reality and in the metanarratives that we (still, stubbornly) use to comprehend it. This extends beyond the plots and settings of our world to the characters themselves: "the image of man," says Bakhtin, "is always intrinsically chronotopic" (85).

In its choice of material and its broad arguments about recent Russian film history, this section of our cinemasaurus privileges the spatial over the temporal. The three contributions are devoted to predominantly spatial categories—empire, ruins, metropoles and colonies, heartlands, borderlands, marginalities, alterities—that have overtaken or at least competed robustly with history and historicity for the attention of Russian filmmakers and filmgoers since the 1990s. This arguable shift followed the perestroika emphasis on the temporal, on dissecting and interrogating the USSR's history, an emphasis that itself can be seen as a reaction in kind to Soviet cinema's own obsessions with historical consciousness.

The chapters by Zhanna Budenkova, Tetyana Shlikhar, and Trevor Wilson also share a concern with Russia's strategies of self-presentation and global self-positioning, a crucial medium for which has been narrative cinema. It can be argued (not uncontroversially) that the pendulum of Russia's self-image has for centuries swung reliably between masochistic self-deprecation and aggressive self-aggrandizement. This temporal metaphor of a clock is lent a spatial element not only by the movement of the pendulum through space but also by the inevitably central role of the country's physical position vis-à-vis the West (and, of somewhat lesser importance to the chapters in this section, the East) in determining the direction and speed of the oscillations.

Budenkova's analysis of the effect of Tajik newcomers on a Russian village in Gennadii Sidorov's *Little Old Ladies* (Starukhi, 2003); Shlikhar's characterization of the humor in 1990s Russian comedies as "a delicate mix of self-study and self-mockery" reliant on encounters between various Us-es and Thems; and Wilson's examination of alternative sexualities (in conjunction with other alterities) as a vehicle for national self-presentation all compellingly portray how post-Soviet filmmakers have engaged with the movements of this hypothetical pendulum using all the tools at their disposal: genre, stereotypes and archetypes, continuity, casting, marketing, and (yes) chronotope.

One of the themes visible when considering these three chapters together is an old and perhaps hackneyed paradox: the equal symbolic importance attached to mundane small spaces (*byt*) and richly evocative vast expanses (*bytie*) in the project of Russian self-regard. This is a site of potential dissonance that Richard Stites (47) dubbed "crowded on the edge of vastness." It lends itself both to concrete metaphorization and visualization (the steppe versus the *kommunalka*) and abstract paeans to the flexibility and the spiritual and intellectual omnivorousness of Russian culture, able to express and project itself simultaneously on a macro- and micro-scale, especially when publicly musing about its own relationship to the world. That relationship is often marked, as Shlikhar points out in her analyses of Nikita Mikhalkov and Aleksandr Sokurov, by prominent examples of cultural borrowing that are not coded as borrowing, or even as participation in global culture, but as a form of righteous assimilation and even bricolage that has taken on a complex set of meanings specific to the condition of post-Sovietness and has been expressed in terms of Russia's (literal) place in the world.

None of this is to say that we should accept Francis Fukuyama's storied announcement of the end of history as a foolproof prism through which to atemporally examine Russian films since 1991; the authors in this section certainly do not. But they each in their own way implicitly highlight how Russia's spatial identity, including geography, infrastructure, topography, and ethnic proximities, bear witness to Sergei Medvedev's observation that Russia "lives under the spell of space" ("A General Theory," 526).

7. Fragments of Empire: The Heartland in Post-Soviet Film

Zhanna Budenkova

In this chapter, concerned with a cinematic representation of Russia's heartland, it is worth mentioning two framing assumptions. One deals with the notion of modern ruins—a notion that extends far beyond a concrete narrative of death and decay and that, nonetheless, is directly important for the films considered in this chapter. A second assumption connects this theme of ruination with a postcolonial reflection characteristic of the mindscape of modern-day Russia striving to (re-)create a range of identities after the collapse of the Soviet Union. Both assumptions determine a specific cinematic language that describes Russia's heartland in post-Soviet cinematography: on the one hand, it demonstrates distinct traces of the preceding era, and on the other, it exhibits the anxieties of Russia's present.

All four films considered in this chapter were shot after the collapse of the Soviet Union: the earliest one, Lidiia Bobrova's *In That Land* (V toi strane, 1997), engages with a specific dissolution of Soviet tropes associated with "village film,"[1] as well as of the Soviet genre system in general. Released at the very end of the twentieth century, *In That Land* does not shy away from reproducing a number of recognizable clichés characteristic of Soviet, and even Stalinist, cinematography, but the air of decay has already touched its monumental

1 The term "village film" is used broadly here, encompassing a range of films from Stalinist comedies whose action unfolds in kolkhoz settings (especially films by Ivan Pyr'ev) to dramas produced in the Stalinist period and beyond, dealing with a theme of communist construction in the village and/or involving a juxtaposition of rural and urban existence. The term "village film" inevitably evokes the better-known term "village prose" (*derevenskaia proza*), a movement conventionally traced to Valentin Ovechkin (1906–68), whose short stories, collected under the title *District Routines* (Raionnye budni) appeared from 1952 to 1956 in the leading journal *Novyi mir* even before Stalin's death in 1953. As a creative movement, village prose was both a style of writing and a thematic concern that departed from the existing conventions of Stalin-era socialist realism in the village-prose writers' focus on traditional Russian village life (both its idealized values and their deterioration), drawn through sharp contrasts between village and city, old and new, spirituality and modern exigencies. The best-known writers associated with the village-prose movement include Fedor Abramov, Vasilii Belov, Aleksandr Iashin, Valentin Rasputin, the early Aleksandr Solzhenitsyn, and Vasilii Shukshin, who figures in the analysis that follows. Increasingly, in the late 1970s and early 1980s, the village-prose movement became associated with nationalist opposition, whether encouraged by some factions within the Communist Party of the Soviet Union (CPSU) or in anti-authoritarian protest against it.

reminiscences, turning them into a form of postmodern bricolage.[2] In three additional films to be examined here, what might be described as the Soviet mindscape is discernable through the surface narrative of modern Russia, for which that mindscape functions both as nostalgia and as nightmare, evoking a modernity that alternatively worships and dreads its own ruins. It may come as a surprise that nostalgia for the Soviet mindscape is also explicit in *Free Floating* (Svobodnoe plavanie, 2006) by the younger (then) *auteur* director Boris Khlebnikov, infusing the film with a specific melancholic tone. As Johannes von Moltke (411) has remarked, the mood of melancholy is typical of films concerned with an aesthetic of ruination: a melancholic mise-en-scène serves to bring "temporal movements of cinema and ruins to a halt," as if to suspend historicity. The notion of suspended historicity is connected to the idea of a ruin's sublimity, which embodies a logic of idealization of the past, important in the production of nostalgia. The anxious component of the films examined in this chapter is constituted in the risk that they may use the Soviet tropes unreflexively, as a trace of consciousness no longer present but not entirely absent: the "ruin consciousness" of the Soviets that keeps haunting the present day.

In his essay "Authentic Ruins," Andreas Huyssen (26) speaks about this ambiguity, proposing the term "authenticity" to describe a modern admiration of ruination as an instrument that grasps the community's imagined past through evidence of its decay. According to Huyssen, the process of ruination, imagined as (re)turning human-made structures into nature, becomes associated with the notion of a nostalgic aura of the past, the sense of lost brilliance and harmony. At the same time, the discourse of authentic ruins bears within itself a threat of lethal suffocation within the constraints of the past, and this threat determines its ambivalent character.[3]

2 The term *bricolage*—building things in an amateur manner without the direct aid of professionals—was reintroduced by Claude Lévi-Strauss (17) to describe a mythopoetic activity that uses "whatever is at hand" to create new "projects" (including ideas). Further elaborating the term, Jacques Derrida ("Structure, Sign, and Play," 258) mentions that it is possible to view *bricolage* as a form of critical language—every discourse actor is essentially a *bricoleur*, building a personal narrative out of existing composite parts. In the current chapter, reliant on this legacy, *bricolage* is understood as a form of nostalgic consciousness that builds cinematic narratives of heartland out of existing Soviet tropes, as well as new ideas that transform these tropes, instilling them with novel meanings.

3 In his analysis of Giovanni Battista Piranesi's etchings *Carceri,* Huyssen ("Authentic Ruins," 26) argues that the modern admiration of ruins has a darker side to it: according to the scholar, the idea of authenticity, which venerated ruins embody, may constitute a "prison of invention" (26), where the bounds of the past cancel out the possibility of innovation.

Both the admiration of ruins and the anxiety around their suffocating potential are often present in the discourse on Russia's heartland in post-Soviet cinema. Recurrently, the heartland becomes an embodiment of the ruination of the Soviet imperial past, which often bears distinct traits of physical destruction, be it a dying village in Gennadii Sidorov's *Little Old Ladies* (Starukhi, 2003) or the ruins of a Soviet school in Andrei Konchalovskii's *The Postman's White Nights* (Belye nochi pochtal'ona Alekseia Triapitsyna, 2014) more than a decade later. At the same time, the deceased empire tends to be presented as a site of desire, whose intensity does not subside even when confronted with the self-criticism in which these films abound. Here the empire attains an organic quality, revealing the logic of identifying the natural with the national, characteristic of the early ethnographic as well as certain nationalistic phantasms. In this identification of the empire with the living organism, the representation of Russia's heartland plays a crucial role.

In his theorization of the national as a narrated category, Homi Bhabha ("DissemiNation," 212) speaks about the imagining of nation as a form in space, or "landscape," which informs the idea of nation with "visual presence." In this respect, it might be argued, the space of Russia's heartland in the films considered here comes as the visual presence of imperial consciousness, which simultaneously repels and attracts utopian longings. Obvious characteristics of the heartland as a remote, nature-laden space activates dichotomies of the traditional and modern, cyclical and linear that help to inscribe it into the narratives of modernity. In present conditions when—one might argue—modernity is experiencing its own ruination, including the demise of the Soviet state as a form of alternative modernity, certain metaphors present in these films may come as part of a broader reflection on the specifics of modernity in Russia. Here the theme of heartland is closely intertwined with phenomena that have sometimes been described as symptomatic of internal colonization, which finds its vivid representation in a specific ethnographical impulse of the films discussed below.

The term "internal colonization" was reintroduced by Aleksandr Etkind to describe a specific Russian reality in which the country's *Volk*, and the peasantry in particular, have been assigned a role of internal "barbarian," whom westernized elites began to Orientalize as a consequence of the reforms of Peter the Great. As a result of the reforms, which contributed to the shoring up of the estate system in Russia, the nobility tended to view peasants from the position of the colonizer: as "wild natives" or, worse, as domesticated animals (Etkind, *Vnutrenniaia kolonizatsiia*, 171), a status that was reinforced by master-slave relations prior to the 1861 abolition of peasant slavery. Drawing on an intellectual legacy that includes ideas developed by the Russian historians Sergei Solov'ev and Vasilii Kliuchevskii, Etkind's view on internal colonization is compatible with related arguments by Geoffrey Hosking and Michael Cherniavsky (119–20), delineating two different imaginings of Russia: as Holy Rus', which embodied the Russian *Volk*, and imperial Russia, the domain of post-Petrine elites, who viewed themselves as in many ways detached from the demotic roots.[4] The divide proved to be enduring and survived into Soviet imperial consciousness: in his essay devoted to the early Soviet cinema, Walter Benjamin ("On the Present Situation") cites Russian filmmakers' belief that the peasants' perception is drastically different from that of the urban population. Here he repeats the filmmakers' idea that Russian peasants are unable to follow two simultaneous narrative strands in film and are capable of following only a single series of images that had to unfold chronologically "like the verses of a street ballad" (14). According to Etkind (*Vnutrenniaia kolonizatsiia*, 8), this account might be taken to confirm the Orientalizing logic regarding the *Volk*, the logic characteristic of internal colonization, adopted by Russian intelligentsia as a westernized cohort.

The view of heartland as something fundamentally different from the imperial center and constructed as culturally and ideologically inferior to it was a popular cliché of Soviet cinematic representation, wherein Moscow occupied the position of a panoptic observer of the rest of the Soviet Union. It is fair to say that a similar perspective, intimately connected to the notion of internal colonization, still underlies the perceptions of many contemporary Russian filmmakers, who continue to view the heartland according to a dyad of metropole/colony relations. Indeed, the imperial perspective has a rich legacy independent of (and prior to) the Soviet tradition in the history of world cinematography, dating back to the early ethnographic projects, to which the post-Soviet heartland films have a surprising affinity. To demonstrate this connection, it is worth briefly turning, for example, to an early ethnographic film, *In the Land of the Headhunters* (1914), by the American filmmaker Edward S. Curtis.

4 In *Tsar and People: Studies in Russian Myths*, Cherniavsky attributes the emergence of the term "Holy Rus'" to the sixteenth century—it first emerged, he argues, in Andrei Kurbskii's correspondence with Tsar Ivan IV. In his writings, Kurbskii used the term to oppose the mass of the country's population—Holy Rus'—to the autocratic tsar. Cherniavsky argues that since then, the term has frequently been used to delineate the totality of the Russian people, as opposed to the ruling elite, including in Petrine times.

Curtis's film offers a bizarre example of the turn-of-the-century "salvage ethnography" aimed at saving traces of American indigenous cultures, believed to be on the verge of extinction due to the unavoidable march of progress. In this context, native cultures were perceived as the prehistory of civilized humanity, and preserving their traces, in essence, meant preserving the history of white civilization (Wakeham, 294). *In the Land of the Headhunters* was Curtis's contribution to this project: in his film, he aspired to show what Native American existence looked like before the intrusive influence of white culture took its destructive toll. To fulfill this mission, the filmmaker created a script including aspects of romance, intrigue, and adventure that, in his mind, could have taken place in the indigenous community prior to white invasion and asked the native people of Kwaqiutl to act that script out for the camera. Apart from using this script, which capitalized on white stereotypes regarding Native American populations, Curtis made the indigenous actors wear commercial merchandise of his time, including mass-produced wigs and nose rings imported from China (Wakeham, 298).

Despite being shot in a different cinematic era and with a different purpose, one might argue that *In the Land of the Headhunters* shares a striking affinity with post-Soviet cinematic imaginings of Russia's heartland. This affinity constitutes itself in a specific colonial aesthetics, realized through the use of a documentary alibi that, paradoxically, only reinforces the constructedness of the cinematic fabric. Just like the Curtis film, post-Soviet imaginings of the heartland occurs along lines of Orientalizing (yet simultaneously westernizing) its inhabitants. Most of the films examined in this chapter employ a cast of nonprofessional actors, usually consisting of the residents of the localities being filmed. As in *The Land of the Headhunters*, they are asked to act out scripts suggested by an urban filmmaker who comes as an outsider to their community.

In That Land, filmed in the village of Verkola, employed villagers to play roles as themselves under different names—for example, the main protagonist, the shepherd Skuridin, is played by Dmitrii Klopov, a real shepherd in the village; similarly, the part of a former prisoner is given to a real former inmate. Although the directorial imposition of the plot structure remained strong, actors were allowed to change certain lines if they seemed inauthentic to them, thus reinforcing the ethnographic impulse of the film as a study of the village life. Likewise, Gennadii Sidorov's *Little Old Ladies* contains both professional and nonprofessional actors. Here the mixed cast serves to emphasize the constructed-ness of the filmic situation, which also carries certain ethnographic overtones: real old ladies of the village, most of whom remain unnamed throughout the film, participate in the demonstration of specific village rituals, including mourning and gossiping. Last, *The Postman's White Nights* also works as a combination of professional actors and villagers playing themselves, reproducing the casting choice of Konchalovskii's earlier film, *The Story of Asya Klyachina* (Istoriia Asi Kliachinoi, kotoraia liubila, da ne vyshla zamuzh, 1967). Overall, the fact of directorial imposition of a vision of village life on real villagers who, as a result, are enjoined to perform modified versions of themselves for urban audiences can be perceived as a colonizing practice that simultaneously regards the village population as a curiosity in need of cataloging and attempts to structure this population under the rubric of the Other. In this scheme, the inhabitants of the Russian heartland serve as the exotic background of tradition that highlights the modern quality of an urban lifestyle.

While the opposition of village and urban lifestyles is an old trope of Russian cinema, used in both prerevolutionary and early Soviet films,[5] the impulse to produce documentary narratives within the fictional framework (and vice versa) stems most productively from avant-garde experiments of Soviet filmmaking. In his documentary *Kino-Eye* (Kino-Glaz, 1924), the film without "actors and script" (as the viewers are informed by introductory intertitles), Dziga Vertov engaged reenactments in order to create narrative cohesion (for instance, a group of Young Pioneers was asked to reenact Pioneer rituals for the camera). Concerned with "catching life unawares" and rendering "cinema truth," Vertov was generally preoccupied with the goal of ridding the cinema of all artifice, including trained actors,[6] a mission relevant to our analysis. Yet post-Soviet films dealing with the theme of the heartland, by contrast, often use the device to produce a more complex conceptual vision of the post-Soviet and postimperial landscape; here the representation of the villagers as a subject group contains the elements of nostalgia connected to imaginings of a ruined past.

5 In early Russian film and in the cinema production of the 1920s, the city tended to be portrayed as a site of decadence and moral corruption, as opposed to the purity of village existence. The trope can be traced in Evgenii Bauer's short *Child of the Big City* (Ditia bol'shogo goroda, 1914), as well as in the films of the early Soviet period, including Lev Kuleshov's *The Extraordinary Adventures of Mister West in the Land of the Bolsheviks* (Neobychainye prikliucheniia mistera Vesta v strane bol'shevikov, 1924), Abram Room's *Bed and Sofa* (Tret'ia Meshchanskaia, 1927), Fridrikh Ermler's *Kat'ka the Appleseller* (Kat'ka "bumazhnyi ranet," 1926), and others.

6 In his essay "On the Significance of Non-Acted Cinema," Vertov (37) insists that the only valuable cinema is the kind producing "film-objects" that focus on "real life" instead of artificial narratives. For these film-objects "the field of vision is life, the material for montage construction—life, the sets—life, the actors—life."

The Soviet Union We Have Lost: *In That Land*

Shot in 1997, Lidiia Bobrova's *In that Land* comes as a distinct example of a post-Soviet consciousness of ruin. The film reuses several tropes of the Soviet village cinema, including a focus on a strong kolkhoz leader, who battles village vices of inertia and alcoholism. Characteristic treatments of the motif can be found in many Soviet films, including Aleksandr Zarkhi and Iosif Kheifits's *Member of the Government* (Chlen pravitel'stva, 1939), Iurii Egorov's *A Simple Story* (Prostaia istoriia, 1960), Aleksei Saltykov's *The Chairman* (Predsedatel', 1964), and Evgenii Matveev's *Earthly Love* (Liubov' zemnaia, 1974). I should add that, although in several of these instances, a given film may propose the figure of a kolkhoz chairwoman, the female leaders are constantly advised by male communist mentors, a trope that undergirds the patriarchal logic of Soviet ideology.

In addition to the strong kolkhoz leader, a second borrowed theme is the narrative of the "ticket to a sanatorium," frequently found in village films of the 1970s and 1980s. In Vasilii Shukshin's *Happy Go Lucky* (Pechki-lavochki, 1972) and Vladimir Men'shov's *Love and Pigeons* (Liubov' i golubi, 1984), the motif receives characteristic comic treatment similar to that in *In That Land*. Apart from individual motifs, Bobrova's film recycles an entire plotline from the iconic *The Red Snowball Tree* (Kalina krasnaia, 1974), turning Shukshin's film into one of its principal sources. It seems that Bobrova embarked on the task of recreating what the Soviet village film constituted as a genre, reproducing and rethinking its prominent filmic traits. Overall, *In That Land* may be viewed as a specific screen on which nostalgia for the Soviet (cinematic) culture is projected: this screen comes to be a site of mourning for the filmic country that was lost and must be reconstructed as a totality in order for reflection to take place.

Central to Bobrova's film, as an example of what I have chosen to call "ruin cinema" (Moltke), is its attention to a confused temporality: throughout most of the film, we are never entirely sure when the events are unfolding. In one scene toward the end, the viewer is presented with a TV screen with opening credits of the US soap opera *Santa Barbara*, from which we can understand that the action is set sometime after the collapse of the Soviet Union.[7] In introducing Soviet themes into the film, Bobrova fosters this confusion: in essence, the viewers are shown a post-Soviet reality of the village that looks very much like the Soviet village. From the film's

7 *Santa Barbara* was one of the first soap operas screened in Russia shortly after the collapse of the Soviet Union: the broadcast began in January 1992.

action, the viewer understands that the village still resembles a kolkhoz, with Chairman Chapurin as its leader; it is still possible to get a free ticket to a sanatorium if you work well; and the village authorities are still making visible efforts to tackle the village's social ills, such as alcoholism. In the film, post-Soviet reality "pretends" to be Soviet; however, the viewer is also presented with obvious facts indicating the destruction of Soviet forms of consciousness that have died out together with the communist economy.

In Bobrova's *In That Land*, Chairman Chapurin is constructed as a typical Soviet mentor, who strives to move the collective farm forward and to reeducate those populations who are ideologically lagging behind (a group of drunkards whom Chapurin tries to persuade to quit their habit). Despite retaining some characteristics of the Soviet leader, Chapurin finds himself in a new reality to which he cannot fully reconcile himself. Realizing that the old system has collapsed, he believes that his country is now "rolling into the abyss," as he intimates to his wife. Chapurin is visibly upset and inept in the new conditions: he laments that he cannot pay salaries to his fellow villagers anymore ("before, the government gave us money; now we need to earn money ourselves"). As the film unfolds, it turns out that the chairman is also unable to reeducate the drunkards, who die one after another, providing a near-ethnographic demonstration of village funeral rituals.

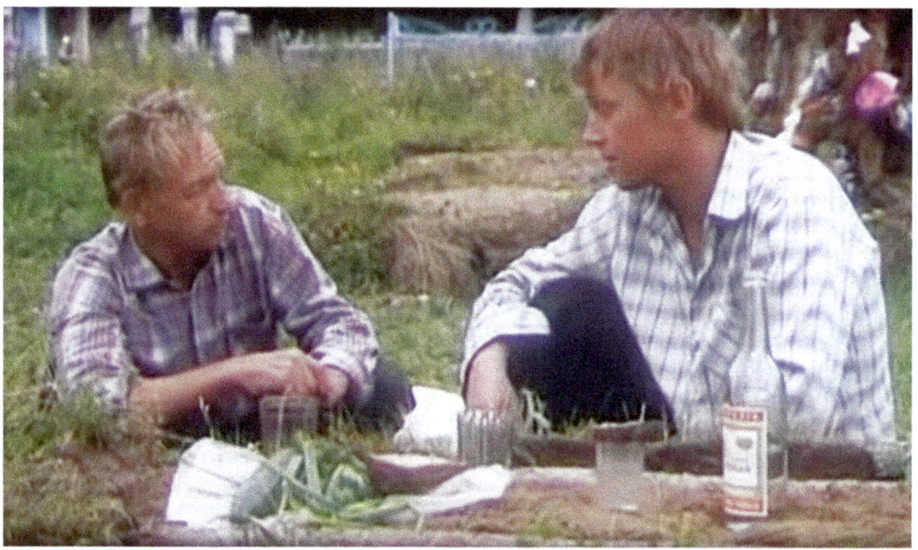

Fig. 7.1. Bobrova, *In That Land.* Local drunkards whom Chairman Chapurin fails to reeducate.

On the one hand, in accordance with Soviet tropes, Chapurin is portrayed as a strong, even monumental personality: when a fire occurs in the village, he is the one who runs into the burning house to save its inhabitants, an act of heroism that buys him the sympathies of his young female secretary, Katia. At the same time, Chapurin is presented in a distinctly less idealistic fashion than kolkhoz leaders in most Soviet films. On several occasions, he is portrayed as a person whose private interests outweigh his communal obligations: despite being married, he contemplates an affair with Katia, and he takes back a sanatorium ticket from Skuridin to please his influential superior. It is clear that the character of Chapurin is constructed as a form of intermediary consciousness, a nostalgic phantasm oscillating between the new reality of post-Soviet Russia and the "ruin consciousness" of the Soviet period. This "ruin consciousness" can be characterized as a patriarchal realm. Despite the monumental depiction of Chapurin, he fails to attain the epic status of his Soviet predecessors. He is distressed by the ongoing historic change whose consequences he cannot control; important decisions in his life are made by his wife, who takes control in times of crisis. Overall, Chapurin as a figure of patriarchal power proves unable to function in the new reality, which lacks the moral clarity and uniformity of the communist period.

Bobrova's film is alternately dismissive and expressive of the previous moral and political hierarchies deeply embedded in the history of Soviet cinema. One such motif would be a direct citation from Vasilii Shukshin's *The Red Snowball Tree*. Shukshin's film narrates the story of a former criminal, Egor Prokudin, who is released from the penal colony and attempts to start a new life in the village where he comes to meet his female pen pal, Liuba. Despite his early prison behavior as a thug, Egor gradually undergoes a transformation under the influence of village life and Liuba's devotion, but his criminal past catches up with him, and he dies at the hands of his former accomplices. *In That Land* borrows this plotline almost entirely, omitting some of its dramatic components: in Bobrova's film, former prisoner Konstantin arrives in the village to meet Raisa, whose mother has engaged in correspondence with him in order to marry off her daughter. Much like Egor in *The Red Snowball Tree*, Konstantin brings his prison behavior with him but gets reeducated in the village, adopting a more peaceful mentality by the film's conclusion. Unlike Egor, however, Konstantin is not killed by his former colleagues; instead, a final scene of the film shows him and his former adversary, Skuridin, leading a peaceful conversation over a wooden "bird of happiness," which the shepherd made with his own hands.

The repetition of the plotline of *The Red Snowball Tree* occurs alongside allusions to other prominent Soviet-era village films released in the recent Soviet past. Among them is Vladimir Men'shov's *Love and Pigeons* (1984), in which we also come across a bird as a symbol of reconciliatory transformation: in Men'shov's film, pigeons that initially provided a topic of contention between a husband and wife become a symbol of their reconciliation and newfound happiness. Unlike in *Love and Pigeons,* in *In That Land* happiness is a crafted state, not something preordained. By introducing a handmade bird in a concluding scene, Lidiia Bobrova sends a hopeful message that, despite all the destruction that the village and the country as a whole are undergoing at this historical juncture, happiness can be "made" by means of conscious effort, replacing the governing logic of the Soviet state with the lambent alternative of individual effort. In this regard, the episode with the bird engages in a dialogue with a previous scene, where Chapurin and his friends sing about being born in the country where they will remain forever.[8] In the lyrics, the word *strana* can be understood both as "country" and as "land," creating a conflation of the global and the local, in both the territorial and the historical sense. Chapurin's song becomes a lament for the USSR, the country where he and his fellow villagers were born and that has recently been lost forever; simultaneously, the lyrics serve as a determination to remain in the land where he belongs, despite the turmoil. Combined with Skuridin's bird, the song signals a positive existential program under conditions of major historic loss, which the film processes and mourns. This work is accompanied by the emergence of cinematic ghosts, fragments and echoes of the films produced in the country that is lamented over, as one laments over a recently deceased relative. In this regard, the film becomes a memory site that processes the loss in real time, instilling old Soviet tropes with new hope and a new ideology.

Imperial Nostalgia: *Little Old Ladies*

Writing about Gennadii Sidorov's *Little Old Ladies,* Viacheslav Shmyrov mentions that the film presents a picture opposite to that in *Farewell* (Proshchanie, 1981), the Stagnation-era Soviet village film by Larisa Shepit'ko and Elem Klimov. Based on the novella *Farewell to Matyora* (Proshchanie s Materoi, 1976) by the village prose writer Valentin Rasputin, *Farewell* narrates the story of a village that is to be flooded for the construction of a hydroelectric power plant.

8 "I will remain in the land/the country where I was born."

The film depicts the plight of villagers who do not want to leave their rural homes and ancestral graves, and it can be viewed as a larger commentary on the destructive toll that modern civilization inflicts on the realm of rural tradition. In contrast, according to Shmyrov, *Little Old Ladies* contains the element of hope, showing the village that briefly revives and celebrates itself. The film's hopeful overtones are largely informed by nostalgic imperial sentiment, which both mourns and revives the phantasm of the Soviet Union, creatively reinterpreting major Soviet tropes.

As in Bobrova's *In That Land*, Sidorov's film is filled with markers of ruination that it both documents and attempts to overcome. The action is set in a dying village whose only residents are a handful of elderly women; the only young person is Mikolka, a boy who suffers from Down syndrome. The village comprises a number of empty houses, abandoned as their residents moved elsewhere or died of old age. The village—with its crooked gates and fences, the piles of unwanted kittle that populate the frame—is abandoned also by the state authorities: it has neither electricity nor radio; in many ways, it lives by the inertia of its prior existence. Compared to its Soviet counterparts, this film seems to have abandoned all possible imperial hierarchies—it shows the village in a state of isolation, both from the former metropole Moscow and from civilization more generally.

Yet among its traces of imperial consciousness is the motif of Moscow, signaled by Pashka, the grandson of the old lady Anna, who dies at the very beginning of the film. Pashka comes to pay his respects to his grandmother's grave and spends a day in the village with Mikolka and other relatives. Working as an actor in a Moscow theater, Pashka is eager to perform in front of his village audience, even when it is unnecessary. During (what is supposed to be) a warm conversation between two relatives, Pashka suddenly recites to Mikolka a monologue of Lermontov's character Pechorin; he reads a poem by Sergei Esenin at Anna's grave, performed in an exaggerated theatrical manner inappropriate for the occasion. Both episodes mark a gaping rift between Pashka and his village folks: Mikolka is unable to appreciate the culture references that Pashka brings, as are the village grandmas, who characterize Pashka as "boneheaded." Overall, Pashka is rendered through a largely parodic lens: always drunk and unable to connect, he abuses the notion of high culture with the low quality of his performances and general ridiculousness of his persona. In his recitation of the Pechorin monologue, he is drunk and shirtless, his semi-naked body occupying half of the screen, creating a grotesquely obscene impression. The depiction of the Muscovite not only accentuates the rift between metropole and heartland; it fails to reproduce the conventional Soviet hierarchy in which Moscow dominates the heartland. It undercuts conventional imperial inequalities.

Apart from ridiculing Moscow, the film also focuses on the institution of the army, traditionally associated with the patriarchal ambitions of state power. Despite their isolation, the village residents manage to maintain contact with a larger reality through a Russian army tank regiment, located in the village's proximity, and the regiment's commander, often referred to as Fed'ka (played by director Gennadii Sidorov himself). The regiment's soldiers are regular customers of the village grannie Fekla, who produces cheap homemade alcohol; they also help make coffins when an elderly resident dies. Despite the fact that cooperation between the old women and the regiment often attains satirical overtones, their tandem seems to compensate for the lack of government support for the village after the collapse of the Soviet Union. Conventionally embodying the disciplining power of the state, the army seems to be an unlikely caretaker in normal circumstances. Yet the army itself is shown in a state of confusion and disorder: the entire regiment drinks; privates fulfill nonmilitary tasks on Fed'ka's orders, including coffin production; the commander himself routinely abuses his power, even threatening to kill one of the soldiers for sleeping with his wife. Like the village, the Russian army functions in a state of disarray and paralysis, suspended between the glorious past of Soviet modernity and the uncertain future of the post-Soviet condition.

As we focus on the "ruin qualities" of the film, we cannot help but mention its identification of empire with an aging organism, destined to live out a natural life cycle. Sidorov's film bears strong allegorical affinities to several other films that take up the trope of the human life span as a form of reconciliation to the death of the Soviet imperial state. Best known of these cinematic allegories, perhaps, is one of Marina Razbezhkina's earlier documentaries, *End of the Road* (Konets puti, 1991). In her film, Razbezhkina conflates the lifespan of the Soviet polity with the life of her character, the eighty-year-old villager Zinaida Gorshkova, who witnessed both the rise and fall of the USSR—that is, the socialist empire on its journey. The choice of a villager does not seem like a coincidence; here the landscape of the countryside embodies the empire itself. The representation of the Soviet empire as a natural phenomenon positions the USSR within a pantheistic understanding of the world, alleviating anxieties associated with the recent dissolution of the communist state. Similarly, in *Little Old Ladies* we encounter a present-day village haunted by the ghost of the Soviet imperial memory system; without the women's living recollections, which still populate the ruins among which they live, the Soviet village will vanish without a trace. In this respect, the increasing isolation of the village plays the role of a utopian island, a place where the organic empire can disappear and reemerge over and over again, following cycles of nature and memory.

The village as an embodiment of the "organic" empire is confirmed by the film's principal plotline: a Tajik family arrives in the village, arousing a mixture of hostility and curiosity in its elderly residents. Unlike the village's natives, the newcomers embody reproductive vitality long absent in this land: the woman in the Tajik family is pregnant with her third child. The relationship between the Tajik family and the Russian locals is informed by a dynamic that is both imperial and xenophobic: the old ladies are repelled by and curious about the newcomers. Moreover, the villagers are willing to patronize them in an imperial manner that the Russian film critic Natal'ia Sirivlia calls "loving, Russian style" (*liubit' po-russki*). The crucial moment comes, argues Sirivlia, after Mikolka burns down the house where the newcomers are settled. His act of arson is inspired by the old ladies' xenophobic gossiping, which the boy interpreted as a call to arms. Devastated and desperate, the Tajik family now becomes a focus of the old ladies' affection: "Now they [the old residents of the village] can feel sorry for them, love them with all their heart, invite them to live in their homes, share their last belongings with them" (Sirivlia).

While the arson leads to the reconstruction of the imperial dynamic between the Russian population of the village and the refugees, its most interesting aspect is situated elsewhere: the young father of the Tajik family is building a small power generator to supply the village with electricity, and toward the end of the film, he succeeds, ending the film with the village community's celebration of their analogue of the "Il'ich lamp."[9] This return to the origins of Soviet modernity with its focus on the countryside's electrification and modernization offers an interesting inversion of the imperial dynamic: unlike the 1920s, when the modernizing impulse originated from the imperial center, now it comes from the Tajiks, the former Soviet periphery. Here again, we deal with the notion of empire as a living organism—to be reconstructed, it needs the vitality of the former "subject group," from which it literally drains energy. This

9 In November 1920, the villagers of Kashin (Moscow region) invited Vladimir Il'ich Lenin to witness the lighting of the village's first incandescent bulb, lit by a rudimentary generator in his presence on 14 November. The electrification of the USSR through the efforts of GOELRO (Russian acronym for State Commission for the Electrification of Russia) came to be known colloquially as "Il'ich's lamp," the naked incandescent bulb witnessed by Lenin, who is himself referred to here affectionately by his patronymic "Il'ich."

neocolonial perspective considers the Tajiks as bearers of a "younger," hence "more vital," type of culture, able to produce tangible results that serve the Russian population. In this regard, the film's village acts as a microcosm of the post-Soviet imperial ambition, which has not departed far from the logic of its Soviet predecessor.

Russian Road Film: *Free Floating*

I would begin this analysis of Boris Khlebnikov's *Free Floating* by suggesting that it belongs to the genre of road movie, traditionally concerned with mobility and a corresponding "aesthetics of curiosity" (Hurault-Paupe, 6). Although *Free Floating* does not resemble a typical road film, its concern with motion (and a resulting transformation of its protagonist) evokes direct parallels with the genre. According to David Laderman (2), US road films are often instilled with a mood of rebellion against an oppressive societal norm, which is rejected in favor of self-discovery. Here the road poses as a "universal symbol for the course of life, the movement of desire, the lure of both freedom and destiny." Some of these notions are explored in *Free Floating*, which centers on a young protagonist, Lenia, who is both lost and alienated but also willing to find his place in the society in the state of post-Soviet confusion. In the film, the road is evoked both literally and metaphorically, posing as an organizing principle in the protagonist's work and search for identity, with its traits of postimperial contemplation.

Lenia's journey of self-discovery, heavily associated with professional self-realization, begins after he and his colleagues are fired from a Soviet-era machine-building plant, which is sold to Americans. Following the Soviet tradition, the episode seems to vilify the US investors, who are said to have bought and closed the plant in order to eliminate a competitor; through the use of irony, we understand that what is really being satirized is the remnants of Soviet thinking. In the episode, one of the workers asserts that the Americans bought the plant because its collective "worked well." This statement deserves little credence, as the opening sequences of the film clearly demonstrate the lack of labor discipline at the plant prior to acquisition. The only person who seems to work is the novice Lenia; others are engaged in meaningless leisure activities, such as collective smoking breaks and meandering about the factory premises.

What is interesting here and in the film more generally is its close attention to the factory workers' mundane, empty routines. The static camera lingers forever on each individual person: a worker lethargically unwrapping an antiquated meat grinder; his colleague slowly turning

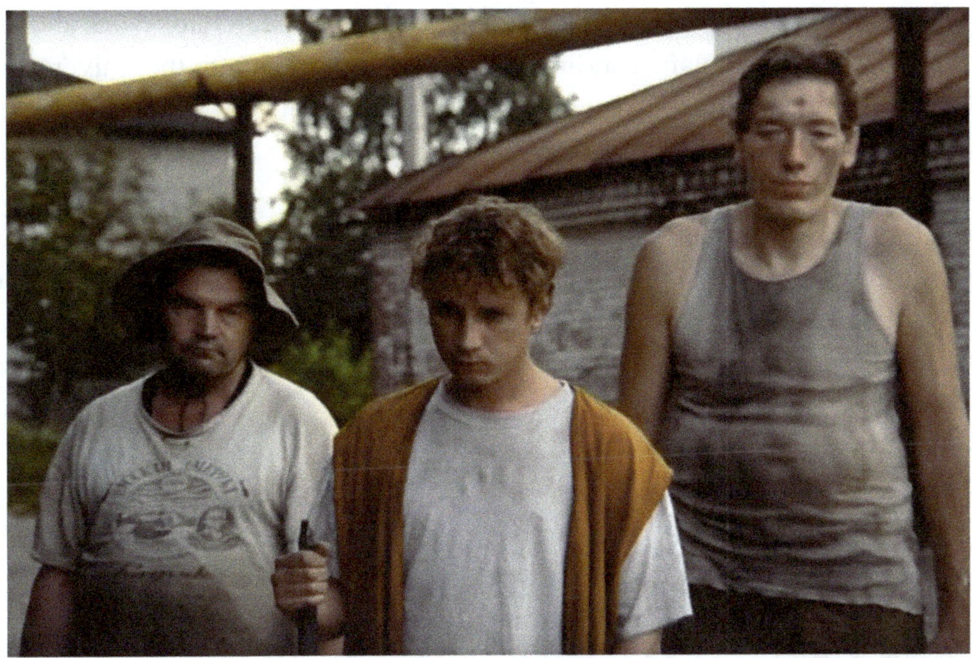

Fig. 7.2. Khlebnikov, *Free Floating*. Lenia and his colleagues from the road repair team.

a beer can into an improvised ashtray. The camera turns into a meditative observer of what is supposed to be the noble routine of labor; in so doing, it both imitates and subverts the habits of the Soviet camera, detailing the labor achievements of shock workers. Here, by contrast, there are neither shock workers nor heroes; rather, the narrative is filled with longing for "real" labor, absent from both ideological and economic landscape of post-Soviet Russia.

Russian film critic Elena Gracheva observes that labor here poses a Platonic ideal: "no one has ever seen it, but everybody talks about it." In addition to being an unattainable ideal, work functions as a staple of self-identification. After leaving the factory, Lenia embarks on a number of short-term jobs, including as a traveling plasterer, a job he rejects after seeing that this work is primarily done by women. The role of the work could be ironically compared to labor in the Soviet films, where a good Communist had to be a good worker. Through an ecstatic experience of work, the Soviet citizen could achieve the heights of class consciousness and social hierarchy (as the heroine does in Grigorii Aleksandrov's Stalinist film *Bright Path* [Svetlyi put', 1940]). Yet labor remains a nostalgic phantasm in the film, impossible in the economic and ideological conditions of post-Soviet, small-town Russia, where the action of

Free Floating unfolds. It is no coincidence that the protagonist's search for work and for identity starts with the demise of the plant, sending its former employees into the universe of entropic "free floating," where employment and identity become a fraught, individual project. In this regard, Lenia's subsequent journey is laden with the anxiety and uncertainty of an atomized existence.

Laderman (4–6) draws an important connection between road films and the key aspects of modernist aesthetics, including an ecstatic belief in technology as a liberating force that can lead the society into the future. The road movies celebrate this belief through the notion of a moving vehicle that brings the character to his transformation. In *Free Floating*, Lenia's search for employment is continuously accompanied by his physical movement on foot and by vehicle or explicit allusions to feet and traveling. First, he sells footwear at a small market; this employment ends abruptly when Lenia decides that he wants to quit. His next attempt as a plasterer is directly connected to traveling by vehicle: Lenia departs by bus, but—on arrival—decides that the job doesn't suit him. He returns home on foot, passing a bizarre sculpture of two white bears, emphasizing the absurdist, even existential, character of Lenia's searches. Next, in a kind of narrative concretization, Lenia joins a team that repairs municipal roads. His foreman Roslov compares the road to a woman, while the repairman is a strange mix of her doctor and lover: the crowbar should not be a tool of "violation," but rather a syringe that "pleases" the road, an allegorical rendition of the road as embodiment of desire. Unsurprisingly, this job becomes Lenia's most lengthy employment before he lands his last job on a barge, in perpetual navigation down the Volga River.

Soviet Modernity Revisited: *The Postman's White Nights*

Andrei Konchalovskii's *The Postman's White Nights* is the most "Vertovian" of the films discussed here. In his essay "The Birth of Kino-Eye," Dziga Vertov reiterates his belief that the "cinema eye" of the camera must serve a single goal: to catch life as it is, without altering it by means of artificial literary scenarios, costumes, or acting. Explaining the existential goal of his technique, Vertov ("Birth of Kino-Eye," 41) writes, "Not 'filming life unawares' for the sake of the 'unaware,' but in order to show people without masks, without makeup, to catch them through the eye of the camera in a moment when they are not acting, to read their thoughts, laid bare by the camera." In an idealization of the cinematic apparatus, Vertov believed in a single "truth" that can and should be rendered by the "kino-eye"; the previous filmic tradition, based on theatrical and literary frameworks, was bourgeois and obsolete.

In *The Postman's White Nights*, Andrei Konchalovskii could be seen as following Vertov's prescriptions closely: from casting a minimum of professional actors (only three in the film, all in supporting roles) to the shooting that involved no script. The camera merely followed a real postman, Aleksei Triapitsyn, in his everyday dealings and introduced a minimum of invented plotlines. According to Triapitsyn (Kichin), the filming process was largely based on improvisation both on the part of the film director and the cast, including the professionals. In his attempt to document village life as factually as possible, Konchalovskii installed static cameras in Triapitsyn's home, as well as in the houses of several other village residents. The cameras' dispassionate gaze recorded the villagers' sleeping habits, waking routines, and an occasional party accompanied by vodka, tea, and a friendly chitchat. It is worth noting that the cameras were mostly installed above the heads of the heroes, the high angle evoking the "God shot." The cameras' positioning does not look like an accident: Konchalovskii's film is instilled with existential symbolism, with distinct traits of both pantheistic and Romantic worldviews, conflating the natural landscape with the divine.

Along with portraying the everyday existence of Triapitsyn and other village characters, Konchalovskii introduces another plane, a distinct authorial view on the essence of the human existence as a spiritual and natural phenomenon. Juxtaposed to the documentary rendition of the visual representation in the film, this plane is intentionally "fictional," facilitated by the film's soundtrack (mostly composed by Eduard Artem'ev, together with Giuseppe Verdi's *Requiem*). Alternately barely discernable and loud, the soundtrack overturns the documentary impulse of *The Postman's White Nights* and renders the film analogous to a painting by William Turner, where the human being is overwhelmed by a sublime natural landscape, framing the human within the magnitude of God's creation of the universe. In a similar fashion, Artem'ev's music, gentle and otherworldly, evokes a transcendental reality that looms over the characters' everyday concerns.

From minute eight, when the music first engages with the natural beauty of Lake Kenozero, to the very end of the film when we hear the *Requiem*, the soundtrack punctuates moments when the divine comes into a close contact with the human and the mundane. It comments on the sublime natural landscape of Kenozero, appears again at a villager's death, and in a morally ambiguous episode when Triapitsyn learns that his longtime friends had stolen his

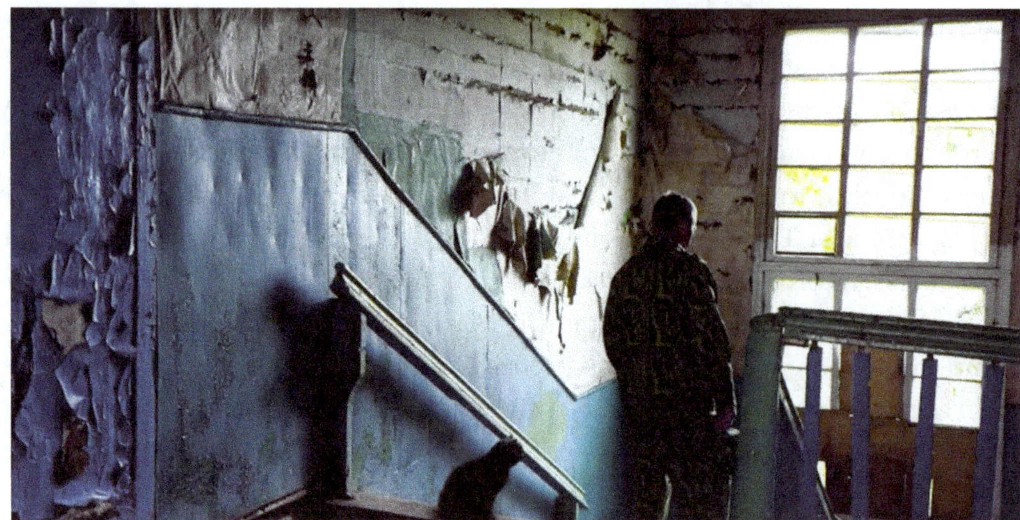

Fig. 7.3. Konchalovskii, *The Postman's White Nights*. Aleksei Triapitsyn in the ruined building of his Soviet-era school.

boat engine. In all the musical episodes, Triapitsyn figures as a direct participant: he observes the natural beauty of his land; he mourns his deceased neighbor and the failing friendship. As the real-life intermediary between the villagers and the "big land" (from which he delivers newspapers, letters, and pensions), Triapitsyn is a kind of provincial Charon, connecting the dying village with the urban space that still inherits the future.

An encounter of the "documentary mundane" with "fictional divine" makes up the ontological framework of *The Postman's White Nights*, highlighting a specific aspect of what I have been calling "ruin cinema." In a dream sequence, Triapitsyn sees himself in the ruined building of the Soviet school where he and his friends underwent initiation into the communist collective many years ago. In the sequence, the postman visits the building, now dilapidated and forgotten, and hears fragments of Soviet songs he sang in childhood. This oneiric scene poses the Soviet past as a nostalgic vision, both beautiful and ephemeral, organized as a form of mnemonic collage. While ruined and lost forever, its lingering in dream and memory reinstitutes this modernity as an active part of Russia's present. This Soviet modernity is preserved, too, by the film's theme of the space industry, still able to launch rockets into the beyond. The village is located next to a real launching facility in Plesetsk, which the postman Triapitsyn visits in hopes of asking assistance with finding the stolen engine. The space industry is signaled again toward the end of the film, as a rocket takes off into the sky, underscored by a return of the same otherworldly soundtrack. It is a deeply ambiguous turn, granting Soviet modernity—with its idealization of cosmonauts and outer-space achievements—a second chance at transcendental status, an eternal empire that inherits the sky. In his own version of imperial ambition, Konchalovskii steps beyond Sidorov's organic, dying empire. Instead of the Soviet empire as a mortal body, Konchalovskii's deceased country is an immortal soul, an allegory that is arguably a little more troubling.

Filmography

Aleksandrov, Grigorii, dir. *Bright Path* (Svetlyi put', 1940).

Bauer, Evgenii, dir. *Child of the Big City* (Ditia bol'shogo goroda, 1914).

Bobrova, Lidiia, dir. *In that Land* (V toi strane, 1997).

Curtis, Edward S., dir. *In the Land of Headhunters* (1914).

Egorov, Iurii, dir. *A Simple Story* (Prostaia istoriia, 1960).

Ermler, Fridrikh, dir. *Kat'ka the Appleseller* (Kat'ka "bumazhnyi ranet," 1926).

Khlebnikov, Boris, dir. *Free Floating* (Svobodnoe plavanie, 2006).

Konchalovskii, Andrei, dir. *The Story of Asya Klyachina* (Istoriia Asi Kliachinoi, kotoraia liubila, da ne vyshla zamuzh, 1967).

———. *The Postman's White Nights* (Belye nochi pochtal'ona Alekseia Triapitsyna, 2014).

Kuleshov, Lev, dir. *The Extraordinary Adventures of Mister West in the Land of the Bolsheviks* (Neobychainye prikliucheniia mistera Vesta v strane bol'shevikov, 1924).

Matveev, Evgenii, dir. *Earthly Love* (Liubov' zemnaia, 1974).

Men'shov, Vladimir, dir. *Love and Pigeons* (Liubov' i golubi, 1984).

Razbezhkina, Marina, dir. *End of the Road* (Konets puti, 1991).

Room, Abram, dir. *Bed and Sofa* (Tret'ia Meshchanskaia, 1927).

Saltykov, Aleksei, dir. *The Chairman* (Predsedatel', 1964).

Shepit'ko, Larisa, and Elem Klimov, dirs. *Farewell* (Proshchanie, 1981).

Shukshin, Vasilii, dir. *Happy Go Lucky* (Pechki-lavochki, 1972).

———. *The Red Snowball Tree* (Kalina krasnaia, 1974).

Sidorov, Gennadii, dir. *Little Old Ladies* (Starukhi, 2003).

Vertov, Dziga, dir. *Kino-Eye* (Kino-Glaz, 1924).

Zarkhi, Aleksandr, and Iosif Kheifits, dirs. *Member of the Government* (Chlen pravitel'stva, 1939).

8. Russia on the Margins?

Tetyana Shlikhar

In his seminal volume *Crossing Borders: Modernity, Ideology, and Culture in Russia and the Soviet Union,* Michael David-Fox (49–71) asserts that Russian and Soviet modernity was an "intelligentsia-statist project," in which state-sponsored transformations were wedded to Westernized elites' attempts to overcome Russian backwardness, a kind of enlightenment from above.[1] In spite of transnational exchange, as well as ardent engagement with European culture and selective appropriation of Western innovations, the gap between Europe and Russia could not be measured simply by a single linearity—that is, an accounting of the "progressiveness" or "backwardness" of either of them.[2] Where does Russia fit vis-à-vis Europe? What anxieties do Russians bring to the act of juxtaposition to Europe? What could be said about Russian identity today, and how is it revealed in Russian contemporary cinema?

The answers are complicated by Russia's imperial tsarist and Soviet histories, which are in many ways contradictory and at the same time intertwined with each other. Although in pre-Petrine Russia, Europe was viewed at times as an enemy inferior to Moscow (as the true locus of Christianity),[3] the preeminence of European civilization was textually acknowledged from the

1 The Russian intelligentsia, David-Fox (*Crossing Borders*) argues, was a central element in Russian-Soviet modernity, predicated on deep, structural features of Russian historical development: the autocratic, yet largely Westernizing state; the powerful tradition of state service; and competition and perceptions of difference with Europe and the "West," which became a central feature of Russian identity in the nineteenth century.

2 In the twentieth century alone (that is to say, bracketing Petr Chaadaev, as well as his Westernizer/Slavophile heirs), "backwardness"—and cultural backwardness in particular—has a rich scholarly, political, and ethnographic tradition, both internal to the Soviet Union (with reference to its ethnonationalities) and external to it (with reference to the country itself vis-à-vis the West). The twentieth-century intellectual legacy cannot be adequately characterized here; I refer only to the key figure of Mikhail Gershenzon (1869–1925), whose "A Correspondence between Two Corners" (1920), co-authored with Petersburg School Symbolist Viacheslav Ivanov, became a key point of reference for these debates. For details of the internal Soviet debates—in which the conceptual advocacy of "cultural backwardness" (1932) and its terminological exclusion (1934) were a mere two years apart—see Martin; and Wixman.

3 See Østbø. In chapter 6, "Nataliia Narochnitskaia—Inverting the Myth," Østbø (177) discusses Narochnitskaia's conservative ideas about the myth of Moscow as the "Third Rome," and emphasizes that "more than anything

eighteenth century onward by the Russian Empire's attempts to join the Western community.[4] As Soviet power was consolidated in the twentieth century, the attitudes of its political leaders toward Western polities became increasingly inflected both by a rising xenophobia (of which the Iron Curtain was, in part, a symptom) and by concomitant aspirations to overtake Europe. It was precisely these aspirations that articulated Russia's vulnerabilities.

An anti-Western and antibourgeois orientation played a significant role in Soviet cinema during the Cold War (from roughly 1946 to 1991), and this confrontation can be extended in Russian cinema into the post-Soviet period (Fedorov). According to Fedorov, for example, a content analysis of Russian films made from 1992 to 2016 reveals a prevalence of three plotlines: (1) Russian characters are attracted to the West as a site of a better life; (2) post-Soviet Russia is a poor country with low standards of living, especially in the 1990s; and (3) Russian secret-service members and/or loyal citizens fight Western spies and criminals. Yet in contrast to many of the earlier Soviet confrontation films of 1946–91, Russian cinema of the 1992–2016 period was nurtured not only by conflict plots—espionage, mafia, or military antagonism—but also by stories of cooperation and mutual assistance between Russia and the West, portrayed nevertheless as deeply contrasting to each other. Whatever the balance between one cinematic example and the next, Russian cinema of the post-Soviet period indisputably inherited many of the Soviet traditions in its attitude toward the West: the image of the West is most often an image of the Other, often a hostile Other, averse to Russian civilization (Fedorov). In the meantime, contemporary Russian cinema has also nurtured a vision of Russia as a unique and exceptional culture. Russian spirituality and high moral values are often contrasted to the rationality and utilitarian mentalities of Western culture. Ultimately, it is through this "inherent uniqueness" that Russia is superior to the West.

Engaging with this line of analysis, this chapter discusses interrelations among six films (three pairs) as they may be located within the following categories: (1) "Laughter Therapy: On the Border of the Fallen Empire," focusing on Iurii Mamin's *Window to Paris* (Okno v Parizh, 1993) and Aleksandr Rogozhkin's *Peculiarities of the National Hunt* (Osobennosti natsional'noi okhoty, 1995); (2) "High Investments in the Resurgent Empire" discussing Aleksandr Sokurov's

else, her account demonstrates what she perceives as the moral (eternal) superiority of Russia, as against the moral (eternal) inferiority of the West."

4 For a lively discussion about Russia's geographical positioning between East and West, see Bassin.

Russian Ark (Russkii kovcheg, 2002) and Nikita Mikhalkov's *Barber of Siberia* (Sibirskii tsiriul'nik, 1998); and (3) "Imperial Ambitions and Anxieties: The Ukraine Syndrome," concentrating on Vladimir Bortko's *Taras Bulba* (2009), with some remarks on Aleksei Balabanov's *Brother 2* (Brat 2, 2000). Although these films—either as pairs or as an entire set—are deeply incompatible with each other in terms of genre, historical setting, or distribution goals, together they provide an opportunity to explore some recent patterns in Russia's self-definitions. What the films arguably share is a preoccupation with border narratives or travel narratives, elaborated with an accompanying self-exploration. Notably, males, cows, bears, and other animals are deemed worthy of these explorative journeys, but—generally speaking—not women. What these films have in common, furthermore, is anxiety about Russia's status vis-à-vis Europe, the United States, and the near-abroad, bolstered by intermittent claims to a unique civilization and a yearning for restorative isolation.

Laughter Therapy: On the Border of the Fallen Empire

The gradual fall of the Soviet Union between 1988 and 1991, with its accompanying disillusionment about the promised communist future, engendered in cinema a cluster of farcical representations of life on the border between "then" and "now." Laughing at oneself became a way to speak about the weaknesses and vulnerability of a society at a loss. The sudden opening up of the borders between Russia and the West after many years of separate coexistence led to an accelerated exploration of cultural differences. Iurii Mamin's *Window to Paris* and Aleksandr Rogozhkin's *Peculiarities of the National Hunt* both feature farcical imaginings of such cultural encounters, the material and spiritual dimensions of envy toward the Western world, as well as the perception of Russia's uniqueness and inimitability, on which some measure of pride could be re-established. As Aleksandr Shpagin points out, these two films were the first to contribute to the Russian national idea and national consciousness. Both Mamin's *Window to Paris* and Rogozhkin's *Peculiarities of the National Hunt* represent a "cheerful humiliation of oneself. The audience thus felt an incredible pride in self-effacement."[5]

5 See Aleksandr Shpagin's contribution to the discussion at the 2003 Russian Film Symposium held at the University of Pittsburgh (*Arrogance and Envy*) in Sirivlia and Stishova.

The collapse of the Soviet empire gave hope to a project of Russian nation building, distinct from Western civilization but no less worthy. In these two films in particular, Russia finds itself on the margins in its effort to understand its new place in the world community. In these comedies, margins do not appear as a territory on which to restore the lost imperial superiority but rather as a place to explore the constructed nature of identities. The setting at the margins, thus, does not imply a straightforward fantasy of marginalization and inferiority.

Iurii Mamin, *"Window to Paris"*

In *Window to Paris,* Iurii Mamin creates an image of Russia on the crossroads of vast change after the disintegration of the Soviet Union and the frustrations associated with it, all inflected by the postmodern turn that became increasingly evident in the late twentieth century. The film tells a comic story about a schoolteacher who shares a communal apartment with a working-class family in early 1990s St. Petersburg. One day, a passageway opens from their poor apartment leading directly to Paris. As the characters enjoy this sudden opportunity to travel, they learn that the window will close soon. The film thus offers a metaphor for Russia's bouts of modernization and encounters with the West.

In his discussion of postmodern historiography, Patrick Hutton (11) reminds us that "there had been too much displacement, destruction, and death in the wars and economic crises of the twentieth century to contend that somehow all of these disruptive forces might be adapted to a framework of history as an ongoing and uplifting journey." Nowhere is this assertion more apt than in the territories of the former USSR. The temporal vector of the film, therefore, was no longer set in the bright socialist future; neither was it nostalgic for the past. Instead, it created a memory of the "present" of the early 1990s. This present, in the meantime, transmitted gloomy implications about the past and vague visions of a renewed capitalist future, with its inherent acceleration of technology and telecommunications, for which the window to Paris in the film might be seen as an ironic, symbolic representation. "The past cannot give us what the future has failed to deliver," maintains Andreas Huyssen ("Present Pasts," 37); what remains is the present. Marginality is the main feature of the film's temporal and spatial dimensions, questioning the historically precarious position of Russia in the post-Soviet space.

Mamin's *Window* establishes a clear delineation between Russia and Europe, initially construed as a contrast between a barbaric East and a civilized West. As Edith Clowes has suggested, echoing a long tradition of interpretation, "this east-west axis is a construct of Russian modernity, a three-hundred-year span during which Russian national identity has become divided, complex, and highly interesting" (12). Russia's marginality and its citizens' disorientation are clearly articulated throughout the film, and yet an air of transition is evident in the modernizations, cultural aspirations, and political reforms of the film's timeframe of the early 1990s. After seventy years of Soviet rule and official xenophobia vis-à-vis Western culture, Paris is represented as cognitively unattainable, distanced not only geographically but also politically and culturally. When a spatial glitch miraculously allows easy access to Paris, the Western capital stands in for a completely different world. On their first visit to Paris, the dwellers of the St. Petersburg communal apartment are amazed by the variety of food available to the French, as well as luxury clothing and vehicles. Contrasted to post-Soviet St. Petersburg, Paris at first glance serves as the epitome of European abundance, culture, and welfare, from which Russia is separated not only spatially but also temporally, since it lags behind Europe "by two hundred years," as one character claims.

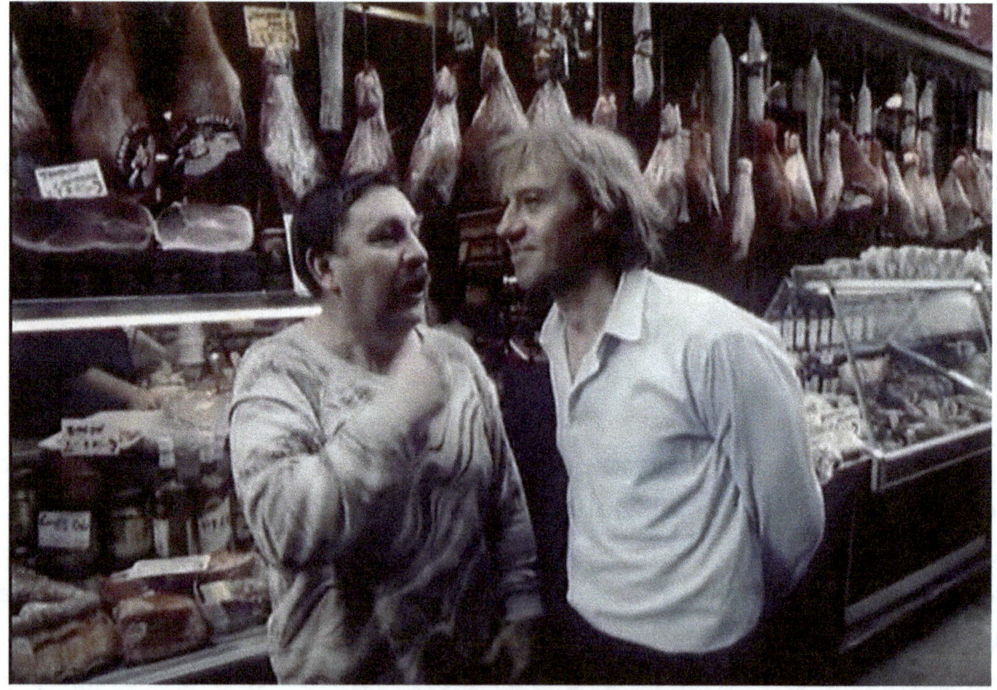

Fig. 8.1. Mamin, *Window to Paris*. Amazement and contempt of Western abundance.

At the same time, in the film's logic, this gap can never be bridged. The Russian characters, landing in Paris for a limited time, try to derive the most from their visit, on any terms whatsoever. Mamin's comedic representation of Russian citizens is a fierce satire on the harsh circumstances in which ordinary people found themselves by the end of the Soviet period. In the film, Russians quickly adapt to life in Paris, making money and taking home everything that seems to have no owner. A French woman, by contrast, has a hard time when she lands in St. Petersburg, since she, used to a comfortable European life, is not ready for post-Soviet modes of survival. Indeed, even the film itself comprises two unbridgeable texts: two versions, one for the domestic consumption, the other—a shorter film with a different title *Russian Salad* (Salades russes, 1994)—for a French audience, omitting scenes in which the Russian visitors speak negatively about the French. As a collage of stories that can exist separately, the film is indeed a "Russian salad."[6]

In Mamin's film, post-Soviet access to the West is an opportunity for farcical exaggeration: children at school are taught management and marketing; huge banknotes of foreign currencies replace paintings on the walls. Capitalist values, including the aphorism "time is money" replace the communist legacy of the past. Traces of xenophobia and Western antagonism suggest, however, that elements of a Soviet mentality are still present. The slogan "Russia for Russians" at a communist demonstration reminds the viewer of the late Soviet era. Situating Russia on the temporal border between the communist past and the capitalist future, the director shifts the film's tonality so as to question the value of pro-Western transformation. In spite of the blessings of European life, Mamin's film suggests, the dirty and unfriendly homeland may still be preferable. The film's implicit message encourages new generations to change Russia, striving for a European level of culture at home, rather than leaving home in search of a better life abroad.

And while the Russian side of the window to Paris—discovered in an old woman's apartment—serves as a symbolic border demarcating Russia and Europe, the idea of travel is nevertheless devalued. As Emma Widdis has suggested in a different context, "the myth of foreignness holds no more appeal; Russia is reinstated as the central 'home'"; "the myth of travel is revealed to be essentially a chimera," so "the key to contentment is reconciliation with your immediate, local environment" (72). In spite of all the downsides of Russian reality,

6 See more in Molchanova.

Mamin's film suggests, there is ultimately no need to go anywhere or compare oneself to the West, because Russians can be satisfied with what they have.

The farcical representation of Russians in Paris underscores the abyss between cultured Europeans and backward Russians, yet laughter provides the therapeutic effect of calming anxiety. A clear margin between "theirs" and "ours," marked by the window border as a passage to Paris, operates as a medium for self-study, as if the window were also a mirror. From a different perspective, the film reveals the narrative return of Soviet xenophobia: the Russian characters admire Parisian affluence yet envy those who have allegedly deprived Russians of those goods.

The dissipation of Western society, in the meantime, is contrasted to the high spiritual values of Russians. Although St. Petersburg is a dark place whose people may also be mired in petty-bourgeois values and alcohol, the city is still preferable to the tidiness of Paris. As the characters realize that they do not belong to this foreign world, they also understand they have something better—values that give them the right to be proud of their homeland. Exceptional spirituality enables Russia to stand out among Western countries. The genre of comedy, in the meantime, supports the message of reconciliation, enhancing it through contrasts and derision, while leading the viewer toward the necessary conclusion.

While there is much more to be said of this film (and of this topic in relation to Mamin's work), let us move ahead for the time being to an instance that examines related and contrasting dimensions of this common theme of laughter therapy.

Aleksandr Rogozhkin, *Peculiarities of the National Hunt*

A second relevant comedy from the 1990s is Aleksandr Rogozhkin's *Peculiarities of the National Hunt*. In terms of history, 1995 is notable for a number of events, among them NATO's expansion to Eastern Europe and the Victory Parade on Red Square in Moscow attended by major world leaders, including US President Bill Clinton. There is a certain rapprochement between Russia and the West, yet the tension persists. In Rogozhkin's film, a Finnish Russophile named Raivo decides to participate in a real Russian hunt. Instead of what he expects—a hunt conducted in the best Russian aristocratic tradition—Raivo finds himself encountering rampant drinking and most unusual adventures. The actual hunt, despite the film's title, is of secondary importance. In his dreams, Raivo still imagines a Russia grounded in the literary texts he has read. For him, Russia is associated primarily with the nobility of imperial times. Yet the Russia Raivo encounters is already a post-Soviet country, a confounding amalgam of Soviet/Russian with allegiances neither entirely Eastern nor Western (Elena Prokhorova). In his dreams, Raivo imagines Russia as an elite Westernized culture, with imperial subjects conversing in French and the hunt as a highly ritualized endeavor—in particular, with drinking in an elegantly aristocratic manner. Indeed, Raivo's associations, grounded in an imagined, but historically ill-defined imperial culture, might be seen as wholly compatible with Mikhalkov's *The Barber of Siberia*, set in the reign of Alexander III, which I discuss below. The marginality of Russia is underscored by the film's diegetic location, somewhere near the border between Russia and Finland. This border eventually serves as a border between other dyads besides Russia and Finland: a border between sincerity and irony; between past and present; and between the Westerner's imaginings and Russia "as it is," with no trace of Raivo's Westernized empire.

Is this the same country that Pushkin or Tolstoy depicted? Is there any connection to the West? The stock archetypes of Russia present in the film—the vodka, the bathhouse, the

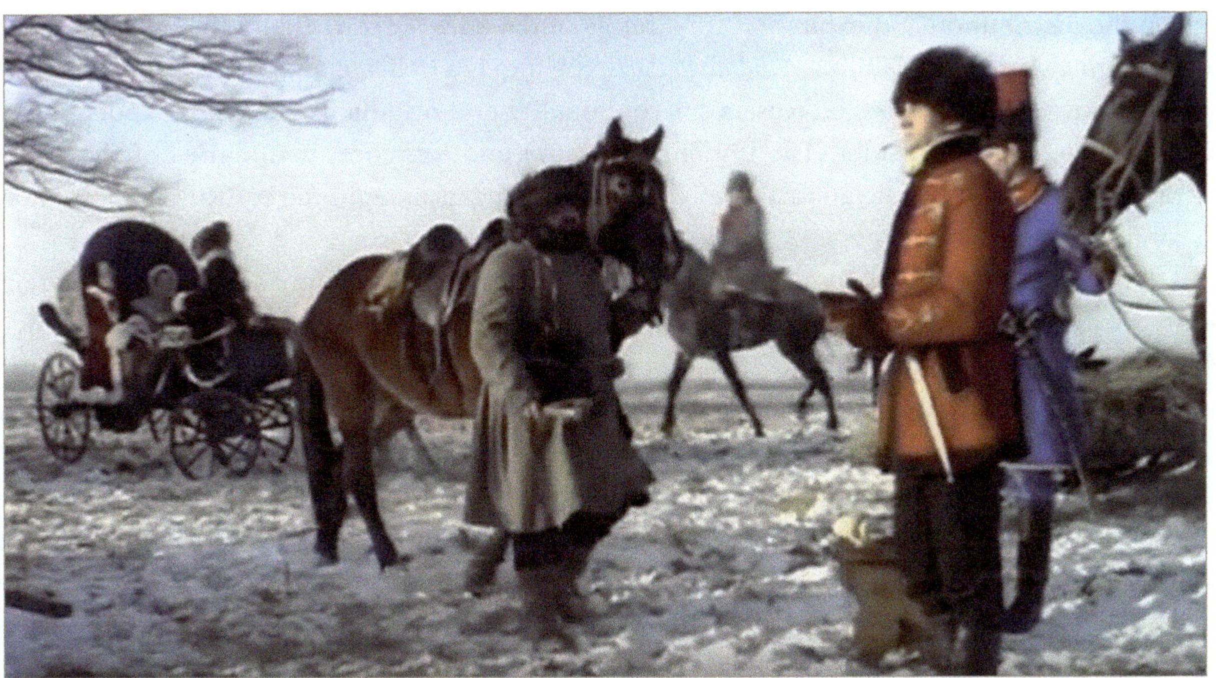

Fig. 8.2. Rogozhkin, *Peculiarities of the National Hunt*. Russian hunting in Raivo's dream.

drunken bear—draw on Western stereotypes of a backward Russia, in contrast to Raivo's idealistic vision, embedded in a schoolbook love for Russian culture. Yet the film's "reality" is also highly conditional: Rogozhkin's ironic comedy is more a *stiob* (mockery) of contemporary Russia than a realistic representation. In this carnival world, a cow is transported in a bomber; a baby bear blocks the way out of the bathhouse; an encounter with two silent *lubok*-style females is accompanied by a drink fest that substitutes for the hunt itself. As Birgit Beumers argues, "drinking may be without a purpose, but it is a habit [that] makes social and national differences disappear, lifts temporal boundaries in bringing together past and present, and annihilates the borders between animals and humans. The world returns to its purest form, without any boundaries or limits" (*Russia on Reels*, 80). Drinking in the film is a foundation for friendship of the peoples; it unites Russians and foreigners, transcending even the drive to prove superiority over the Western world or to raise national self-esteem.

In the spirit of the pattern evident in much of the 1990s, Rogozhkin mocks the traditions of imperial Russia that reappear throughout the film in Raivo's dreams. The image of contemporary Russia, in the meantime, proffers a Russia easily legible to Russians, who—given the distribution and exhibition constraints of the era—were virtually the only audience of the film.[7] Much like Mamin's *Window to Paris*, the film is a delicate mix of self-study and self-mockery, with an emphasis on Russia's exceptionality and originality that cannot adequately be perceived by an outsider. The undefined spatial and temporal boundaries of the film's setting, furthermore, create an imaginative world serving as an epitome of "Russianness" and a confidence in its uniqueness.

If we may look ahead to the closure of the twentieth century, we might argue that, in a larger framework, Rogozhkin's *Peculiarities* belongs to his national explorations of the 1990s, which he continues in such later films as *Peculiarities of the National Fishing* (Osobennosti natsional'noi rybalki, 1998), *The Checkpoint* (Blokpost, 1998), and *Cuckoo* (Kukushka, 2002), among others. But by *Cuckoo*, a change is evident. Set during the Second World War, *Cuckoo* creates a memory about wartime, in which communication among different cultures is ultimately impossible. While in *Peculiarities of the National Hunt*, there is still a possibility for understanding through drinking together, in *Cuckoo*, communication between the Finnish soldier Veikko, the Red Army captain Ivan, and the Sami woman Anni leads only to misunderstanding and confusion. Although the

7 See kino-teatr.ru (http://kino-teatr.ru/kino/movie/ros/4815/annot/).

film features elements of comedy, especially in relation to the cultural differences between Veikko and Ivan, this is a wartime drama with much more serious and more philosophical implications. The film's historical background, rather than a depiction of the "1990s present," is instead a pronounced shift that will become increasingly evident in the Russian cinema of the 2000s.

High Investments in the Resurgent Empire

In the cinema of the late 1990s and early 2000s, a different pattern becomes more evident among new film offerings: the comparative impulse weakens, while the exceptionalist drive grows stronger. Russia has become an exceptional cultural space, unique and distinct from the rest of the world. With bigger budgets allotted to the film industry, the stakes are higher for the establishment of an image of Russia on a par with or superior to the West. Aleksandr Sokurov's *Russian Ark* and Nikita Mikhalkov's *The Barber of Siberia* present Russia as a major cultural axis around which the rest of the world might be seen to rotate. While in early 1990s cinema, Russia was repeatedly pictured as looking for its place on the world map, now its main concern is increasingly to negotiate its place as an equal-or-superior center vis-à-vis an imaginary West, itself viewed from what might be described as Russia's imperial skepticism. In the films we examine next, the turn toward the historical context is a significant shift, since it gives the directors an opportunity to turn to the Russian past to support present-day imperial imaginings rather than to disparage contemporary conditions.

Aleksandr Sokurov, *Russian Ark*

In his *Russian Ark,* Aleksandr Sokurov explores the uneasy issue of the cultural proximity of Russia to Europe in the historical period from Peter I to the Great Patriotic War (roughly concurrent to World War II). Historically, the year of the film's release (2002) was marked by the establishment of the euro as the new currency of the European Union and the Russian Orthodox Church's campaign against the Catholic Church for allegedly working, in conjunction with the United States, to attack Russian Orthodoxy. There was a tendency toward a more radical delineation of Russian culture from European values. In Sokurov's film, an unnamed narrator, known only as the Time Traveler, wanders through the Winter Palace in St. Petersburg.

The narrator implies that he died in an accident and is a ghost drifting through the palace. In each room, he encounters real and fictional people from various periods. He is accompanied by a French aristocrat who represents the Marquis de Custine, a historical nineteenth-century French visitor to Russia.

The film's primary focus is the director's journey through time and space in the pre-Soviet imperial culture preserved at the Hermitage. The itinerary of the journey is, however, highly selective, focusing predominantly on the rooms dedicated to Russia's "European self" (Condee, *Imperial Trace*, 176). According to Oleg Kovalov, "the Petersburg cultural life is presented very selectively in the film—its deep themes and motifs are turned outside, like a glove." As Beumers (Review of *Russian Ark*) notes, the director disregards the Hermitage's holdings on Russian history before Peter the Great, as well as the years of Soviet rule (with the exception of the Great Patriotic War) and post-Soviet Russia. This selectiveness is a strategic move toward the construction of a certain memory in the present about Russia's past, based on forgetfulness and amnesia of other sides of history, including its rich indigenous and peasant culture. Barbie Zelizer has argued that forgetting is "considered not as a defect or deficit practice but a valued activity that is as strategic and central a practice as remembering itself. Forgetting reflects a choice to put aside, for whatever reason, what no longer matters" (220). As Russian cinema contributes to a project of official state building, deeply indebted to the production of a mythical empire with long coherent history, this coherence relies on a highly strategic selection of facts and an associated amnesia about the uncomfortable or "irrelevant" pages in history. The recurrent attempts to deny certain pasts or remake the past by way of remembering or forgetting are consequences of the existence of competing memories or adoption of new political lines. While Sokurov's film cannot be reduced to a project of "official state building," neither is it aloof from participation in the state's imperial memory system.

As much as Sokurov's film is designed as a journey, its narrative is again a kind of self-study, an exploration of a Russia positioned on a cognitive border and in search of recognition. The Time Traveler's anxieties about inferiority to Europe are the underside of the film's sustained reclamation of its cultural primacy. Both the French aristocrat and the Time Traveler, who speaks with Sokurov's voice, guide the viewer around the Hermitage, engaging in a dialogue that contests the achievements of Russian culture. Where the French aristocrat sees a European trace in every piece of Russian art, and even wonders whether he is in the Vatican, Sokurov's voice insists that the site is even better—it is Russia. As Dmitrii Komm mordantly remarks, the Time Traveler's argument resembles a low-quality advertisement in which one product is promoted at the expense of the other by its shameless disparagement. Sokurov's emphasis on the imperial legacy of the country inevitably underscores its commitment to elite culture, yet therefore implicitly sets the stage for the French aristocrat's counterargument against Russia's unique contribution in comparison to the West.

Necessarily, therefore, the French aristocrat contends that the imitative nature of Russian art dominates the collection: he sees Raphael's style, for example, in several of the Russian paintings. Although the foreigner's caustic exclamations suggest that Russians do not have ideas of their own, the Time Traveler remains reserved in his comments. While the French aristocrat is arrogant and his remarks are biting, the Time Traveler replies quietly, at times merely echoing the stranger's words, confident that the truth is on his side. Russian tsars were Russophiles, he responds, but they also wanted to dream about Italy. The Hermitage was created for such dreamers; this is why an Italian flair endures in elite Russian art. Every foreign statement of doubt regarding Russia's originality has its response, creating a story of Russia's exceptionality and (in the Time Traveler's view) the authenticity of its culture. In his review of the film, Andrei Plakhov underscores that "although the ark of art is defined as Russian by the director, it is built by Europeans while the Russian state, according to the director's commentary, is an 'adolescent in the civilized world'" ("'Russkii kovcheg'").

"Why do you want to join European culture? Why do you need to follow the mistakes of Europe?" the foreigner exclaims as he enters a room with Italian sculptures. The irony is this: the French aristocrat's remarks echo the Russian Slavophiles, who disputed the necessity for Russia to join Europe.[8] Revealing a less sympathetic stance, the foreigner mentions he has read Pushkin in French and his works are nothing special. As for Russian music, the composers are all Germans. In implicit counterargument, as one scholar puts it, the film's soundtrack "attempts an integration of imperial European with Europhile Russian culture similar to its project in visual arts: work of Russian composers is inter-edited with works of Purcell and Telemann and performed by the Mariinskii Theatre Orchestra" (Condee, *Imperial Trace*, 176). Moreover, Komm argues, Sokurov has most successfully realized a state project of establishing the foundational continuity of Russian culture, despite the Bolshevik intervention and the

8 The Pan-Slavist ethnologist and philosopher Nikolai Danilevskii is one of several thinkers who eloquently contrasted Russia's uniqueness to the materialism and individualism of Europe.

ravages of the Great Patriotic War: the family of Nicholas II is set alongside the Soviet museum administration. This overriding drive for continuity, of course, is not exceptional to Russian culture: as Jeffrey K. Olick and Joyce Robbins have argued, "the past is produced in the present and is thus malleable" (128). Memories of the past encompassed by history go hand-in-hand with politics and are never free from construction. "Political traditions are validated through some sense of a stable past," stresses Zelizer (227).

While the West gets most of the Time Traveler's attention, the imaginary East receives much less: the Russian imperial narrator adopts a stance of superiority to the militarily inferior East. The film's imperial reception of the Persian ambassadors, who have come to apologize to the Russian court on the occasion of diplomat-playwright Aleksandr Griboedov's murder, is thus transformed into a symbolic celebration of Russia's dominance over "Asia." Through Sokurov's lens, Russia is an empire both culturally superior to Europe and militarily more influential than Asia. It stands out in the international arena as a unique power whose marginality between Europe and Asia is the advantage of an elite culture.

In this regard, the use of the Russian *russkii*, not *rossiiskii*, in Sokurov's title is a revealing ideological choice. As Geoffrey Hosking (9) and others maintain, these two adjectives refer roughly to the distinction between "ethnic" and "imperial" Russianness. The distinction further assigns to *Rus'* a preimperial Russian identity rooted in the people, land, and church, while *Rossiia* most typically refers to the state and to the multinational imperial Russia ruled over by an *imperator* (rather than a tsar). The Hermitage, as the film's "ark" of Russian culture, preserves the elite art of the Russian Empire, with no reference to the culture of the people (*narod*). In this sense, the film's title (*Russkii kovcheg*) is ideologically misleading: why, one might reasonably ask, not *Rossiiskii kovcheg*?

Nikita Mikhalkov, *The Barber of Siberia*

Nikita Mikhalkov's *Barber of Siberia* shares with Aleksandr Sokurov's film an attempt to wed contemporary cultural identity to both Russia's imperial past and Western enlightenment. Unlike Sokurov's film, which makes a cinematic case in favor of a greater respect for mutual differences and accomplishments, Mikhalkov's work is committed to portraying Russia as culturally superior to the West, and to the United States in particular. It is notable that 1999 in Russia was marked by the bicentennial of Pushkin's birthday, a key moment in the story of Russia's claim to a unique literature. Set in late imperial Russia, Mikhalkov's film tells a story of love between a Russian military cadet, Andrei Tolstoi, and an American woman, Jane Callahan, who comes to Russia to assist Douglas McCracken, an obsessive engineer in search of a patron to sponsor his invention, a timber-harvesting machine that will potentially destroy Russian forests. The powerful General Radlov is eventually entranced by Jane's beauty and wants to marry her. Tolstoi and Radlov become rivals for Jane's love, given eventually to the young cadet, and the two spend a passionate night together. In the wake of several misunderstandings, Tolstoi attacks the general, who arrests his young rival on false charges and banishes him to hard labor and exile in Siberia. The entire story, we come to understand, is framed as a letter that Jane writes to her son, a cadet at a US military academy, after many years in which she has kept these events secret.

In his analysis of the film, Stephen Norris argues that Mikhalkov sees Russia's eastern traditions, not those of its west, as "more truly 'Russian'" (*Blockbuster History*, 32). The emphasis on nobility and elite culture, fused with all the familiar stereotypes of Russianness existing in the West aims explicitly to manifest the uniqueness of Russian culture. As Condee argues, "counterpoised to an effete and profligate Western Europe, his Russia is assertively different in its healthy barbarity. Counterpoised to the United States, Mikhalkov's Russia is assertively European in its exquisite conservation of high culture" (*Imperial Trace*, 86). Unlike Sokurov in *Russian Ark*, Mikhalkov attempts to amalgamate the elite culture of Russian nobility with the folk culture of the masses, rendering a further collection of stock stereotypes—especially in the Carnival (Maslenitsa) episode, with its pancakes, caviar, and jumping Petrushka—utterly predictable. The result is the impression that the film was made not by a Russian director but by a foreigner who had decided to project everything he knew about Russia onto the screen.

The elite tastes of the protagonist Andrei Tolstoi are revealed in his love of opera, shared with Jane, an American woman traveling to Russia. Indeed, his participation in a cadet performance of Gioachino Rossini's *The Barber of Seville* would become a turning point in his life. The imperial culture reaches its apogee in the pompous reception of the military corps by Alexander III, whose every detail is perfectly staged and rehearsed. As in *Russian Ark*, the ceremonial moment is not so much narrative as spectacular, reflecting back for the viewer's admiration examples of elite Russian culture and then (in a cameo performance by Mikhalkov) of Alexander III himself, set off by picturesque aerial shots of the ceremony from a bird's eye view, replete with golden church domes in the foreground.

In a "society of the spectacle," as Guy Debord presciently defined the emerging postmodern world already in the 1960s, film—as a medium heavily reliant on visual qualities—acquires high value in representation of certain ideologies. Debord argued that the present age "prefers the sign to the thing signified, the copy to the original, representation to reality, the appearance to the essence." Thirty years after (and culturally removed from) Debord's polemical writing, the spectacular nature of the ceremony in Mikhalkov's film makes empire alluring to the viewer, who is invited to join in this spectacle and share memories about the glorious times of the Russian Empire. These mediated memories available to viewers regardless of their ethnic background, skin color, gender, or religious affiliation are, in Alison Landsberg's terms, "prosthetic memories." Landsberg contends that "mass culture enables the production of prosthetic memories, memories that give people access to events that are not their 'natural' or biological inheritance" (109). The term is productive in connection with the imperial implications in Mikhalkov's film, since what Landsberg considers prosthetic memories also has the propensity to unite an audience despite its inherent differences. As she emphasizes, "the power of mass cultural sites also lies in their ability to engage spectators across racial lines, to create prosthetic memories even in those to whom the memories do not 'properly' belong" (109). *Barber of Siberia* provides memories calling for empathy with the empire, but as a film aimed not only at an entirely Russian audience but also targeting Western viewers, it also aims to convince its foreign viewers of the genuine beauty of the Russian imperial past and lead them to share these memories, agitating—at times circumspectly, at times directly—for Russia's superiority over the West.

The visual citation of Orthodox cupolas in Alexander III's ceremonial scene is another strategy by which the imperial identity is invoked, since the official Church was administered in tandem with the secular imperial order, affirming the mythology of Moscow as the Third Rome. As Nikolai Berdiaev pointed out, "'Russians' are defined by 'Orthodoxy'" (38), and Russia was the only remaining true Orthodox state. Russia's religious mission, furthermore, became linked to the strength of the Russian state, whose sole ruler was the tsar.[9] For all the tumultuous changes since Berdiaev's day, one might argue that—in this respect—little has changed. As Katarzyna Jarzynska argues, present-day Russian nationalism "exists in a highly fragmented, non-homogenous state, characterized in the most general terms according to the

9 See a more detailed discussion of Berdiaev's ideas in Østbø, 61–63.

two 'lines' of thought, an imperial-Orthodox line and an ethnic line which encompasses the broadest views of particularly Putin-era nationalism" (1).

The strategic emphasis that Mikhalkov places in the film's discourse on Russia's religiosity, superior intelligence, and high culture is contrasted to US cultural stupidity—another stereotype deeply engraved in Russian minds since Soviet times. The comedic representation of the US sergeant establishes the cultural poverty and backwardness of his fellow countrymen, in contrast to Cadet McCracken's integration (through Mozart) into European culture. As half-Russian, half-American, he is fortunate to have inherited his father's affinity for elite culture. When his mother, Jane, tells the sergeant that Andrew's father was Russian, the latter exclaims: "Ah, that explains a lot." Whatever the young man's Russian parentage could explain to the sergeant, he makes the assumption that Mozart was also therefore Russian. Mikhalkov's Russia is thus not only culturally unique but also progressive and Westernized in its own fashion. As Mikhail Brashinskii points out, it is only Russians who are confident that "their 'Russianness' can explain anything." Much as in Sokurov's *Russian Ark,* the true European cultural legacy is appropriated by Russia to produce the image of exceptionality and parity, if not superiority, to the geographic West.

Antagonist Douglas McCracken's timber-harvesting machine, in the meantime, is a Western symbol, swallowed up by Russia's imperial expanses. The infinite landscapes of the Siberian forest in the opening and closing shots manifest the power of Russia to counterpoise Western incursion, analogous in some respects to the visit of the Foreigner in Sokurov's *Russian Ark*. Made at the end of the 1990s, *Barber of Siberia* is a vivid example of Mikhalkov's vision of Russia's orientation in post-Soviet times. Completely disregarding revolutionary and Soviet history, Mikhalkov, like Sokurov, focuses predominantly on Russia's imperial heyday.

The "visit of the foreigner to Russia" is a recurring trope that helps to define Russia both from within and from without—from the outsider's point of view. In *Russian Ark*, the foreigner's skepticism about Russia's cultural originality locates the value of Russian culture within Western civilization, as well as narrates the story of its development as beginning with Peter the Great's innovations. In *The Barber of Siberia,* by contrast, Jane's visit to Russia emphasizes the gulf between Russia's European culture and that of the United States; the visit reveals Russia's uniqueness, albeit through the same stereotypical artifacts with which the West usually associates Russia. As a very different contrast, a "broken Russia" is imagined by Rogozhkin (*Pecularities*), in which Raivo is caught between his vision of an imperial, Westernized Russia and the jarring contemporary realities he encounters. A fourth variant (*Window to Paris*) is a post-Soviet and postimperial Russia, disconnected from the West—indeed in some respects, a complete opposite. The dark portrayal of Russia in *Window* underlines a transitional stage in Russian cinema, revealing its exceptional spiritual richness in contrast to the degraded morals of the West. In each instance, and in very different ways, Russia's social anxieties—emerging from its perpetual comparison to the West (and to Europe in particular)—receive onscreen consolation through self-regard, a recurrent element of which is the affirmation of superiority and uniqueness, brought into focus most starkly on a symbolic border between the imaginary East and West. Let us now turn to our third set of preoccupations, where we invoke a different (and more controversial) model of the West.

Imperial Ambitions and Anxieties: The Ukraine Syndrome

As early as the Kiev street protests of November 2004, the twenty-first century had begun to witness a redefinition of "borderland," one that (I argue) involved a profound inversion of marginality. Scholars disagree about the historical origins of the name "Ukraine,"[10] specifically whether it designates "border" or "region." This dispute need not concern us here, except for the fact that we are witnessing a contemporary redefinition of "border" that increasingly situates Russia at the margin of a Europeanizing Western Ukraine. By the late 2000s, Russia's aspirations to form a united community of Slavic "brotherly peoples," encompassing Ukrainians and Belorussians into a larger Russian world, were imperiled by an independent nation-state that was already in the early 2000s increasingly developing its own national identity. Anxieties about the newly established borders and inability to control the territories of the neighboring countries triggered incidents of violence in relation to Russia's neighbors (Ukraine and Georgia, in particular) as a response to the threat of marginalization vis-à-vis these new nation-states. This is an enormous topic, worthy of its own monograph; for our purposes here, however briefly, our interests coalesce around this question: what traces of this

10 The year 1187 marks the earliest appearance of the word "Ukraina," tied to the death of Volodymyr Hlibovych (ruler of the Principality of Pereiaslavl') and contained in the Hypatian Codex. The name has historically been taken to mean "borderland," from the Proto-Slavic *krai* (edge), although this etymology was challenged as early as 1936 by Serhii Shelukhin, who contended that the origin merely meant "region," not "border." See Shelukhin.

shift do we see on the screen and how does the industry itself articulate the growing concept of Ukraine as a cinematic neo-border?

Aleksei Balabanov, *Brother 2*

The year 2000 was a "border year" in Russian history, with the Second Chechen War providing high ratings for Vladimir Putin as presidential candidate and his eventual election as president. By the early 2000s, Russia's uncertainty about its imperial future, with a Westernizing Ukraine on its southern border clearly perceptible, began to make passing appearances in cultural texts, including ones under examination here. Aleksei Balabanov's *Brother 2* is a curious early Putin-era example. A sequel to Balabanov's Russian crime thriller *Brother*, the film revisits the same protagonist, Danila Bagrov, who learns from his army buddy Konstantin Gromov of dire family circumstances: Konstantin's twin brother Dmitrii, a professional US hockey player, has been swindled into an exploitive contract. Several days after the conversation, Danila finds Konstantin dead; to avenge his friend and find justice, Danila travels to the United States.

Although the Ukrainian theme in Balabanov's *Brother 2* is only a secondary plotline, it is a key element in our examination. The Ukrainian line fits well within the film's larger narrative of travel from periphery to center (here, from Moscow to the United States), as well as the all-permeating Russian patriotism revealed in the film's recurrent lines of Iurii Pavliukov's patriotic poem "This Is My Homeland" (Eto—Rodina moia) running as a leitmotif throughout the plot. According to Alena Solntseva, the idea of the reestablishment of justice is the central idea driving the main hero's actions: "he has to protect old people, women, and children; he has to kill bad people and defend 'our' people. Those who are not 'ours' are bad, they are strangers."[11] In spite of all its flaws, Russia is ultimately accepted by the heroes as the only homeland, while Ukrainians are portrayed to us as traitors who have forsaken their homeland for a better life in the West. In his film, Balabanov provocatively conflates Americanness with defective Russianness: characters speak Russian but are neither Russian nor good people. Danila Bagrov meets the first such character in New York when a Jewish immigrant sells Danila a defective car. The second cluster of defective Russians are Ukrainian gangsters who

11 See the full interview with prominent film critics in Fanailova.

(in Balabanov's universe) speak defective Russian—that is, Ukrainian; this is what westernization of Ukrainians is about.

Bagrov's older brother exterminates one of the Ukrainian gangsters in a Chicago émigré restaurant restroom ("You, bastards, will pay me for Sevastopol").[12] The film itself was prohibited from exhibition in Ukraine after the 2014 Crimean annexation because of its disparaging image of Ukrainians. The Russian discourse around Crimea (and the necessity for its return) circulated long before the territory's actual annexation. In this respect, one might argue that Balabanov's film turned out to be a prescient example of the current memory wars enacted in Russian and Ukrainian cinema.

In one famously untenable assertion, Samuel Huntington once assured us that "if civilization is what counts . . . the likelihood of violence between Ukrainians and Russians should be low. They are two Slavic, primarily Orthodox peoples who have had close relationships with each other for centuries" (38). With regards to the current Russia's military actions in Eastern Ukraine, this hypothesis is in retrospect risible: Russia's imperial ambitions run counter to Ukraine's national aspirations. And while Russian media repeatedly aims to minimize borders between Slavic peoples, the result is a relentless effort to absorb Ukraine into its realm of representation. How this dynamic will continue to play itself out on the screen and in the intricacies of media production is one of the most challenging issues of Russian contemporary cinema.

Vladimir Bortko, *Taras Bulba*

By the early 2000s, Russian cinema had acquired a key role in sustaining a recognizable identity. The importance assigned to cinema as a medium for identity construction is evident from the huge investment in films promoting state ideas. Vladimir Bortko's *Taras Bulba* is a distinct example of imperial loyalties, condensed into a classical narrative undergirded by historical background. Based on Nikolai Gogol's novel *Taras Bulba* (1835, 1842), the historical drama is set in the sixteenth century, when Ukrainian Cossack warriors defended their lands against the advancing Polish armies. A Cossack leader Taras Bulba kills his son, a traitor who has joined the Poles because of his love for a Polish woman.

12 Here Balabanov provides a visualization of a famous quotation by President Vladimir Putin, who at the beginning of his presidency promised to fight terrorists everywhere, even in the outhouses (cited in Brown).

Bortko's film essentially claims that there is no such thing as Ukrainian identity. Ukraine simply serves the role of Russian territory (as "border," not "region"), which the West tries to annex away from Russia. While the film makes a clear statement about Russian patriotism, it also enters into a dialogue about the contested borders between Russia and the West, essentialized as Catholic Poland. By the time of Bortko's 2009 film, the tension in Russo-Ukrainian relations was nothing new; the Orange Revolution of 2004 was already far in the past.

By then, the film's logic seems to suggest, there was no need for Vladimir Bortko to exterminate Ukrainians in his film, because they did not exist as a separate people. As Ellen Barry points out, "Mr. Bortko aimed to show that 'there is no separate Ukraine,' as he put it in an interview, and that 'the Russian people are one.'" After the film's Russian premiere, nationalist politician Vladimir Zhirinovskii suggested that the film was better than thousands of books and thousands of lessons; that everyone who watched the film would understand that Russians and Ukrainians are one people; and that the enemy is the West (Barry). Bortko's film became, on the one hand, a quintessence of Russian imperial imaginings about its own superiority; and on the other, an embodiment of its anxieties about the potential loss of its ancient history, including the legacy of Kievan Rus' and a Cossackdom that it had shared with Ukraine. This anxiety is compounded by the ever-growing divide between Russia and Ukraine, as Western Ukraine subsequently took a more radical turn toward Europe in 2013–14.

The recurring "Russian land" and "Russian faith" throughout Bortko's *Taras Bulba* thus became a proclamation of imperial power, a kind of filmic equivalent to the shirtless Putin. The film was highly acclaimed by conservative film critics as a paragon of the historical film, although both Gogol's novel and Bortko's film have a very distant relationship with archival history. Instead, they both represent a fascinating instance of imperial vision—which, in Bortko's case, is also well supported financially by the state budget. The heroes of Bortko's film are Ukrainian Cossacks who fight against an enemy from the West and, when they die, speak as one about the "Orthodox Russian land."

The Russian appropriation of Gogol in Bortko's adaptation is evident even before the film begins. The Russian tricolor at the film's beginning, followed by an acknowledgment of support from the Russian Ministry of Culture, is followed by a narrative "epigraph": a black-and-white flashback features Taras Bulba (the Ukrainian actor Bogdan Stupka) lecturing his Cossack regiment about true comradeship, a monologue from the novel learned by heart

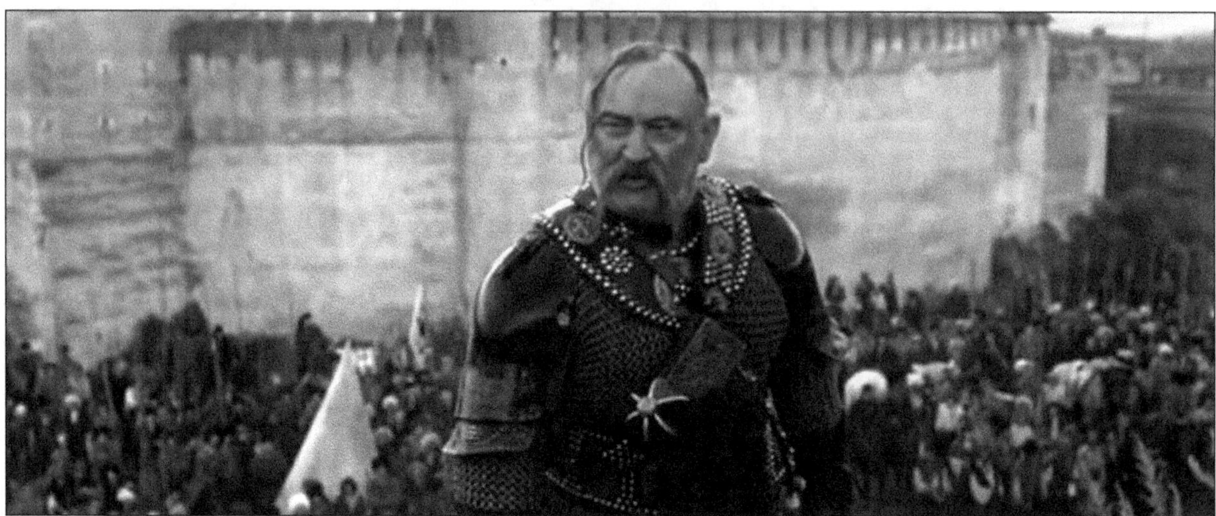

Fig. 8.3. Bortko, *Taras Bulba*. Fight for the Russian land!

by generations of Soviet schoolchildren. Its choice is ideologically explicit, since Taras Bulba speaks about the unity of the Russian people, and his words are generally a panegyric to the Russian land (*russkaia zemlia*), which in the viewer's mind immediately establishes a connection to contemporary Russia, especially after the image of the Russian flag.

With the Russian imperial implications already inscribed in Gogol's *Taras Bulba*, Bortko enhances the novel's ideology with meanings contemporary to the twenty-first-century spectator. As Andrei Plakhov ("Ballada") points out, Gogol's novel is "pure poetic hooliganism aiming to replace Homer's epos with legends and myths of the sixteenth-century Zaporozhian Host, whereas Bortko's attempt to 'rewrite Gogol' and add motivation to his free legendary world ended in an embarrassment." Gogol's dual Russo-Ukrainian identity, coupled with Bortko's own dual identity as a Ukrainian-Russian director, resulted in a deeply Russian patriotic interpretation of the novel and the historical past associated with it; it likewise created a shared memory of exclusively Russian Cossacks who fought for the Russian land against the Poles (the metonymic West). Although this is a narrative of defeat, it promises a great victory to come, and hence enforces the Russian identity and the unity of the people. Here one might recall Reinhardt Koselleck's argument that defeat can, "by virtue of an inverse logic, raise a challenge to identify, precisely out of defeat, with the fatherland for whom the fallen had given their lives" (297).

The potential for equivocation in the novel *Taras Bulba* is grounded in the fact that Gogol himself wrote two versions of the novel. In comparison to the first redaction that appeared in the *Mirgorod* cycle (1835), the later, revised version (1842) features a drastically different agenda. Whereas the first edition of the novel portrays Cossacks as free people fighting for Ukraine, the second version explicitly promotes Russian-identified virtues and incorporates a putative Russian spirit into the image of Cossacks. According to Saera Yoon, "the Cossacks in the 1842 *Taras Bulba* completely internalize a form of the Russian identity. They have adopted the patriotically charged epithet 'Russian' to describe themselves, and in so doing express their animosity toward Poland within the framework of the opposition between Russia and the West" (431). Yet Gogol never completely discarded his sympathies toward the Ukrainian alternative, less supportive of state control. As Edyta Bojanowska comments, "his historical texts often feature a duality between the gestures of support toward official ideology and points of tension with it" (102).[13]

The Cossack era (the general scholarly consensus here assigns this period to the fifteenth through eighteenth centuries)[14] is an important historical period for the formation of Ukrainian national identity. It is true that the history of Cossackdom is shared by Ukraine and Russia, yet as Serhii Plokhy (194) indicates, the roles Cossacks played in the historical development of these two Slavic peoples is different. "In Russia, the Cossacks remained a marginal factor in national history, border warriors who challenged the Russian state on a number of occasions, but eventually were defeated by it. In Ukraine, the Cossacks were those who took upon themselves the difficult task of defending the national religious and cultural traditions against the attacks of foreign states, which culminated in the creation of a polity of their own."

After the release of Bortko's film, it was immediately denounced in Ukraine as a film made to Russian state order and since 2014 the film has been banned from public screening. The

13 The negative image of the Poles in Gogol's text partially explains why film adaptations of the novel have always been problematic, especially in Soviet times. Sergei Bondarchuk had dreamt of filming *Taras Bulba* for many years, but when he offered his script in 1971, it was eventually rejected by the Soviet Ministry of Culture with advice to find a different literary work for screen adaptation; he made his film *Steppe* instead. The decision to make a film adaptation of the novel in 2009, one might argue, is a sign of weakness, a representation of the empire's increased impotence and anxieties, recoded as its alleged might. See also Klekhovskii.

14 The Cossack movement has hardly been monolithic from the very beginning of its existence. Gogol's novel discusses specifically Zaporozhian Cossacks, who lived in today's central Ukraine. This group was forcibly disbanded in the late eighteenth century, with most of the population relocated to the Kuban region. In addition

film aroused resentment among Ukrainian intellectuals, who saw it as an encroachment on Ukrainian national memory. According to the State Agency on Cinema of Ukraine, Bortko's *Taras Bulba* "distorts historical events, falsifies and discredits the Ukrainian national idea, and is generally blatantly anti-Ukrainian, as well as questioning the existence of the Ukrainian people" (Kokotiukha).[15]

The fight for Gogol as a national Ukrainian poet *versus* Gogol as a Russian national poet will never end, with each side struggling to acquire the full right to the writer's legacy. The bicentennial of Gogol's birth in 2009 was widely commemorated in both Russia and Ukraine. And a Ukrainian film version of *Taras Bulba* by Petro Pinchuk and Ievhen Berezniak, *A Song about Taras Bulba* (Duma pro Tarasa Bul'bu, 2009) could not stylistically and financially be more unlike Bortko's Hollywood-style historical blockbuster. Pinchuk's and Berezniak's work is a low-budget film with its main focus on Ukrainian spirituality and national unity. Ukraine's low state investment in the film industry is also indicative of the fact that cinema in Ukraine is not yet a primary source of identity formation at this historical stage, unlike in Russia, where state-subsidized film has increasingly become an imaginative space for imperial fantasies about its superiority and national unity.

* * *

The six films discussed in the chapter, therefore, explore in very different ways the dynamics and evolution of Russian imperial imaginings about itself starting in the early 1990s, when reconstitution of the new empire was accompanied by anxiety about both its lowered status in the world cultural arena and its retreat from the center of post-Soviet countries. If the late Putin era finds itself able to make higher investments in the state film industry and in historical drama as the primary genre of "national" cinema, then this tension between resurgent aspirations and cumulative frustrations at the frontier will only be aggravated. In this respect, such works as Andrei Maliukov's *The Match* (Match, 2012), Fedor Bondarchuk's *Stalingrad* (2013), Kim Druzhinin and Andrei Shal'opa's *Panfilov's 28* (28 panfilovtsev, 2016),

to the Kuban Cossacks, there existed also the Don Cossack Host, Terek, Yaik, and other Cossack formations, diverse in their goals and composition, as well as their periods of existence. See more in Grau. The origins of the Cossack movement are also elaborately discussed in Seaton; and Longworth.

15 See also Stepula; and Kraliuk (9).

Sergei Mokritskii's *Battle for Sevastopol* (Bitva za Sevastopol', 2015), and Anton Megerdichev's *Going Vertical* (Dvizhenie vverkh, 2017) are harbingers of what is to come.

Filmography

Balabanov, Aleksei, dir. *Brother 2* (Brat 2, 2000).
Bondarchuk, Fedor, dir. *Stalingrad* (2013).
Bortko, Vladimir, dir. *Taras Bulba* (2009).
Druzhinin, Kim, and Andrei Shal'opa, dir. *Panfilov's 28* (28 panfilovtsev, 2016).
Maliukov, Andrei, dir. *The Match* (Match, 2012).
Mamin, Iurii, dir. *Window to Paris* (Okno v Parizh, 1993).
Megerdichev, Anton, dir. *Going Vertical* (Dvizhenie vverkh, 2017).
Mikhalkov, Nikita. *Barber of Siberia* (Sibirskii tsiriul'nik, 1998).
Mokritskii, Sergei, dir. *Battle for Sevastopol* (Bitva za Sevastopol', 2015).
Pinchuk, Petro, and Ievgen Berezniak, dir. *A Song about Taras Bulba* (Duma pro Tarasa Bul'bu, 2009).
Rogozhkin, Aleksandr, dir. *The Checkpoint* (Blokpost, 1998).
———. *Cuckoo* (Kukushka, 2002).
———. *Peculiarities of the National Fishing* (Osobennosti natsional'noi rybalki, 1998).
———. *Peculiarities of the National Hunt* (Osobennosti natsional'noi okhoty, 1995).
Sokurov, Aleksandr, dir. *Russian Ark* (Russkii kovcheg, 2002).

9. Contending Alterities: Drag Show, Roma Camp . . .

Trevor Wilson

"Visibility is a trap."
—*Michel Foucault, Discipline and Punish*

Imagine, for the sake of argument, two distinct genealogies of the critical use of "alterity" operating within the post-Soviet field. The first would begin somewhere within the historical rhetoric of early Soviet anti-imperialism. Inaugurating what Terry Martin (68) describes as the "affirmative action empire" of the Soviet Union, party leaders at the Eighth Party Congress in 1919 first wrestled with the important question of self-determination among Soviet national minorities in the wake of the Russian Empire. What we have come to understand, if only telegraphically, as "alterity," understood here as the abstract category of relation between differing social identities, became officially endorsed through resolutions passed in 1923 at the Twelfth Party Congress as well as at a special Central Committee Conference on Nationalities Policy, henceforth referred to in official Soviet policy as *korenizatsiia* (roughly, "indigenization"), ensuring the support for local languages and cultures and the state promotion of local ethno-national intelligentsia (73–74). As Martin convincingly argues, despite a sharp shift in rhetoric toward explicitly Russocentric policy in the 1930s, including the famous claim of Russia's status as "first among equals" in the Soviet family of nations, the Soviet Union succeeded in varying degrees throughout its lifespan in maintaining an intricate interplay between the enforcement of a deeply centralized state apparatus and the promotion of former colonial national identities. The continued existence of autonomous republics within the Russian Federation, such as Tatarstan or Chuvashia, illustrates the enduring legacy of this national relation, although violence in republics like Chechnya and Dagestan, for example, as well as recent crackdowns on national language programs, raise doubts as to the future of this image of state-approved national alterity.

To this first genealogy of alterity, I add a second one, germane to nearly the entire corpus of Western critical theory. Emerging concomitantly with the long process of decolonization, the emergence of the "Third World" and the Cold War after the Second World War, philosophical critiques of normativity based on socially constructed categories of racial, sexual, and generally "othered" difference have fueled an entire cottage industry of thought surrounding the question of alterity. While its history is far too broad and varied to describe here in full, inherent in this genealogy is the claim of a mutual constitution for the subject and its other, so that several of its major ideational waypoints included the resurgence, thanks to Alexandre Kojève, of the Hegelian "master/slave" dialectic in French existentialist thought (most prominently in Simone de Beauvoir's *The Second Sex* [Le deuxième sexe, 1949]); Georges Canguilhem's work on defining "normal" and "pathological" in the biological sciences, which would in turn influence Michel Foucault's examination of *biopouvoir* and the knowledge-power nexus in its relation to normativity; and Frantz Fanon's use of psychoanalysis to describe the postcolonial self-perception of the black subject in *Black Skin, White Masks* (Peau noire, masques blancs, 1952).[1] As critical theory and, within it, fields such as queer and postcolonial theory have entered Russian academic discourse since the Soviet collapse, its reception has oscillated between, at one end of the spectrum, its convincing use to critique contemporary Russian culture from a dizzyingly diverse number of perspectives and, at the other end of the spectrum, its blanket dismissal as a Western epistemology whose features fail to address the unique nuances of the former Second World.

Of course, these two genealogies of Otherness are admittedly not completely self-contained, and are often even in direct contact and contestation, yet they are nonetheless immediately recognizable and legible as discrete ideological agents circulating within the former Soviet space. I argue here that the interaction between these two genealogies—at times reconciliatory, at other times openly hostile—has shaped the contours of representation of Russia's "Others" in post-Soviet cinema. Perhaps the most significant distinction, operationally useful in a discussion of these two visions of the Other in post-Soviet culture, is one which Eve Kosofsky Sedgwick (88) has described as between minoritizing and universalizing. Sedgwick's distinction is an attempt at a more nuanced debate within Western feminism between essentialism and constructivism. In her argument, theoreticians of alterity rhetorically choose to imagine an Othered identity either as fixed, distinct, and separatist (essentialist, minoritized) or as "an issue of continuing, determinative importance in the lives of people across the spectrum" (constructivist, universalized) and therefore equally important in the constitution of the

1 A very broad but useful description of this trajectory in French theory can be found in Descombes.

hegemonic subject (2). The idea is not to claim one view as true and the other false but rather to identify the stakes of their strategic deployment in political and cultural representation.

Arguably the former, minoritizing view has long dominated the discourse surrounding alterity in Russian culture, with its obvious thematic semblance to "indigenization" as understood in the logic of the autonomous republic. Yet cinematic portrayals of Russia's Others have increasingly emphasized alterity as a more flexible category of post-Soviet life, grounded in the theoretical claim that we are actually talking about ourselves when we talk about an Other. This discursive conflict has produced intricate depictions of alterity particularly with regards to sex and class, two vectors of identity that hardly have any naturalized, "separatist" geographic deployment, but that are nonetheless mapped spatially when represented on screen. The need for a spatial framing of Otherness reflects an ongoing rhetorical quid pro quo between the two genealogies of alterity and speaks to the heart of the problem of cultural differences on screen. Are these differences "separatist," with a minority population distinguishable from the majority, or are they "integrative," based on liminality and the possibility of the minority's centrality within majoritarian culture? To put it more bluntly: are Russia's Others external to Russian culture, or are they essential to its very definition?

Ol'ga Stolpovskaia and Dmitrii Troitskii, *You I Love*

The historical portrayal of non-normative sexuality within post-Soviet Russian cinema serves as a particularly useful example of this oscillation or hesitation between the two articulations of Otherness. Often, though erroneously,[2] considered the first Russian gay film, *You I Love* (Ia liubliu tebia, 2004) directed by Ol'ga Stolpovskaia and Dmitrii Troitskii, narrates a complicated love triangle among Timofei, Vera, and Iliumdzhi, a young *Gastarbeiter* from Kalmykia, who awakens Timofei's latent bisexuality with his heavily Orientalized behavior: exotic dancing, mudras, and pronounced general cultural atavism, such as sleeping in a zoo and a total ignorance of how to use an ATM. Particularly telling are the negative domestic reviews of the film, which frequently tinge homophobia with racism around the addition of a Kalmyk character: "let's have the protagonist out of nowhere turn out to be gay. You know what, that's

2 Iurii Pavlov's *The Creation of Adam* (Sotvorenie Adama, 1993) precedes *You I Love* (2004) by over a decade yet is only rarely considered for this title, perhaps because it lacked the international release of the latter, which premiered in the Panorama program of the 2004 Berlinale Film Festival.

great, *pourquoi pas*? And let's have him begin to sleep with not just a friend, but . . . but with . . . for example, an Eskimo. No, even better, with a Kalmyk, that's kind of more fun. And have the Kalmyk work in a zoo and never wash" (Barabash). Critics often objected not to the offensive, stereotype-laden portrayal of a non-Russian on screen but rather to the implausibility of the love affair, as well as the unsuitability of the Kalmyk role, with one critic arguing the Kalmyk was not portrayed as "wild" enough: "he clearly lacks savagery. Which is understandable, as the actor is neither a young boy nor a Kalmyk. He is part Russian, part Chinese, graduated

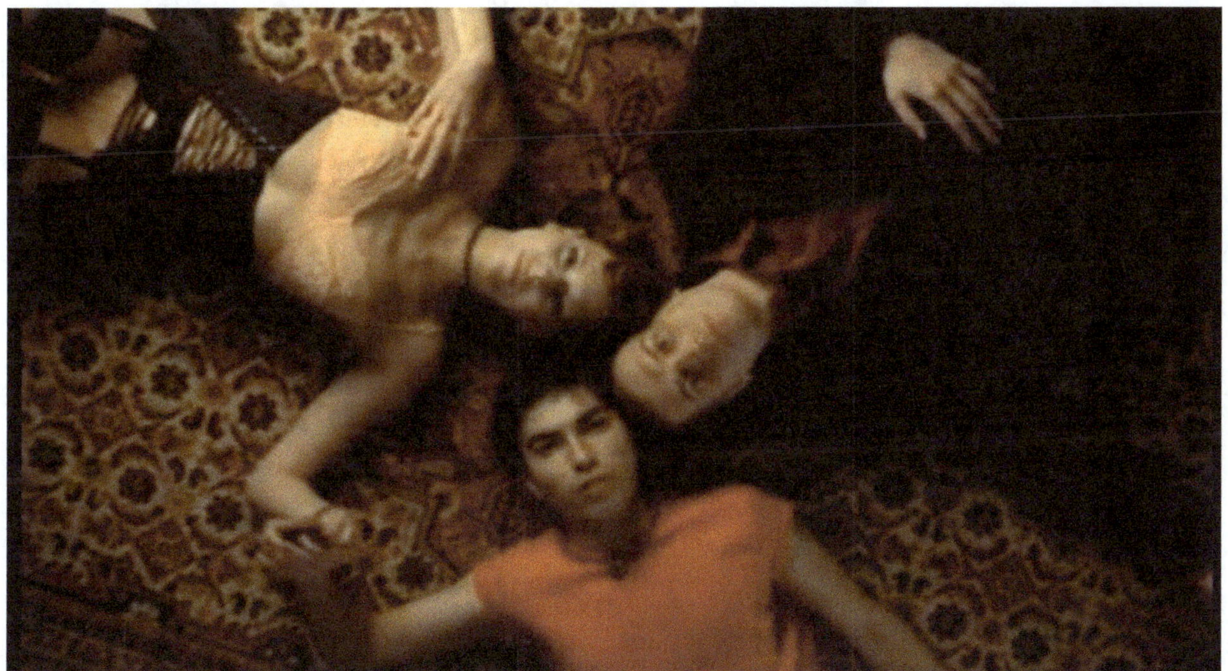

Fig. 9.1. Stolpovskaia and Troitskii, *You I Love*. Vera, Timofei, and Iliumdzhi's love triangle.

from the institute a while ago, and works as a lawyer" (Raiter).

This landmark Russian film is striking in its sustained insistence that the viewer interpret queer sexuality through overt geopoliticization. Protagonist Timofei works for a foreign advertisement agency in Moscow, where his boss is a gay African-American man named John, and his parents have relocated somewhere abroad. In its imagined geography, the film jostles between these two poles of sexual non-normativity: should queerness be read as a product of non-Western sensual permissiveness, dancing swarthy boys in the vein of André Gide's 1902 novel *The Immoralist* (L'immoraliste) and Vladimir Makanin's 1994 story "Captive of the Caucasus" (Kavkazskii plennyi); or should it be read as a yet another sign of Western corruption and the perversions of liberal Gayropa and the United States? One of the film's most poignant scenes depicts Timofei and Vera enjoying a threesome at a decadent gay party hosted by John, who is not only their third's boyfriend but is confusingly clad in traditional African garb. Between crude gags on the hilarity of Western sexual extravagance are interspliced scenes of Iliumdzhi sitting outside Timofei's apartment, distraught at the idea of having lost Timofei as a lover and dreaming of his childhood, chasing sheep in Kalmykia. The film struggles to negotiate Timofei's sexuality between these two geopolitical positions, and in so doing reveals the contradictions in crafting a representation of a "uniquely Russian" sexual alterity.

Iliumdzhi and John here are symbolic portrayals of what Sedgwick defines as minoritizing approaches to queer sexuality, albeit with contrasting results. Their Otherness is one that is separate and concise, which, if necessary, is easily quarantined so as to prevent wider contamination. Indeed, the film encourages an associative chain where the semiotic sign of Otherness passes from homosexuality to foreign national and back again, yet the Russian specificity of this move lies in the fact that it is *not only* a rehashed orientalist trope of an imperial hangover but also a statement of Russia's own relationship to the West. In the final moments of the film, after Vera has more or less given her consent to a loose form of bigamy, Timofei and Iliumdzhi prepare to leave for a lovers' trip abroad (and although Timofei won plane tickets from his company to a location of his choosing, the viewer at this point is generally convinced they are traveling West), when suddenly they receive a phone call at the airport that Iliumdzhi's father has died. Their voyage to Kalmykia for the funeral turns out to be a trap, set up so that his family can enlist him in the army and save him from a homosexual relationship with his Russian partner. If in the film's beginning, Timofei, and furthermore Vera, whose narrative motivation is entirely deprived of psychological elaboration, are representative of a stable Russian midway point between the East-West poles of sexual license, the film concludes with a dramatic shift toward Russian tolerance of sexual alterity vis-à-vis a homophobic Kalmyk family.

This narrative ploy reiterates in one fell swoop what Joseph Massad (37) describes as the modernizing shift in the historical discourse of Orientalist sexuality: "while the premodern West attacked the world of Islam's alleged sexual licentiousness, the modern West attacks its alleged *repression* of sexual freedoms." Here the contemporary Russian queer film is capable of occupying both of these positions at once—that is, defending against moral depravity and (at the same time) advocating for social tolerance, precisely because it obfuscates two competing views of social alterity, encompassing within itself a vision of cultural autonomy ("things are done differently here/there") *as well as* a vision of itself as a modernizing, progressive former colonizer.

This necessarily endows a certain mutability to Timofei's sexuality, which the film, in its relatively limited stylistic repertoire, can only portray as his latent bisexuality. To a certain extent both colonizer and colonized, in that he is seen perpetually fleeing from Western impositions of homosexuality while defending his own from Eastern homophobia, Timofei oddly comes to embody Sedgwick's "universalized" Other. His alternative sexuality suggests a fluidity within even the most stable definitions of Russian sexuality: you, too, might someday fall in love with someone of the same sex.

Feliks Mikhailov, *Jolly Fellows*

Five years later, the queer collective seen in Feliks Mikhailov's *Jolly Fellows* (Vesel'chaki, 2009) attempts to find a similar universalizing definition of non-normative sexuality, albeit with different narrative conceits. The film is an open-faced remake of the Australian cult classic *The Adventures of Priscilla, Queen of the Desert* (1994), an attempt to humanize the lives of drag queens whose campy, feather-boa-clad performances on the Moscow stage would otherwise disqualify them for any sympathy on the behalf of the more traditionalist Russian viewer. Mikhailov instead, through the narrative device of a newspaper journalist interviewing the queens about their lives, digs into the contradictions, motivations, and even mundanities that define their lives as fellow human beings who just happen to be drag queens.

Otherness here attempts to present itself as a universalizing act, exemplified in the film's tagline: "each has his faults" (*u kazhdogo svoi nedostatki*), in turn a translation of the phrase "well, no one's perfect," from the famous crossdressing scene in Billy Wilder's 1959 film *Some Like It Hot*.[3] It would be difficult, however, to argue that this attempt is successful: despite attempts

3 *Some Like It Hot* holds cult status in the former USSR, beloved for its cultural taboos and kitschy, over the top performance by Marilyn Monroe. Wilder's film was first purchased during the Thaw in 1963, rereleased in the 1980s, and was the only film starring Marilyn Monroe to be released in the Soviet Union in general.

to "normalize" the queens, Mikhailov relies on the most facile stereotypes surrounding gay men, so that homosexuality truly feels like a world apart. Indeed, the film broadly assumes that there is little daylight between a drag queen and a gay man; that gay men are necessarily implicated in accusations of pedophilia; and that a gay love narrative must conclude in the tragic revelation that one partner has contracted HIV.

Addressing these preconceived notions of homosexuality would not in and of itself be a bad thing, given their stubborn persistence in public perceptions of male homosexuality, were it not that the film does not challenge them in any direct way or even provide psychological complexity to the characters beyond these plotlines. As Marko Dumančić describes it, the film is structured around a "hetero-queer tension," which prevents any universalizing of non-normativity and instead pits "hetero and queer characters against each other in a battle of the wills." This is most clear in the film's final scenes, where the queen Roza is murdered by a prospective lover who turns out to be avenging the death of his child at the hands of a pedophile, all while Roza's other drag-queen friends are running into literal and figurative final battle with a troop of homophobic mechanics. These rigid oppositions undermine the film's presumably sincere attempt at reconciling its audience to the lives of a queer Russian counterculture.

While the film certainly holds a pride of place within any history of gay Russian cinema, and while Mikhailov should be given credit for an attempt at a nuanced portrayal of queer culture, the fact remains that homosexuality is so deeply conflated with drag culture that narration of one is narration of the other. As the journalist asks the queens around a café table to describe their decisions to perform drag, their personal narratives almost entirely avoid any mention of sexual partners or gay romance—in fact, the only plot point to address sexuality is when Fira's partner confronts her with the discovery of Fira's HIV status, breaking up with her abruptly, with almost no reference to their relationship whatsoever, prior to this narratively cheap revelation. Otherness in the film, therefore, operates not through the spectrum of intimacy, as in *You I Love*, but rather through performativity.

Two personal narratives in the film in particular merit analysis for the manner in which they betray a cultural eclecticism underlying Russian queer performativity. The first is Lara, one of the oldest queens in the troupe. Lara narrates to the journalist how he first came to drag through participation as a student in a Komsomol concert for a party functionary, in which, due to a shortage of performers, he was forced to play the role of a Roma woman in a Romani dance. In a bland music hall in front of an equally bland audience of Soviet officials, Lara performs an image of the Other, characteristic of the most conventional depictions of Russian Romanticist orientalism.

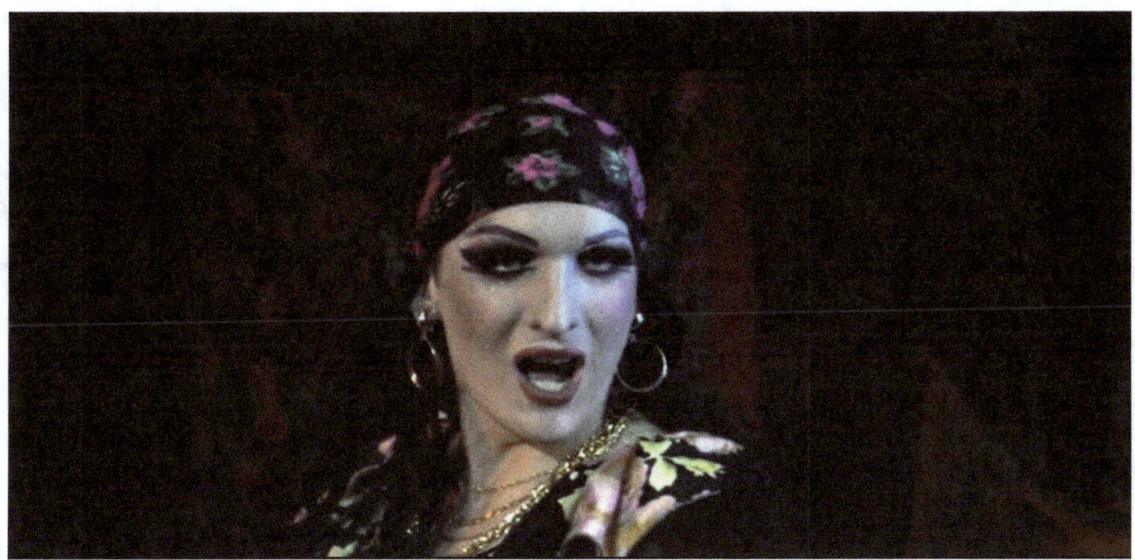

Fig. 9.2. Mikhailov, *Jolly Fellows*. Lara performing in her Roma drag.

She dances in a circle around a campfire to a song titled "Gypsy Love" (Tsyganskaia liubov'), and the intimacy she performs with her male dance partner recalls the Pushkin poem "The Gypsy," which imagines a brief but passionate love affair between the Byronic hero Aleko and the exotic gypsy Zemfira in a Bessarabian camp during Aleko's exile from (his notion of) civilization. Mikhailov grounds this queer narrative within the framework of a domestic variety of orientalism for the same reason that Iliumdzhi is essential to Otherness in *You I Love*: alterity in Russian cinema must rely on a logic of geographical, even national displacement in order to render itself legible to the audience.

The second personal narrative in *Jolly Fellows* speaks particularly to this same problem of geography. Liusia comes from a backwater village far from Moscow, so that the "problem" of her decision to become a drag queen, let alone come out as gay, is articulated explicitly through the lens of center and periphery. When Liusia decides she is tired of life in Moscow and wishes to return home, she is seen off by her friends at the train station in full drag, yet the train to the periphery is the stage for her meticulously undressing out of her persona, so that—in leaving the train bathroom, and Moscow in general— she henceforth passes as a regular man. On arriving home, Liusia learns that his family, in particular his mother, has fallen into a state

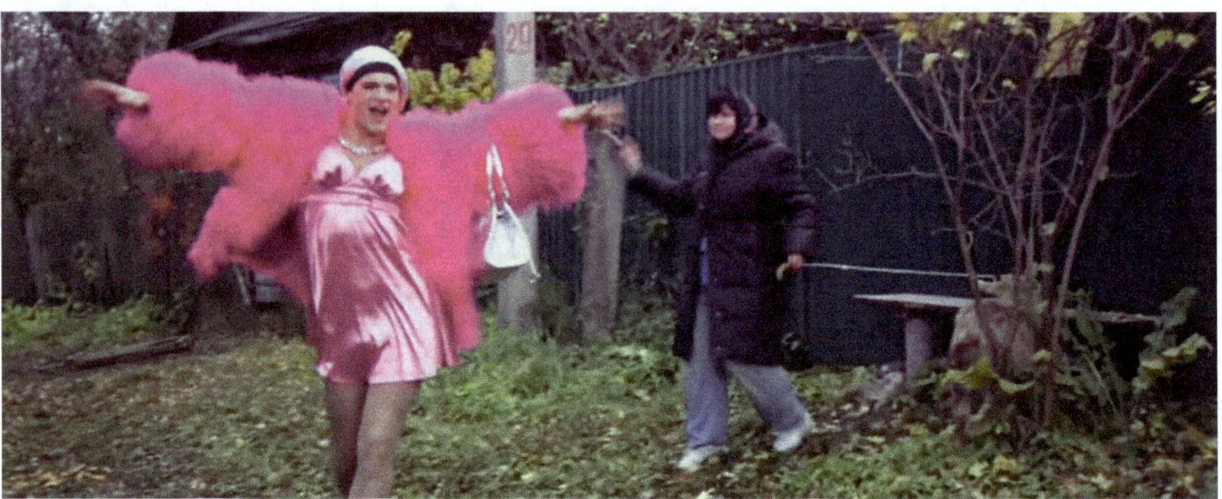

Fig. 9.3. Mikhailov, *Jolly Fellows*. Liusia dances through her hometown.

of total disarray and alcoholism since the death of his father. Visual cues—dilapidated fences and heaps of empty liquor bottles—inform the viewer that Liusia's family life in the country has quickly eroded. It is unclear whether the dysfunctional tragedy of the periphery should be considered the "cause" of Liusia's decision to don drag, as she has never previously revealed her decision and we are led to believe that the family's downfall has been recent. Nevertheless, drag represents her liberation from the confines of her rural familial village, as exemplified in the film's most iconic scene, where Liusia surprises her family in drag one morning and breaks free from their control over her by literally busting down the gate and strutting through the village to Gloria Gaynor's *I Will Survive*.

Granted, the trope of LGBT characters moving to metropolitan locales for the freedom to be their authentic selves is widespread and certainly transcends Russian specificity.[4] One cannot help but wonder, however, whether there is not some sort of exchange between queer

4 Scott Herring, for example, tackles this trope head-on in his *Another Country*, which theorizes queerness outside of a necessary link to cosmopolitanism.

alterity and peripheral alterity as they are presented in the film: what, for instance, separates the gypsy camp from the peripheral village? The former, with which Mikhailov identifies queer alterity, represents a form of subjective freedom away from social norms, whereas the latter, from which queer alterity must break free, threatens the queer Other with uniformity and despair. Where does Moscow, home of the whole drag troupe, find itself in this ideological deployment? Just as in *You I Love*, the film establishes "normative," metropolitan Russia as a median between two geographically defined depictions of alterity, both of which are essential to its very constitution. Indeed, just as Kalmykia and Gayropa are simultaneously integral to any definition of modern Russia and constituted as Russia's abject Others, so, too, are the gypsy camp and the peripheral village both deployed as inclusive and exclusive to the ideological image of Russia and difference.

Sergei Taramaev and Liubov' L'vova, *A Winter Journey* (2013)

These contradictions are addressed directly in Sergei Taramaev and Liubov' L'vova's *A Winter Journey* (Zimnii put'), the latest film to earn the designation of "queer Russian cinema" for its portrayal of same sex love. *A Winter Journey* has also garnered unfortunate historical significance—the film was denied a distribution license from the Ministry of Culture in August 2013, just months after President Putin's signing of the "anti-gay propaganda" bill. Although, after the initial ban, the film did receive distribution rights for audiences eighteen years or older, the politics surrounding the film prevented its wider viewing in theaters and at festivals across Russia, notably including Kinotavr. Despite this, the film received effusive praise, and several notable prizes, at those festivals that did manage to screen it.

The film follows an unusual romance between Erik, a classical vocalist at a conservatory who is preparing a performance of Franz Schubert's song cycle *Winterreise* (A Winter Journey) for a major competition, and Lekha, a homeless Moscow transplant who has just recently relocated from a stifling, unnamed provincial town. Erik is a near picture-perfect image of the disillusioned metropolitan, so profoundly saturated in Western culture that his life has paradoxically slowly drifted into a destructive self-caricature of alcoholism and immorality. Echoes of Silver Age decadence can be found in his portrayal and the film's general cinematography, with the dens where Erik and his gay friends hang out decorated in flowers and mirrors, elaborate bedding, and one friend running around in a mask parodying fin-desiècle *japonaiserie*. While too early for the Silver Age, the choice of Schubert as the film's through-composition is likewise not accidental—the composer's elevation of traditional German *Lieder* signified a larger Romantic fixation on the naïve, often articulated through the rift between the modern subject of culture and the innocent love object in nature. The simple if powerful love expressed in *Winterreise* is therefore paralleled by the fascination Erik feels for Lekha and his innate energy as a stereotypically "untamed" ruffian.

The juxtaposition of Erik and Lekha is arguably so successful in the film precisely because it recalls a laundry list of similar oppositions historically at work within Russian culture: the sentimental and the naïve, the metropole and the periphery, consciousness and spontaneity. These oppositions have been so firmly embedded into the rhetoric of modernity that it feels natural to watch a contemporary interpretation of same-sex romance take up its form. In the beginning of the film, Erik is chastised by his instructor for failing to take up the spirit of Schubert in his performances. He is instructed to follow three simple commands if he wishes to succeed: "sleep, walks, Schubert." Erik instead chooses to go on a drinking binge, the beginning of his descent into the thrilling chaos that surrounds Lekha's life in Moscow, and at the following rehearsal Erik's performance is hailed as a masterpiece. Erik's instructor incorrectly suggests asceticism as a method for understanding Schubert, whereas real understanding of the Romantic spirit of the songs lies in a search for the powerful truth of everyday passion.

Paradoxically, then, Lekha's influence becomes the means by which Erik can finally understand the message of Schubert's songs, yet the very same influence will also destroy him. Lekha is unhinged and prone to violent outbursts, and his behavior serves to alienate Erik from his career, his family, and his friends when the singer decides to join Lekha in his lawlessness. Erik's Orientalized "gaze into the abyss" to connect with Lekha will give him remarkable insight into the power of lived experience, yet it will ultimately sever his final connection to the "civilized" world. Although the film has ostensibly nothing to do with colonial entanglement, this romance recalls two of the most famous depictions of same-sex desire in Western Modernist literature, both of which imagine sexuality as operating along the same binary operation as the colonialist power differential. The first is again Gide's *The Immoralist*, wherein French scholar Michel chases an authentic sense of self throughout North Africa, finding it only among young Arab boys in the remote oases of the Maghreb. As Edward Said (*Culture and Imperlialism*, 192) described the novel, Michel "comes to terms with his eccentric sexuality by allowing it to strip him not only of his wife, Marceline, and career, but paradoxically of his will. . . . Gide explicitly connects Michel's self-knowledge with his experiences of Algeria, which are causally related to the death of his wife, his intellectual reorientation, and his final, rather pathetic bisexual forlornness."

The second reference, however, is perhaps more instructive. Unlike Gide's Michel, Erik already acknowledges his homosexuality, and the search for authenticity has little to do with a sexual self-discovery. Instead, the film invokes class conflict as a means of narrativizing sexual alterity. In E. M. Forster's *Maurice* (1913–14, first published in 1971), the eponymous wealthy protagonist falls in love with Alec, a working-class gamekeeper. While throughout the novel Maurice struggles to understand his sexuality within the conservative mores of early twentieth-century England, engaging with but ultimately renouncing the images of homosexuality he finds in university circles and high society, he eventually finds release through an escape into obscurity with Alec. The novel concludes with the two of them never to be seen again, so that reconciliation of their two worlds necessitates their complete disappearance. *A Winter Journey* at first suggests a similar fate for Erik and Lekha, as the two plan an escape from Erik's music career and Lekha's criminal record by running away to India. To finance the trip, they rob Erik's mentor, who himself offers a template for the type of educated, cosmopolitan gay man Erik could have become had he continued to develop his musical career. Their trip, as well as their romance, collapses at the last minute due to Lekha's hesitancy to commit to their relationship. After having kissed Erik, their first moment of realized intimacy on screen, Lekha panics, violently insults Erik, and escapes into the night, leaving Erik to drink himself to death on a snowy Moscow street.

A Winter Journey refuses reconciliation of these two worlds: while there remains the speculation that Lekha could, after all, experience same-sex desire toward Erik and therefore disrupt the binary opposition in which homosexuality is viewed as a product of cosmopolitan, Western decadence averse to working-class culture, in the final instant the film pulls away from this conclusion. Nevertheless, the film still leaves open the tense possibility of cross-contamination: it was, after all, Lekha who initiated the kiss, and the reasons for his disavowal of the romance at the last minute suggest some ideological impediment larger than himself at work. The film therefore, to return to Sedgwick's terminology, reenacts a conflict between minoritized and universalized visions of alterity, with queerness both decidedly estranged from working-class identity and nearly diffused across lines of difference. In this light, *A Winter Journey* mimics the culture clash of the traditional buddy film, where two personages are forced together despite dramatic cultural differences, seen more recently in Avdot'ia Smirnova's comedy *Kokoko* (2012). While *Kokoko* is not a queer film per se,[5] it stages the same oppositions as *A Winter Journey*, where social difference is nearly reconciled through a homosocial relationship—this time between Liza, a researcher at the Kunstkamera Museum in St. Petersburg, and Vika (Yana Troyanova), a rough but "authentic" provincial woman who lacks the ability to read social cues of bourgeois society. Like Erik, Liza is the perfect image of the metropolitan intelligentsia—her work as an ethnographer at the museum bleeds seamlessly into her fascination with Vika, whose Otherness becomes a project for Liza as she attempts to acclimate her new roommate to St. Petersburg educated culture. Unlike *A Winter Journey*, however, *Kokoko* attacks the assumptions of the metropole, with Liza quickly becoming an antagonistic figure when her helping Vika is revealed to be more out of self-interest than out of any genuine concern for her behalf. Lekha's final attack on Erik, in contrast, appears completely lacking in opportunism.

A comparison between the two films is intriguing: both represent (sexual, socio-economic) alterity as an opposition that simultaneously threatens to vanish and perpetually reignites into conflict. *A Winter Journey* denies resolution to the protagonists' romance, and Erik's binge drinking at the conclusion parallels his drinking in the film's opening scenes. Likewise, the homosocial romance between Vika and Liza in *Kokoko* begins at the police station, where in the opening of the film Liza vindicates Vika after the latter is falsely accused of stealing Liza's purse; it will end there as well, after their problematic friendship has finally eroded into an all-out fight, resulting in Vika's second imprisonment. Although Liza, as before, decides to bail out her friend, Vika screams to be left inside the jail instead of being brought back into contact with Liza, suggesting that perhaps Liza's civilizing project has done more harm than good in the long run. Lekha may similarly have benefited from Erik's nonintervention. Regardless, both films remind the viewer that several centuries of the Russian intelligentsia's fascination with the masses have done little to break the cycle of our engagement with this framework of alterity—its application to the discourse of sexuality is recent but not necessarily novel.

5 Both Smirnova and Anna Mikhalkova, the actress who plays Liza, have denied an overtly romantic affair between the two protagonists. The precise nature of their relationship remains up for interpretation, however, as critics have described it as "plus and minus combining in a boiling cauldron of friendly (and in the extreme romantic) bonds" and identified its continuity with a larger theme in Smirnova's work of "a love story between people speaking different languages, men and women, the upper and lower classes, the *intelligentsia* and the *narod*" (Maliukova, "Pogovorim").

It is therefore difficult not to imagine the preceding cinematic depictions of alterity as having at their base an understanding of Otherness rooted in imperial Russian experience. Ronald Grigor Suny (25) describes the relationship as: "a particular form of domination or control between two units set apart in a hierarchical, inequitable relationship, more precisely a composite state in which a metropole dominates a periphery to the disadvantage of the periphery. If peripheries are fully integrated into the metropole, as various medieval Russian principalities were into Muscovy, and treated as well or badly as the metropolitan provinces, then the relationship is not imperial." The fact that historically, as indicated above, alternative sexuality has been "territorialized" on screen speaks to this lingering influence. This does not, of course, deny the possibility of nuanced portrayals of queerness, yet the mediation of empire nevertheless dictates a spatial framing of Otherness, so that alterity as a universalized condition remains both tantalizingly possible and structurally illegible.

I would argue in conclusion, however, that two recent films elude this model and present more universal paradigms of sexual alterity: Aleksei Chupov and Natal'ia Merkulova's *Intimate Parts* (Intimnye mesta, 2013) and Ivan Tverdovskii's *Zoology* (Zoologiia, 2016). Neither film addresses queer sexuality directly through a same-sex relationship, yet they are stark depictions of Otherness as occupying a central place in the constitution of contemporary Russian identity on screen.

Aleksei Chupov and Natal'ia Merkulova, *Intimate Parts*

In *Intimate Parts*, Chupov and Merkulova attack the hypocrisy of what in the United States has come to be called "morality policing." The film is both an ode to a sexual revolution within a newly emergent Russian middle class and a critique of state-sanctioned efforts—some of which turned out to be simultaneous to the film's festival premiere—to repress sexual freedom. Roles such as Liudmila Petrovna (Iuliia Aug), chairwoman for the Committee on Morality, draw direct parallels to contemporary morality crusaders such as Elena Mizulina or Vitalii Milonov, although Chupov and Merkulova have been hesitant to admit an immediate inspiration for their depictions of authority (Larina). The film nevertheless critiques the notion that sexual promiscuity (homosexuality, polyamory, even a childless marriage) is somehow immune to the very mechanisms that enforce its prohibition. Although Liudmila seeks to prosecute an artist named Ivan (Iurii Kolokol'nikov) for the immorality of an erotic exhibition where he hangs massive photos of his subjects' genitals, she is simultaneously portrayed as sexually voracious, draining her vibrator completely of its batteries.

This relationship between social taboo and social norm, and the role transgression plays in the very constitution of these norms, speaks to the heart of earlier critiques of normativity in its postwar discussion of alterity in France and elsewhere. As Georges Bataille (*History of Eroticism*, 48) describes in his treatise on sexual transgression, "the object of the prohibition was first marked out for coveting by the prohibition itself: if the prohibition was essentially of a sexual nature, it must have drawn attention to the sexual value of its object (or rather, its erotic value)." In the film, the psychologist Boris (Timur Badalbeili) diagnoses each of the men he treats with "reward deficiency syndrome" (*sindrom defitsita udovletvorennosti*), characterized by a compulsive need to amplify one's stimulation due to a decreased feeling of pleasure. This deficiency manifests itself in the film through two clusters: first, Aleksei's (Nikita Tarasov) unhappy marriage and his fetishistic infatuation with a mentally disabled street vendor (Anastasiia Kholodniakova); second, Eve (Ekaterina Shchlegova) and Sergei's (Aleksei Chupov) need to seek out a third romantic partner, a sexual adventurousness that looms over their inability to conceive.

To return to our earlier proposed model, *Intimate Parts* does not therefore minoritize sexual difference but rather places it at the heart of the formation of normative Russian identity. Unlike, for example, the relationship triangle among Timofei, Iliumdzhi, and Vera in *You I Love*, the threesome of Eve, Sergei, and—as the plot develops—a male circus performer (Pavel Artem'ev) in the film is neither geopolitically displaced nor needlessly exoticized, but rather essential to understanding the sexual and moral problems facing contemporary Russia: familial crises, birth rates, and romantic dissatisfaction. Indeed, it is these very "problems," expressed in sexual difference, that sustain our understanding of Russian society in its entirety.

Ivan Tverdovskii, *Zoology*

Tverdovskii's *Zoology* does not possess the same breadth of subject matter as *Intimate Parts*, yet its governing message on difference bears similarities to the earlier film. The film tells the story of Natasha (Natal'ia Pavlenkova), a lonely middle-aged woman whose only solace lies in interacting with the animals at the zoo where she works. Lacking social and romantic success, one day Natasha wakes up with a tail-like appendage and begins to come into herself as a person, including through a burgeoning romance with her radiologist, Petia (Dmitrii Groshev). Simultaneously Kafkaesque and Gogolian, *Zoology* parodies these authors' grotesque depictions of the inherent estrangement of modern life. Natasha passes through each societal apparatus (the hospital, the church), which in turn—as Althusser would frame it—ideologically "hails or interpellates concrete individuals as concrete subjects" ("Ideology," 47): that is, transforms the individual into a subject capable of normative state control. Yet despite this gauntlet, run through the ruling ideology, Natasha initially finds her tail not to be some monstrous deviation from the norm but rather a source of self-confidence and even pride. It is only in the final moments of the film, when she realizes that Petia's attraction to her has only been the result of his fetishizing of her new appendage, that Natasha feels truly estranged and othered by her difference. This leads her to amputate the tail. The film leaves the viewer uncertain not only about her survival but even whether she has gone through with the decision.

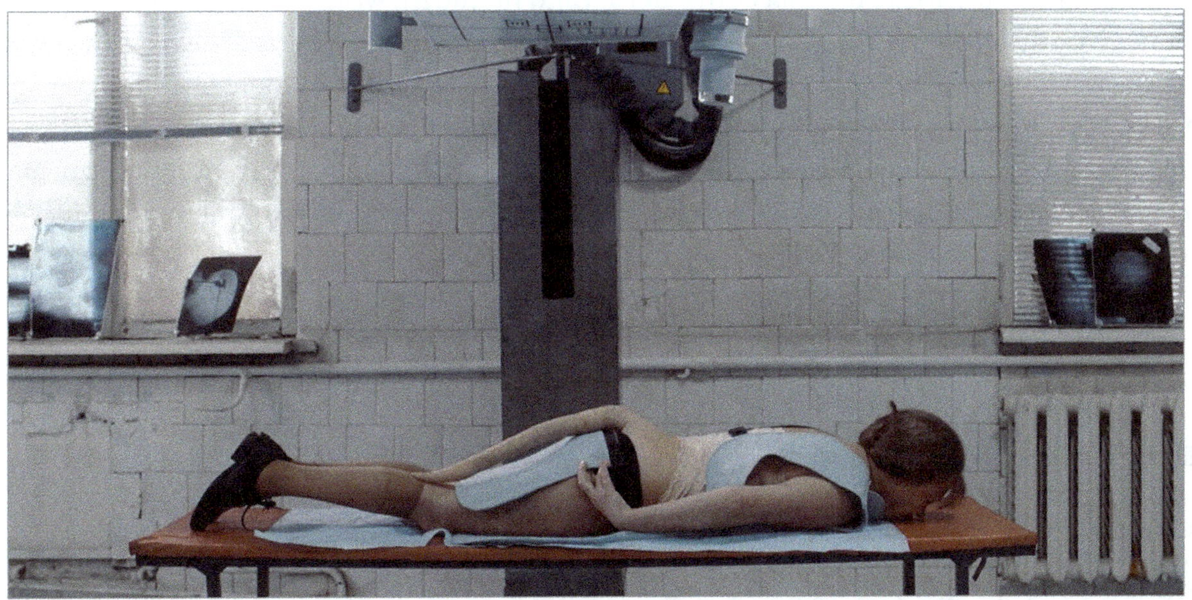

Fig. 9.4. Tverdovskii, *Zoology*. Examining Natasha and her appendage.

Zoology succeeds in presenting Otherness as universal in its absurdity—the most mundane of us could one day wake up with a monstrous deformity, yet perhaps our happiness will emerge as we have taken joy in our "deformities" instead of struggling to adhere to social norms. Although this chapter has almost exclusively discussed the question of sexual alterity, it should be mentioned that this paradigm of difference potentially addresses other identities: Tverdovskii's metaphorical transmogrification could easily extend into his treatment of dis/ability in his *Corrections Class* (Klass korrektsii, 2014).

Regardless of the axis of identity, the allegory of the freak tail in *Zoology* recalls the double bind of Otherness and visibility. It is indeed a difficult question where the boundary lies between, on the one hand, visibility as an expression of the celebration of difference and, on the other, visibility as a Foucauldian expression of the spectator's power in the pursuit of knowledge. Natasha's journey toward acceptance of her new appendage reiterates the former, whereas Petia's objectification of it resonates with the latter. Are we, as viewers, not also complicit in Petia's perverse pleasure at the sight of the tail? Must a love story between a gay Kalmyk and a Russian always be unethically ethnographic?

It is surely no coincidence that both Natasha and Iliumdzhi work at zoos in their respective films, given that their Otherness has reduced them to dehumanized objects of display, including by us as viewers. Any surmounting of the impasse in a representation of difference will necessitate grappling with the various legacies of diversity operating in contemporary Russia. Unsurprisingly, these complicated questions are implicit in contemporary Russian cinema's own articulation of alterity and will undoubtedly shape the discourse of identity politics on screen in the next several years.

Filmography

Chupov, Aleksei, and Natal'ia Merkulova, dirs. *Intimate Parts* (Intimnye mesta, 2013).
L'vova, Liubov', and Sergei Taramaev, dirs. *A Winter Journey* (Zimnii put', 2013).
Mikhailov, Feliks, dir. *Jolly Fellows* (Vesel'chaki, 2009).
Pavlov, Iurii, dir. *The Creation of Adam* (Sotvorenie Adama, 1993).
Smirnova, Avdot'ia, dir. *Kokoko* (2012).
Stolpovskaia, Ol'ga, and Dmitrii Troitskii, dirs. *You I Love* (Ia liubliu tebia, 2004).
Tverdovskii, Ivan, dir. *Corrections Class* (Klass korrektsii, 2014).
———. *Zoology* (Zoologiia, 2016).

Part Four

THE IDEOLOGICAL OCCULT

Framing Essay

Petre Petrov

A dead space station is tumbling on a low orbit above the Earth. There is no crew on board; the station has been piloted remotely for some time. An electrical malfunction has now disabled all its systems; the interior is an icy high-tech cave. No longer controlled by its terrestrial stewards, the station is just a human-made meteorite menacing the world with disaster. Two astronauts are sent on an apparently suicidal mission: to take control of the gigantic dead thing and bring it back to life. In an act of high-stakes levitational coitus, their spaceship couples with the station's wildly gyrating corpus. As power is restored, the ice inside melts (the water has to be mopped off with rags made from the previous crew's uniforms). A last-minute tragedy is averted through a do-it-yourself exercise in open space: the rescue mission's commander, hammer in hand, does battle with a rugged, Soviet-made metal fixture; he succeeds in knocking it off just before the oxygen supply runs out, freeing up the sensor that controls the station's solar batteries.

This is the narrative kernel of Klim Shipenko's *Salyut-7*, a 2017 cinematic recreation of an actual drama that played out in the Soviet space program during 1985. Of a high-production gloss but low intellectual and artistic substance, the film is perhaps most successful as an allegory for cultural politics in contemporary Russia. There a rescue operation has been under way for nearly two decades now, its goal to reestablish contact with a platform once evacuated, defunct, and feared lost. The platform in question is, of course, that of empire (the Soviet conquest of space, for which *Salyut-7* served as a hub, provides a near-literal rendition). Set adrift by the fall of the Soviet Union, the imperial idea had been largely frozen during the 1990s, a time of social chaos, economic collapse, and numerous geopolitical retreats. If one wished to complete the allegorical picture, one could see the mission control center of Shipenko's film as a figuration of Putin's Kremlin, and the cosmonauts tasked with the dangerous undertaking as stand-ins for those cultural agents of today brave and capable enough to thaw out and restart the ideological machinery of empire. In this sense, it is a felicitous fact that the troubled mother ship bore the name *Soyuz* (Union); for the most hazardous aspect of the reclamation job is certainly that of ideologically coupling the Russia of today to the ambiguous legacy of the Soviet Union.

Russian cinema has played its part in this cultural adventure. The three chapters constituting the current section of the volume shed light on some of the deeds involved. They analyze some of the ways in which big- and small-screen film productions of the Putin era have performed state-conscious ideological work. The section's title, "The Ideological Occult," replays in a more scholarly register that same theme of regaining contact with a lost dimension, of reestablishing control over an unresponsive object. The reference is to Peter Brooks's pathbreaking study of the "melodramatic imagination" and its pivotal concept of the "moral occult." Rather than tracing factographically the beginnings of melodrama, Brooks has constructed an ideal genesis: the imagination constitutive of the genre is to be understood as a reaction to the crumbling of religious authority and the moral order that authority had sanctioned. As the advance of modernity strips the world of its mythic trappings, it also gives rise to anxiety; the void triggers desire for the very thing that has been taken away. The moral occult is what comes to fill the void. It proclaims and dramatizes the idea that beneath the disenchanted surfaces of the mundane, under the rubble of decommissioned religious creeds, the forces of good and evil continue their eternal contest. "The moral occult is not a metaphysical system; it is rather the repository of the fragmentary and desacralized remnants of sacred myth" (Brooks, 5).

The phrase "ideological occult" gestures toward an analogous dynamic in Russian culture of the post-Soviet period. The void this culture confronts is the one left after the socialist state and its official ideology crashed out from the stage of history. As was the case in the aftermath of the French Revolution—the historical focus of Brooks's theorization—the moment of rebellious freedom and forward-looking exhilaration quickly gave way to the doldrums of conservative melancholy. (These are not necessarily the discrete phases of a temporal succession; the two impulses can, and do, coexist in the same historical moment, and even in the same individual.) It is debatable whether the Putin regime possesses anything worth calling "ideology," that is, a coherent system of political notions that are not just espoused but also systematically implemented. What is beyond debate, however, is that it acts in response to an acutely felt need for order, including ideological order. In a most general sense, the ideological occult *à la russe* can be taken to mean the need to perceive, behind the *seeming* homogenization of the post-cold-war world picture, an ever-same pattern of essential forces, an ongoing geopolitical *agon*, in which Russia has always been destined to play a cardinal part. If the genre home of the moral occult is melodrama, that of the ideological occult is conspiracy theory, arguably the most fecund form of cultural production in today's Russia.

Just as the moral occult is not a metaphysical system, its terminological cousin should not be taken as referring to an actual belief system or a *Weltanschauung.* It too is fragmentary, made up of scraps, traces, echoes. The three chapters that follow collect and examine such fragments across a varied lot of contemporary films: patriotic historical dramas, sci-fi thrillers, "emergency" films, feel-good holiday movies. The majority are state-sponsored blockbusters, financed through the Cinema Fund or the main TV channels. Most of them reimagine Soviet-era realities, characters, or conventions. All of them attempt to capture the motile affects of an imperial past in order to create what was once sloganized as "cinema for the millions." The ideological messages one can read in these films are often hung uncertainly between the pathos of the meaningful and the knowing opportunism of a PR stunt. The images of the heroic that this cinema proffers hang uncertainly between popular Western and Soviet prototypes, between conscious mythmaking and unconscious *lubok.* The advanced technologies of Hollywood storytelling and cinematography, marketing campaigns, and franchising coexist uneasily with crude, make-do efforts of reheating the Russian Idea. The improvised solutions of Shipenko's rescue mission—rags and hammer—come to mind.

10. Past, Present, and Posthumous Fathers: Cinepaternity Reloaded

Theodora Trimble

Those familiar with Russo-Soviet filmmaking will be no strangers to discussions surrounding the evolving relationship between cinema, the state, and what has come to be called cinepaternity (Goscilo and Hashamova). Alexander Prokhorov ("Myth") and Seth Graham ("Models"), for example, trace Soviet cinema's preoccupation with father figures in its efforts to reshape images of the Soviet family from High Stalinism to the Thaw and Stagnation. Such interests, as they note, are reflective of extensive processes beyond the thematics of the screen, within the film industry, and in culture more broadly. As Graham (72–73) argues,

> The pre-perestroika cinematic family . . . when broken, was almost invariably portrayed as such owing to a clearly defined historical process or event, most commonly the Great Fatherland War or the Russian civil war. Absent fathers were (so to speak) ever-present in Soviet war films and revolutionary-historical films, for reasons that are far from mysterious. Moreover, the familial ruptures . . . were typically depicted so they could then be repaired by the establishment of new family units . . . or alleviated by the formation of alternative communities . . . [S]uch narrative arcs demonstrated both the possibility of overcoming obstacles via adherence to Soviet values and the historically determined progression from strictly biological to other types of intimate collectives.

Keeping such studies in mind, this chapter considers Russian filmmaking's stake in the patrimonial structure and what it reveals at this cultural moment. Who are contemporary cinema's symbolic fathers?

Whereas conversations around this question have typically focused on the loss, replacement, and absence of fathers—celluloid, digital, or symbolic—this chapter instead proposes that cinepaternity is, in one way or another, robustly present on the contemporary Russian screen. Cinema's fixation on paternity often demands a relationship between popular culture and politics: that is, charismatic celebrity figures—political, historical, and fictional—of whose prominence we are reminded through an event or crisis that threatens the stability of the ideological apparatus. In the case of recent Russian films, the event almost always signifies the apprehension around the fall of the Soviet Union and thus, through a set of cinematic choices, warrants the suffusion of the celebrity father trope on screen.

Since 2011—that is, after Putin's announcement that he would seek a third, now six-year term, as president—Russian cinema has engaged in the construction of a new model of cinepaternity. In this spirit, the film industry engaged in the production of big-budget pictures that combine commercial appeal and Hollywood-style stardom with an ideological agenda of using the father-son relationship as a cypher for the reinvigorated and expanding Russian state. In this chapter, I focus on two clusters of films that broke box-office records and are particularly symbolic in the reenactment of a neo-Soviet brand of this new cinepaternity. The first cycle consists of sports films about Soviet-era epic victories at world sports events. The star athletes and their mentors and coaches are male, the spirit is patriotic, and anti-Americanism is the default sentiment. The second cycle consists of disaster films, in which male characters save the community from a catastrophe. Following Nancy Condee ("Cold Snap"), I call this second type of films "the emergency film," rather than simply the Hollywood-style disaster film. Condee contends that these emergency films invoke natural and technological disasters in order to guide the viewer to the situation where there is seemingly only one solution—to obey the orders of state authority. At the center of the emergency film is "the principle of exceptional compliance—obeying urgent orders, trusting the emergency crew, preserving the hierarchy."

Both film cycles find the usable past and inspiration for their narratives in the late socialist Cold War era. Most of these films link Russia's present with the glorious Soviet past in order to reinforce historical continuity with patriarchal lineage, thus obfuscating the radical break between the Soviet Union and post-Soviet Russia, driven by market capitalism. Several of these big-budget pictures are produced by Nikita Mikhalkov's Studio TriTe, directed by Nikolai Lebedev, and/or sponsored by the federal television Channel Russia-1 (Rossiia). As in the late Stalinist era, the big-budget films of the mature Putin period claim to be loosely based on true events, and the promotional campaigns often create media events around the celebrations of these past achievements. As Condee ("Cold Snap") observes, "In these recent . . . Russian films, the injunction to consent is particularly compelling because . . . the plot is based on real events: the first 1965 spacewalk; a 1972 Soviet Olympics victory; a 1985 Soviet space emergency. . . . Reassuringly, it often involves a historical triumph over the United States."

I argue that in both sports and emergency films the male protagonist played by a film star is designed to become a role model for moviegoers only after the protagonist himself is remolded by the imperative to obey the state. My case studies examine two films that each employ a major Russian film star (and heartthrob), Danila Kozlovskii, in the roles of father figures in the making, who are, in their own ways, part of the larger story of contemporary patrimony in Russian cinema. I first discuss Lebedev's *Legend No. 17* (Legenda No. 17, 2013), in which Kozlovskii plays the Soviet hockey star Valerii Kharlamov. Next, I analyze Lebedev's film, *Flight Crew* (Ekipazh, 2016), in which Kozlovskii plays a Russian pilot, another Soviet-era role model resurrected by the contemporary Russian media industry.

* * *

For Soviet audiences, Olympic stars belonged to one of the highest orders of public figures and role models. One may reason, then, that Soviet society had leading, robust athletes (and implicitly the fittest population) in the world—who also served as a point of pride for Soviet citizens. Unlike in the West, where commercial sport agents were responsible for supporting the athlete's image and negotiating salaries, in the Soviet case, it was the state that offered perks for highly desired and successful athletes. The state came to view top athletes able to successfully compete at international events as a weapon in the ideological war with the West or—as Tony Shaw and Denise Youngblood (184) have described it—"Soviet sport as Cold War proxy."[1]

The Soviet sport movement was extraordinarily successful in its Olympic ventures and the importance of its hockey team to state pride cannot be overstated.[2] The Soviet team was coached for many years by Anatolii Tarasov, the "Father of Russian Hockey," who was largely

1 Shaw and Youngblood note that Soviet sports films favored team sports, such as soccer or ice hockey, because they focused on the spirit of collectivism into which talented but spontaneous individual had to be integrated. A common plotline in such films is the conflict between the collective and a rogue team member who fancies himself a star. In this respect, the post-Soviet version of sports films, such as *Legend No. 17*, which glamorizes individual hockey stars such as Kharlamov, is a peculiar and eclectic narrative that attempts to reconcile residual Soviet collectivism with the star vehicle. The outcome ends up being somewhat confusing ideologically.

2 The group flourished in World Cup competitions, national championships, and world championships, but the team's victories at the Olympics made USSR hockey a force to be respected in the global athletics sphere. The team won its first Olympic gold medal at the 1956 Games in Cortina d'Ampezzo, Italy, earned its second gold in 1964 in Innsbruck, and continued to be victorious until 1980, when they were defeated by the US team in Lake Placid.

responsible for creating the team from scratch. His impact on the prestige of the sport was transformative—and crucial—in the development of Soviet sport tradition after the end of the Second World War.[3] The real Valerii Kharlamov was Tarasov's prodigy and one of the top players for CSKA Moscow (Tsentral'nyi sportivnyi klub armii) from 1967 to 1981, until Kharlamov died in a car accident at a tragically young age. Kharlamov was an unstoppable, active player at the time of his death, at the peak of his career and Soviet hockey. During his time on the team, Kharlamov's accomplishments included eight gold medals in eleven world championships, eleven out of fourteen national championships, and two gold medals at the Olympic Games.

Such accomplishments speak not only to Kharlamov's talent but to the weight of his stardom in the international sports arena, as well as to his symbolic power in representing the superiority of the Soviet way of life over that of the West. After the 1972 Olympics, where Kharlamov led the Soviet team to victory, the National Hockey League (NHL) had two teams propose $1 million offers for Kharlamov, who was only twenty-four years old.[4] Kharlamov's fame, both in the Soviet Union and Canada, canonized his reputation as one of the greatest Soviet athletes of all time, a hero at home and a global celebrity. Although he became one of the most coveted athletes by teams abroad, Kharlamov never defected.[5] His posthumous stardom, however, has taken on new meanings since the collapse of the Soviet state.

3 Robert Edelman writes: "Perhaps [Tarasov's] greatest gift was an ability to turn disadvantages into advantages. He overcame the Soviets' ignorance of traditional tactics by developing an entirely new style of play. Similarly, he was able to surmount the lack of training facilities by inventing a wide variety of cross-training routines. Finally, he was able to articulate his ideas in written form so that the first generation of Soviet coaches, players, and fans could apply them relatively quickly throughout the entire country" (117).

4 Considering that the league's top players were earning only $12,000–15,000 per season, the offer was quite staggering. Only one player, Bobby Hull, had been offered the kind of money that was proposed for Kharlamov and he was nearly ten years older than the Soviet athlete, whose only experience playing against NHL players was during the eight-game Summit Series, also in 1972, in which the Soviet national team shocked the Canadians with their competitive edge. "Forced to reassess the quality of Soviet players, NHL executives went from dismissing them to offering unbelievable sums for one: at the same time as Toronto's owner said he would pay $1,000,000 for Kharlamov, he professed that he could not 'afford to pay' his incumbent star $150,000" (Soares 35–36).

5 Kharlamov lived in the era during which signing an individual contract with a Western ice hockey club was not an option for a Soviet athlete. This opportunity appeared only during Gorbachev's perestroika in the late 1980s.

Couched in Russian national interests and in those of Russia's reputation on the international stage, the Sochi Winter Olympics kindled nostalgia for the victorious years of the Soviet Olympic teams, while simultaneously creating a space for a sense of reenergized national pride. The preparations for the Games also served as the inspiration for staging such sentiment in cinema and reintroducing the Soviet athlete as the ideal contemporary role model. If Olympic athletes were the brightest stars of the former Soviet state, then cinema was the ideal venue to recollect those memories, one in which successful stars could take on new significance in accordance with the anticipated Olympics and its attendant political interests.

Soviet athletes became protagonists of state-sponsored blockbusters, a hybrid between Hollywood cultural practices and familiar narratives of state nationalism. Kharlamov was ideal for this role because he represented a perfect usable past—Soviet triumph during the Cold War—and was a recognizable international celebrity. In his work on Russian blockbusters and the state, Stephen Norris (*Blockbuster History*) traces the recent Russian blockbuster as work that conveys a national spirit or message through popular cinema, an invocation of the Russian government's central role in leading the nation, and contemporary state nationalism. Norris wrote his seminal monograph about Putin's blockbusters of the 2000s when the regime had just started cutting its teeth on restaging the glorious Russian and Soviet imperial pasts. By Putin's third presidential term, blockbusters themed around sports, maritime, aviation, and space exploration became cyphers for the brewing rivalry with the West. The connections, Norris argues, are "far from coincidental," as the process of recent Russian cinema in many ways is akin to "what Vladimir Putin discovered to be useful in his presidential administration: patriotism and the past sell" (*Blockbuster History*, 5).[6] This cultural platform of combining patriotism and the past has been realized most vividly in recent cinema through Soviet athletes who were the admired stars of international sport culture, its political stakes, and its Olympic objectives.

Although sports films were certainly not the main genre of Soviet cinema, they were an ideal format for performing the anxieties of the Cold War: the "us" vs. "them," or Soviet citizens

6 "Historical blockbusters generated widespread discussions about patriotism and belonging in the new Russia. Filmmakers, producers, screenwriters, composers, and other people involved in the cinema industry all attempted to articulate their vision of a 'patriotic' film. They did so by traveling to the past" (Norris, *Blockbuster History*, 16).

vs. the West. While other genres of late Soviet cinema sought to untangle more complex, deep-seated cultural questions, the sports film, as Shaw and Youngblood have written, were "'socialist realist' in style and content." As they argue, "The master plot of such films is that of an inspirational coach who takes a talented but immature athlete (usually a young man) and teaches him the Soviet values of hard work and discipline. The young man often has been 'discovered' by talent scouts on a collective farm or elsewhere in the provinces and is brought to the 'center' (Moscow or Leningrad) to train. . . . The plot focuses on character-building as much as on winning, but victory is almost always the result, the implicit message being that the superiority of Soviet values leads to sporting triumph" (180).

In view of the centrality of the paternity trope for *Legend No.17*, its major narrative line links Tarasov, the tough but fair coach and a true father figure, and Kharlamov—his best disciple. To foreground the importance of the father-son connection, Lebedev introduces false father figures who temporarily separate the star athlete from his true mentor. Tarasov's main antagonist is the party functionary, Balashov, who supervises ice hockey on behalf of the Communist Party. He tries to manipulate Kharlamov into betraying Tarasov and signing a complaint against him. Moreover, Balashov demands that Kharlamov's Red Army Club throw the game to please Leonid Brezhnev, the weak and aging leader, who allegedly roots for the other team. Eventually, Balashov fires Tarasov, thus depriving the Soviet team of its father figure before it goes to Canada to face the brutal enemy. Appropriately, the film depicts Canadians as giant and ape-like hockey players. But the seeds of robust cinepaternity have been planted. During the decisive game, through masterful cross-cutting Lebedev establishes an almost supernatural connection between Tarasov in Moscow and his team in Canada. Drawing movements on the ground with a stick in Moscow, the true father orchestrates the movements of the Soviet players on the ice rink across the ocean and leads Kharlamov and his dream team to victory.

Legend No. 17 was the first successful example of resuscitating this genre memory, the goal of which is to foster the Cold War spirit of ideological competition. The film reintroduces the Cold War enemy into the present day and reminds us of the platform of superiority of Soviet values through sport. The sports film, moreover, realized even more success as a contemporary genre in *Going Vertical* (Dvizhenie vverkh, 2017) and in *Lev Iashin, the Dream Goalkeeper* (Lev Iashin: Vratar' moei mechty, 2019). The former, directed by Anton Megerdichev, turns to the 1972 Olympics, guiding the viewer through a reimagination of the Soviet victory over the United States in basketball. Megerdichev's blockbuster became the highest-grossing Russian film of all time on its release. As in *Legend*, Megerdichev's film presents us with the mentor-apprentice relationship, another celebration of the victorious past and a gesture toward the familiar socialist realist template. In Vasilii Chiginskii's *Lev Iashin*, we again see the revival of the sports drama, this time through soccer and another biopic about the most famous Soviet soccer player, Lev Iashin.[7] As in case of the Kharlamov biopic, the biopic about Iashin is connected with the persona of the Russian president. Indeed, according to *Gazeta.ru*, Putin gave the producers the idea of making a film about the legendary Russian goalkeeper (Kulinicheva).

Lebedev, who succeeded in initiating the revival of the sports film, owes much of his reputation and good fortune to his other mentor in the industry—the head of Mos'film Studio and an ardent supporter of Russia's president, Karen Shakhnazarov. Shakhnazarov chose Lebedev to direct the 2001 war film *Star*, as a young director who at the time showed promise in delivering a popular hit that would erase any confusion about the existence of disputed cultural narratives dealing with the Second World War. *Star* was widely celebrated by Russian viewers, and as Norris ("Guiding Stars," 164) notes, spawned a chain of successful films that readdressed the war and its legacy.[8]

Not surprisingly, Lebedev has been widely celebrated for his films and has received much public praise from Putin himself. The director's work has been recognized through numerous awards at film festivals and nominated for an array of accolades, on top of the fact that *Star* and *Legend*, two at first seemingly different films, both received the State Prize of the Russian Federation. His *Flight Crew*, moreover, was the highest-grossing film at the Russian box office in 2016.

With respect to *Legend*, in its efforts to provide a reconstruction of Kharlamov's celebrity text, it is fruitful to recall the image of the star described by Richard Dyer: "From the perspective of ideology, analyses of stars—as images existing in films and other media texts—stress their structured polysemy, that is, the finite multiplicity of meanings and affects they embody and the attempt to so structure them that some meanings and affects are foregrounded and others are masked or displaced" (3). In extending Dyer's model to Kharlamov's present-day celebrity

7 Notably, one of the most cherished Soviet sports films was also about soccer: Semen Timoshenko's *The Reserve Player* (Zapasnoi igrok, 1954), a musical comedy cautioning the Soviet viewer against the perils of individualism.

8 Some reviews, moreover, even "labelled Lebedev's film 'guiding star' because of Shakhnazarov's eager use of state funds to make his product, his unabashed attempt to shape remembrance of the Great Patriotic War, and Vladimir Putin's concurrent uses of the war to build patriotism" (Norris, "Guiding Stars," 164).

in the film, his "star text" suggests the component parts of political culture in today's Russia as reflected in cinema and other media: national pride, the merging of the celebrity image with "fatherhood," and Putin's leadership as head of state.

Kharlamov's posthumous image has been the face of a series of cultural events circuitously linked to the Russian-hosted Games. But three additional issues are worthy of brief mention here. First, Kharlamov's biopic, *Legend No. 17*, enjoyed overwhelming popularity in Russia and was screened recurrently on Russian television. Second, Kharlamov was publicly acknowledged as a national hero by President Putin, who celebrated the athlete's birthday and endorsed the film with great enthusiasm. Third, Putin carried out a televised performance at a hockey gala on his own birthday in 2015, during which he appeared to be performing the hockey star's celebrity identity. Despite the fact that these events occurred both before and after the Olympics, the megaproject of the Sochi Winter Games gave the state an opportunity to initiate and continue to spark a reawakening of Kharlamov's popularity in cinema for the purposes of promoting Russian pride and cult of the leader in popular culture. The state's resurrection of Kharlamov's star text, as well as its desire to replot that narrative according to contemporary political and national interests, reflects one of cinema's most obvious ventures: the investment in cultural figures and celebrities as potential symbolic fathers. It suggests the presence of a growing patrimonial network: if previous cinematic "eras" have insisted that cinepaternity is teleological, then cinema in Putin's Russia reimagines this paternal lineage as more of an eternal cycle, one that offers the head of state as the sire of directors, actors, and posthumous stars as a way to synthesize the Soviet era with the present.

Produced by Nikita Mikhalkov's TriTe—Mikhalkov himself being an ardent Putin supporter—TV Channel Russia-1, and the Federal Cinema Fund, *Legend*, like Lebedev's other films, features a star-studded cast of the most popular actors in contemporary Russia. Kozlovskii, the actor selected for the lead role of Kharlamov, also works in the United States.[9] Kozlovskii, who prepared for months on the ice with staff trainers at his disposal in order to play the "dream role" of Kharlamov, has been subtly critical of the merging of the celebrity with the political in Russia (Grachev).[10] As a biopic, the film drew skepticism from scholars and

9 Kozlovskii starred in Mark Waters's *Vampire Academy* (2014).

10 Kozlovskii comments: "Athletes today do not become national heroes, at least not to the extent that they did in Soviet times. Times have changed, and sports too. Now professional sport is big business, with its own rigid laws, its own goals. It is moving farther and farther away from the true laws and values of sports and I, for one,

film critics, who took issue with *Legend*'s overtly jingoist overtones as a work that is simply part of Putin's political machine. Elena Stishova ("Adrenalin") noted, "The downside of the success of *Legend No. 17* has already appeared—President Putin personally ordered a biopic about Lev Iashin, also a legendary athlete. Perhaps we will have a string of pictures about the aces of Soviet sport. . . . So what is the result? That our future is our cursed past."

Others have criticized the film for its eagerness to invent biographical details about Kharlamov's life.[11] On the one hand, the scriptwriters invent conflicts that never existed; on the other, they varnish the Soviet past, creating an idealized and ultimately quite conflict-free Soviet chronotope for the generation that lacks firsthand experience of living under socialism. Sergey Dobrynin's review of the film, for example, asserts that "the Putinist attitude toward the Soviet Union is highly ambivalent—it tries to wed communist nostalgia for the glorious imperial past with a nominally anti-communist rhetoric." The reviewer notes that the makers of *Legend* put together a theme park of late Soviet life and that it cares about being attractive for the visitors more than about conveying any sense of authenticity.

But is this a matter of falsehood perpetuated by the Russian state or a studio using government money? Or —a more familiar sin—a matter of the biopic as a genre that is deeply indebted to its Hollywood traditions? Dennis Bingham writes: "Private behaviors and actions and public events as they might have been in the person's time are formed together and interpreted dramatically. . . . The genre's charge, which dates back to its salad days in the Hollywood studio era, is to enter the biographical subject into the pantheon of cultural mythology, one way or another, and to show why he or she belongs there" (10).[12]

am losing interest in it. Previously, for example, I could call myself a soccer fan, if not an avid one, and now—no, it's boring. When athletes are in politics, seriously considering their knowledge enough to make important state decisions—it's funny and sad" (Grachev).

11 Sergey Dobrynin writes: "A deal is struck between Soviet sports authorities and the NHL on having a 'super series' between Canada and the USSR. (In fact, no one called it a 'super series' in 1972—not in the Soviet Union—but the linguistic anachronisms abound in this film; modern-day slang is especially jarring.) Before that event, however, the Soviet team plays at the 1972 Winter Olympics in Sapporo, triumphantly, and upon return, is forced to participate in a rigged game with Spartak. The players are supposed to lose because, they are told, Leonid Brezhnev, who attends the game, is a Spartak fan. There never was such a game. Brezhnev was a fan of CSKA (Kharlamov's team), not Spartak. Tarasov quit the national team leadership in 1972 and would be fired from CSKA in 1975, for different reasons. Kharlamov would get in his first (non-fatal) car crash in 1976, and it will not be politically or emotionally related."

12 George Custen argues: "Given all the possible variables—star casting and available personnel, censorship, the

Yet this false set of choices—conniving Russian statecraft, Hollywood's honored legacy—is not a simple set of decisions. After all, Bingham's analysis of the biopic suggests that the genre's importance to the building of a celebrity mythology lies precisely in its potential for crafting national and political platforms. The notion that the biopic offers a frame of reference for celebrity influence, with a strong emphasis on the subject's personality, therefore, invites a closer look at the rhetoric that Russia's president uses in his celebration of Kharlamov's achievements and his public endorsements of Lebedev's film.

On the eve of the 2013 Youth World Hockey championships, Putin himself appeared in a televised presentation of Lebedev's film to the Russian team. Prior to the screening, he greeted the young players with a brief introduction:

> Tomorrow our national youth team begins the world hockey championships, and we felt that on this day it would be appropriate to present the new film by our filmmakers, a film made about our outstanding hockey player. But probably not everyone knows the most important thing that made him the way he was is his character, because the doctors gave him as a child quite a tough diagnosis—heart disease. And not only did he deal with it, but he became an outstanding player, and not only on our team but in global hockey. ("Putin")

In this speech, the president underscores three components of Kharlamov's star image as he wishes to craft it in contemporary Russia. First, he refers to Kharlamov as "ours," dissolving the divide between the current youth who were not alive during the time that Kharlamov played and former generations of Soviet athletes. His speech thus suggests a multigenerational Russian family—Kharlamov as an admired precursor and Putin himself as the paternal custodian of his new image. Second, the president highlights that what made the star outstanding is not his talent but, rather, his character. That character is evident in the fact that Kharlamov, as the

power of some producer's point of view, legal considerations—that can influence the shape of a life on film, how do these films situate themselves as historical narratives? . . . The title . . . serves the function of avowing that the film that follows is true. This convention of the biopic, the introductory assertion of the truth, serves as a reminder of a fact so obvious that we might overlook it: that most films made in Hollywood are not supposed to be taken as true. This use of the title sets up one of the genre's distinctive qualities, a claim to truth. The title also sets up the moment of a life when we can witness the birth of a particular talent—seldom the character's literal birth . . . It seemingly permits the viewer to be present at the creation, witnessing the birth or the first display of the traits that will make the older version of the biographee famous" (51).

president asserts, persevered despite the health challenges he faced at a young age.[13] Third, Putin emphasizes Kharlamov's impact on *global* hockey, drawing attention to his status as a celebrity on the international stage, his achievements at the Olympic Games and other world competitions, and thus his contemporaneous importance. Kharlamov, as Putin makes clear, should be the inspiration for young hockey players and, by extension, a father figure and role model for Russian citizens.

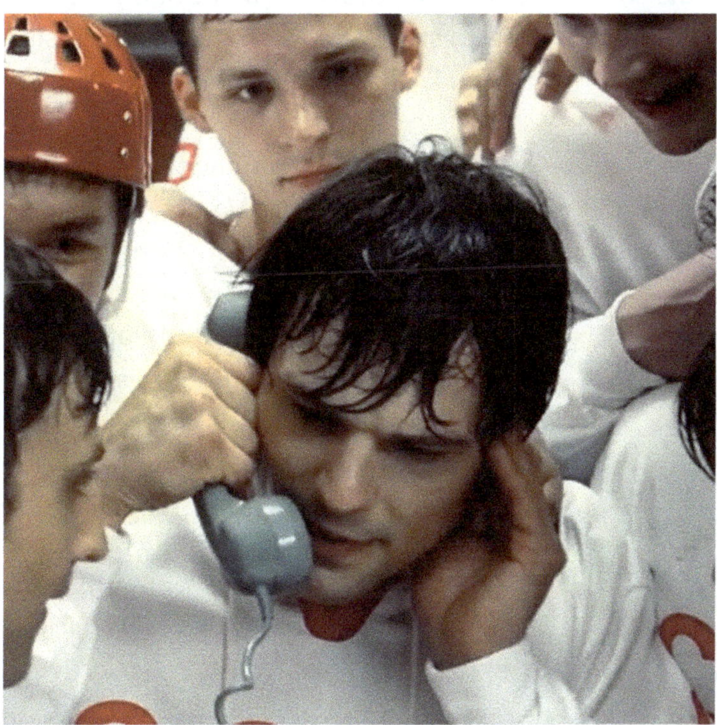

Fig. 10.1. Lebedev, *Legend No. 17*. Legend narrates the Soviet victory.

One particular moment at the beginning of the film is particularly relevant, as it relates to Putin's fixation on Kharlamov as a potential father figure. The film opens in Spain in 1956, a nod to the fact that Kharlamov's mother was Basque and the hockey star spent part of his childhood with her in Bilbao. Just as the local tradition of the Running of the Bulls is about to begin, the young Kharlamov, who is safely standing on an apartment balcony high above the streets with his parents, spots a stranded puppy below, directly in the path of the bulls. "Valera" races to the street to scoop up the puppy just in time to save it from the animals' rampage. He is furiously scolded by his mother. Nevertheless, the scene sets up two guiding ideas for the way in which the viewer is meant to interpret the film. The hagiographic moment suggests, first, that Kharlamov's moral compass was formed from a very early age, setting up a framework to underscore the positive

13 As Dobrynin notes (and criticizes), this message about Kharlamov's character is recurrently emphasized in the film. Kharlamov "is told . . . that he can achieve anything, as long as he really wants it—the maxim that will later be repeated by his girlfriend and by his coach."

aspects of his personality. In this way, nationalist sentiment is fused with Kharlamov's good character. The scene, second, reminds the viewer of Putin's own celebrity image in which he is frequently photographed with young animals. It is well known that Putin is an animal lover, and this subtle yet unmistakable reference to his benevolent side initiates a viewing of the film that connects national pride with Putin himself. It also, however, draws an association between the Soviet star, Putin as father of the contemporary Russian state, and Russian state interests.

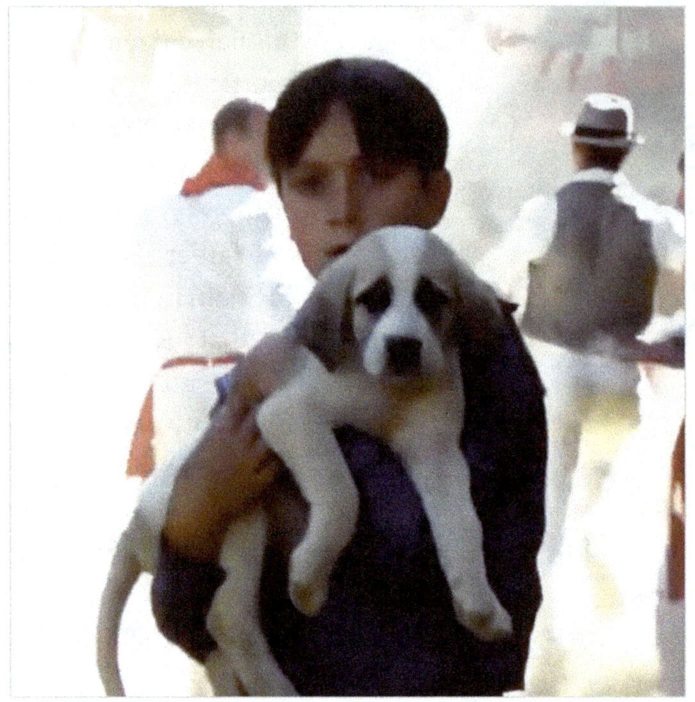

Fig. 10.2. Lebedev, *Legend No. 17*. Valera rescues the puppy.

* * *

While the publicity campaign around *Legend No. 17* established the Soviet celebrity as a symbolic father figure shining his aura onto the middle-aged but athletic father of the Russian nation, this present-day father still lacked a proper young disciple in the present. What would be the cultural logic behind such a character?

Fast forward to 2016 and the premiere of Lebedev's next blockbuster, *Flight Crew*, the highest-grossing film at the Russian box office that year. A remake of Aleksandr Mitta's 1980 original work of the same name, *Flight Crew* was inspired by another popular genre that emerged from the reeducation narrative in Soviet cinema: the aviation film.[14] As John McCannon's work demonstrates, the achievements of

14 Patrimonial lineages are complex and numerous in the texts I am examining. Nikolai Lebedev claims Aleksandr Mitta as his teacher and his life-long mentor (Uskov). *Flight Crew*'s ending credits open with a dedication to Mitta: "With gratitude to Aleksandr Mitta for his lessons in creativity and inspiration." Notably in the same interview, Lebedev contends that his *Flight Crew* is not a remake of Mitta's 1980 film. Be that as it may. More importantly, Lebedev's *Flight Crew* forms a dyadic relationship with *Legend No. 17*—the foundational text for establishing the new trope of cinepaternity for the visual economy of the Putin era.

pilots occurred in a context of interest in aviation in the Soviet Union. The obsession with flying was, in turn, part of an even larger movement around frontier expeditions of discovery and conquest in the 1930s and 1940s. Although similar public fascination around flying occurred in North America and the rest of Europe, as McCannon argues, the process of creating Soviet explorer-heroes was inextricably tied not only to state agendas but to Stalin's own interest in aviation. Such interest naturally translated well to the big screen of Soviet cinema.

As in *Legend*, in *Flight Crew* Lebedev cast Kozlovskii in the star role, but this time Kozlovskii plays a young military pilot, another popular Soviet celebrity hero. Aleksei Gushchin, who is fired from the Russian Air Force for failure to follow orders issued by a corrupt commanding officer, undergoes a series of life-threatening challenges and ultimately performs a dangerous rescue mission as the pilot of a passenger aircraft. He is eventually dismissed from that position as well, once again for violation of command by the corrupt owner of the private air carrier where Gushchin works. In the end, after multiple tests of his strength of conviction and stamina, Gushchin is rewarded with a job at the government-owned Aeroflot.

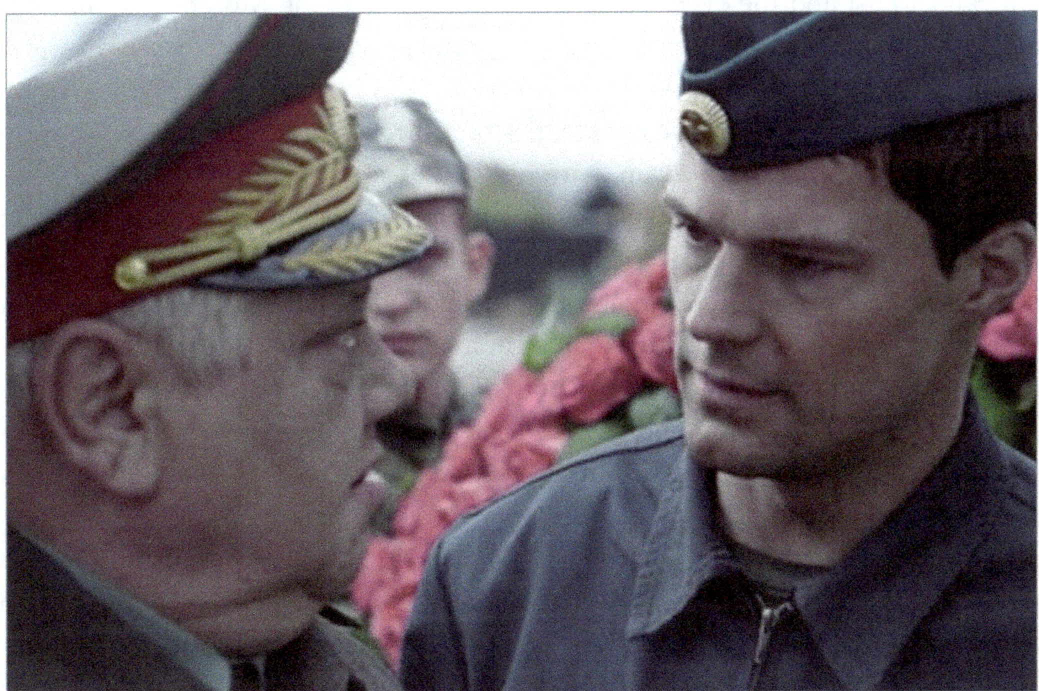

Fig. 10.3. Lebedev, *Flight Crew*. Gushchin talks to his commanding officer.

The disaster in Putin-era emergency films conveys a number of easily readable ideological messages. First, as with the Soviet-era films, social and natural disasters occur outside Soviet/Russian borders. Second, Lebedev repeats everything twice, including disasters. First, Gushchin and his senior colleague Leonid Zinchenko (Vladimir Mashkov) fly on a rescue mission to an African nation where a military coup has just happened. While Gushchin tries to save every civilian, Zinchenko follows bureaucratic procedures regarding the rescue of international workers. The locals stay behind and are executed by the military. In the second and climactic disaster, the two men finally get it right, according to Gushchin. Notably in the scene of volcanic eruption on a foreign tropical island, Lebedev deviates from the Soviet original. For spectacular and ideological reasons, Gushchin and Zinchenko each fly a plane with rescued civilians, Russian and foreign. Zinchenko flies a Soviet-era cargo plane, Gushchin flies a post-Soviet Russian-made jet liner. When the Soviet-era plane runs out of fuel, the two men arrange a specular midair rope transfer of people from the Soviet to the Russian plane. Spectacle aside, Lebedev milks the scene for all of its ideological potential. He creates literal lines of connection between the heroic Soviet past and the even more heroic Russian present. Moreover, Zinchenko, who up to this point was stuck in a bad pre-Putin masculinity crisis, is reborn as a man and a father. It is not surprising that his rebellious and mischievous son is the first to embrace him after the mission is accomplished. *Flight Crew* mends these ruptured patriarchal bonds.

Flight Crew presents us, once again, with one of Lebedev's favorite narrative devices: the trope of the spontaneous youth traveling from periphery to center, who is reeducated—or repatriated—under the guidance of the state. But the Moscow to which Gushchin arrives is noisy, chaotic, and, in some ways, foreboding. His biological father—a semiretired Soviet-era aircraft designer—however, conveniently lives in a penthouse apartment in one of the Stalin-era Seven Sisters buildings, a space that is both symbolically and visually Soviet. The Stalin-era skyscraper establishes spatial and social hierarchies and a value system, codes the film's landscape, and marks the role of the state in redirecting the young hero's work ethic and sense of discipline.

In the same vein, just prior to Gushchin's arrival in the city, we are introduced to the film's political and cultural investments in another way. During the opening sequence, the overfreighted air force plane, which Gushchin is flying, must eject a portion of its goods on Gushchin's orders. What is jettisoned from the cargo hold turns out to be *the* status symbol of the post-Soviet middle-class: a brand-new black BMW. The crashing of the car into the river below signifies less a rejection of capitalist merchandise than a remark on misplaced cultural habits. The dumping of the vehicle serves as a broader suggestion of the need to dispose of generational values.

While *Flight Crew* is almost completely void of female lead characters, many "false fathers" appear in the film. Zinchenko, the officer who supervises Gushchin at the passenger airline where he works for the majority of the film, has an unruly teenage son, Valerii (Sergei Romanovich), who spends his days working out in his room, seducing his English tutor, and avoiding his parents. During a conversation in which Zinchenko suggests that he go to flight training, Valera responds that he does not wish to be a *taksist* (taxi driver) like his father. Through this dialogue, Zinchenko is coded as the absent role model, a father focused on his work, which has no meaning beyond being the breadwinner. The son needs a male role model, aka a hero. Given Valera's behavior and the mention of taxi driving, it is difficult not to view this moment through the prism of Pavel Lungin's 1990 cult film, *Taxi Blues* (Taksi-bliuz): Valera does not want to follow in the footsteps of his father, who came of age during perestroika and the early 1990s. Zinchenko is automatically cast off as belonging to the "wrong" generation, that group of men whose decisions to embrace capitalism cost the Soviet Union its status of global superpower.

Flight Crew, in fact, is punctuated at every juncture by men who fail to represent model examples: Gushchin's first boss, the corrupt Air Force general, who uses the Russian government's military planes for his own business transactions; the oligarch, Gushchin's second boss, who must be ejected from the plane in order for it to take off; Valerii's father, who has his priorities in the wrong places. Each of these figures represents a type of false father who incarnates the radical transformation of Russia during the reforms of the 1990s. Ultimately the false patriarchy represents capitalism as impeding the development of the robust and healthy body and mind of the hero for the new era—the pilot on government service.

Perhaps most notable are the cameos of true fathers and mentors in the film. Aleksandr Mitta, Lebedev's teacher, if only briefly, appears in one of the earlier scenes. Even more striking, Lebedev himself plays the role of the pilots' supervisor at Aeroflot. The director's appearance signifies a connection in the fictional narrative between the state—represented in that scene through the aviation company—and its young male citizens. Lebedev's part also suggests something more revealing in terms of the current state of the Russian cinema industry: the director's self-perceived role in serving as liaison between the state and its celebrities. The film's

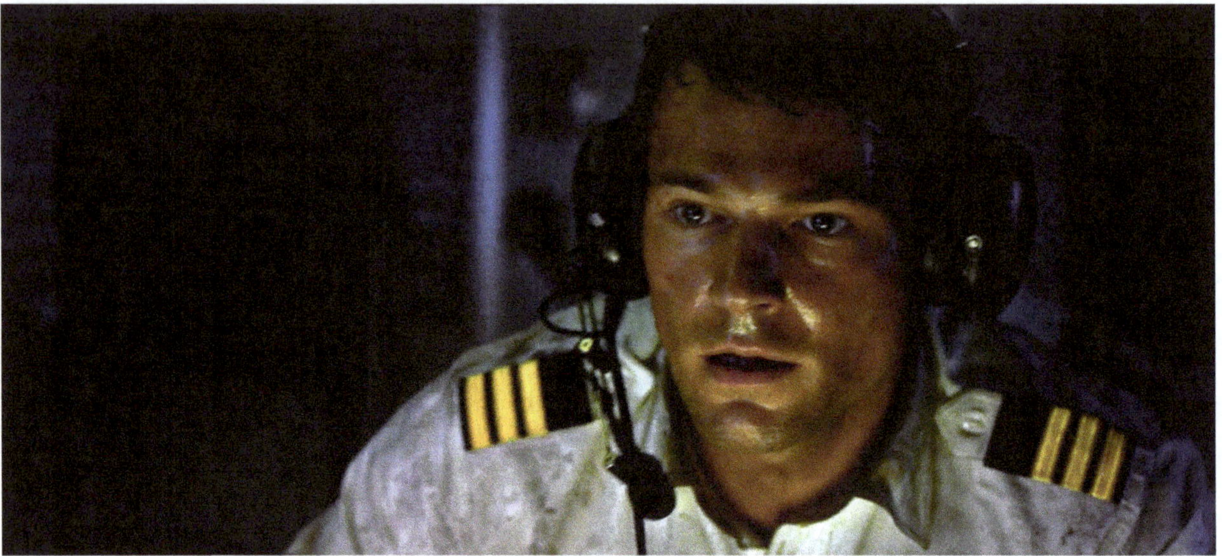

Fig, 10.4. Lebedev. *Flight Crew*. Gushchin pilots a rescue mission: questioning the orders of the false father.

message, despite the many ways in which it appears, is actually quite simple: the "fathers" of the early 1990s got it wrong. Rather than following in their footsteps, one should turn, instead, to the state for guidance and mentorship.

We can see this thread from start to finish in the film: Gushchin's "reward" is to be transferred from a privately owned airline company to the state-owned Aeroflot. The rejection of false fathers is further reinforced by the misogynistic treatment of women in the film. Women appear in supporting roles and simply lack the ability to make any meaningful decisions. Zinchenko's wife, for example, does not have a career or any independent existence on screen. Naturally, she is incapable of raising her male child properly. The woman on the plane—who has two small male children—does not support the crew's decision to attempt the rescue of the old Soviet aircraft. Her children, however, make the "right" decision. To pay lip service to gender equality, Lebedev introduces a token female pilot, Sasha, who cannot even park her own car and needs Gushchin's assistance to escape the tight spot. In the beginning, Sasha still flies planes. Over the course of the film she is reeducated in her own way and learns to be a "real" woman: her only role at the film's end is to admire her love interest—Gushchin—as the hero for the new era.

* * *

Both the sports film and the emergency film establish a new regime of paternity and link it with the blockbuster plot. Soviet fathers—such as Tarasov in *Legend* or Gushchin's father, a Soviet aircraft designer, in *Flight Crew*—are validated and juxtaposed to individualist money-grabbing father figures from the gangster nineties (*likhie devianostye*). *Flight Crew* brims with father figures, both good and bad, but the director contributes an innovative technique to the production of symbolic paternity. He depersonalizes paternity and links it, rather, to the corporate identity of Aeroflot, a state-controlled company—a benign Russian outpost of neoliberal capitalism. The last shot of *Flight Crew* depicts two protagonists, Gushchin and his older colleague Zinchenko, as trainees in Aeroflot climbing ropes toward the sky. In the sky, we see an airplane in Aeroflot livery as the embodiment of a new, better Russia, now in strong male hands.

The new paternity seeks its legitimacy in tradition, the most familiar of which is steeped in Soviet rituals, embracing the new advantages of media and celebrity cultural tools to produce a charismatic make-believe. Yet the new paternity is at the same time supernatural, quick to turn to violence if challenged, and grounded in equal measure in the charisma of Hollywood-inspired popular culture.

As in Viktor Pelevin's *Generation P*, the father of the nation does not exist for the subjects of the Russian Federation outside concerted and ongoing digital creations, a *Gesamtkunstwerk* for the twenty-first century, a metainstallation of which Boris Groys would approve. Robustly glorified in the Russian and international media, the president's popularity has assumed several archetypes of stardom paradoxically connected to both Hollywood and the Soviet tradition: the hunk, the product, the strongman, and the ideologue (Goscilo, "Ultimate Celebrity," 35). Some films set the serious action film about robust state paternity in the present, such as Vasilii Serikov's 2014 *22 Minutes*, about Russian Blue Berets fighting terrorism. Others, like Roman Prygunov's *Dukhless* (2012) and *Dukhless 2* (2015), accomplish the same goal by embracing lighter, comic-strip aesthetics of the father-son relationship. In Prygunov's film, the protagonist Maks Andreev, an unscrupulous banker, learns about the importance of patriotic business ethics from Putin himself, who visits under the guise of a superman figure, traversing space and time.

Putin's patriarchal claim is consistently confirmed in his appearances at carefully orchestrated media events that ostensibly promote cinematic premieres but turn these into a glorification of the Soviet past, thus positioning the father of the nation as heir and keeper of such a past.[15] If ritualizing the past in Soviet times meant heroicizing the leaders, then, as the head of state, Putin celebrates the past by offering gratitude to the living stars of Soviet sports and the aerospace industry.[16] Dead celebrities, such as Kharlamov, are faces of this ritual.

As the 2014 Sochi Olympics approached, it became clearer that every invocation of Soviet athletic glory was meant to contribute to the cult of the true athletic leader—Putin, the incarnation of the new media paternity. For example, the president gave a 2013 public speech, marking what would have been Kharlamov's sixty-fifth birthday, the release of Lebedev's film, and the upcoming Sochi Olympics.[17]

> One of the brightest and most talented players in hockey history, Valery Kharlamov was an idol to millions of his fans. . . . Today Valery Kharlamov's name, his successes and achievements, are the pride of our sporting world and entire country. I am sure that CSKA hockey club, Russia's ice knights, will continue to honour Valery Kharlamov's rich heritage and develop the tradition he founded. And younger players will look up to this legendary player and wonderful person. ("Greetings")

Just as Medvedev served as a placeholder for Putin's presidency from 2008 till 2012, Kharlamov's name in Putin's speech is the cypher of Putin's own celebrity and authority embedded in tradition. Putin's rhetoric, here again, underscores Kharlamov's potential to serve as a role model for Russian youth, and his impact and reputation for the state. As Christel Lane maintains:

> Besides strengthening the legitimacy of the . . . system and political elites by emphasizing the traditional nature of their authority, the . . . system of ritual also serves to stabilize power relations in other ways. It functions to disguise conflicts of interests between elites and various social groups and keeps them latent. Ritual accomplishes this by transmitting definitions of social relations made by political elites which structure the perception of social reality by those who take part in ritual performances. (215)

15 I understand "ritual," in this context, to mean a ceremony, actions or behaviors consistently followed by a person or a group of people. See Lane's analysis (213) of legitimacy and power through socialist ritual.

16 A number of Olympic champions, such as Alina Kabaeva, Irina Rodnina, Vladislav Tretyak, and cosmonauts, such as Valentina Tereshkova, are elected to the State Duma.

17 See Ssorin-Chaikov, 359.

In drawing these connections, Putin's speeches dissolve the divisions between the elite and the public, obfuscate the sharp break between the Soviet and the post-Soviet eras, and produce neo-imperial memory texts for mass consumption.

It is noteworthy that Putin accomplished this aim on his own sixty-third birthday, 7 October 2015, which he celebrated on the ice at a gala hockey game in Sochi, well attended by state officials, legendary sports stars, and former NHL hockey players. Broadcast on state-run television, Putin skated out on the ice, fist-bumping other members of the team. The news story about Putin playing hockey at the gala in Sochi was titled *Legend No. 11*, the number under which Putin appeared on the ice and invoked Lebedev's title (Zarubin). Putin's speech after the match was showcased as the central event of the evening on federal television channels, all while he entertained a roar of support from other players pounding their hockey sticks against the ice.

> Thanks to our hockey stars of Soviet and Russian times, this project became a success. Thank you, dear friends, for your contribution to the development of the Night Hockey League. And of course, I welcome and congratulate the fans, like me—for example, people who do not engage in such a professional sport as do our outstanding players. What I want to say is that I thank you not only for your personal participation but also for the fact that you, by example, motivate millions of our citizens to engage in physical culture and sports. Anyone who moves toward victory will be sure to achieve it. Good luck to all. (Zarubin)

Here Putin shifts from a ritual of gratitude toward the star figure and instead *becomes* the celebrity, "who moves towards victory and will be sure to achieve it." In so doing, he uses his own celebrity status to humble his image against that of Kharlamov's ("fans, like me, . . . who do not engage in such a professional sport as do our outstanding players"). The action of publicly thanking—and subsequently becoming—a sports celebrity legitimates Putin's own star power in the cultural and political sphere, and therefore his current political interests in creating a space in which points of Soviet pride seamlessly become notions of Russian grandeur.

In "The Celebrity Politician," John Street poses the question, "In a world in which pop stars are increasingly portrayed as, or behave like, politicians, does it make equal sense to think of politicians as pop . . . stars?" (85). Street's inquiry homes in on the inseparability between popular culture and politics in contemporary culture, the intersection not only between political figures and stars but between mass culture and national interests. In this aspect of today's Russian cinema, it is clear that Russian filmmaking's stake in the patrimonial structure is inseparable from state interests and the necessity of veiling the cultural rupture between the Soviet period and post-Soviet society. Through two distinct cycles of big-budget, state-sponsored films that saturate the screen with celebrity mentors—the sports film and the emergency film—it is possible to understand the ways in which the Soviet celebrity holds value for the face of Russia in contemporary culture and cinema, and for the ways in which it strives to be integrated into a symbolic lineage of national pride.

Filmography

Chiginskii, Vasilii, dir. *Lev Iashin, the Dream Goalkeeper* (Lev Iashin: Vratar' moei mechty, 2019).
Ginzburg, Viktor, dir. *Generation P* (2011).
Lebedev, Nikolai, dir. *Flight Crew* (Ekipazh, 2016).
———. *Legend No. 17* (Legenda No. 17, 2013).
———. *Star* (Zvezda, 2002).
Lungin, Pavel, dir. *Taxi Blues* (Taksi-bliuz, 1990).
Megerdichev, Anton, dir. *Going Vertical* (Dvizhenie vverkh, 2017).
Mitta, Aleksandr, dir. *Flight Crew* (Ekipazh, 1980).
Prygunov, Roman, dir. *Dukhless* (2012).
———. *Dukhless 2* (2015).
Serikov, Vasilii, dir. *22 Minutes* (22 minuty, 2015).
Timoshenko, Semen, dir. *The Reserve Player* (Zapasnoi igrok, 1954).
Waters, Mark, dir. *Vampire Academy* (2014).

11. New Auteurism: The Case of Mikhalkov and Bekmambetov

Olga Mukhortova

> The only effective liberation . . . begins with the recognition that there is nothing that is not social and historical—indeed, that everything is "in the last analysis" political.
>
> —*Fredric Jameson, The Political Unconscious (20)*

Contemporary Russian auteurism—assuming "Russian" in the loosest possible sense—has three lead protagonists: one stayed in Odessa; a second went to Hollywood; a third flourished in Moscow. This chapter is—for the most part—the story of the second and third *auteurs*—Timur Bekmambetov and Nikita Mikhalkov—and how their examples have shifted the ways in which we understand Russian auteurism.[1]

* * *

In "Multiple Modernities vs. Neo-Traditionalism," Michael David-Fox traces several streams of debates on Russo-Soviet history; the first is concerned with modernity's alleged elements of universalism; the second with a model of particularism in Russian culture. David-Fox then discusses the weaknesses of Shmuel Noah Eisenstadt's alternative of "multiple modernities," which enables an account of the conceptual differences of modern phenomena within the Soviet empire. In my chapter, and in agreement with David-Fox, I use the concept of "entangled modernities," articulated by Göran Therborn and others, requiring a shift away from similarities or distinctiveness in favor of "mutual appraisal and interaction across borders" (David-Fox, "Multiple Modernities," 1).

In this last view, Russo-Soviet culture is entangled with, inter alia, a larger European modernity. Among the strengths of this model is the fact that it begins to account for phenomena

1 The Odessa-based auteur I have in mind is Kira Muratova. She would be perfect for the discussion of Soviet and Russian film auteurs alongside, for example, Andrei Zviagintsev and Aleksandr Sokurov. I consider these three film auteurs examples of high-modernist European-inspired film authors and, for the sake of my argument, focus instead on Mikhalkov and Bekmambetov.

of modernity—let us telegraphically suggest they include industrialization, dissemination of education, systems of medical support, mechanisms of urbanization, and ideas connected with progress and utopianism—as ones that deliver results often apparently unrelated or even oppositional to those evident in other European cultures. Conflicting models of authorship as a manifestation of individual agency, enacted by Russian cultural figures who forged them from, among other practices, Western sources in the seventeenth and eighteenth centuries, belong to this concept of modernity as well.

When we talk about authorship in cinema, we usually imagine the high-modernist auteur director from Sweden, France, or Japan.[2] French critics from *Cahiers du cinéma,* by contrast, were inspired by Hollywood directors such as John Ford or Howard Hawks, who worked in a genre-driven film industry.[3] In this chapter I argue that, while Mikhalkov and Bekmambetov do not fit the profile of the absorbed (even neurotic), narrative-breaking auteurs of the high-modernist model, they very much fit the model of the industry craftsmen who manifest their auteur signature in both their artistic output and commercialism. If there is no contradiction between having an individual vision and collaborating with the commercial and state ideological apparatus, it could be argued that the filmmaker can still manifest his or her individual agency while channeling state or corporate agendas. Hence the title, the protagonists, and argument of this chapter.

"Entangled Auteurship"

Emergent in the mid-twentieth century as only one aspect of a larger reevaluation of the status of subjectivity, the idea of the film auteur—understood as the center of highly personalized film production and the point of creative power— became a key concept that entered the Soviet cultural landscape in connection with the very limited Soviet exhibition of French cinema in the 1960s. A decade earlier, in 1954, François Truffaut had published his article on *la politique des auteurs* and initiated the discussion in which André Bazin, Claude Chabrol, Jacques Rivette, and Eric Rohmer actively participated, turning reader interest to the value of Hollywood. The concept of *auteur* initiated not only a new classification of films but also a new optics of watching

2 The theoretical literature is immense, but one can find a detailed history of the auteur in Sellors.

3 See, for example, Editors of *Cahiers du cinéma* and Rivette.

movies. Instead of paying attention to genre characteristics and aspects of film narrative, auteurist criticism offers instead a focus on the director's style, tracing patterns of mise-en-scène construction; recurrent work with particular artists; lighting techniques, and so on. This change of optics empowered the director and the cameraman, who in the Hollywood studio system had more often appeared as one of many hired professionals. This empowered auteur turned into a structuring figure who proposed a unified, individually ascribed authorship in the collective process of film production. In this new configuration, the director appears as the main figure of the filmmaking process as he or she constructs the essential features of a film, now perceived as more art than entertainment in this paradigm (Elsaesser, 4–6).

The status of auteur is thus by no means merely a stylistic matter. David Bordwell notes that the auteur "becomes a formal component, the overriding intelligence organizing the film for our comprehension" (777). When an auteur encounters conventions of genre cinema—for example, in the case of John Ford, Nicholas Ray, or Howard Hawks—authorial motivation starts competing with and redefining narrative conventions of the genre film. This authorial motivation is a structural feature of the auteur filmic text, and in Bordwell's view this feature provides a unifying vision.

As auteurism migrated eastward, its core features swiftly found creative examples in, most prominently, the films of Andrei Tarkovskii, whose Soviet and international acclaim and cultural influence served as the bedrock of auteurism during the Soviet era. In "*Auteur* Cinema during the Thaw and Stagnation," Eugénie Zvonkine discusses Soviet cultural factors influencing auteurism during this period, emphasizing two elements in particular.[4] First, she notes the crucial relation between the individual and the collective that locally contributed to the negotiations and outcomes of auteur cinema in its struggles with Soviet film censorship. Second, Zvonkine explores the fundamental (and often politicized) role of the scriptwriter, framed by the specific logocentric system of Soviet cinema production. We will return to the issue of logocentrism shortly; I would first restrict our focus to the debates within auteur cinema and its gradual changes.

Writing on the opposition of auteur cinema and genre cinema in the Russo-Soviet film industry, Dawn Seckler has argued that Soviet auteur cinema functioned as a kind of productive

4 Among Soviet auteur filmmakers, Zvonkine discusses Marlen Khutsiev, Andrei Konchalovskii, Kira Muratova, Andrei Tarkovskii, and others.

antagonist to *zhanr* (genre) cinema, which had often historically served as a politically engaged supporter of the Soviet state: "the narrative limitations intrinsic to Soviet genre cinema during the 1930s and 1940s functioned as a mechanism of political suppression" (30) that continued in the later periods of Thaw and Stagnation. Seckler further maintains that the decade of 1985–95 was a time of prosperity for auteur cinema, prosperity that was connected with emergent freedom of speech, the fall of the Soviet Union, and (ironically) the collapse of an industry (in production, distribution, and exhibition) that would otherwise have supported genre films.

Yet post-Soviet auteurism might be seen as functioning quite differently from the auteurism of the late Soviet era, being situated in drastically different social and cultural contexts. Post-Soviet Russian cinema industry resignified auteurism, forming its own version of an auteur and auteur cinema, in which global film structures and practices increasingly interacted and coexisted more intricately with local cultural phenomena.

As might be expected, there is no agreement among Russian film critics and practitioners concerning the boundaries between mainstream genre cinema and auteur cinema, or concerning the cultural roles that they respectively fulfill. One of the few things on which critics agree is that the actual films do not fit neatly into the apparent binaries of genre/auteur cinema. Producer Alexander Rodnyansky, president of the major Russian film festival Kinotavr, emphasizes, for example, that it is through auteur cinema that the Russian film industry connects more broadly to global film trends. In fact, Rodnyansky (Dondurei, "Kinopokaz") asserts, "Russian auteur cinema is connected to auteur cinema of any other country more than to Russian genre films." Yet while the global nature of art cinema has always been a point of departure for the reflections about the nature of "international film language," the exact status and identity of the Russian auteur very much depend on political and economic context.[5] Sitora Alieva in turn emphasizes the diversity of models that constitute Russian auteur cinema: "Nowadays

5 Film critic Anton Dolin ("Kak russkie rezhissery") explains the meaning of *avtorskoe kino* as a recognizable continuity: "an uncompromising state of mind. The author expresses himself and does not care about anything else. Moving in a different direction from everyone else, [the auteur] does not make any compromise at all or makes this compromise only if it is driven by the author's internal desire." Andrei Plakhov (*Kino*, 62) insists that post-Soviet auteur cinema serves as the engine for the Russian film industry: "The springs that move Russian mass and social cinema forward lie in authors' films and even experimental movies." Using auteur cinema as a synonym of arthouse film, Sitora Alieva, the Kinotavr program director, points out that it supplies other types of Russian films by professional directors: "It is vital to support auteur cinema because it serves as a talent foundry. Many blockbuster directors start with arthouse. Russian cinema industry will die without auteur cinema."

auteur cinema is very diverse. Answering the question about art cinema, many students cite Tarkovskii as an example. However, times are changing: now we have a lot of film schools and directions of auteur cinema, which clearly differ from each other."

The most important legacy of the Soviet era was initially the absence of private enterprise as an alternative to state funding of the auteur and cinema at large. As many recent examples demonstrate, such as the public debate around the release of Aleksei Uchitel"s *Matilda* (2017), the use of government money implies a certain type of co-authorship with the state and its ideology on topics of state concern, such as Russian Orthodoxy, imperial history, or Russian patriotism writ large. While migrating first into Soviet Thaw cinema and intertwined with more local ideas of author and authority, socialist values, distinctive social structures, and a state-led cinema industry system, the ideas of the auteur and auteur cinema later came to underscore the auteur's symbolic power within an increasingly corporatized yet politically divided contemporary landscape. For that reason, while not necessarily directly engaged in activism, Russian auteur directors who seek state funding must choose how to situate themselves in relation to the state's increasingly explicit ideology. Meanwhile, as a more constant counterweight pressure, Western film festival prizes that might be awarded at Cannes, Venice, and the Berlinale continued significantly to influence not only Western theatrical preferences for the Russian director as an "author" or "master," but also Russian state recognition of talent for potential funding (Prikaz, 184).

While retaining some of the earlier (one might say) isolationist features of the singular auteur, some contemporary auteur cinema became engaged in complex ways with a contrasting set of cultural values associated with the patriotic blockbuster.[6] For all their signature differences, two "blockbuster-auteur" directors, Nikita Mikhalkov and Timur Bekmambetov, increasingly came to occupy prominent places in post-Soviet filmmaking. Highly regarded by film audiences in the 2000s, Bekmambetov's *Night Watch* (Nochnoi dozor, 2004) and *Day Watch* (Dnevnoi dozor, 2006) obtained the status of the first Russian blockbusters (Norris, *Blockbuster History*, 176). The two *Watches* earned, respectively, $16,239,819 and $31,965,087 in Russian box-office returns.[7] Mikhalkov's sequels to his Oscar-winning *Burnt by the Sun* (Utomlennye solntsem, 1994) likewise appeared as important milestones in film production in a different but no less

6 Hereafter I use this term that I borrow from Stephen Norris's seminal work (*Blockbuster History*).

7 The box office outside Russia consists of $17,711,196 and $6,897,630. All data are from Kinopoisk.ru.

important way.[8] Mikhalkov has converted his distinctly recognizable Soviet auteur signature into the most expensive blockbusters of the post-Soviet period—including *The Barber of Siberia* (Sibirskii tsiriul'nik, 1998), *Burnt by the Sun 2: Exodus* (Utomlennyie solntsem 2: Predstoianie, 2010), and *Burnt by the Sun 2: Citadel* (Utomlennye solntsem 2: Tsitadel', 2011). The film industry site Kinopoisk cites an estimate of €33,000,000 (no dollar figure cited) for *Exodus* and $45,000,000 for *Citadel.* In this way, auteur cinema appears as a foundational, uniting recourse for further development of the Russian post-Soviet cinema industry, rather than an oppositional element inside a binary construction of Soviet filmmaking.

For the mass audience, in the realm of promotion and exhibition the name of a director-auteur comes increasingly to serve as a brand, offering some guarantee of quality in a movie theater and even attracting potential young filmmakers to a film education. Increasingly, the contemporary offerings at VGIK (Gerasimov Institute of Cinematography) face educational competition from the likes of Nikita Mikhalkov and Marina Razbezhkina (this list could be much longer), losing what was once a virtual monopoly for state film education. Thus in the contemporary Russian filmmaking industry, the concept of *auteur,* on the one hand, preserves its elite application among film professionals to empower the figure of a director. On the other hand, the auteur has become a means of marketing to mass film audiences.[9]

Not surprisingly, two of Russia's most successful auteurs, Nikita Mikhalkov and Timur Bekmambetov, ended up establishing studios that produce their creative output. These studios have a particular vision of filmmaking behind them, an industrial extension of the auteur beyond the features of the filmic text itself, and beyond the director to the level of a studio "signature." In the West, this is recognizable: the new Hollywood knows several examples of auteurs who combined filmmaking with entrepreneurial talent (Stephen Spielberg, George Lucas, Spike Lee). In the USSR, an attempt to invent producership as part of auteurist identity could analogously be found in the instance of Grigorii Chukhrai, who, together with Vladimir Pozner Sr., established the Experimental Creative Unit as a quasi-autonomous auteurist studio.

8 The 1994 film won the Cannes Film Festival's Grand Prix and the Best Foreign Film Oscar.

9 In the USSR, filmmakers were trained at directors' workshops run by either VGIK or the Higher Courses for Directors and Scriptwriters. Andrei Tarkovskii and Vasilii Shukshin studied with Mikhail Romm; El'dar Riazanov studied with Grigorii Kozintsev, and so on. Maria Belodubrovskaya (6, 7, 13) contends that even under strict state control, while trying to build an assembly-line model similar to Hollywood, Soviet filmmaking remained artisanal, driven by the figure of the director, as both the creative consciousness and a mentor of future filmmakers in creative workshops (*masterskie*).

Its financial success and challenging pictures triggered an alarmed response and resulted in the closure of the Experimental Unit in the 1970s.

In post-Soviet Russia, the usual mismatch between the auteur and financial success was—in at least some instances—overcome. The most evident cases, Mikhalkov's and Bekmambetov's studios, continue to produce highly profitable pictures. In the case of Mikhalkov's TriTe, such films as *Going Vertical* (Dvizhenie vverkh, 2017) or *Flight Crew* (Ekipazh, 2016) became box-office hits and impeccable ideological commodities. These *auteur* ventures maintained a comfortable symbiotic relationship with the ideological needs of the government.

Logocentricity and Russian Auteurism: The Case of Nikita Mikhalkov

In *Imperial Sublime*, Harsha Ram traces the genealogy of the poet-prophet figure, claiming its cultural influence as a constituting feature of imperial order. Ram (*Imperial Sublime*, 4) argues that the poet-prophet connects Russian literature to empire in several ways, among them poetics, affect, and imperial geography. Even in the poem's coming-into-being, the poet is constrained with empire's demands for art to promote its might:

> Initially rooted in the vicissitudes of court life, the imperial academy, and state policy, Russian poetry began . . . as a *subject of empire* [emphasis mine]. While its subsequent history would take it far beyond its early role as the clarion of victories won and treaties signed, the traces of the Russian *poet's original subjection to autocracy* [emphasis mine] and its expanding realm would linger, subtly marking the poet's responses to a range of interconnected issues.

From the inception of modern Russian literature, the imperial idea and emperor's figure define and authorize the concept of authorship. The figure of a poet-prophet emerges as tightly connected with the imperial culture, continues through Russian cultural tradition, and still holds power as a part of contemporary culture. The poet-prophet figure as an ideal and powerful author was established as a canonical figure in Aleksandr Pushkin's "Prophet" (Prorok, 1826) and Mikhail Lermontov's "Poet" (Poet, 1838), then followed by Nikolai Nekrasov's "Poet and Citizen" (Poet i grazhdanin, 1855). In recent popular culture, this figure reappeared as a postmodern character in Dmitrii Bykov's television project *Citizen Poet* (Grazhdanin Poet, 2011) and other fora.

From the 1960s onward, the poet-prophet figure came to empower the concept of *auteur* in cinema, holding enormous symbolic sway in an apparent continuum of cultural influence over nearly two centuries. Mikhail Yampolsky argues that Russo-Soviet "film mentality is essentially logocentric . . . here the influence of our world-focused cultural tradition is felt. Russian culture is verbal rather than visual" (11). In the era of cinema, film was poised to inherit from literature many of the functions promoting state and empire.

Son of the writer Sergei Mikhalkov, Nikita Mikhalkov started his directorial career with two auteurist renditions of the most profitable international genre models—the Western in *At Home among Strangers, a Stranger at Home* (Svoi sredi chuzhikh, chuzhoi sredi svoikh, 1974) and melodrama in *Slave of Love* (Raba liubvi, 1975). Notably, both films claimed to celebrate two of the most ideologically validated narratives: the October Revolution and the Russian Civil War. After the fall of communism, Mikhalkov's films serve as the brightest examples of the imperial discourse as it has been appropriated by Russian cinema. In *Burnt by the Sun: The Film Companion*, Birgit Beumers examines Mikhalkov's 1994 film, together with other works that focus on his "state authorship," most evidently his performance of the emperor in *The Barber of Siberia*:

> Mikhalkov idealizes the pre-Revolutionary past and the figure of the tsar as the father of all Russians. He cast himself in the role of Tsar Aleksandr III, a reactionary and nationalist ruler . . . Such a portrayal is significant both in the context of Mikhalkov's political 'ambitions' and in light of the absence of a father-figure in so many contemporary Russian films of the post-Soviet period, when soldiers no longer know what they are fighting and dying for. (4)

As film auteur, Mikhalkov plays multiple roles in the production. He is the director, the producer, the studio owner, and the actor who plays the emperor. Mikhalkov's embodiment of Aleksandr III continues the long tradition of the imperial poet-prophet partaking in the aura of state power.

Notably, Mikhalkov's 1998 role appears at a historical moment—I would argue—that is between two imperial periods: the Soviet era (1917–91) and the neo-imperial era beginning (let us say) in 2012 with Putin's third term as Russia's president. The role fills in a twenty-year "imperial gap" (1992–2012), revealing Mikhalkov's aspiration to fill the shoes of the absent emperor, at least on the screen. With this role, Mikhalkov deploys his authoritative power as director-auteur and combines it with his symbolic capital from Soviet cinema to create an imaginary field that projects the imperial past onto the not yet imperial present of 1998 (the film's release year).[10] Emphasizing this feature in Mikhalkov's work, Condee writes: "His cinematic Russia is a fraught reminder that the years from Chekhov through Bunin to Gor'kii could (for very few) be ones of cultural continuity rather than rupture" (*Imperial Trace*, 87). For Mikhalkov, what matters is the continuity of the empire.

The imperial auteur envisions this continuity in the mise-en-scène of his *Barber.* One of the most symbolic settings of the film is the replica of the Cathedral of Christ the Savior, featured prominently in several scenes. The original cathedral was erected as a monument to the empire's victory over Napoleon's army and was destroyed on Stalin's orders in 1931. Several historians writing about the film noted that the construction of the cathedral's replica after the fall of communism served as a symbolic gesture of epic proportions to reinstate the imperial power of Russia (see, for example, Merridale, 379; and Norris, "Tsarist Russia," 102). Stanislav Rostotskii notes concerning *Barber of Siberia*: "The role of *The Barber* in the context of Russian cinema is similar to the one that the Christ the Savior occupies in Moscow cityscape. With all its pluses and minuses, this is undoubtedly a pleasing-to-God [*bogougodnyi*], large-scaled, and expensive edifice."

Mikhalkov's staging of landscapes is often tightly connected with the protagonist, who acquires the features of a poet-prophet. Ram argues: "the prophetic mode in Russian romantic poetry remains connected to an imperial geography" (*Imperial Sublime*, 9). In his dilogy *Burnt by the Sun*, in *The Barber of Siberia*, and later in *Sunstroke* (Solnechnyi udar, 2014), Mikhalkov frequently places the imperial landscape in close connection with the main character, recycling the poetic trope that enhances his cinema with imperial tropes.

In *Burnt by the Sun*, for example, Mikhalkov inserts his protagonist (played by himself) into a classic Russian landscape, familiar from nineteenth-century nationalist Romantic paintings. The director depicts this river landscape as a place of happiness and as a locus for the idyllic father-daughter cathartic relationship. In this frame, Mikhalkov emphasizes his role as a father not only for his daughter but metonymically toward the whole of Russia. In another shot, Mikhalkov appears as a mighty, engaged patriarch, a well-known military commander, and the leader of local community. He even helps the locals to rescue their harvest.

10 Here I understand the term "symbolic capital" as residing "in all the markets in which economic capital is not fully recognized, whether in matters of culture, with the great art collections or great cultural foundations, or in social welfare, with the economy of generosity and the gift" (Bourdieu, "Forms," 245).

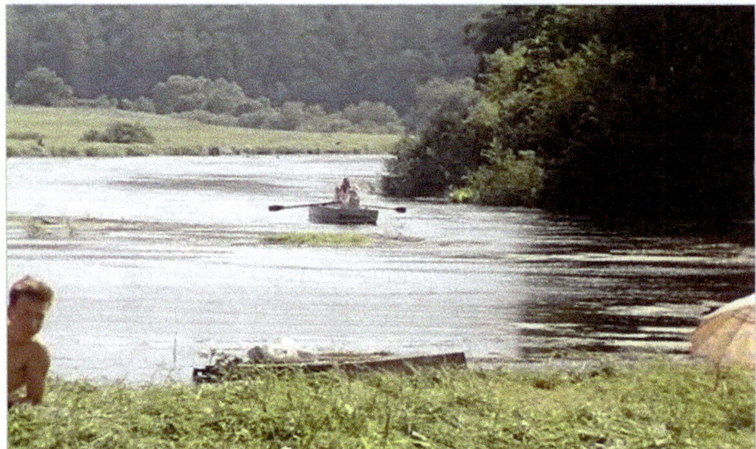

Fig. 11.1. Mikhalkov, *Burnt by the Sun*. The river view.

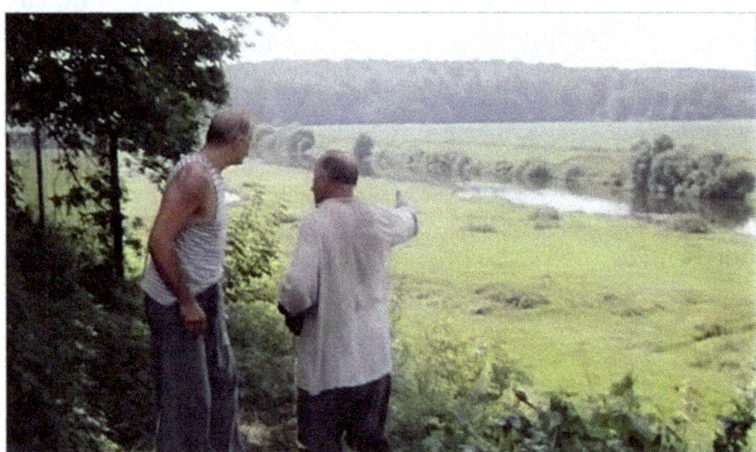

Fig. 11.2. Mikhalkov, *Burnt by the Sun*. Kotov and a peasant.

The endless river and landscape suggest space without borders for miles and centuries, an empire-building fantasy underwritten by the dominant horizontal axis and the human height of the camera angle to express an imaginary space of equality and prosperity. Yet it is important to note that, through the landscape, the director lends coherence to the collective, headed by the division commander Kotov, the patriarch of the land, elaborating his essentialist ideas of nationhood.[11] The horizontal layers are lent coherence by the vertical protagonist, suggesting

11 In using the term "national idea," I imply that Mikhalkov in his film presents this idea as the basis for developing an imaginary community. Here one can observe a situation in which ethnic/national and imperial cannot be truly separated from each other and work as mutually supporting structures.

a ready stewardship over the land, the imperial gentry at the edge of the estate, as the heartland of an imperial world order.

Later this utopian land repeatedly appears in the protagonist's dreams. Kotov conjures it up recurrently in the second part of the dilogy. In Mikhalkov's *Sunstroke,* the protagonist, a nameless White Army officer, dreams of his riverboat journey in sunny imperial Russia while sitting in captivity in Crimea, occupied by non-Russian and godless Bolsheviks. The only thing left are his sublime dreams, in which the empire is alive and the rivers are full of steamboats. In *Barber of Siberia* the auteur finishes his work with another visual metaphor for the epic expanses of Russia—the endless coniferous forests of the Siberian taiga. In this oneiric sequence, the film's protagonist runs through the taiga, where he has found true family, the power to procreate, and ultimately happiness in this epic world.

The ever-expanding land of the empire as the foundation of an imagined collective, with the patriarch as the source of unifying power, also reveals the vertical axis of imperial hierarchy as a form of affect inherited from nineteenth-century Russian poetry. Ram describes this affect as the imperial sublime that connects poetry and politics: "An experience of poetic inspiration is thus presented as analogous to the political power it then describes: impersonal, absolute, a vision that soars to embrace the expanding realm" (*Imperial Sublime,* 5). Throughout two decades of Mikhalkov's filmmaking, the acting style of the film author (as well as that of the actor Oleg Men'shikov) reveals an exaggerated manner that can be compared to the highest register of the Russian language in ceremonial odes in praise of the emperor.

The imperial sublime that underlies the characters' long monologues veers in the direction of the political sermon. Raptured upward by the sublime, the director and lead actors enjoy the pleasure of self-admiration, drawing the viewers in the vortex of imaginary glory. This mechanism is once again reminiscent of the effect of the poetic sublime: "Tapping the lexicon of religious exaltation and courtly praise," Ram writes, "the sublime [pulls] the speaker and the listener into a shared identification with an object of wonder" (*Imperial Sublime,* 21). In this amalgam of film art and state political dreams, Mikhalkov not only promotes himself as an auteur, a socially and politically influential figure, but also reproduces and puts to work an inventory of imperial tropes, most spectacularly as Alexander III in *The Barber of Siberia.*[12]

12 Leonid Parfenov famously mocked the second inauguration of Vladimir Putin as the coronation of a tsar, cross-cutting modern-day footage with the imperial parade scenes from *The Barber of Siberia.*

Tapping into the long historical trajectory of Russian literature's political unconscious, the director simultaneously raises his status as an auteur and a star, visually serving as a modern-day substitute for the absent emperor.

Bekmambetov: Transnational Auteur?

Bekmambetov shares with Mikhalkov entrepreneurial talent and international success, not only as a filmmaker but also as a producer and businessman. We may look for analogues in other cultures outside Russia (such major auteur directors as Akira Kurosawa or Jean-Luc Godard come to mind), but in Russia Mikhalkov and Bekmambetov set a new standard for what it means to be an auteur in the new market-driven Russia.

Bekmambetov's career was launched at the very start of early neo-capitalism: after a perestroika-era debut, in the mid-1990s he produced a successful series of commercials for the Russian Imperial Bank. These brief clips, all about the rise and fall of world empires and their creators, were at the same time succinct and spectacular. The commercials caught the eye of film critics and even international film festivals. In a sense, Bekmambetov's career follows a logic analogous to such Soviet avant-garde artists as Dziga Vertov and Lev Kuleshov, who learned montage cinema by editing footage during the Russian Civil War. Bekmambetov's training took place during the battles for the cause of capitalism.

Already these early-career projects manifested Bakmambetov's signature style, in particular his ability to experiment with visual art forms, cinema being just one of such forms. Bekmambetov's commercials fused music video aesthetics with epic narration. In the *Watches* dilogy (*Night Watch* and *Day Watch*), Bekmambetov tried his hand at producing the Russian version of the fantasy genre by fusing Russian and Soviet stories with Hollywood-style technical sophistication. In *Day Watch*, he demonstrates his auteur style: for example, in the scene of the red sports car driving at breakneck speed along the glass wall of a Moscow skyscraper. With the help of computer-generated imagery (CGI), Bekmambetov often visualizes physically impossible situations, such as defiance of gravity.

Another distinct feature of Bekmametov's filmmaking is the prominence of humor even in genres and scenes that are far from comic, lending Bebkmambetov's style a postmodern, commercial touch absent in Mikhalkov's films. In the same sports-car scene from *Day Watch*, Bekmambetov freezes the spectacular, violent narrative to insert a microscopic sight gag. The car leaves a scratch on the window pane, and the scene cuts to the inside of the room, where a cleaning woman tries to remove the same scratch from the inside. The comic effect comes from two parallel interpretations of the event running simultaneously: the vampire driver in her red car leaves a scratch mark on the outside of the skyscraper's window pane, while the ordinary cleaning woman makes a futile attempt to remove the scratch, never realizing its supernatural origin.

Here Bekmambetov plays with a theme that is central to the dilogy, one that he shares with Mikhalkov: the separation of the world of ordinary humans and that of superheroes, be they fantastic beings or officers of the empire. The sports-car driver and the cleaning woman are separated not by the glass window but by the incompatible temporalities of the events in the world of the Light and Dark warriors. While both auteurs have introduced superheroes to the realm of the new Russian filmmaking, a fundamental difference now reveals itself between Hollywood and their new Russian superheroes: Superman and Wonder Woman are figured as socially equal to the rest of their community; they just possess certain extraordinary abilities. The creatures from the *Watches* are above the law as it exists for ordinary human beings. Several contributors to Boris Kupriianov and Maksim Surkov's *"Watch" as a Symptom* (Dozor kak simptom), a scholarly collection dedicated to the release of Bekmambetov's dilogy, have emphasized that the elite world of the *Watches* operates outside Judeo-Christian ethical imperatives, while mere humans follow the laws of the state and God (Ryklin). Ryklin notes that the Light and Dark others treat humans as disposable energy containers—that is, as batteries.

As members of an elite, Bekmambetov's superheroes mend the traumatic break between the Soviet and post-Soviet eras. In his previous life, Geser—the leader of the Light Forces— served as a Soviet minister. The separation between the ordinary and the extraordinary is reinforced by hierarchies superimposed by such references from the Soviet period. No moral judgement is passed. Yet Bekmambetov adds an ironic postmodernist touch to his ideological gestures. The information about Geser's Soviet career is available only if the viewer watches the final credits that roll to Uma2rmaN's fusion song, summarizing the film in a mode comprehensible to the younger moviegoer.

To return once again to the issue of logocentrism, Bekmambetov's relationship to this tradition is of a somewhat different nature. He draws on popular literature and culture as well as on government television sponsorship. His first blockbusters were based on bestselling fantasy novels by Sergei Luk'ianenko and funded by federal television Channel One. In fact,

Channel One Russia chief executive officer (CEO) Konstantin Ernst and his producer Anatolii Maksimov had originally invited Bekmambetov to direct the already thought-out project (Karakhan, "Zhazhda"). The state-controlled Channel One produced and promoted the dilogy. For many film viewers, the dilogy appears to be tightly connected to its literary source. Boris Groys refers to the inseparability of the films and the novels: "My problem as a viewer is that I have read the trilogy before, and I cannot imagine how both films could be watched without reading all three novels. I do not see the films as self-sufficient" ("Beseda," 217).

Ernst explains that "in Luk'ianenko's *Watch*, the point of our interest was not the genre but an opportunity to catch a strong basic construction, which we could replicate as we wish" (Karakhan, "Zhazhda"). As is clear from the CEO's explanation, the novels attracted him because they dealt with the Cold War rivalry in fantasy-novel mode: in the novels, the treaty between the Light and Dark Forces was signed fifty years prior to the events—that is, around the beginning of the Cold War. Many of the Light Forces had served in the KGB during Soviet times. The defeat in the Cold War as the formative trauma of the 1990s and the rise of the market as a new economic order constitute the key narrative lines that Channel One leadership embraces. Yet references to the Cold War, as well as fictional attempts to revise its outcomes, were softened in the cinematic rendition of the novels. In the films, the treaty between the Light and Dark Forces was signed in the Middle Ages. Thus the films cultivate dual audiences. For the global viewer, the films are fantasy narratives with Russian mise-en-scènes. For post-Soviet viewers, still very aware of Soviet-era material culture and the Cold War–era Manichean universe, the film appeared as a revisionist narrative of the defeat in the Cold War, not unlike D. W. Griffith's famous 1915 blockbuster *The Birth of a Nation*.

Equally important is the confrontation between the Light and Dark Forces as a circumstance that is not relegated to the past but offers the viewer a framework for the interpretation of the present. In the film, the Lights ride a cyberpunk, Soviet-era Zil truck; the characters wear shabby Soviet-style utility workers' uniforms and exist in Soviet-style apartment and office spaces. In contrast, vampires drive Western cars, dwell in Western-style living spaces, and run contemporary businesses while consuming human blood. As Ernst insightfully points out, the films did not adapt the novels but "invited the audience to play with them" (Karakhan, "Zhazhda") as with Legos, including the fact that the myths were prepackaged for the audiences.

I designate Bekmambetov a postcinema auteur because, among other reasons, he is interested in screen culture beyond the traditional cinematic text in a movie theater. In his

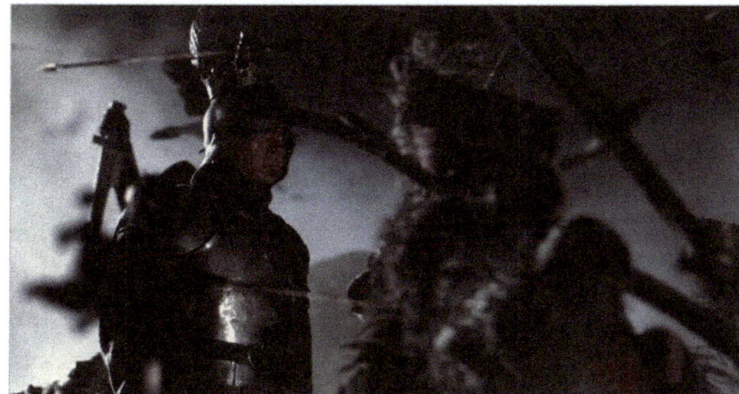

Fig. 11.3. Bekmambetov, *Night Watch*. Geser on the battlefield.

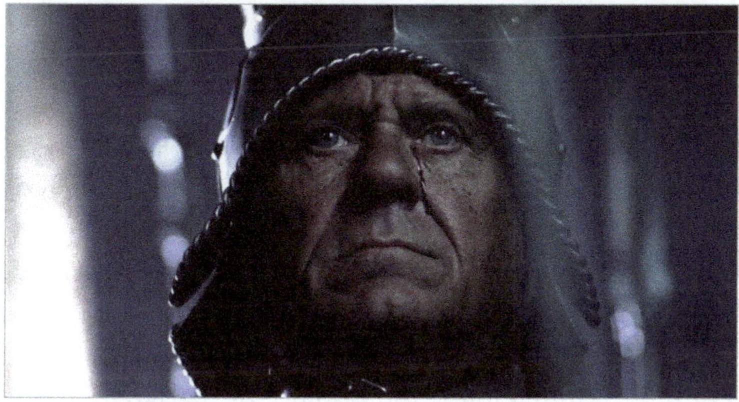

Fig. 11.4. Bekmambetov, *Night Watch*. Geser's portrait.

comedy franchise *Six Degrees of Celebration*, the narrative is motivated by the digital map of Russia, where events are connected and intersect following the logic of Internet browsing. The software product *Prezi* is an inspiration for this kind of storytelling.[13] Bekmambetov's 2018 project *1968.Digital* is the first mobile documentary series about key people and events that changed the course of global history. The series imagines these historical personages owning and using a cell phone to tell their story on the smartphone screen. The viewer experience is framed by the screen and the specific app used by the character: "Andy Warhol shares photos of his exhibitions on Instagram; Mick Jagger releases future hit songs on SoundCloud; Yuri Gagarin chats and posts photos on VKontakte" (*1968.Digital*). Notably, Bekmambetov demonstrates his signature style, a playful and humorous attitude toward both the narrative

13 For a detailed discussion of the *Six Degrees of Celebration* franchise, see Beach Gray's chapter in this volume.

and the technologies used to visualize it. Bekmambetov's Bazelevs Studio collaborates on *1968. Digital*, for example, with major global media players, such as BuzzFeed News.

Since 2015, Bekmambetov has been developing films in what he calls Screen Life, a new format in which the narrative is presented on computer screens (so-called "screen movies"). The major narrative premise and visual feature of such films is the fact that they take place solely on computer screens (Satubaldina): Aneesh Chaganty's psychological mystery-thriller *Searching* (2018), for example, is shot from the point of view of smartphones and computer screens, consisting of fictional found footage. Bekmambetov's talent as an auteur-entrepreneur is evident in this innovative project, shot on a shoestring budget of one million dollars but already reaping sixty-four million dollars in sales.

Film Auteurs for the New Empire?

Stephen Norris (*Blockbuster History*) identifies the patriotic blockbuster set in Russia's past as a central mode for the production of a usable past in Putin's Russia. While both Mikhalkov and Bekmambetov, as the film auteurs for a neo-liberal Russia, do not fit neatly into this niche, their films share a number of key ideological features central to Russia's new hegemonic ideology. These are the artists who do not mind casting aside the high-modernist mask of an independent artist in order to engage both commercial genres and state ideologies. First and foremost, the concern at the core of their filmmaking is the stability of patriarchy—be it a military unit, social brotherhood, or the father-son relationship.

Second, both Mikhalkov and Bekmambetov share the temporality of "never too late." In contrast to the melodramatic temporality ("too late") marking some of Mikhalkov's earlier work, the male protagonists of these two authors often now travel into Russia's historical past to fix the mistakes that led to the crisis in the present. If in classical melodrama, the protagonist suffers the consequences of exercising her agency in the past, Mikhalkov's and Bekmambetov's male characters are capable of mending and erasing the unusable past. The crumbling city of Moscow cannot be rescued unless the protagonist travels back to 1992 to erase the historical mistake and restore patriarchal continuity. Boris Groys formulates this trajectory for Bekmambetov, though his remarks could just as accurately refer to both directors: "I believe this film does not answer any question of the current reality, because it ends with the appeal to turn the past into the nonexistent and vice versa: to turn the nonexistent into the past, to return backward. In fact, it is indicative for Russian thought to formulate social and political programs as projects of return, as a search for the turning point, where everything went the wrong way" ("Beseda," 223). For both *auteurs*, a binary vision is fundamental to the proper functioning of the imperial imaginary. This binarism is not even personified ("hero"/"enemy"), as in many Hollywood films. Instead, it is tribal: the hierarchy is clear; the male leader is never in doubt; the dyad instead is only "us" and "them."

Finally, to maintain this patriarchal edifice, eternal war must be waged as the new normal, in an epic time embedded in a heroic past, the only mode of existence for real men. Any peacetime present is an illusory surface, hiding the true state of reality.

In Bekmambetov's *Night Watch* and *Day Watch*, war appears as a perpetually unresolved power play between good and evil, influencing all sides of contemporary life. For Mikhalkov, war belongs to the historical past as a treasured heritage, a time of hero-fathers who survey every centimeter of imperial landscape. And if Bekmambetov's war is invisible to ordinary humans, it is just as eternal and pervasive as Mikhalkov's paradigm of war. It is through this patriarchal triumphalism that both *auteurs* have contributed to the resurgence of filmgoing in modern-day Russia. Though Mikhalkov's own recent films have been far from successful, his studio—with its top-grossing blockbusters—has made an invaluable contribution to a cinema in which heteronormative masculinity finds empire to be its natural habitat.

Filmography

Bekmambetov, Timur, dir. *1968.Digital* (2018).

———. *Day Watch* (Dnevnoi dozor, 2006).

———. *Night Watch* (Nochnoi dozor, 2004).

———. *Six Degrees of Celebration* (2010).

Chaganty, Aneesh, dir. *Searching* (2018).

Mikhalkov, Nikita, dir. *At Home among Strangers, a Stranger at Home* (Svoi sredi chuzhikh, chuzhoi sredi svoikh, 1974).

———. *The Barber of Siberia* (Sibirskii tsiriul'nik, 1998).

———. *Burnt by the Sun* (Utomlennye solntsem, 1994).

———. *Burnt by the Sun 2: Citadel* (Utomlennye solntsem 2: Tsitadel', 2011).

———. *Burnt by the Sun 2: Exodus* (Utomlennye solntsem 2: Predstoianie, 2010).

———. *Slave of Love* (Raba liubvi, 1975).

Uchitel', Aleksei, dir. *Matilda* (Matil'da, 2017).

12. *Elki*: The Most Profitable Franchise of the Putin Era

Beach Gray

The *Elki* series of films (here "elki"—pronounced "yolki"—is Russian for "New Year's trees") has become the most successful film franchise in the history of the Russian Federation.[1] As of August 2018, the inventory includes six independently released feature films, one spinoff film,[2] a planned seventh film,[3] individual pages on Facebook, VKontakte, and Odnoklassniki; and promotion on the Bazelevs Studio Twitter page.[4] The films of this comedy franchise are blockbusters. The peak thus far in terms of box office receipts has been *Elki 3*. It is the fourth highest-grossing domestic Russian film since 1991,[5] the year of the collapse of the Soviet Union

1 *Elki*, which literally means "fir trees," has associations with the New Year's tree that Russophone people often put up in their homes for the holiday. It has a striking affinity to the western Christmas tree. The symbol is an ideal brand since it has all of the positive associations of the Soviet and post-Soviet New Year's holiday but no particular political or religious affiliation.

2 The six films are *Six Degrees of Celebration* (Elki, 2010), dir. Timur Bekmambetov; *Elki 2* (2011), dir. Aleksandr Baranov, Levan Gabriadze et al.; *Elki 3* (2012), dir. Levan Gabriadze, Aleksandr Kott et al.; *Elki 1914* (2014), dir. Timur Bekmambetov, Aleksander Kott et al.; *Elki 5* (2016), dir. Timur Bekmambetov, Aleksandr Kott, et al.; and *Elki 6* (Elki novye, 2017), dir. Aleksandr Karpilovskii, Dmitrii Kiselev, Zhora Kryzhovnikov, et al. The spinoff is *Paws, Bones, & Rock'n'roll* (Elki lokhmatye, 2015)—literally, "Shaggy New Year's Trees"—dir. Maksim Sveshnikov.

3 *Elki 7* (dir. Anna Parmas et al.) premiered on 27 December 2018. For state funding confirmation, see http://www.fond-kino.ru/news/proekty-kinokompanij-liderov-utverzdennye-popecitelskim-sovetom-fonda-kino-v-2018-godu/.

4 VKontakte and Odnoklassniki (Russian for "in contact" and "classmates," respectively) are state-regulated Russian social media outlets, in some respects similar to Facebook in their structure and organization. The official website of the *Elki* franchise is elki-film.ru, although this website covers only the first three *Elki* films. For more information on the later films, see bazelevs.ru. The feeds and pages on social media often change quickly, but the most current ones (as of July 2018) are on Facebook, https://www.facebook.com/elki.novie/; VKontakte, http://vk.com/elki_novie; Odnoklassniki, http://ok.ru/elkinovie; and Twitter, https://twitter.com/bazelevscompany?lang=en.

5 As of July 2018, *Elki 3* is the fourth most lucrative domestically produced film in Russia since 1991. *Six Degrees of Celebration* earned over $22 million at the box office with a theater attendance of just over four million. See www.kinopoisk.ru/film/493768/. *Elki 2* and *Elki 3* surpassed these figures with $26 million and $38 million at the box office, and (respectively) just under five million and just over five million theater spectators. See www.kinopoisk.ru/film/573817/ and www.kinopoisk.ru/film/652659/. Since then, the box-office numbers have

and the gradual start of a predominantly capitalist mode of film production.[6] The films are funded in part by Russian state television and produced by Timur Bekmambetov.[7] Each family-friendly film is composed of a series of short interlocking vignettes, a host of domestically famous actors, and plots that emphasize the magic of the New Year holiday. This holiday is both the temporal setting and the release time for these films, with the result that *Elki* as a franchise is impossible to ignore. It is simultaneously a highly publicized event in Russian popular culture and one of the barometers of what is and is not encouraged in the state-controlled cultural landscape of contemporary Russia. These films primarily target a Russophone audience, inside and outside the Russian Federation.[8]

Beyond the fact that these films are influential in their own right, why devote analysis to them? They are, after all, light-hearted commercialized comedies with little influence outside Russia. There are two reasons why these films merit greater attention.

First, the *Elki* films *stake a claim on depicting New Russia*, a clear self-image of a nation with growing global political and economic influence. This representation goes beyond the categories of "post-Soviet" or "neo-West." Rather, the films create a hyperreality that highlights all of the positive aspects of contemporary Russia while subduing the negative ones. To make sense of this cinematic world, the first section of this chapter examines four underlying narratives about Russia that these films tacitly advocate: Russia is a place now free of trauma; inaction is the best action to advance in Russian society; Russia is once again a global empire with expanding

dropped off but are still significant: *Elki 6* earned just over $16 million, while *Elki 5* earned over $13 million, and *Elki 1914* surpassed the $12 million mark. For a list of the most lucrative films and box office earnings, see "Samye kassovye fil'my," *KinoPoisk*, www.kinopoisk.ru/box/best_rus/view_all/1/.

6 On early post-Soviet film production, see Beumers ("Cinemarket") and Condee ("Cine-Amnesia" in *Imperial Trace*, 49–84).

7 Before the first *Elki* installment, *Six Degrees of Celebration*, in 2010, Timur Bekmambetov was already the most prominent big-budget film director in Russia, with the success of the Russian blockbusters *Night Watch* (Nochnoi dozor, 2004), *Day Watch* (Dnevnoi dozor, 2005), and *Irony of Fate 2* (Ironiia sud'by: Prodolzhenie, 2007). Bekmambetov garnered international recognition by the success of the US, German, and Russian co-production *Wanted*, with Angelina Jolie and Morgan Freeman.

8 The *Elki* films have consistently been released in Estonia, Kazakhstan, Lithuania, and Ukraine, but rarely outside of the former Soviet and East European bloc. See "Six Degrees of Celebration (2010): Release Info," "Yolki 2 (2011): Release Info," and the other IMDb.com webpages in Works Cited. Most interestingly, the latest film, *Elki 6*, has been released in Cyprus, a country in which Russia has growing political and economic influence. See "Yolki novye (2017): Release Info."

borders; and Russia is a nation with a value system opposite to that of the West. The first three narratives are a blueprint that models how to come to terms with the Soviet past, live in the Russian present, and anticipate the future for Russia, respectively. The fourth narrative ties the first three narratives together by showing what it means to be Russian—in the past, present, and future—through the subtle promotion of a conservative, nationalist value system.

Second, these films use a *new model of film production*. This model is a hybrid of capitalist venture and state-sponsored investment. It is sustainable economically (each film will make profits at the box office), and it is viable politically (each film supports state ideology). In the second section of this chapter, I break the model down by analyzing four specific aspects: production, exhibition, marketing, and funding. These "real" aspects of the films' creation and promotion dovetail with the narratives described above. For each aspect, I focus attention on the way it supports each of the four specific narratives. The franchise's practices of production reinforce the narratives in the films. The Bazelevs Studio, therefore, practices what it preaches. The effect is to legitimize a franchise that has no direct literary or cinematic antecedent.

The *Elki* franchise is, in many ways, the inverse of a Western film franchise. Its protagonists are "regular people" rather than superheroes, such as Batman or Superman.[9] Although *Elki* films fulfill genre expectations and create their own series of myths,[10] the franchise is, ultimately, set in a refraction of the "real world," rather than in a fantastical realm or a science-fiction universe as in, for example, *The Lord of the Rings* or *Star Wars*.[11]

Another key difference is the lack of merchandising for the *Elki* franchise, whose producers seem more interested in supporting state narratives than selling commodities.[12] And, of course, the *Elki* franchise benefits from the unambiguous support of the Russian state. To some extent, this difference is informed by historical paths: in the United States, franchise cinema

9 For a discussion of the *Superman* and *Batman* film franchises over time, see Booker.

10 For a thorough discussion of the genre of New Year films in Russo-Soviet cinema, see Beumers, "Father Frost." See also DeBlasio, "New-Year Film."

11 Throughout this chapter, I draw on the work of Kristin Thompson, who theorizes on franchise film in the Hollywood context. See especially Thompson, 1–13.

12 In contrast to the heavily merchandized Hollywood franchises, the *Elki* franchise takes on the identity of a low-key, friendly "noncapitalist" venture. Through this act, the franchise suggests that performing a public good by providing family-friendly entertainment for the New Year's holiday is more important than making money. The fact remains, however, that the *Elki* films are high-grossing.

came about after the purchase of Hollywood studios by large corporations and international conglomerates in the late 1970s (Thompson, 5), while in Russia it has appeared in tandem with the rise of the Bazelevs Studio and the success of domestic blockbusters in the 2000s. This argument does not attempt to rehearse the notion that Russia is somehow stuck in the past. Rather, it points out that the Russian film industry will, necessarily, have a trajectory different from that of Hollywood because the state will, for the foreseeable future, have a hand in the funding and messaging of high-budget domestic cinema.

Four *Elki* Narratives That Sell: Myths for the Past, Present, Future, and All Time

Myth for the Past: Soviet Trauma Is Erased in New Russia

The formula for coming to terms with the past is simple: that which was traumatic in the Soviet Union no longer exists in New Russia.[13] Contemporary Russia is completely different from the Soviet Union, according to the *Elki* franchise. The Soviet institutions that produced suffering, pain, and persecution are changed. They are now a source of lighthearted amusement rather than trauma. These institutions include the police, jail and the prison system, the GULag, the army, and even the psychiatric ward, which the KGB used to incarcerate opposition figures.

The most salient corollary to this formula is the characterization of the police as a transformative institution for wayward young men. In *Six Degrees of Celebration*, a thief is arrested but then escapes by donning the clothes of a policeman. On the run, he dodges into a cellular telephone store. A robbery takes place, and the thief-turned-policeman comes to the rescue and foils the crime. An older police officer finds the thief and releases him, once he realizes the thief has done a good deed. In *Elki 1914*, the same actor (Artur Smol'ianinov) plays the role of a police officer, but in a different time period. The taxi driver in *Six Degrees of Celebration*, who kidnaps pop star Vera Brezhneva, becomes a police officer by *Elki 2*, in which he assists an older couple to reunite. In *Elki 3*, a police officer matures under the guidance of an older officer and becomes a father. These representations clash with the bribe-seeking,

13 This section grows out of an argument made in Gray, "Levan Gabridze et al."

exploitative reputation of law enforcers that often occurs in the cinema of the 1990s (or in some lived social reality).

The franchise's image of the police pairs with a light-hearted depiction of jail. Jail is represented as a merry place where falsely accused people meet on the eve of the New Year. They quickly unravel the series of misunderstandings that caused incarceration in the first place. In *Elki 2*, the police chief's daughter is locked in a cell to keep her from visiting her boyfriend. A professor of international relations joins her. He was arrested for attempting to climb the New Year's tree to prove his love to his girlfriend. In *Elki 3*, a young woman is arrested for allegedly stealing from another woman's bank account at an automated teller machine (ATM). The young woman is released when the husband of the second woman arrives to explain that he withdrew the money to buy his wife a gift. Jail does not lead to prison, which is not even depicted. Rather, it is a liminal space that symbolizes the anxiety of characters who seek to unite with their romantic interests for the holiday. Jail is a place in which characters learn to trust police officers, stern state authorities who turn out to be benign.[14]

References to the GULag do not dig up past trauma either. Rather, they are opportunities for humor and the reeducation of characters. In the episode in *Six Degrees of Celebration* referenced above, the song "Magadan" by Vasia Oblomov plays nondiegetically when the thief initially is caught. Since the thief is released eventually for performing a good deed, the joke is light. He never actually goes to Magadan, the epitome of GULag horror. In *Elki 3*, two male teenagers who try to dodge selective service are sent to Ratmanov Island, also in the far northeast, adjacent to Alaska. The remoteness of the location suggests GULag exile and the deprivation experienced by guards as well as prisoners. The episode focuses, however, on the felicity of the New Year holiday. The girlfriend of one of the characters and her grandmother surprise the two men with a visit. All four enjoy skiing together. Potential trauma turns into fun. Military service becomes an inconvenient responsibility, but one that does not threaten physical or psychological harm.

In fact, a subtler reference to the GULag is the decentered system of city connections that the film features. It is a perverse palimpsest that does not mention its predecessor, the infrastructure

14 Hollywood is best known for depicting police officers as comic and often slapstick figures because of their inaptitude as agents of modern institutions. Bekmambetov's comic cops differ radically from Hollywood cops. In their bonding with—and reforming of—criminals, they are the heirs of Soviet cops, sugary cinematic militiamen.

that contributed to the building up of many Soviet cities. An unsettling implication of this argument explains an episode in *Elki 2* in which a couple separated in the Soviet Union reunite in New Russia on Red Square. The discovery of a misplaced letter initiates the woman's search to find her long-lost lover again after forty years—and she succeeds. The unspoken therapeutic message is that those loved ones who disappeared during Soviet times are not really lost. They are out there somewhere. It was all due to an unintentional failure of communication rather than incarceration or execution by the state.

Even the psychiatric ward becomes a place of humor, where Zhenia (Sergei Svetlakov) and Boria (Ivan Urgant) end up because of mistaken identity. A potentially horrible fate is punctuated by flirtatious quipping with the attendant nurse and an escape plan by the two protagonists, who are able to hide the incident from their wives. What bodes to be a traumatic life-altering event turns into an episode of male bonding. Any actual trauma present in contemporary Russia is absent from the screen, both in this episode and the franchise more broadly.

Myth for the Present: Fairy Tales, Ivan the Fool, and Faith in New Russia

The myth for the present in the *Elki* films promotes passivity. It maintains that inaction and faith are the best ways to achieve one's dreams in contemporary Russian society. Ivan the Fool, a character from Russian folk tales, is the device that expresses this myth. Ivan the Fool is seemingly naïve, yet he always succeeds in his endeavors. He marries the rich princess by sheer force of blind luck and a refusal to play by conventional societal rules. His appeal is in his devil-may-care attitude. He obtains wealth not through hard work, but through being in the right place at the right time and not asking too many questions.

It makes sense that a character who does not remember the (traumatic) past and has no psychological depth most adequately embodies the myth for the present.[15] In fact, fairy- and folktale references in the *Elki* films abound, with frequent appearances of Father Frost and Snegurochka (respectively, the Russian counterparts of Santa Claus and his little granddaughter), albeit costumed. Furthermore, the vignettes rely on a folktale structure in which romantic stories unfold in a linear fashion and end in "marriage" (the couple getting

15 On the lack of psychological depth as a defining feature of the folktale, see Lüthi, 12.

together).[16] And most importantly, there is a clear delineation between good and evil, even if that evil is mostly sidelined. Moral ambiguities do not exist in this cinematic world.

It is not so much Ivan the Fool himself who features as a character in these films, but rather Ivan the Fool's modus operandi that appears. In *Six Degrees of Celebration*, it would seem that the protagonist is able to deliver the message through the interconnectivity of cellular phones and the power of the "six handshakes" to connect any one person to any other. In fact, it is thanks to the sheer good fortune of the connection of a caretaker in the orphanage to a guest worker on Red Square that then Russian President Dmitrii Medvedev receives the message on time. *Elki 2* is based on a similar premise, since the fulfillment of romantic desire comes through blind hope on the part of both the older woman and the older man, who meet on Red Square after almost forty years, itself a magic number in folk tales. In *Elki 3*, Facebook "likes" and "the boomerang of good" (a karma-like concept) lead to the resolution of the central vignette.

These episodes find a parallel in a folktale in which Ivan the Fool posts an embellished message at a crossroads. He boasts about killing forty "warriors" after he kills forty flies.[17] Knights greater than he pass the crossroads, read the note, and take his meaning literally. They join ranks with him rather than challenge him. These knights do most of the work for Ivan the Fool, who is able to defeat his enemies and marry the princess in the end. What begins as a silly joke brings about an unexpectedly favorable outcome far out of proportion to the effort applied. The message within the films is that faith in a small initiative at the right time is more powerful and likely to lead to results than sustained and organized efforts over longer time periods. This message encourages the apolitical use of technology, whether through cellular telephones or social media. Rather than a post at a crossroads, it is the social media post that magically resolves problems in these films.

There are two important corollaries to this motif. The first has to do with ethnic hierarchies. Within the *Elki* films, the characters who channel Ivan the Fool are ethnically Russian. Characters whose names and appearances suggest they belong to other ethnicities, such as the Central Asians who work in the orphanage and on Red Square, are present as magic helpers rather than as full-fledged characters. In this regard, the fairytale aspect has a dark side, since the magic only works if you are a "real" Russian. Even though Russian ethnicity is a genetic myth,

16 For one of the formative descriptions of the structure of folk tales, see Propp.

17 See "Ivanushka, the Little Fool."

it is still a powerful social construction. Despite the interconnectivity and implied equality of all people that the films promote, a clear ethnic hierarchy places Russians at the top.

The second corollary is generational. The fairy tales include elderly people, but they are sexless and powerless, while also supportive and benevolent. Bekmambetov's franchise freely acknowledges that neo-liberal Russia has been built for younger people in terms of technologies, public spaces, pace of change, the speed of information, and the circulation of people within the country. The only place for the elderly in these narratives is as comic sidekick or magic helper. Baba Mania (present in the vignettes with the skier and snowboarder) is included in films for comic relief—never, of course, as a commentary on a dilapidated social structure that struggles to provide for the retired. An older man in *Elki 3*, Nikolai Petrovich, suppresses his own need for care in order to help the young girl who is keen to meet her sweetheart for the New Year. Nikolai Petrovich wishes her well with a Facebook message, thus integrating the elderly at least in the fictional world of social media and thereby into modern Russia.

Myth for the Near Future: New Russia, a Constellation of Cities with Expanding Borders

The myth for the future in the *Elki* films is that Russia will return to its place as a global superpower and expand both its influence and its geographic borders. This myth is expressed by depicting Russia as a constellation of cities. The Russia of the future is decidedly urban, and its citizens are technologically on a par with the rest of the world. In this cinematic space, each city is equally important. Despite ambitions for expansion, there is no threat of potential war or even violence. The myth of Russia's bright future ties into the promises of the myths of the past and the present. There will be no trauma in the future, just as all Soviet trauma is now erased. Passivity is and will be the best strategy for moving forward. The absence of potential conflict associated with this expansion has a parallel in the absence of conflict within the vignettes.

The *Elki* films are the first cinematic franchise that represents contemporary Russia as this constellation of cities. Every *Elki* film begins with a map of contemporary Russia in which regional capitals, the major cities in which the vignettes take place, are illuminated against a black background.[18] When transitions are made from vignette to vignette, the map is shown

18 The exception to this rule is *Elki 1914*, set in the year 1914. A map appropriate to the time setting (replete with prerevolutionary orthography) takes the place of the usual map.

again, with lines connecting cities that are linked by cellular telephone calls or social media messages from one character to another.

The projection on screen actually parallels demographic trends in Russia.[19] Villages rarely appear. This model of movement from city to city contrasts with the Stalinist cinematic trope of center and periphery, in which characters sought to reach Moscow. Although *Six Degrees of Celebration* ends in Moscow, and *Elki 2* begins there, the journey to Moscow is not necessary for the majority of characters. They usually remain in or return to the city in which they already find themselves. Many episodes reveal that since each Russian city is every bit the equal of another, characters do not need to change their physical location—just their mindset. And the only reason to move in the first place is for love. The clearest example involves two Ekaterinburg teenage sweethearts, who have been communicating over Skype. One pretends he is in Cuba, while the other acts as though she is in Switzerland. They both discover that each has been lying and later meet by chance. They realize that they actually live in the same city. Characters discover that their home cities are, counterintuitively, the best places to be. Since they are Russian cities, they are the locations in which New Year's miracles are most likely to occur.

The *Elki* films retrospectively reveal a story of Russian geopolitical influence on the world stage, in which ambitions of expansion increase with each successive film.[20] The conceptualization of Russia as a constellation of cities naturalizes these ambitions, since any Russian-speaking city can be included even if it falls out of the internationally recognized sovereign borders. The first two films are set in several cities within the borders of Russia and include Kazakhstan and Tajikistan—arguably, Russia's sphere of influence. They studiously avoid the contentious areas of the Baltics, Georgia, and Ukraine. *Elki 3* expands west to include a vignette in London, and east to include one in Shanghai. In each of these two vignettes, characters must reject the foreign place and its soulless pursuit of money to return to Russia. The point, however, is that these characters had business dealings in these locations. Geopolitically, London and Shanghai represent places that have significant economic ties to Russia. They communicate affluence with less potential for military conflict than continental Europe, the United States of America,

19 For a thorough discussion of the way in which contemporary demographics in Russia centers around cities, see Schulmann.

20 *Elki 6* is the notable exception in which the geographical frontiers of Russia, for once, are not expanded within the film.

or the Middle East. These inclusions characterize Russia as a member of the economic elite nations with political clout. Projecting *economic* influence is just as important as expanding actual physical borders.

As the series progresses, the expansion becomes bolder and more in concert with Russian ambitions. *Elki 1914* (the fourth film), set in 1914, reclaims the pre-Soviet past and creates nostalgia for the Russian Empire. A provocative step occurs in the setting of one of the vignettes in Anapa, a Russian town on the Black Sea as close to Crimea as possible while still remaining in the Russian Federation. Russian military forces invaded Crimea in the same year that *Elki 1914* was made (2014), although before the film was released. The film naturalizes the real-world event by reminding the audience that Crimea was part of the Russian Empire and that adjacent Anapa has always been in Russia proper.

Elki 5 continues this trend to literally new dimensions. This expansion does not engulf the borders of sovereign nations. Rather, the projection is to the only geographical spaces that have not been carved up by nation-states: the Arctic and Outer Space. One story is set on a natural gas extraction rig in the Arctic Ocean;[21] another is set at the International Space Station.[22] Gazprom and Roskosmos sponsored the film.[23] The idea is not so much to resurrect Soviet dominance of space as to bring into play Russia's control of the Arctic region and the extraction of its natural resources, which has been an economic key to Russia's reemergence as a global superpower. Expansion in each film, therefore, claims increasing influence and expanding borders for Russia without openly advocating military action or dissolving international treaties.

Given the way in which this franchise engages with audiences virtually and caters to a Russian-speaking demographic, it would seem that the best model to conceptualize the nation for these films would be to return to Benedict Anderson's notion of imagined community. Rather than the printing press, the system of film distribution and the RuNet (Russian Internet) provide the physical and virtual spaces in which audiences connect with the films. This

21 The move is part of a larger geopolitical agenda to claim large parts of the Arctic Ocean and the North Pole that may be rich in natural resource deposits. Russia has literally planted its flag in the region. See Parfitt.

22 There has been a recent uptick in Russian movies set in outer space. See Klim Shipenko's *Salyut-7* (Saliut-7, 2017) and Dmitrii Kiselev's *Spacewalk* (Vremia pervykh, 2016) (Bazelevs Studio). Like *Elki 5*, *Salyut-7* is sponsored by both Russia-1 and Roskosmos. *Spacewalk* is produced by the same studio as the *Elki* films, Bazelevs, and the director, Kiselev, has worked on several *Elki* films.

23 Gazprom is the Russian state natural gas corporation. Roskosmos is the Russian equivalent of NASA.

connection is based on the Russian language and a shared post-Soviet experience, rather than Russian citizenship per se.

The strange aspect to this conceptualization, though, is the lack of cultural signifiers to stamp the nation as specifically Russian, except for the folktale motifs already discussed and the *elka* (fir tree) itself. In the past, as Boris Grois (*Utopiia*) and Aleksandr Etkind ("Bremia") contend, members of the Russian elite have defined themselves in part through an internal colonization of the village folk, an Other who adhered to different customs, spoke a different kind of language, and had a different set of values. In the *Elki* films, by contrast, the motif of the "authentic villager" is not resurrected or deconstructed; it is completely absent. To be Russian is to be urban and to be urban is to be tech savvy, but in a way that leads to closer communication with fellow Russians rather than dissidence against the Russian state and/or alignment with the global West. The new unifying principle is a type of *sobornost'* (congregationalism) that is not based on a particular philosophical-religious teaching but on a type of popular morality, the "boomerang of good" from *Elki 3*. Within this philosophy, there is a surface desire to be apolitical but the tacit agreement to accept the authority of the state. This *sobornost'* is a distinct kind of imagined community: its participants actually congregate, even if that congregation occurs in a defined, virtual space.

The Myth for All Time: The State and Private Enterprise Are Joined in Matrimony

There is a fourth myth within the *Elki* franchise that combines the previous three and answers a pressing existential question for the post-Soviet Russian subject: what does it mean to be Russian when the lived reality of socialism and the ideals of communism are now gone? And this question is not just about identity. It is about understanding the recent past, navigating the present, and preparing for the future in terms of the political and economic system in which subjects find themselves. The myth that the franchise advocates is that the strong Russian state and new capitalist enterprise are in harmony because, ultimately, the state keeps business in line. The metaphor for this relationship between business and the state is matrimony.

This narrative is realized in vignettes that sustain the structure of a fairytale and, as such, often end with "marriage"—that is, the beginning of a formal relationship. The curious aspect of this choice, however, comes in the gendering. Many of the male heroes in the *Elki* stories directly represent state authority, while many of the corresponding female love interests of these male characters are connected with capitalist enterprise and technology. The result is often a symbolic marriage of state and private interest on screen through likable young characters, but one in which the state is in the position of authority at the top of the hierarchy, just as the husband is "the head of the household" in a traditional marriage. The metaphor and what it represents reinforce each other. They provide an unspoken counterdistinction to the model of the West, in which the state does not necessarily hold all the power over private enterprise and the traditional marriage, dominated by the husband over the wife, is less often represented as the ideal dynamic.

In *Six Degrees of Celebration*, the thief (Smol'ianinov) who escapes jail, donning the uniform of a police officer, dodges into an Evroset' cellular telephone store to hide. When the store is robbed, the thief plays the role of the police officer and foils the robbery, saving the young woman who works in the store. The cellphone business, gendered as female, is a damsel in distress who must be "rescued" by the representative of the state who, ironically, is also a thief. The vignette is both an endorsement of state authority and an advertisement for Evroset'. Just as the two young characters who represent the state and business get together by the end of the film, government and state authority are shown in a healthy and appropriately functioning relationship as well, in which the police protect legitimate businesses from criminals.

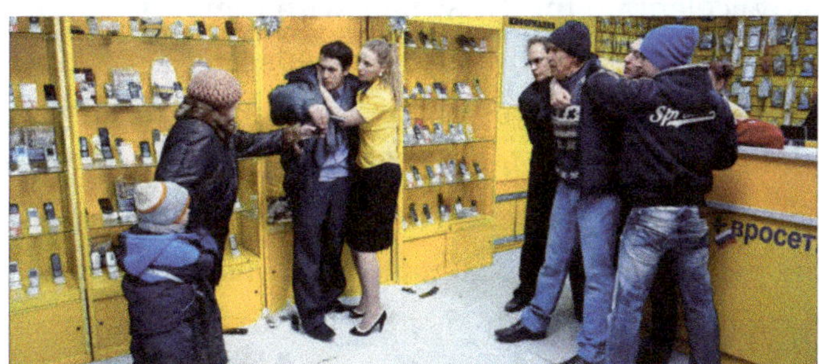

Fig. 12.1. Bekmambetov (producer), *Six Degrees of Celebration*. The female love interest comforts the thief in police officer's clothing after he foils the robbery.

The valence of this comedic episode shifts, however, when the actual social history of Evroset' is taken into consideration. The original owner of the company, Evgenii Chichvarkin has claimed that *siloviki* (enforcers) from the Russian Ministry of Internal Affairs repeatedly attempted to blackmail Evroset' by seizing its mobile telephones.[24] Although Chichvarkin wrote a letter to then President Vladimir Putin asking for protection, he claims he was ignored. Chichvarkin appealed to the US Department of State, and then Secretary of State Condoleezza Rice even

24 For Chichvarkin's side of the story, see Dud'.

raised the issue with Putin. Eventually, Chichvarkin sold the company in 2008 for a fraction of its yearly revenue to oligarch Aleksandr Mamut and fled to London amid allegations of kidnapping.[25] It is unknown the extent to which the filmmakers of *Six Degrees of Celebration*, which was released in 2010, were aware of this history. The lighthearted lack of conflict in the film, however, is at odds with a complex history of conflict between state officials and a private actor, in which the state clearly dictated the terms and conditions for a business to operate and caused a private businessman to flee the country.[26]

Just as there are clear hierarchies of gender in these films, other episodes that involve romantic relationships reveal attitudes about ethnicity and orientation. In *Elki 3*, the protagonist of one vignette is an ethnically Russian male police officer involved in a mixed union with a Central Asian woman. The valence of the film comes out clearly when the police officer chooses the name of their child. He dismisses the suggestions from his wife's relatives for a Tajik name in favor of the Russian name Ivan. The wife has no speaking part. Although marriage between ethnicities is acceptable and even endorsed, the franchise still observes a hierarchy of ethnicity, national origin, and language.

Elki 3 encourages multiculturalism and marriages of mixed ethnicities of a certain type, but the messaging on sexual orientations that are not expressly heterosexual is less ambivalent. In *Elki 3*, Boria (Urgant) and Zhenia (Svetlakov) celebrate the New Year with their wives after their escape from the psychiatric ward. At the stroke of midnight, they separately kiss their respective wives. Boria motions as if to kiss Zhenia, who responds by backing away and reminding Boria that "hey, that's for next New Year!" (*eto uzh na sleduiushchii Novyi god!*), an ironic statement that reveals what is acceptable under the contemporary political order. On the one hand, it is markedly homophobic, making light of homosexual male relations. On the other hand, the joke ("for next New Year") subtly suggests that the film is in line with a state agenda that could change over time. It is a slight ironic nod to a younger generation of viewers who may fancy themselves more cosmopolitan.

25 According to *Kommersant''*, Mamut bought 100 percent of the company for $1.25 billion, $850 million of which went to pay the reported company debt, leaving Chichvarkin with $400 million. According to the same article, the total revenue of Evroset' for the year in 2007 was $5.6 billion. See Khodonova and Bordiug.

26 Sadly, the episode does not end there. In 2010, Chichvarkin's mother Liudmila Chichvarkina passed away in Moscow. Despite evidence that she had been assaulted just hours before her death, no homicide investigation was ever carried out. See "Mat' Chichvarkina."

The Creation and Marketing of the Franchise

Production: The Evening News Format and the Resurrection of Television

In Bazelevs Studio's innovative mode of production, different teams produce disparate and seemingly unrelated content that is later edited into a final product. In some ways, this approach mirrors the system of production for the television evening news format. Television is the vehicle for this process despite the negative associations it had at the end of the Soviet period, when both the television set itself and what it broadcast came to symbolize the failures of the Soviet system. The actual object was not as technologically sophisticated as its Western and Japanese counterparts. And its broadcasting went silent in times of political crisis, when prerecorded versions of *Swan Lake* played on air instead of live coverage of events as they unfolded. It is no coincidence that state television Channel Russia-1 is a major sponsor of the *Elki* franchise and appears in the opening credits of each film. The rebranding of television programming correlates to the myth for the past, which proclaims that Soviet trauma has now been erased in the New Russian present.

At the heart of the franchise is head producer Timur Bekmambetov, a director who made his name in the 1990s by producing television commercials and music videos at a time of low cinema attendance and production.[27] The model for the *Elki* vignettes could be traced to this encounter with new visual formats. All of the several interlocking vignettes in each *Elki* film, however, have their own director, cast, and cinematographer(s), as well as lighting, costuming, and makeup crews. Every story is a film unto itself that can be edited, included, or excluded at will. Ostensibly, this system leads to greater economic flexibility and lowers costs, since no one director or actor can halt the show.[28] Although the model prioritizes financial sustainability over ideological messaging, it also has a socialist legacy beyond the evening news format. This mode of production has the real effect of employing many people and functioning as a school for younger directors and other production professionals. For many, it is not a first chance, but a mid-career move that allows them to earn money and pursue more controversial projects, or

[27] The most famous of these commercials were the series entitled *World History: Bank Imperial,* shot from 1992 to 1997. Bekmambetov also produced two music videos for songs by Russian rock singer Iuliia Chicherina, *Tu-la-la* (2000) and *Zhara* (2000).

[28] It is a solution to the problem that had confronted Bazelevs with the sequel to *Wanted*—the sequel was stalled because star Angelina Jolie would not commit to the film. See Douglas.

simply films with lower budgets. A prime example is Aleksander Kott, who worked on several *Elki* films and then moved to direct his own project, *The Test* (Ispytanie, 2014), a feature film about Soviet atomic bomb testing on the Kazakh steppe. The *Elki* film narratives tell fairytales, while the film production itself acts out a narrative of personal social advancement in lived experience for those who work on the film. It is an evolution over the Soviet system of film director education. The directors who work on the *Elki* films are apprentices in Bekmambetov's master studio.[29]

Vesti—which plays on Russia-1, the television channel that sponsors the films—is the television program in New Russia that most closely aligns with the *Elki* franchise. It goes without saying that *Vesti* and Russia-1 are owned by the state and receive directives from the Kremlin. The digital sheen of bright piercing blue (a clear rebranding in tune with global news formats after the fall of communism) pervades both the *Elki* films and the news outlet *Vesti*. *Vesti* even appears in *Elki 3*, when an international news story about the central vignette

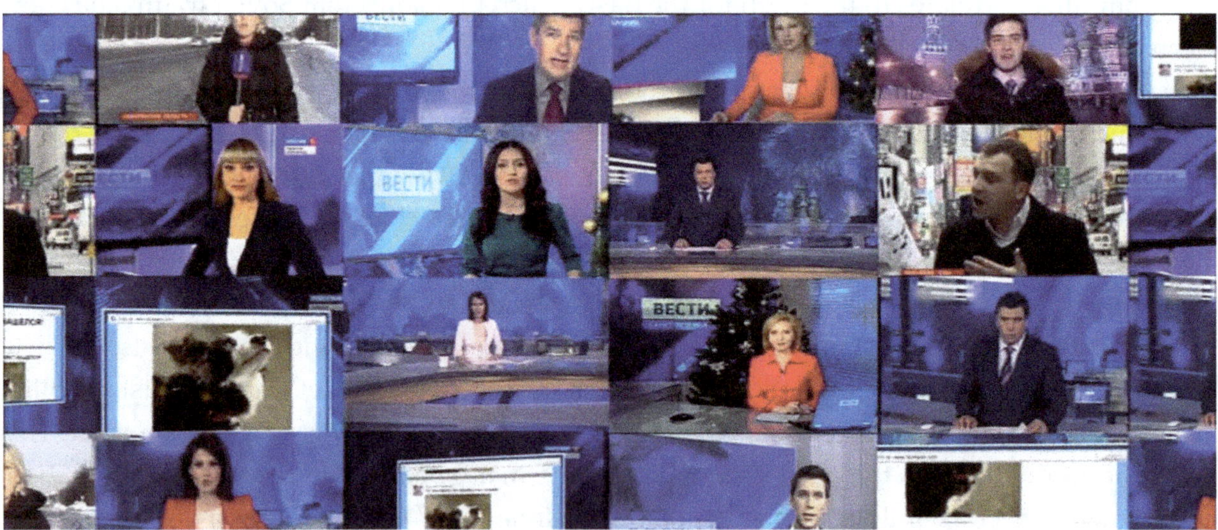

Fig. 12.2. Bekmambetov (producer), *Elki* 3. Each local *Vesti* news outlet reports an event from the central vignette.

breaks. Furthermore, a news outlet features prominently in *Six Degrees of Celebration* when (then) President Dmitrii Medvedev appears on screen to resolve the plot and deliver a secret

29 About the role of film workshops led by major Soviet or Russian filmmakers, see Mukhortova in this volume.

message in his New Year's congratulations to the country. Despite the gap between fiction and nonfiction, the *Elki* films share a similarity to state-controlled news programming in Russia: they are simultaneously entertainment and state messaging.[30] They represent "real-world" Russia as a place with opportunities for advancement, and with an honest and benevolent state that enforces the rule of law. The *Elki* films are produced quickly and regularly, and they rely on a host of actors, most of whom—similar to news anchors—may be replaced with no significant damage to the end product.

The exceptions to this rule are, of course, the franchise's major stars, Ivan Urgant and Sergei Svetlakov, both of whom had made their careers in television before cinema,[31] and who appear in each film except the spinoff. In the Russo-Soviet context, cinema has been closely linked with theater, especially the cross-pollination of actors and production workers. Bekmambetov and the *Elki* franchise are, by contrast, intimately linked with television, specifically at the level of funding and production.

The connection to the television evening news format has two repercussions. The first is about capacity. This model can handle a higher volume for a larger audience (target audience = every citizen) in a shorter time than a traditional film, especially since the genre routinely demands neither stunts nor special effects. The second point is about content. The lines between fiction and nonfiction blur: the lacquered simulations subtly begin to seem true to life. The loyal subject of the state and the active consumer of commodity goods suddenly become conjoined.

Marketing in a Transmedial Landscape: "Elki" Adapts to the Latest Platform

The myth for the present concerns apolitical orientation and passivity. It is embodied in the *Elki 3* episode, in which Facebook "likes" magically resolve the central vignette. The power of the latest social media platform has a parallel outside the franchise in the way that the films are marketed. Each film is a document of the time of its production, in which the latest technological device is at the heart of connecting the vignettes. These devices change with the times.

30 See, for example, infotainment morning shows such as *Good Morning!* (Dobroe utro!) on Channel One Russia and *Morning of Russia* (Utro Rossii) on Russia-1.

31 Urgant is most famous for his late-night show *Evening Urgant* (Vechernii Urgant); Svetlakov for his participation in the sketch variety show *Comedy Club* and the game show *KVN*.

The social media campaigns of the *Elki* franchise aim to keep fans engaged with the franchise year-round, rather than just at the New Year's release. For *Elki 3*, an official *Elki* website from which one could access Facebook, Instagram, Odnoklassniki, Twitter, and *VKontakte* facilitated sharing material related to the film. For *Elki 1914*, free online video games were associated with the franchise ("Elki 1914"). Pages and feeds were uploaded throughout the year and provided space for the community of *Elki* fans to interact with the franchise and each other. In the months leading up to the release of *Elki 3*, fans were encouraged to tag photos on Instagram, showing their love of the New Year's spirit. Beginning in September and concluding before the release of the film, a winner was announced each week, with the corresponding photograph posted on the official website ("Avtory"). These contests advertise for the film with little financial investment. They reify the notion that actions in the virtual world of social media can have real effects in the physical reality of lived experience.

Social media and the Internet have also deeply influenced the visual aesthetic of these films. The mise-en-scène—with its attention to white space, digital sheen, and product placement—

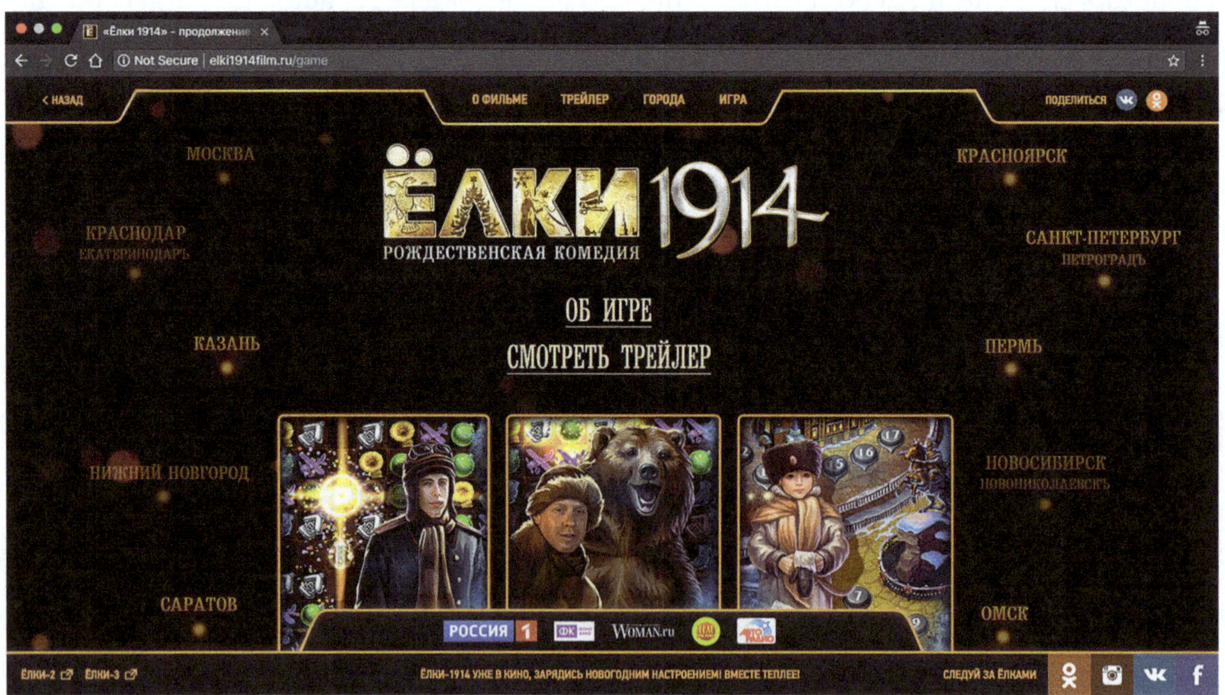

Fig. 12.3. *Elki 1914* website. The website links to franchise pages on *Odnoklassniki*, Instagram, *VKontakte*, and Facebook.

begins to look like an ideal webpage. Characters are constantly on their devices: at first, cellular telephones, then tablets and computers. In *Elki 6*, most of the footage is shot by the young protagonist who turns the camera on himself, a reference to the latest trend of users live-vlogging their daily activities for an online audience.[32] Technology is, in fact, the centralizing hero of the film. It is the character that connects all other characters and ultimately allows good deeds to flourish. All of the action occurs against the background of a digital sparkle, a high-production value that is updated with every new addition to the series.

This does not mean that television as a technology becomes outdated—rather, it remains the lifeblood of a franchise in which other technologies are constantly changing. These films are conducive to being replayed on television, especially for screening after the Soviet classic film *Irony of Fate* (1975) that plays every year in Russia on the New Year. The *Elki* films may run in the background, without demanding too much attention as people continue to celebrate into the night. Similar to New Year's trees themselves, they are props that add to the holiday with bright, digital tinsel. Although each film is made for the present and to reflect the present, it is also structured to occupy a place in the recent past when the time comes. The goal is to connect to that positive legacy of Soviet culture that does not have associations with trauma. And part of the potential nostalgia for these films is the way in which they encapsulate a specific time period with technological devices that quickly become dated.

Distribution and Exhibition in the Constellation of Cities

The methods of distribution and exhibition for the *Elki* franchise cater to the constellation of cities themselves, which has become a demographic trend in Russia. These practices point to a future that is optimistic, even if that future is only in the short term. This section discusses three ways in which the films draw on the concept of *sobornost'* mentioned previously in this chapter. Social media promote the franchise and organize fans to participate in events of congregation in physical reality. This very process of congregation in the real world mirrors the actions of characters portrayed on screen.

32 See also in this volume Mukhortova's discussion of Bekmambetov developing a new film genre, which the filmmaker calls the "screen life" genre.

The clearest example of *sobornost'* concerns the (predominantly) Russian cities that are the settings for the films' vignettes. They are often regional capitals and, more importantly, the locations of large multiplexes where the films play. Cities drive exhibition, the congregation of people in cinema theaters to watch each film when it is released. For *Six Degrees of Celebration,* premieres were scattered over a few dates in December, so that regional cities that feature in the film's diegesis could have their own individual premieres (Gray, "Timur Bekmambetov"). New *Elki* installments often include new cities, but the "usual suspects" have remained. Since the equality of cities is paramount to the ideology of the film franchise, marketing events usually occur in several different cities rather than a single one. The governing mood is conflictlessness. Any rivalry among cities is dissolved through the acts of communication and congregation.

Two additional real-life marketing events intersect with exhibition and serve as further examples of *sobornost'*. Their organizing principle is literally the depiction of the audience on screen. During the summer before *Elki 3* was released, production crews visited several regional cities in order to film fans collectively organized to form the shape of a single letter. A crane shot took footage from a bird's-eye view, and the letters were later composited to form the phrase "Happy New Year" in Russian. Each letter and the composited digital image appear at the end of *Elki 3.*[33] The act of organizing fans in a public physical space in their home city was, itself, a rehearsal for going to the premiere of the film. Of course, the expectation is that people filmed in each letter would invite friends and family to see them in the film. This exhibition practice also contains an ideological message: "Happy New Year!" is a slogan that unites the country through a shared national heritage without associations to a specific ethnicity or religion. The phrase is then literally made up, on screen in *Elki 3*, of an urban Russian population. The unspoken point is that the real heart and soul of New Russia is in the city, the only place with opportunities for visibility and—by extension—social advancement and a viable future.

The other marketing and exhibition strategy that reifies *sobornost'* is evident in *Elki 2*. Several months before the release of the film, fans were encouraged to send in home videos of how they celebrate the New Year (Gray, "Dmitrii Kiselev"). At the end of *Elki 2*, the chosen films

33 The Russian cities are Ufa, Magnitogorsk, Krasnodar, Ekaterinburg, Perm', Voronezh, Irkutsk, and St. Petersburg. Almaty (Kazakhstan) was the only location not in Russia. Each letter consisted of at least five hundred individuals. See "S''emki."

were then played in the credits, suturing fans into the film to blur the lines between a fantasy projection of life in Russia and actual lived reality. The reward for the best story was a round-trip ticket from any city in Russia to any other city in Russia. This prize makes real the notion that Russia is merely a constellation of cities with not much in between. Even if one's starting point and destination are not major cities, all Russians—the contest suggests—are connected through the cities closest to them.

The mythology of the future is simple in these latter two examples: the future holds an immediate reward because you, the spectator, will experience the joy of literally appearing in the film. In the greater context, the myth of a bright future devoid of violence is supported by a film franchise that interacts with spectators and responds to them. The model in this respect is more bottom-up than top-down. Even though the producers of the film have the final say, this form of interaction suggests that Russia has become a more open society that responds to everyday people, even as the state becomes more controlling of citizens and intrudes into their everyday lives. This invasion occurs eerily through the trackable technological devices that the films show citizens so happily using.

Funding and Advertising: The State Wins the Messaging Battle with Corporations

The *Elki* franchise relies on both corporate sponsorship and state subsidy. This hybrid of private and public investment means that both corporations and the state have a stake in the messaging of the film. It is a combination that ties all of the loose ends of this franchise together. Corporate sponsorship appears in the form of product placement. The traces of state subsidy in the films themselves, however, are more difficult to pin down, but they relate to the narratives discussed in the first section of this chapter. Over the arc of the *Elki* franchise, state messaging has taken an increasing share, to the extent that the primary corporate sponsors of *Elki 5* are state-owned Gazprom and Roskosmos.

Even in the first *Elki* film, the dominant "advertisement" is arguably an endorsement for the benevolence of the state in the form of a cameo by then Russian President Dmitrii Medvedev. A television screen within the diegesis mediates his presence as a reminder to the audience that he is more of an "advertisement" with a specific message than a character within the film. In addition to being an endorsement of the state, this episode shows the way in which television as a particular technology is divorced from its negative Soviet associations and rebranded with

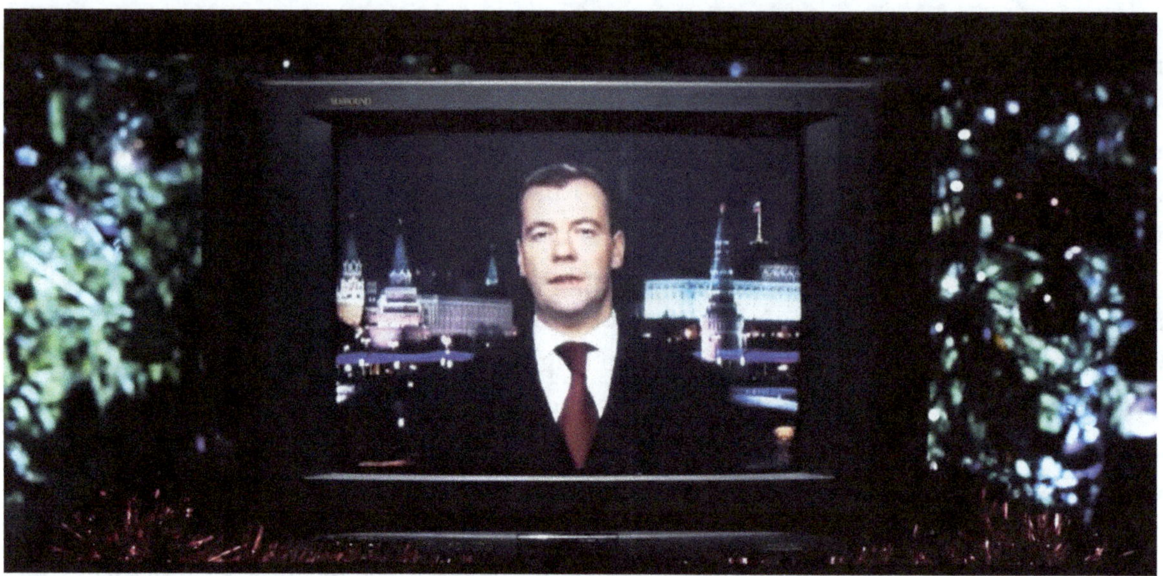

Fig. 12.4. Bekmambetov (producer), *Six Degrees of Celebration*.
President Medvedev delivers the secret message at the stroke of midnight.

positive associations for the state. The highest state official, the president, listens to and does a good deed for the humblest citizen, the orphaned child. This characterization of the technology of television also sets the stage for each successive social medium to be subsumed under the aegis of the state without necessarily being a tool of pure propaganda.

Product placement occurs throughout the *Elki* series of films, and yet a projection of Russian affluence seems more important than selling specific commodities. This fact occurs most clearly with product placements for S7 airlines and Yakutia Diamonds in the vignettes with Urgant and Svetlakov in *Six Degrees of Celebration*. As the *Elki* series progresses, certain corporate sponsors fall out. McDonald's, for example, appears only in the first film. Mercedes features in the third installation but not the fourth, fifth, or sixth. Here geopolitics speaks louder than money. The product placement for Evroset' in this context is chilling, even if the filmmakers and producers were unaware of the history of its founder, Chichvarkin. It is a reminder that cooperation with the state is the only road to success—pure enterprise without state oversight cannot be allowed to exist, especially when it comes to products at the heart of technology, entertainment, and communication. The telecommunications and film industries are not so disparate in the greater context of New Russia's economy.

* * *

In the introduction to this chapter, I argued that the *Elki* franchise could be seen as an inverse of the Western model of the film franchise. Yet producer Timur Bekmambetov's cross-pollination with Hollywood has deeply influenced the visual aesthetic and production mode of these films. *Elki* cannot be divorced from this Hollywood context, but it also cannot be separated from its own cultural and politico-economic context, not only from Russia of the Putin era, but from the Soviet Union as well. In a certain sense, the *Elki* franchise has become a fulfillment of the Soviet ideal for cinema: a (basically) controlled economy produces films that both bring in revenue and promote a series of state-approved messages. The most important of these messages is to trust the state for economic fulfillment and a stable status quo.

Filmography

Baranov, Aleksandr, Levan Gabriadze, et al., dir. *Elki 2* (2011).
Bekmambetov, Timur, dir. *Day Watch* (Dnevnoi dozor, 2005).
———. *Irony of Fate 2.* (Ironiia sud'by. Prodolzhenie, 2007).
———. *Night Watch* (Nochnoi dozor, 2004).
———. *Six Degrees of Celebration* (Elki, 2010).
———. *Wanted* (2008).
———. *World History: Bank Imperial* (Vsemirnaia istoriia: Bank Imperial, 1992–97).
Bekmambetov, Timur, dir. Performer Iulia Chicherina. *Tu-la-la* (2000). Music video.
———. *Zhara* (2000). Music video.
Bekmambetov, Timur, Aleksandr Kott, et al., dir. *Elki 5* (2016).
———. *Elki 1914* (2014).
Burton, Tim. *Batman* (1989).
———. *Batman Returns* (1992).
Dobrodeev, Oleg, Evgenii Kiselev, et al., creators. *Vesti* (1991–present). Television show.
Donner, Richard, dir. *Superman* (1978).
Gabriadze, Levan, Aleksandr Kott, et al., dir. *Elki 3* (2012).
Jackson, Peter, dir. *The Lord of the Rings: The Fellowship of the Ring* (2001).
———. *The Lord of the Rings: The Two Towers* (2002).
———. *The Lord of the Rings: The Return of the King* (2003).
Karpilovskii, Aleksandr, Dmitrii Kisilev, Zhora Kryzhovnikov, et al., dir. *Elki 6* (Elki novye, 2017).
Kiselev, Dmitrii, dir., *Spacewalk* (Vremia pervykh, 2016).

Kononov, Iurii, dir. *Good Morning!* (Dobroe utro!, 1997–present). Television show.
Kott, Aleksandr, dir. *The Test* (Ispytanie, 2014).
Lucas, George, dir. *Star Wars Episode IV: A New Hope* (1977).
———, creator. *Star Wars Episode V: The Empire Strikes Back* (1980).
———, creator. *Star Wars Episode VI: Return of the Jedi* (1983).
Oblomov, Vasia, perf. *Magadan* (2010). Music video.
Parmas, Anna, Timur Bekmambetov, Egor Baranov, et al., dir. *Elki 7* (2018).
Riazanov, El'dar, dir. *The Irony of Fate, or Enjoy Your Bath!* (Ironiia sud'by ili S lekhkim parom!, 1976).
Schumacher, Joel, dir. *Batman Forever* (1995).
———. *Batman & Robin* (1997).
Shestakov, Igor', prod. *Morning of Russia* (Utro Rossii, 1998–present). Television show.
Shipenko, Klim, dir. *Salyut-7* (Saliut-7, 2017).
Sveshnikov, Maksim, dir. *Paws, Bones, & Rock'n'roll* (Elki lokhmatye, 2015).
Svetlakov, Sergei, performer. *Comedy Club* (2005–present). Television show.
———. *KVN* (1995–present). Television show.
Urgant, Ivan, performer. *Evening Urgant* (Vechernii Urgant, 2012–present). Television show.

Part Five

INTERVIEWS

The Mediascape: Alexander Rodnyansky
(CEO, AR Films, Non-Stop Production)

In 2017, *Variety* named you among the 500 "most influential business leaders in the global entertainment industry." No one (except perhaps Timur Bekmambetov) has worked so effectively in a global market. Has the profession of media leader reached the historical moment when the young executive must be trained on a transregional scale in order to survive? Is "school" an archaic concept?

Absolutely not. I would say that the opposite is true: to be truly global you have to be as local as possible. The global market today is driven by local content that achieves international success not because it was engineered to be transregional, but rather because it grew from a very personal experience of someone who can share his story with the world in a way that is both reflective of his culture and relatable to people around the globe. That is the trick, and you can't really teach it. On the other hand, if you try to be global you will most certainly fail.

You have written (IndieWire and *Vedomosti*) that the US viewer seeks authentic social issues, whereas the Russian viewer more often prefers fantasy. But the United States is the Land of Hollywood, a place where inauthenticity and sugar coating are historically what our cinema does best. Is the US viewer maturing, or are you too "severe" toward your own (Russian) compatriots?

The tradition of both Hollywood and Soviet cinema was founded on bringing reality to the screen, trying to reflect on the state of the world and human nature. And both industries, when it was appropriate, sugarcoated reality for mass consumption, but the true art still existed. In modern Russia, this tradition is still mostly absent, as the Russian mass audience prefers escapism to honest conversations. If you believe that cinema has a certain therapeutic function—it diagnoses the problems and offers the audience a chance to talk about them, to think—then our contemporary audience is a patient who refuses to see the doctor. Having said that, I would add that, as an older audience flocks to Russian film theaters, we start to see how modern, serious Russian drama gains more and more popularity—still on the fringes of the industry, and in no way in competition with mainstream genre, but there is growth as reflected by the box office.

It was difficult to predict (in the early 1990s) that Kinotavr would become the leading regional festival. But what were its key moments of crisis? Were its most serious crises external to the festival (for example, 1998 or 2008) or internal to its identity as a festival?

During the 1990s, Kinotavr was a festival whose main function was to promote rare Russian films made during that time, to make the audience aware of their existence before they were released on VHS. There was no theatrical industry and no other way of distribution. The festival was an event mainly because of the Soviet stars who attended it, and it was the only place where you were able to see Russian films on the big screen. It all changed when *Titanic* was released and when the Russian theatrical industry began taking shape and growing. Soon Russian films were again released theatrically and—in this new reality—I decided to change the focus of the festival and make it national. It was, so to speak, a full-service agency for blooming talent: young directors would debut with their short films, would come back with their first features, and a few years later would win the best prize of the festival. Hundreds of reporters from every possible media attend the festival every year, and in terms of positive marketing, this has had a tremendous effect on every film screened. But it is also a place where new talent is discovered, and important issues of our contemporary life are discussed and analyzed in film. External economic events have affected us, but only in a limited financial way: they never affected our core ideas or concepts.

The Festival: Sitora Alieva
(Program Director, Kinotavr)

You have had extraordinary training: actress, academic, scriptwriter, promoter, editor (*Iskusstvo kino*), and now artistic director of the largest national film festival. What advice would you give today to those seeking to "find their place" in the contemporary cinema process? Is it "life experience" (as in Maxim Gorky's *My Universities*) or institutional training?

Technology changed the way that we perceive cinema, and the Internet changed the way that films are distributed. Today anyone is a director and everyone is a distributor, so I believe that everything is important: institutional education, personal experience, and most importantly an understanding of what cinema is in the twenty-first century. To quote Gilles Jacob, the previous general delegate (1978–2004) and president (2001–14) of Cannes Film Festival: you need to watch every film, read every book, and become who you really are.

Your task is (on the one hand) to advocate for difficult films but (on the other) to support the film industry's health as a commercial venture. Has this contradiction become easier in recent times (or more difficult)?

Today there is no such contradiction: a talented director can work in any film genre, radical art or mainstream. Contemporary global experience shows that directors do just that, moving from one sector of filmmaking to another and back.

US viewers know Eisenstein (*Battleship Potemkin*), Tarkovsky (*Stalker*), and Sokurov (*Russian Ark*). They do not know Russian comedy or (more broadly) Russian blockbusters. Be our professor: choose for us one post-Soviet Russian comedy and one blockbuster that should be taught in any US university seminar on Russian cinema.

For comedy, I would nominate *The Land of Oz,* written and directed by Vasilii Sigarev, a thoughtful and funny film about life in Russia's provinces. And for a blockbuster, I'd say *Stalingrad* is the most important one. The Battle of Stalingrad changed the way that modern wars are conducted, but—more importantly—the film by Fedor Bondarchuk changed the way that modern Russian films talk about the Great Patriotic War. From a technological standpoint, *Stalingrad* was masterful, an amazingly shot film. And for the first time, a German character was not just a personification of evil but an actual human. This is a new way of exploring character for contemporary Russian films.

The Exhibition Space: Paul Heth
(CEO, Rising Star Media; Karo Film Holding)

What was the event or opportunity that drew you to the Russian industry in 1993?

Believe it or not, it was more happenstance or fate that I ended up in Russia. In 1993, I had finished my commitment to the army, was doing some work for a businessman in Los Angeles. He in turn asked me to visit Russia to check in on a timber project he had invested in the Far East of Russia. Although I did not stay in the timber industry, while visiting Moscow on this assignment, I got the idea about starting a cinema and the rest is history!

The top three 1990s cinema challenges, most would agree, were piracy, piracy, and piracy. Beyond these, what were the obstacles you encountered? Who turned out to be good local (Russian) collaborators, as you figured out a path ahead?

The obstacles were manifold. I would say the main three challenges other than piracy were:

- The cost of capital—meaning, the scarcity of investment capital—was a massive challenge. The cinema sector is generally a modest-margined retail business, so it was very hard (at the time) to find investors who were willing to accept longer payback periods.
- Lack of malls or retail developments to develop and place cinemas in, as mass retail and malls themselves each took, on average, five to seven years to plan, construct, lease out, and open. This was an early-on challenge, as I bet all I had on the premise that multiplexes were vital to revitalize the Russian cinema sector. Soviet cinema had been focused on classic single-screen movie theaters. I believed that, like other large, global cinema markets, the modern multiplex offering a variety of films would reengage moviegoers. I am glad to say I was right.
- Lack of films, both locally produced and Hollywood produced. In the early 1990s, I had to buy independent films one at a time in LA and bring them in on a plane week by week. In the early 2000s, we convinced the Hollywood majors to open local offices and distribute directly into the market. As the market grew, local production began to increase output little by little and began to break out with some hits.

Many say that the top three challenges today facing the Russian cinema are market share (currently around 23%), a low per-capita penetration of screens, and a need for more content (to fill both the screens and the seats). Do you agree with this assessment? What does it overlook?

I do not agree fully with this view.

- I would rather have a sustainable flow of quality films than just sheer quantity. I do believe local market share will level out in the next few years to 30–35 percent.
- Same challenge as I mentioned earlier is the lack of more mall/mass retail infrastructure. In the last few years, real-estate development was slowed considerably by the stagnation and recession in the overall Russian economy.
- Bit of a concern about the Russian Ministry of Culture trying to protect local films by blacking out certain release dates of the Hollywood blockbusters. This is ill advised, as film selection by moviegoers is based on quality, no matter who is the producer. For all consumer products, achieving success or failure in a market economy is based on consumers voting with their wallets. We see now Russian blockbusters out-grossing Hollywood films on certain dates. We also see Hollywood films out-grossing Russian films in the same manner. Our moviegoers have an expectation that all films have to have high production values and high-caliber storytelling.

The Film Journal: Birgit Beumers
(*KinoKultura*, UK)

Do *KinoKultura* contributors East and West often see cinema differently? Is there a "Western view"? What about an "academic view," as opposed to that of critics and journalists?

My favorite answer to all black-and-white questions is: it all depends—or, to speak with film technology: I prefer color. In any case, I never distinguish authors by nationality or background—geographical, academic, or disciplinary—since I think it's unproductive. First of all, we often have Russian authors who have lived and/or studied abroad. Second, to what extent would an American or British scholar of Russian culture have a different view from a Russian scholar, and where would the difference be? We have all spent lengthy periods of time in Russia, and surely our views are "tinted" or "toned." The question suggests national or educational categories I don't share. Good film analysis transcends borders and focuses instead on the subject of the review or the article and contextualizes it. Often an Asian context can be more helpful in a film analysis than a Western/European/American one; often local knowledge helps, but not always—sometimes it obscures the view. That's one of the reasons why we have the "double view" rubric, where we publish sometimes different and sometimes similar perspectives on the same film: to highlight precisely that convergence and divergence of views does not necessarily have to do with East and West. What is really important is to get a range of different authors and to encourage younger scholars to try their hand at writing a review, so they have a starting point for further writing of a different nature, be that journalistic or academic.

Having said this about a universal critical discourse, there is, however, one issue that arises more in Russian critical discourse than in Western views: the almost obsessive measure of the film against reality. I keep being reminded of the time when, in the late 1960s, "workers of the agricultural sector" (Soviet-speak for peasants) were called to a screening of Andrei Konchalovskii's *Asya Klyachina* and to a rehearsal of Iurii Liubimov's stage production of Boris Mozhaev's *From the Life of Fedor Kuzkin* to assess and evaluate the authenticity of the film/show to condemn it with the words: "it's not like that in real life." Well, no, it's not, because it's a work of fiction. Similarly, and over thirty years later, a Kazakh viewer was outraged to see the character played by the very same Samal Esliamova—who just garnered the first-ever Best Actress award in Soviet/post-Soviet cinema history at Cannes for *Ayka*—wash her hair with kefir: he cried how wrong this was, and that they do have shampoo in Kazakhstan. Sure. A bottle of shampoo in a yurt in the middle of the steppe would have been so much more authentic and convincing! This kind of measurement on a scale reminiscent of socialist realism, trying to ensure that what we see is what we have in life, is not only obsolete but also extraneous to critical discourse. However, when writing for an international readership, much of this pseudorealistic comparison disappears from the reviews.

Concerning critics and journalists, there is another, maybe more important factor to consider: the profession of the film critic or film journalist has changed quite dramatically over recent years, with the development of online publications and blogs, and the closure of many high-quality (and high-profile) print editions. This is a different topic, though, on which a debate should be had: maybe a topic for an article! *KinoKultura* encourages authors to write in an informed manner and in whatever detail they think is necessary; hence there is no limit on the length of the review, unlike in papers and journals. Yet many contributors find it difficult to write within a specific time frame, and you sometimes wonder what they would do in the shoes of a journalist, who often has to write a review within forty-eight hours or a more comprehensive piece within a week. It is a very useful skill to acquire.

While the focus of *KinoKultura*—its "close-up shot," so to speak—is contemporary Russian cinema, the journal often aims more broadly to take stock of Central Eurasian cinema and its festivals, including the cinemas of the Caucasus, the Baltics, and Central Asia. How has the regional profile evolved over the years, since its founding? Has the journal reached its "regional limits"? If it has reached its "regional limits," are there new ideas that you are considering for special issues?

The special issues on the cinematographies of the new "Central Europe" and the former Soviet states that had gained independence after the collapse of the USSR were originally the idea of Vladimir Padunov, who at the time was the journal's co-editor (2003–8). When I launched the journal, it was intended to focus on Russian cinema, because there was so little information on new Russian films; and the little that was there came in the form of printed journals and bulletins rather than online. This was 2002–3, before the boom of the Russian art house and before the rebirth of the Russian film industry with the legendary *Night Watch*. So *KinoKultura* set out to cover new Russian cinema, and the first five issues were only about the thin harvest of Russian films. At the time we also listed "films in production" and had an information page on the film industry ("Novosti"), which folded when this was competently done on Russian sites and therefore redundant. The same is true for lists of new books on Russian cinema, both in Russian and English.

Within the framework of *KinoKultura,* I published in 2004, with permission and at the initiative of Gulnara Abikeyeva, some of the texts from her book on Central Asian cinema (*The Heart of the World*), which had been published in English translation with a very low print run, and which gave an overview of the state of cinema in an even lesser known geographical region. At that point, Vladimir Padunov came up with the idea to invite two of his colleagues, Elzbieta Ostrowska from the University of Alberta and Martin Votruba from Pittsburgh, to guest-edit issues on Polish and Slovak cinema, respectively. These special issues were published within a month of each other, at the end of 2005. I remember that Martin Votruba, who sadly passed away quite recently, played a key role in suggesting a special issue (even though the Slovak issue came second in sequence). In 2007, another two special issues later, we did a little "coup" with the Romanian issue coinciding with the enormous surge of attention to Romanian cinema when Cristian Mungiu's *4 Months, 3 Weeks, 2 Days* (2007) won the Palme d'Or and Cristian Nemescu's debut feature *California Dreamin'* took the award from Un Certain Regard—in the same month as the launch of the Romanian special issue, which covered recent developments of a cinema that had not (yet) been written about widely in English. It has been a great privilege to have several special issues published in collaboration with and with the support of National Film Centers. Moreover, two of the special issues have subsequently been published in book form.

After Vladimir's departure from the journal, I continued the special issues, with some issues on Central Eastern Europe and venturing more intensively into the former Soviet republics, which had by now acquired sufficient infrastructure and produced enough films to fill a special issue. There are two republics, Belarus and Lithuania, that have not been covered through special issues; the edition on Belarusian cinema is in the making. There is probably enough new output now to justify separate editions on some of the Central Asian republics, and there is also an argument for second editions for some countries covered over ten years ago. At the same time, the work with authors specializing in national and regional cinematographies has also meant that more films (especially from Georgia, Kazakhstan, Kyrgyzstan) get reviewed in the regular editions of the journal, so that coverage of the most prolific film industries is guaranteed.

A new aspect is the regional cinemas in autonomous republics and regions of the Russian Federation, and we have carried both articles and reviews on films from Buryatia, Sakha, and Tatarstan, and will continue to do so and highlight the work done and the developments accomplished in those regions.

***KinoKultura* has been the central English-language periodical for building an international community of writers—from first-year PhD students to internationally known critics, journalists, scholars, and industry figures. What kind of intergenerational conversation is this? Is the journal read by critics beyond Moscow and St. Petersburg?**

The journal's readership is mostly from North America, followed by Europe, and then Russia and Asia. Statistically we cannot see where the readership comes from in terms of precise locations, just by country, so it is impossible to say where the readers in Russia sit.

By engaging authors from various countries, I hope to bring together and give opportunities to people who embark on writing about film and who will have an opportunity to measure themselves against more advanced writers from Slavic and film departments, but also professional film critics, and this includes people writing in Yakutia and Kyrgyzstan, Australia and Europe—as long as it enables them to reach out to a readership beyond their own country. As an editor, I am profoundly grateful for recommendations for and suggestions from new authors. In some regions, I depend on the phenomenal support from local film "activists," such as Gulnara Abikeyeva and Gulbara Tolomushova, who ensure that Central Asian and Kyrgyz cinema are incredibly well covered on *KinoKultura* and have their place on the "map."

It may seem that *KinoKultura* is a journal of contemporary cinema, while your other initiative, *Studies in Russian and Soviet Cinema* (SRSC), is dedicated to cinema history. Is that the case? How distinct are their profiles?

SRSC is indeed quite a different project. It is a scholarly journal on the history of cinema—prerevolutionary, Soviet, Russian, and from the post-Soviet space— which appears in three issues per year and carries only articles (no film reviews), but in addition scripts (issue 1), documents (issue 2), and book reviews (issue 3). While *KinoKultura* also publishes articles, these tend to be of a different nature: there are pieces about individual filmmakers or about festivals ("festival reports"); there are different formats, such as interviews or video essays; there are publications that involve statistics and data analysis; there are papers from roundtables; and articles of an early-stage research nature where the author wanted to experiment and try out a different approach. We also tend to publish texts linked to anniversaries, such as thirty years after Tarkovskii's death, or the centenary of the Revolution. Articles undergo a single review process instead of the double-blind peer review by at least two anonymous reviewers that is required for most scholarly journals.

SRSC was launched after *KinoKultura*, and even though a lot of debate went on at the time about the difference between the journals, I think it has become quite clear whether an article would be better suited for *KinoKultura* or *SRSC*, or the other way around. By 2006, *KinoKultura* was in full swing, with a steady flow of articles and reviews (the film industry was also picking up). Massoud Yazdani, the founder of Intellect publishing in Bristol, was expanding his portfolio of journals, which would become quite stunning, especially in film and media, design and visual arts. When I proposed a journal on Russia cinema, he supported it instantly, and it was basically a question of picking a cover design. Massoud had an incredible vision in terms of publishing strategies and futures, competent and inspiring, and with a competence in which you could trust and on which you could rely. I will never forget his commitment to the cinema of Central Asia, first by allowing a special issue of *SRSC* for the Open Doors program at Locarno IFF (2010), and later by commissioning a *Directory of World Cinema* on Central Asia, knowing only too well that it would not really be a bestseller but saying that the region deserved attention. Massoud sadly parted from this world far too early. Before he did, he transferred a bunch of his most established journals to Routledge, which was seeking to expand its journal titles in film studies. *SRSC* was among them. And although Routledge meant a totally different class of distribution and production, I was sad to leave The Mill in Fishponds, Bristol, where *SRSC* started; and with it some of the flexibility that you have with smaller publishers.

However, Routledge's experienced production team has made a genuine effort (and taken some leaps) to accommodate our special requirements.

As editor-in-chief, I have three co-editors, a fabulous book review editor (who must not be forgotten, although it is tempting, because I never need to think of that side of the journal), an editorial board and an advisory council. My two columns of support sit to my right and my left, or geographically to the east and to the west of Bristol: the always inspiring and enthusiastic Julian Graffy in London, who has come up with more than one idea for special features; and the amazing Richard Taylor in Swansea, who has taken on a range of document sections and translated more than one could expect any co-editor to do. Thanks to their support in the background, I can focus on other things, such as actively attracting young scholars to the journal. Indeed, I often call the purpose of conference attendance "paper-shopping," in the sense of encouraging promising paper-givers to consider a submission to the journal. In that same spirit, and with the support of the editorial board acting as jury, we have run a competition for the best graduate essay for volume 5; then for volume 8 the competition was in parallel with the Russian State Institute for Cinematography (VGIK) in Moscow; and in volume 11 we held a competition only for staff and students of VGIK. This has encouraged a number of scholars and meant that some new names have appeared in print, and it has brought to the fore some energetic Russian scholars, who continue to put forward new ideas. The sections on scripts and documents are very good platforms for young scholars to try their hand at editing and translating: Eugenie Zvonkine, Daria Ezerova, Nina Sputnitskaya, and Anna Kovalova have all presented and introduced scripts; Natalie Ryabchikova and Peter Bagrov have led entire document sections. *SRSC* is also keen on special issues, themed or event-based—like the upcoming special issue to mark the centenary of VGIK—and it is a fine opportunity once again for young and experienced scholars to try their hand at guest editing, as Justin Wilmes has recently shown with his Vyrypaev cluster.

If you were to choose one aspect of Russian cinema that has markedly changed in the past five years—whether in the production/exhibition sector or a matter of thematic emphasis—what would it be?

I guess Russian cinema has changed gradually and steadily over the last twenty years, turning from an artistic to a commercial product, while the Russian market literally rose from the ashes to the sixth-largest in the world. So in that sense, globalization would be a key word for an aspect that has changed Russian cinema, but it goes hand in hand with the phenomenon of "blockbusterization." Yet what for the West is a sinister attempt at political control to facilitate patriotic messages in cinema could also be viewed as the rise of a different system from that of Hollywood and the American diet prescribed by the increasingly US-controlled distribution sector in the country. Something like France's quotas, only on a smaller scale and not numerically controlled.

Another sector that has changed already (and will continue to change) is the film press—another topic for a research project. Cinema is always in flux, in terms of production, of distribution, of ideas and of technologies, but not in the way in which films are written about. In film studies we foreground quantitative analysis and audience studies; from philology departments we get texts often made up of plot summaries, yet we have moved well beyond that through multidisciplinary approaches. Few writers/critics pay attention to the changes not only in digital technologies but also in computer effects: for example, Bekmambetov's new software for screen capture (Screenlife); or the implications of mo-cap, ventures into VR and AR, and so on—that is, the world of cinema, rather than the world on screen.

In terms of film history, one aspect that deserves more attention is that of film education and film schools. Maybe with the centenary of the world's oldest film school, VGIK, the ball will get rolling. *SRSC* has a special issue in 2019 on VGIK, in the hope of setting things in motion. However, things have moved in a slightly different direction within the institution itself, which has closed its research department, the Scientific-Research Institute of the Cinematic Arts (Nauchno-issledovatel'skii institut kinoiskusstva, NIIK). Most of our colleagues have lost their jobs or moved to the Museum of Cinema, into a department and roles that will have to be newly defined. Several contributions in the special issue look at the history of *kinovedenie* (film scholarship), drawing attention to the need for film history, a discipline that is increasingly disappearing from film schools but is vital for the development of film art and for the emergence of a young generation of scholars. Looking at current submissions for both journals as well as the *Cinemasaurus* project, something's going right.

What kind of cinema (medium, genre, topic) would you like to see more of in the next several years? "What have we lost" and what could we hope to see?

I don't work with shopping lists—neither in the supermarket nor for my paper shopping. I don't have any wishes or regrets about what we see or don't see on screen. We have what we get. Take it or leave it. However, I have an innate curiosity and I want to be taken aback, surprised, and shaken up. In a sense, I don't want to get what I want, because that would be much too comfortable. The task of a film critic is to analyze why we get what we have. Otherwise, we should be making films rather than watching them. Natasha Merkulova's and Aleksei Chupov's *The Man Who Surprised Everybody* is my film of the year 2018, for the man who did surprise, and for showing us how highbrow viewer expectations can stop you from missing the point, or rather that canard . . .

One aspect that worries me is the state of film criticism (see also above, where I talk about film history), both in Russia, where training in the history of cinema is relegated to less than a footnote in the various curricula, and in Europe. Students should know things (besides how to google) and look attentively at archival stuff. Fortunately, there are quite a few young scholars both in Russia and in the Anglophone world who pay attention to the sources and who care about the possibilities we have to reconstruct cinema's history through documents. Anna Kovalova is a point in case, having just produced an article for *SRSC* to introduce the script and libretto for a lost film (Meyerhold's *The Picture of Dorian Gray*) and equipping us with a toolkit of how this can be done.

The Film Symposium: Vladimir Padunov
(Russian Film Symposium, US)

How has the Russian Film Symposium changed since its inception in 1999? Has it seen different stages of development? Different preoccupations or themes? Has it changed as Russia itself has changed?

It was 1999. It was a different world. Films were still on 35-mm celluloid and portable viewing was on VHS cassette tapes. And there were probably still dinosaurs roaming the street at night. By 2018, the world had changed. Digital had fully replaced analog: DVD, Blu-Ray, streaming, and DCP prints. It's a different planet (but I still miss the dinosaurs!).

In these two decades, the symposium changed as well. Actually, it started changing during the very first symposium. When we set out, Nancy and I naively assumed we could handle a three-day event with five films and three Russian participants on our own. It would be a snap. But reality is never kind. So first we had to pull in one graduate student in the Slavic Department to assist us (website—we really didn't know what that was back then; posters and t-shirts—old folks' thinking), then two, then four. Since then, the symposium has exploded. It now lasts seven full days, screens twelve films (eight on subtitled DVD and four on DCP), and has two roundtables. The organizing committee now includes graduate students and faculty from a range of departments—English, Film and Media Studies, French and Italian, German, and, of course, Slavic. That is just an "internal" explanation.

The external one is more complicated. The first symposium was simply called "New Russian Cinema." There were very few new Russian pictures released that year, so it was not difficult to select five debut films by young directors. But as the Russian film industry slowly began to reorganize itself and to encourage new studios with some private capital investment, selection became more difficult. So we started grouping films, sometimes by genre, sometimes by topic, sometimes by studio, etc. After five years of focusing on contemporary films, we decided to do a historical retrospective ("Arrogance & Envy: Anti-American Cinema under Communism and After"). This was the first time that we screened an early Soviet silent film (Kuleshov's *The Extraordinary Adventures of Mr. West in the Land of the Bolsheviks* [1924]). We decided not to use canned music and opted for live musicians. For *Mister West* we used an accordionist. In subsequent retrospective years for silent films we have used an improvisational jazz ensemble and a thereminist.

What has been the role of Kinotavr in shaping the subsequent decisions for the Russian Film Symposium? How does Kinotavr's "harvest" shape what you are interested in screening the following year?

Kinotavr is the premier festival for Russian films in the world and has been central to the activities of the symposium since its inception. Nancy and I have been guests of the festival since 1994, and our twenty-four years there have introduced us not only to a multitude of new Russian films, but also to virtually all of the major players in the Russian film industry—from directors, scriptwriters, and actors to a very wide swath of film scholars and critics to heads of production studios and distribution companies—many of whom have been guests of the symposium over the decades. But the "mother lode," of course, are the films. The work of the Selection Committee for Kinotavr has become more difficult with every passing year. As film production has grown from barely a dozen in 1994 to well over a hundred in 2018, its task of choosing the twelve to fourteen best films released annually for the competition program is daunting, but it also provides participants the opportunity to view these films in an ideal setting.

The morning-after press conferences for competition films screened the day before (frequently including both production crews and cast members), as well as the roundtables for film scholars, critics, and journalists are exceptionally valuable. The ability to listen to the views of the films' producers and participants firsthand cannot be overrated; the opportunity to listen to the kinds of questions posed by Russian critics is fundamental material to non-Russian film scholars.

But in addition to the competition screenings, over the years Kinotavr has also hosted a number of parallel programs; these have included retrospectives, forgotten films, debut films, student films, short films, and especially important: the free evening outdoor screenings for the residents of Sochi of popular blockbuster films released during the year.

Is there a "Symposium film," typical of the Pittsburgh effort? What is off-limits? What are the patterns?

There are a number of directors and actors that the symposium has assiduously tracked over its years: Aleksei Balabanov, Renata Litvinova, Nikolai Lebedev, Sergei Makovetskii, Alexei Mizgirev, Kira Muratova, Larisa Sadilova, Vasilii Sigarev, Iana Troianova, etc. At the same time, the symposium has placed an emphasis on debut films by young directors or directors who have switched their professions in the industry (for example, Rustam Ibragimbekov and Aleksandr Mindadze, both of whom worked for most of their careers as scriptwriters before directing and both of whom have been guests of the symposium).

Many of my colleagues at the university, and especially in the Film and Media Studies Program, are convinced that we screen only the "darkest" films released in Russia; that our goal—deliberate or not—is to traumatize audiences. And yet they come year after year and have begun to include contemporary Russian cinema in their courses.

Over the past five or six years, since the reinstatement of puritanical and repressive injunctions on Russian culture (anti-LGBTQ legislation, language sanitization laws, the banning of a host of topics and themes, the refusal to issue certain films a "release certificate"), we have gone out of our way to screen these films during a symposium. At times it has been difficult to negotiate with studios about screening films, the language of which had been "brought to state standards" (either by redubbing the dialogue or by bleeping out words), in their original version. But so far we have succeeded. Nothing is "off-limits." Show us the limits, and our goal will be to cross them.

How has the profile of the Russian guests changed over twenty years? Is the symposium principally a training ground for young cinema scholars, a meeting place for East and West, or a showcase for new films?

The profile has not changed, because there never was a profile to begin with. The goal has always been to invite members of the Russian film industry, whether they were active in film production or film reception. There was one unwritten proviso: always invite new people (a proviso, I admit, we have broken on a couple of occasions). For the first symposium we invited two debut film directors (Larisa Sadilova and Aleksandr Bashirov—who was already a well-established actor) and Irina Shilova, the managing editor of *Kinovedcheskie zapiski*, the leading nongovernmental scholarly film journal in Russia.

Since its founding in 1999, the primary goals of the symposium have been twofold. First, the symposium strives to cut across institutionally constructed "fields of study" in visual culture (art history, communication, cultural studies, film and media studies, photography, and Slavic studies). Our objective is to create during the time of the symposium a number of spaces around a selected group of Russian visual texts that are conducive to establishing and maintaining an active interdisciplinary dialogue among cultural producers and scholars from a variety of disciplines. Second, the symposium attempts to bridge the gap that is traditionally assumed to separate the public (and public's) experience of visual texts from the professional (and professional's) experience. Our objective here is both to involve the rapidly growing local community of Russian-speaking émigrés in the ongoing conversation and to gain access to the untapped and undervalued body of "private or intimate" knowledge they bring to their encounters with Russian visual culture.

In its twenty years, the Russian Film Symposium has screened more than three hundred films (feature films, documentaries, and shorts); has brought five Russian directors (Vadim Abdrashitov, Aleksandr Bashirov, Khusein Erkenov, Rustam Ibragimbekov, and Larisa Sadilova) and the US director George Romero, as well as two of Russia's leading scriptwriters (Aleksandr Mindadze and Rustam Ibragimbekov, now also directors), a film actor (Sergei Makovetskii), a conceptualist performance artist (Dmitrii Prigov), and two directors of film production studios (Sergei Chliiants and Evgenii Gindelis). Forty-seven of Russia's most prominent film critics, historians, and theorists have attended and participated in the symposium over the past twenty years. In addition to the entire faculty of Pitt's Film and Media Studies Program, forty-nine leading scholars of Russian cinema have also participated in the symposium, including participants from Austria, Australia, Czechia, Germany, Hungary, the United Kingdom, and the United States. Finally, delegations of undergraduate and graduate students from Oberlin College, the University of Arizona, the University of Virginia, and Yale University have participated.

The Russian Film Symposium is—among other things—a weeklong dialogue with our colleagues from Russia (critics, journalists, film scholars). Why would Russian colleagues come across the ocean to talk with a collection of foreign strangers?

I suppose curiosity is the driving impulse: What is an American Slavist? What sense do Americans make of "our" cinema, "our" culture? What do "they" not get? The opportunity to experience one's culture sympathetically through the eyes of the "other" rarely comes along. The Russian colleagues who have participated in the two decades of the symposium chose to grab it.

But once the conversations begin, something else kicks in: bonding over words and ideas, over food and drink. The informality of the week-long dialogue (and there is virtually no free time) also produces a kind of professional intimacy that extends well beyond the event itself. Generations of our graduate students have maintained relationships (both personal and professional) with the Russian scholars, critics, and journalists who have participated. At the same time, the Russian participants have the opportunity to meet and engage with some of the most important US, European, and Australian scholars of Russian cinema, who are also, more often than not, in Pittsburgh for the first time in their lives. So it is a neutral space. The only fully grounded participants during the week are the members of the University of Pittsburgh community; everyone else is on a "busman's holiday"—a working vacation.

Once the Symposium is ended, are there collaborations that began in that weeklong meeting? What is its usefulness as a site of connection, networking, or engagement?

In 2001, the symposium published two sixty-page booklets (*Necrorealism* and *Springtime for Soviet Cinema: Re/Viewing the 1960s*), each consisting of a new article by one of the organizers and a translation of a major article by a Russian film scholar. Once they were sold out, we uploaded them as PDF files on the symposium website for free downloads. Twice the online journal *KinoKultura* has published collections of articles prepared for the Symposium: *Melodrama and Kino-Ideology* (no. 17 [2007]) and *The Ideological Occult* (no. 21 [2008]). In 2017, Nevafilm Research in St. Petersburg organized an internship for one of the organizers who was working on a PhD dissertation on contemporary Russian cinema. Even more importantly, the contacts that young scholars acquire at the symposium give them ideas and enrich their research for years to come.

KINO-GRAFIK

From the editors: Several excellent timelines of Russian cinema already exist, most notably Birgit Beumers's *A History of Russian Cinema* (260–91). Our Kino-Grafik is not so much informational as dialogic. It encourages the reader to speculate about three categories: (1) the year's prizes across competitions (note that the more nationalistic Golden Eagle begins only in 2003); (2) the (potential) relevance of mass media's Word of the Year (WoY); and (3) the relevance (or irrelevance) of a single political event. In this spirit, Kino-Grafik intends to stimulate new research questions, not to confirm existing ones.

Year	Kinotavr	Nika Main Prize	Golden Eagle Main Prize
1990 Podol'sk	*Revenge*	*Ashik Kerib*	—
1991	*Sons of Bitches*	*The Asthenic Syndrome*	—
1992	*The Sun of the Sleepless*	*Promised Heaven*	—
1993	*Encore, Once More Encore!*	*Encore, Once More Encore!*	—
1994	*Little Angel, Make Me Happy!*	*Makarov*	—
1995	*Peculiarities of the National Hunt*	*Passions*	—
1996	*Prisoner of the Mountains*	*Peculiarities of the National Hunt*	—
1997	*Brother*	*Prisoner of the Mountains*	—
1998	*Time of the Dancer*	*The Thief*	—

For the non-Russian-speaking reader, many of the WoY would entail exhaustive cultural explanations; we have chosen for the most part not to burden this (intentionally) whimsical Kino-Grafik with such an apparatus. Our sources for the WoY vary but include such familiar venues as Leonid Parfenov's television series *Lately 1961–2003: Our Era* [Namedni 1961–2003: Nasha Era] and Mikhail Epshtein's rubric "Word of the Year" [Slovo goda] in *Novaia gazeta*, as well as the web journals *Snob*, *Meduza*, and other media outlets. As with other WoY compilations, such as that of Oxford Dictionaries, our WoY is ultimately subjective, intended not as a statistical report but rather as a reference to the preoccupations of a given year.

Word(s) of the year	**One event of the year**
Makdonal'ds *legginsy* *lambada*	12/VI-90. First Congress of People's Deputies of Russia declares Russia's sovereignty from the USSR.
novye russkie *gumanitarnaia pomoshch'*	8/XII-91. Belovezha Accords, dissolving SU
vaucher	1/I-92. The government lifts price controls
zakaznoe ubiistvo *evroremont*	IX-X-93. Constitutional Crisis
klubit'sia [to hang out in clubs] *gastarbaiter* *mobila* *piramida*	2/IX-94. First Chechen War
bratva *zhit' po poniatiiam*	1/IX-95. NATO expands into Eastern Europe
mylo (e-mail) *iuzer*	3/VII-96. Yeltsin reelected
transh	Yeltsin and Jiang Zemin sign declaration on multipolar world order in the 21st century.
defolt	17/VIII. Central Bank of Russian declares default.

Year	Kinotavr	Nika Main Prize	Golden Eagle Main Prize
1999	Golden Rose: *Checkpoint* Pearl of the World (Grand Prix): *Moloch*	*Of Freaks and Men*	–
2000	Golden Rose: *Luna Papa* Grand Prix: *His Wife's Diary*	*Khrustalev, My Car!*	–
2001	Golden Rose: *Tender Age* Pearl of the World (Grand Prix): *Poisons, or the World History of Poisoning*	*His Wife's Diary*	–
2002	Golden Rose: *War* Grand Prix: *Lover*	*Taurus*	–
2003	Golden Rose: *Little Old Ladies* Grand Prix: *Chic*	*The Cuckoo*	*The Cuckoo*
2004	Golden Rose: *A Driver for Vera* Grand Prix: *My Stepbrother Frankenstein*	*The Return*	*The Return*
2005	*Poor Relatives*	*Our Own*	*72 Meters*
2006	*Playing the Victim*	*The 9th Company*	*The 9th Company*
2007	*Simple Things*	*The Island*	*The Island*
2008	*Shultes*	*Mongol*	*12*
2009	*Wolfie*	*Hipsters*	*Wild Field*
2010	*Truce*	*A Room and a Half*	*Hipsters*

Word(s) of the year	One event of the year
riazanskii sakhar (explosives)	4/IX-99.Apartment bombings; Second Chechen War
vertikal' vlasti *Kursk*	26/III-00. Putin elected president of Russia.
Delo NTV	Gazprom takes over NTV
Nord-Ost	EU recognizes Russia as a market economy (Ledeneva 11)
siloviki (cf. Western media discussions of Khodorkovsky's arrest).	25-X-03. Mikhail Khodorkovsky is arrested.
Beslan	XI-XII-04. Orange Revolution in Ukraine
Severnyi potok (Nord Stream)	20-VII-05. Putin denounces political activities of NGOs financed from abroad.
glamur	7-X-06. Anna Politkovskaia gunned down in Moscow.
tandem	Putin nominates Medvedev as successor.
krizis	7-12-VIII-08. Russo-Georgian War
perezagruzka	16-XI-09. Tax lawyer Sergei Magnitskii dies in Moscow prison.
laik	1-X-10. Customs Union is formed in Moscow (Belarus, Russia, Kazakhstan)

Year	Kinotavr	Nika Main Prize	Golden Eagle Main Prize
2011	*Indifference*	*The Edge*	*How I Ended This Summer*
2012	*I Will Be By Your Side*	*Once upon a Time There Lived a Simple Woman*	*Elena*
2013	*The Geographer Drank His Globe Away*	*Faust*	*White Tiger*
2014	*Test*	*The Geographer Drank His Globe Away*	*Legend No. 17*
2015	*About Love*	*Lovely Hans, Dear Peter*	*Sunstroke*
2016	*The Good Boy*	*Paradise*	*About Love*
2017	*Arrhythmia*	*Arrhythmia*	*Paradise*
2018	*Core of the World*	*Anna›s War*	*Salyut-7*

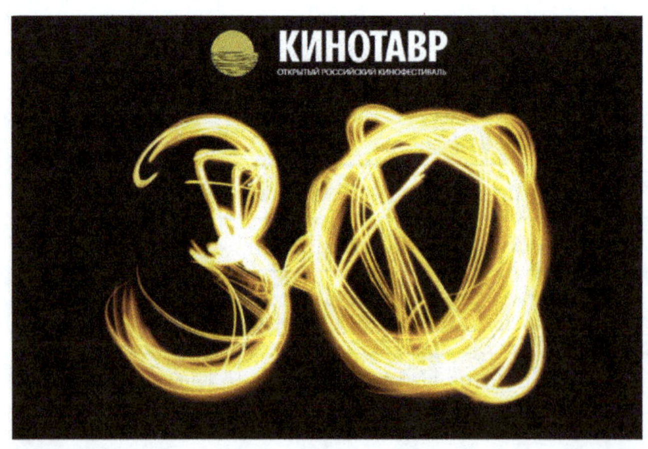

The emblem of the festival "Kinotavr—30", Sochi, June 9—16, 2019

Word(s) of the year	One event of the year
belaia lenta (symbol of opposition. Putin responds, naming it "a condom")	XII-11. Protests against falsified Duma elections
Bolotnaia *inostrannyi agent*	21-II-12. Pussy Riot punk prayer. 4-III-12. Putin elected president of Russia.
zakon podletsov (Dima Yakovlev Law)	21-XI-13 Euromaidan Revolution in Ukraine begins.
Krymnash (cf. Parfenov's *Namkrysh*) *Evromaidan* *russkii mir* *Novorossiia*	18/III-14 Annexation of Crimea; beginning of war in Eastern Ukraine.
Nemtsov most *vata, vatnik* (Kremlin supporters)	27-II-15. Boris Nemtsov is murdered near Kremlin.
Deneg net, no vy derzhites'	5-IV-16. Putin signs the law to establish National Guard, the internal military force to protect public order in case the police cannot handle the situation.
renovatsiia *Onvamnedimon*	Russian athletes doping violations scandal. Russian national team suspended from Winter Olympics.
toksichnyi	Sanctions against Russia for poisoning the Skripal family in London

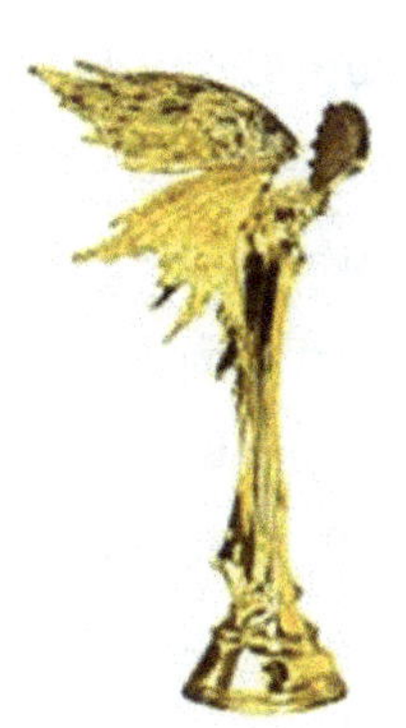

Prize of the film award "Nika"

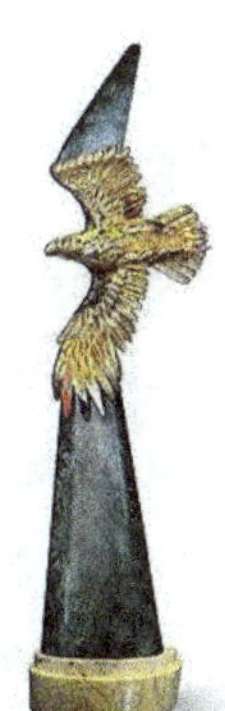

Prize of the film award "Golden Eagle"

NOTE ON THE CONTRIBUTORS

Sitora Alieva is artistic director of Kinotavr, Russia's largest national film festival. In addition to an appointment as Russia's official delegate to the Rome International Film Festival (2007–10), she has served on the juries of the Andrey Tarkovsky International Film Festival (Zerkalo), the Berlinale (Berlin International Film Festival), Karlovy Vary International Film Festival, Minsk International Film Festival (Listapad), Venice International Film Festival, the Warsaw Film Festival, and other film events—in sum, more than thirty international and Russian juries in the last twenty years (the only professional woman in Russian cinema today who has achieved this level of international recognition). She has served as a film expert for the Russian Ministry of Culture and an academic lecturer at film schools and universities in the United States and South Korea, as well as throughout Central Asia and Europe.

A graduate (1987) of the Gerasimov Institute of Cinematography (VGIK) in scriptwriting and film history (Evgenii Surkov's workshop), Sitora Alieva had worked for Tajikfilm before moving to Moscow to join the elite film journal *Iskusstvo kino* (1993–96). In 1993, she was invited by Mark Rudinstein's Kinotavr festival conglomerate to serve as the company's film program coordinator. Appointed from 1999 to 2005 as director and member of the selection committee for Kinotavr's International Film Festival Faces of Love and the International Children's Arts Festival Kinotavrik (Little Kinotavr), Sitora Alieva also served as executive director (2002–5) for the Open Russian Film Festival Kinotavr. When Kinotavr was acquired in 2005 by Alexander Rodnyansky, Sitora Alieva became the permanent artistic director of the Open Russian Film Festival Kinotavr. It is to her credit that an extraordinary slate of filmmakers was screened in Russia for the first time, even before recognition by a Cannes Palme d'Or or an Academy Oscar. These filmmakers include such outstanding figures as Hungarian director Ildikó Enyedi, Iranian director Asghar Farhadi, Mexican director Alejandro G. Iñárritu, Polish-UK director Paweł Pawlikowski, and Thai director Apichatpong Weerasethakul. Sitora Alieva is considered among a small handful of key people advancing new Russian cinema today on the international film festival circuit.

Birgit Beumers is professor emeritus in film studies, Aberystwyth University, Wales (UK). She specializes in Russian culture, cinema, and theater and the cinemas of the former Soviet territories. Her publications on Russian film include *A History of Russian Cinema* (2009), and she has edited *Directory of World Cinema: Russia* (2010, 2014) and *A Companion to Russian Cinema* (2016). She is editor of the book series KINO (Bloomsbury), and KinoSputniks (intellect) as well as the journals *KinoKultura* and of *Studies in Russian and Soviet Cinema.*

Zhanna Budenkova's professional background includes journalism and documentary film production. Her research interests include the development of the science fiction genre in the USSR, as well as the postcolonial implications of contemporary Russian cinema. She is currently working on the theme of air-mindedness in Soviet and post-Soviet culture (including film). Her annotations for the Pittsburgh Russian Film Symposium engage a range of recent festival films, including Kantemir Balagov's *Closeness* and Ivan Tverdovskii's *Zoology*. Apart from this, she is working on the themes of body politics in Russian actionist art and its implications for the Russian Internet.

Nancy Condee's work includes *Imperial Trace: Recent Russian Cinema,* as well as articles in *The Washington Post, The Nation, New Left Review, Sight and Sound, PMLA,* and such Russian journals as *Iskusstvo kino, Novaia gazeta, Novoe literaturnoe obozrenie, Seans, Voprosy literatury,* and *Znamia.* Her edited and co-edited collections include *Soviet Hieroglyphics: Visual Culture in Late 20c. Russia* (1995); *Endquote: Sots-Art Literature and Soviet Grand Style* (with Marina Balina and Evgeny Dobrenko [2000]); *Antinomies of Art and Culture: Modernity, Postmodernity, Contemporaneity* (with Terry Smith and Okwui Enwezor [2008]); and *The Cinema of Alexander Sokurov* (with Birgit Beumers [2011]).

Robert Crane's work dealing with theater and cinema in the Soviet Union and its successor states has been published in *KinoKultura, Performing Arts Resources, Text and Presentation, Theatre Journal,* and *Theatre Survey*. He has served on the organizing committee of the Russian Film Symposium since 2007. He teaches in the School of Drama at Carnegie Mellon University, as well as the Slavic Department of the University of Pittsburgh.

Daria Ezerova is a postdoctoral research scholar at Columbia University. She completed her PhD dissertation (Slavic, Yale University), "Derelict Futures: The Spaces of Socialism in Contemporary Russian Literature and Film," in June 2018. She is a specialist on twentieth-century and contemporary Russian literature and cinema. Her publications have appeared in *Senses of Cinema, Kinokultura,* and *Seans*. She is an organizer of the Russian Film at Yale series and the Yale Slavic Film Colloquium, as well as a series of screenings at the annual convention of the Association for Slavic, East European, and Eurasian Studies (ASEEES), where she is currently president of the ASEEES Working Group on Cinema and Television.

Seth Graham is associate professor of Russian at University College London. He has written about Soviet and post-Soviet cinema for *Studies in Russian and Soviet Cinema, Studio Filmoznawcze, KinoKultura*, and several essay collections. He is co-editor of *KinoKultura*.

Beach Gray is a media analyst for Novetta Advanced Analytics. He holds a PhD in Slavic Studies (2016) and a PhD Certificate in Film Studies (2016) from the University of Pittsburgh. His research interests include advertising and consumer culture in contemporary Russian visual media, object theory, and documentary cinema. His work has been published in *KinoKultura* and *Slavic and East European Journal*.

Paul Heth began his career in the motion picture industry in Moscow, in 1993, shortly after the breakup of the Soviet Union, launching Russia's first English-language, Western-style theater in the lobby of the Moscow Radisson Hotel. By 1996, Heth was partnering with Eastman Kodak on a new venue, Kodak Kinomir (Kodak Cinema World), built to resemble a theater from Hollywood's golden era. Heth served as president and chief financial officer, and under his leadership Kodak Kinomir became one of the highest-grossing and most profitable cinemas in the world. By 2000, Heth was collaborating with National Amusements, the parent company of Viacom and CBS, to form CineBridge Ventures, with Shari Redstone as chief executive officer (CEO). A second collaboration with Redstone and National Amusements was Kinostar Cinemas, for which, as co-founder and CEO, Heth received the Pacesetter Lifetime Achievement award and the American Chamber of Commerce Businessperson of the Year. In 2012, Heth organized a group of private equity partners in purchasing Karo Film Group, a leading Russian cinema operator. As CEO, Heth developed the largest cinema venues in the country and led Karo Film Group through an extensive expansion. Heth was one of the co-producers, with Sony Pictures, of Fedor Bondarchuk's *Stalingrad* (2013), then the highest-grossing film in the history of Russian cinema.

Olga Kim has published in *Studies in Russian and Soviet Cinema, Senses of Cinema,* and *KinoKultura.* She serves as co-editor for the journal *Digital Icons: Studies in Russian, Eurasian, and Central European New Media.* Her PhD dissertation deals with the issues of aesthetics and history in the *tableau* cinema of the Soviet peripheries during late socialism. Her research interests also include the early Soviet avant-garde, new media, and Central Asian visual culture.

Olga Mukhortova is an Assistant Professor at the Defense Language Institute (Monterey). Her work on cinema and literature has appeared in *KinoKultura, Studies in Russian and Soviet Cinema,* and *Slavic and East European Journal.* Her dissertation discusses the construction of the contemporary Russian star system with an emphasis on such figures as Renata Litvinova, Sergei Bodrov, Nikita Mikhalkov, and Andrei Zviagintsev.

Stephen M. Norris is Walter E. Havighurst Professor of Russian History and director of the Havighurst Center for Russian and Post-Soviet Studies at Miami University (OH). He is the author of two books on Russian history and visual culture: *A War of Images: Russian Popular Prints, Wartime Culture, and National Identity, 1812–1945* (2006); and *Blockbuster History in the New Russia: Movies, Memory, Patriotism* (2012). He has also co-edited five books on Russian history, most recently *Museums of Communism: New Memory Sites in Central and Eastern Europe* (forthcoming in 2019). He is currently researching a project on the Soviet political cartoonist, Boris Efimov (1900–2008).

Vladimir Padunov teaches in the Film and Media Studies Program and the Department of Slavic Languages and Literatures at the University of Pittsburgh. Since 1999 he has been the director of the Pittsburgh Russian Film Symposium. Together with Nancy Condee, he directed the Working

Group on Contemporary Russian Culture (1990–93), supported by the American Council of Learned Societies and the Social Science Research Council. His work has been published in the United States (*The Nation, October, Wide Angle*), the United Kingdom (*Framework, New Left Review, New Formations*), and Russia (*Voprosy literatury, Znamia, Iskusstvo kino, Novaia gazeta*). His areas of research include Russian visual culture, narrative history and theory, and film history.

Petre Petrov is assistant professor of Russian at the University of Texas at Austin. His primary research relates to Stalinist culture and ideology in the context of the European aesthetic and philosophic modernism. His published work deals with socialist realism, Russian-Soviet cinema, and literary and cultural theory. He is the author of *Automatic for the Masses: The Death of the Author and the Birth of Socialist Realism* (2015) and co-editor, with Lara Ryazanova-Clarke, of *The Vernaculars of Communism: Language, Ideology, and Power in the Soviet Union and Eastern Europe* (2014).

Alexander Prokhorov is co-author (with Elena Prokhorova) of *Film and Television Genres of the Late Soviet Era* (2017) and the editor of *Springtime for Soviet Cinema: Re/viewing the 1960s* (2001). His articles and reviews have been published in *Journal of Film and Video, KinoKultura, Russian Review, Slavic Review, Slavic and East European Journal, Studies in Russian and Soviet Cinema, Art of Cinema* (Iskusstvo kino), and *Wiener Slawistische Almanach.*

Elena Prokhorova is associate professor of Russian at the College of William and Mary, where she also teaches in the Film and Media Studies program. Her research focuses on identity discourses in late Soviet and post-Soviet television and cinema. She is co-author (with Alexander Prokhorov) of the monograph *Film and Television Genres of the Late Soviet Era* (2017). Her publications have also appeared in *Slavic Review, Slavic and East European Journal, KinoKultura, Russian Journal of Communication,* and in edited volumes.

Alexander Rodnyansky is a Ukrainian-Russian producer, director, and media executive with more than thirty films and twenty television series to his credit, including Russia's highest-grossing film ($67 million), Fedor Bondarchuk's IMAX 3D war drama *Stalingrad* (2013). In 2016, he was invited to become a member of the Academy of Motion Picture Arts and Sciences.

Rodnyansky's early career began in documentary filmmaking, with ten feature documentaries that garnered over forty awards internationally and in Russia, including the Russian National Film Award NIKA and the European Film Award (Best Documentary) for his documentary *The Mission of Raoul Wallenberg* (Missiia Raulia Valenberga, 1990). His media initiatives included the 1994 creation of the Ukrainian television network 1+1, the first independent television channel and the leading channel in the Ukrainian television market.

In addition to co-producing (as Alexandre Rodniansky) Régis Wargnier's historical adventure *East/West* (Este/Oeste, 1999), Rodnyansky's early efforts include some of Russia's best-known feature films: Pavel Chukhrai's drama *A Driver for Vera* (Voditel' dlia Very, 2004); Fedor Bondarchuk's action film *The 9th Company* (9 rota, 2005); and his two-part science fiction film *The Inhabited Island* (Obitaemyi ostrov, 2008–9) and Oksana Bychkova's comedy *Piter FM* (Piter FM, 2006).

In 2002, Rodnyansky was chosen to head the US firm Story First Communication (later CTC Media), which operated five channels internationally and was the first Russian media company to offer an Initial Public Offering (IPO) on the National Association of Securities Dealers Automated Quotations (NASDAQ). Leaving CTC Media in 2008, Rodnyansky founded AR Films the following year. Through AR Films, Rodnyansky oversaw three enterprises: the production company Non-Stop Production; the independent-film distribution leader Cinema without Frontiers (Kino bez granits); and Kinotavr, Russia's most important film festival.

In 2011, Andrei Zviagintsev's *Elena*, produced by Rodnyansky's Non-Stop, won the Special Jury Prize in the competition Un Certain Regard at the Cannes Film Festival. Together with Sergei Melkumov, Alexander Rodnyansky produced Bondarchuk's *Stalingrad*. After Andrei Zviagintsev's *Leviathan* (Leviafan, 2014), also produced by Rodnyansky, won Best Screenplay at the Sixty-seventh Cannes Film Festival, the film went on to win Best Foreign Language Film award at the Seventy-second Golden Globe Awards and was nominated for an Academy Award for Best Foreign Film. *Loveless* (Neliubov', 2017), directed by Andrei Zviagintsev and produced by Alexander Rodnyansky, premiered in the main competition at the Cannes Film Festival, where it won the Jury Prize.

Rodnyansky's US production career includes Billy Bob Thornton's drama *Jayne Mansfield's Car* (2012), which premiered in competition at the 2012 Berlinale. Other US films include D. J. Caruso's drama *Goat Island* (2012) and Tom Tykwer's, Lana Wachowski's, and Lilly Wachowski's (as Andy Wachowski) mystery drama *Cloud Atlas* (2012). In 2017, *Variety* included Rodnyansky in its Variety500 index among the 500 most influential business leaders in the global entertainment industry.

Denis Saltykov's publications have appeared in *KinoKultura, New Literary Observer, Sociology of Power*, and such Russian popular websites as Kino-Teatr, Kinomania, and Wonderzine. His research focuses on the ways in which recent Russian cinema is adopting Western models of horror and action films. He also researches unacknowledged Russian films that seem bizarre or socially deviant, thus provoking the audiences to treat the given work as a cult object. Beyond his research career, he is the chief editor of the horror genre website RussoRosso. In addition to PhD study in Slavic, he has studied sociology in the graduate school of the National Research University Higher School of Economics (Moscow). His current research interests include sociological theories of cinema, film genre studies, and politics of contemporary popular culture.

Ellina Sattarova's book- and film-review publications have appeared (respectively) in *Slavic and East European Journal* and *KinoKultura*. Her dissertation examines a corpus of contemporary Russian films (including work by Andrei Zviagintsev, Kirill Serebrennikov, Aleksei Fedorchenko, and Vasilii Sigarev) that comment on the ways in which the state politicizes human life and subjects it to biopolitical regulation. Among her other research interests are Central Asian cinema and the transformation of the trickster figure in Russo-Soviet cinema. In addition to PhD study in Slavic, she received her MA in German Film from the University of Montana (2013). She was on the Organizing Committee of the annual Russian Film Symposium (2013–16) and was invited to introduce and lead the post-screening Q&A for Ella Manzheeva's *The Gulls* (Chaiki, 2015) at the 2016 Silk Screen Film Festival.

Tetyana Shlikhar's research interests include memory studies, historical film, and Russo-Ukrainian relations. Her dissertation deals with memory wars and myths of the past as represented in contemporary Russian and Ukrainian cinema.

Theodora Trimble wrote her PhD dissertation on the role of celebrity figures in Thaw-era Soviet cinema. She has contributed to *KinoKultura* and to *Television beyond and across the Iron Curtain* (edited by Julia Obertreis, Sven Grampp, and Kirsten Bönker; 2016). Her research interests span a range of topics across film, television, and popular culture, including a focus on the intersection between Soviet celebrities and recent Russian cinema.

Justin Wilmes is assistant professor of Russian Studies at East Carolina University. His primary research examines post-Soviet cinema and culture but extends also to Russian drama, translation, and Polish culture. Justin has published in *Russian Literature, Studies in Russian and Soviet Cinema, KinoKultura, Digital Icons, The Pushkin Review, New England Review*, and elsewhere. He serves as co-editor of the journal *Digital Icons*. He holds a PhD in Slavic and East European Languages and Literatures from The Ohio State University.

Trevor Wilson's published work has appeared in *Slavic and East European Journal* and *The Human Reimagined: Posthumanism in Russia* (edited by Colleen McQuillen and Julia Vaingurt [2018]). His film annotations for the Pittsburgh Russian Film Symposium are available online at http://www.rusfilm.pitt.edu/. His main research focuses on the interaction between Russian and French traditions within Russian émigré philosophy in the early twentieth century. In particular, his dissertation addresses the legacy of Russian philosophy in the thought of Alexandre Kojève. In addition to Russian philosophy, he researches shifting theories of sexuality from command to postcommand economies.

WORKS CITED

1968.Digital. http://1968.digital/en/about.

Abdrashitov, Vadim. "Mesto neuznavaemo. Uznavaema voina." Interview by Ella Korsunskaia. *Kinostsenarii*, no. 5 (1997): 136–45.

Abdullaeva, Zara. "Norma: *Strana Oz*, Rezhisser Vasilii Sigarev." *Iskusstvo kino*, no. 6 (2015). http://kinoart.ru/archive/2015/06/norma-strana-oz-rezhisser-vasilij-sigarev.

Abikeyeva, Gulnara. *The Heart of the World: Films from Central Asia*. Almaty: Complex, 2003.

Agamben, Giorgio. *Homo Sacer: Sovereign Power and Bare Life*. Translated by Daniel Heller-Roazen. Stanford: Stanford University Press, 1998.

———. *Language and Death: The Place of Negativity*. Translated by Karen E. Pinkus and Michael Hardt. Minneapolis: University of Minnesota Press, 1991.

———. *Means without End: Notes on Politics*. Translated by Vincenzo Binetti and Cesare Casarino. Minneapolis: University of Minnesota Press, 2000.

———. *Remnants of Auschwitz: The Witness and the Archive*. Translated by Daniel Heller-Roazen. New York: Zone Books, 1999.

———. *"What Is an Apparatus?" and Other Essays*. Translated by David Kishik and Stefan Pedatella. Stanford: Stanford University Press, 2009.

Alieva, Sitora. "Festival'—eto v pervuiu ochered' zritel'—radi nego vse i delaetsia." *Proficinema*, 16 March 2012. http://www.proficinema.ru/questions-problems/interviews/detail.php?ID=121117.

Althusser, Louis. "Ideology and Ideological State Apparatuses (Notes towards an Investigation)." In his *Essays on Ideology*, 1–60. London: Verso, 1984.

———. *"Lenin and Philosophy" and Other Essays*. Translated by Ben Brewster. New York: Monthly Review, 2001.

Altman, Rick. *Film/Genre*. London: BFI Publishing, 1999.

Anastas'ev, Aleksei. "Komiks vremennykh let." *Iskusstvo kino*, no. 5/6 (2017). https://www.kinoart.ru/archive/2017/05-06/komiks-vremennykh-let-viking-rezhisser-andrej-kravchuk.

Anderson, Benedict. *Imagined Communities: Reflections on the Origin and Spread of Nationalism*. London: Verso, 1983.

Anisimova, Irina. "Celestial Wives of the Meadow Mari" (screening notes). Russian Film Symposium. 2014.

———. "'E' Is for Empire: Postmodernism and Imperial Ideology in the Context of the Sochi Olympic Games." *Studies in Russian and Soviet Cinema* (2018): 1–17.

Arkus, Liubov', ed. *Noveishaia istoriia otechestvennogo kino 1986–2000*. St. Petersburg: Seans, 2004.

———. "Seansu otvechaiut: Vremia tantsora." *Seans*, no. 16 (1997). http://seance.ru/n/16/rfc/vt/.

Arnold, Kathleen R. "Domestic War: Locke's Concept of Prerogative." In her *America's New Working Class: Race, Gender, and Ethnicity in a Biopolitical Age*, 73–103. University Park: Pennsylvania State University Press, 2008.

Aron, Leon. "Novorossiya! Putin and His Dangerous 'New Russia.'" *Commentary* (December 2014). https://www.commentarymagazine.com/articles/novorossiya/.

Artiukh, Anzhelika, and Denis Solov'ev-Fridman. "Dukhless." OpenSpace.ru, 25 June 2012. http://os.colta.ru/cinema/events/details/37953/.

"Avtory samykh teplykh photo." *Yolki* [official website]. Bazelevs Studio, 13 December 2013. http://elki-film.ru/vmesteteplee.

Bakhtin, Mikhail. "Forms of Time and of the Chronotope in the Novel: Notes toward a Historical Poetics." In his *The Dialogic Imagination: Four Essays*, ed. and trans. Michael Holquist and Caryl Emerson, 84–258. Austin: University of Texas Press, 1983.

Barabash, Ekaterina. "Seks, lozh' i video." *Nezavisimaia gazeta*, 11 February 2004.

Barry, Ellen. "A Wild Cossack Rides into a Cultural Battle." *The New York Times*, 12 April 2009.

Bassin, Mark. "Russia between Europe and Asia: The Ideological Construction of Geographical Space." *Slavic Review* 50, no. 1 (1991): 1–17.

Bataille, Georges. *Eroticism: Death and Sensuality*. San Francisco: City Lights Books, 1986.

———. *The History of Eroticism* and *Sovereignty*. Translated by Robert Hurley. New York: Zone Books, 1991.

Bauman, Zygmunt. "Violence, Postmodern." In his *Life in Fragments: Essays in Postmodern Morality*, 139–62. Oxford: Blackwell, 1995.

Belodubrovskaya, Maria. *Not According to Plan: Filmmaking under Stalin*. Ithaca: Cornell University Press, 2017.

Benjamin, Walter. "On Language as Such and on the Language of Man." In *Walter Benjamin: Selected Writings*, ed. Marcus Bullock and Michael W. Jennings, 62–74. Cambridge, MA: Belknap Press, 2000.

———. "On the Present Situation in Russian Film." In *Selected Writings, 1927–1930.* Vol. 2, Part 1, ed. Michael W. Jennings et al., 12–15. Cambridge, MA: Belknap Press, 1999.

———. *The Origin of German Tragic Drama*. London: Verso, 1998.

Berdiaev, Nikolai. *Russkaia ideia*. St. Petersburgh: Azbuka-klassika, 2008.

Bergson, Henri. *Laughter: An Essay on the Meaning of the Comic*. Translated by Cloudesely Brereton and Fred Rothwell. Rockville: Arc Manor, 2008.

Beumers, Birgit. "Brother." In *The Russian Cinema Reader*, Vol. 2: *The Thaw to the Present*, ed. Rimgaila Salys, 261–69. Brighton: Academic Studies Press, 2013.

———. *Burnt by the Sun: The Film Companion*. London: I. B. Tauris, 2000.

———. "Cinemarket, or the Russian Film Industry in 'Mission Possible.'" *Europe-Asia Studies* 51, no. 5 (1999): 871–96.

———, ed. *A Companion to Russian Cinema.* Malden: Wiley, 2016.

———. "Father Frost on 31 December: Christmas and New Year in Soviet and Russian Cinema." In *Christmas in the Movies*, ed. Mark Connelly, 185–209. London: I. B. Tauris, 2000.

———. *A History of Russian Cinema*. Oxford: Berg, 2008.

———. "National Identity through Visions of the Past: Contemporary Russian Cinema." In *Soviet and Post-Soviet Identities*, ed. Mark Bassin and Catriona Kelly, 55–72. New York: Cambridge University Press, 2012.

———. Review of *Russian Ark* (*Russkii kovcheg*), dir. Aleksandr Sokurov. *KinoKultura* (2003). http://www.kinokultura.com/reviews/Rark.html.

———, ed. *Russia on Reels: The Russian Idea in Post-Soviet Cinema*. London: I. B. Tauris, 1999.

Beumers, Birgit, and Mark Lipovetsky. *Performing Violence: Literary and Theatrical Experiments of New Russian Drama*. Bristol: Intellect, 2009.

Bhabha, Homi K. "DissemiNation: Time, Narrative and the Margins of the Modern Nation." In *The Blackwell Reader in Contemporary Social Theory*, ed. Anthony Elliott, 291–322. Oxford: Blackwell, 1999.

———. *The Location of Culture*. New York: Routledge, 1994.

Bingham, Dennis. *Whose Lives Are They Anyway? The Biopic as Contemporary Film Genre*. New Brunswick: Rutgers University Press, 2010.

Bird, Robert. "Aleksandr Kott: *Ispytanie* (*The Test*, 2014)." *KinoKultura*, no. 47 (2015). http://www.kinokultura.com/2015/47r-ispytanie.shtml.

Bitton-Ashkelony, B. "'More Interior Than the Lips and the Tongue': John of Apamea and Silent Prayer in Late Antiquity." *Journal of Early Christian Studies* 20, no. 2 (2012): 303–31.

Bobrakov-Timoshkin, Aleksandr. "Zachem Putinu Krym? Krov' i pochva: Postversal'skii sindrom." *Radio Svoboda*, 7 March 2014. https://www.svoboda.org/a/25288816.html.

Bojanowska, Edyta. *Nikolai Gogol: Between Ukrainian and Russian Nationalism*. Cambridge, MA: Harvard University Press, 2007.

Booker, M. Keith. "Chapter 1: The *Superman* Film Franchise," and "Chapter 2: The *Batman* Film Franchise." In his *"May Contain Graphic Material": Comic Books, Graphic Novels, and Film*, 1–29. Westport: Praeger, 2007.

Bordwell, David. "The Art Cinema as a Mode of Film Practice." In *Film Theory and Criticism*, ed. Leo Braudy and Marshall Cohen, 774–82. 6th ed. New York: Oxford University Press, 2004.

Borenstein, Eliot. *Overkill: Sex and Violence in Contemporary Russian Popular Culture*. Ithaca: Cornell University Press, 2008.

Bourdieu, Pierre. "The Forms of Capital." In *Handbook of Theory and Research for the Sociology of Education*, ed. John Richardson, 241–58. New York: Greenwood Press, 1986.

———. *Language and Symbolic Power*. Edited with an introduction by John B. Thompson. Translated by Gino Raymond and Matthew Adamson. Cambridge: Polity Press, 2011.

Brashinskii, Mikhail. "Iz Rossii s liubov'iu." *Seans*, no. 17/18. http://seance.ru/n/17-18/rezhisser-film-kritik-2/sibirskiy-tsiryulnik/iz-rossii-s-lyubovyu/.

Brooks, Peter. *The Melodramatic Imagination: Balzac, Henry James, Melodrama, and the Mode of Excess*. New Haven: Yale University Press, 1995.

Brown, Mick. "Interview with Masha Gessen: Vladimir Putin. The Godfather of a Mafia Clan." *The Telegraph*, 25 February 2012. http://www.telegraph.co.uk/news/worldnews/vladimir-putin/9100388/Vladimir-Putin-the-godfather-of-a-mafia-clan.html.

Central Intelligence Agency. *The World Factbook*. https://www.cia.gov/library/publications/the-world-factbook/geos/rs.html.

Chan, Andrew, "Waking Nightmares: A Conversation with Jordan Peele." *The Criterion Collection*, 24 February 2017. https://www.criterion.com/current/posts/4439-waking-nightmares-a-conversation-with-jordan-peele.

Cherniavsky, Michael. *Tsar and People: Studies in Russian Myths*. New Haven: Yale University Press, 1961.

Chuprinin, Sergei. *Russkaia literatura segodnia: Novyi putevoditel'*. Moscow: Vremia, 2009.

Clark, Kenneth. *Landscape into Art*. Boston: Beacon Press, 1949.

Clemens, Justin. "Language." In *The Agamben Dictionary*, ed. Alex Murray and Jessica Whyte, 116–19. Edinburgh: Edinburgh University Press, 2011.

Clowes, Edith. "Introduction: Is Russia a Center or Periphery?" In her *Russia on the Edge: Imagined Geographies and Post-Soviet Identity*, 1–18. Ithaca: Cornell University Press, 2011.

Colebrook, Claire. "Animal." In *The Agamben Dictionary*, ed. Alex Murray and Jessica Whyte, 22–23. Edinburgh: Edinburgh University Press, 2011.

Conard, Mark T. "Introduction." In *The Philosophy of Neo-Noir*, ed. Mark T. Conard. *The Philosophy of Neo-Noir*, 1–7. Lexington: University of Kentucky Press, 2007.

Condee, Nancy. "Cold Snap (Part II): Russian Film after Leviathan." NYU Jordan Center for the Advanced Study of Russia, "News," 23 July 2015. http://jordanrussiacenter.org/news/cold-snap-part-ii-russian-film-leviathan/.

———. "The Dream of Well-Being." *Sight and Sound* 7, no. 12 (1997): 18–21.

———. "History in a Time of Premeditated Amnesia: The 25th Kinotavr Open Russian Film Festival." *KinoKultura*, no. 46 (2014); http://www.kinokultura.com/2014/46-condee.shtml.

———. *The Imperial Trace: Recent Russian Cinema*. New York: Oxford University Press, 2009.

———. "Knowledge (Imperfective): Andrei Zviagintsev and Contemporary Cinema." In *A Companion to Russian Cinema*, ed. Birgit Beumers, 565–84. Malden: Wiley/Blackwell, 2016.

———. "Mediation, Imagination, and Time: Speculative Remarks on Russian Culture." *Ab Imperio*, no. 1 (2008): 177–92.

Custen, George F. *Bio/pics: How Hollywood Constructed Public History*. New Brunswick: Rutgers University Press, 1992.

Danilevskii, Nikolai. "Evropa li Rossiia?" Chapter 3 of *Rossiia i Evropa*. http://vehi.net/danilevsky/rossiya/03.html.

David-Fox, Michael. "The Intelligentsia, the Masses, and the West." In his *Crossing Borders: Modernity, Ideology, and Culture in Russia and the Soviet Union*, 49–71. Pittsburgh: University of Pittsburgh Press, 2015.

———. "Multiple Modernities vs. Neo-Traditionalism: On Recent Debates in Russian and Soviet History." *Jahrbücher für Geschichte Osteuropas* 55, no. 4 (2006): 1–36.

De Lauretis, Teresa. "The Violence of Rhetoric: Considerations on Representation and Gender." *Semiotica* 54, no. 1–2 (1985): 11–32.

DeBlasio, Alyssa. "The New-Year Film as a Genre of Post-war Russian Cinema." *Studies in Russian and Soviet Cinema* 2, no. 1 (2008): 43–61.

———. "Roman Prygunov: *Soulless* [Dukhless 2012]." *KinoKultura*, no. 39 (2012). http://www.kinokultura.com/2013/39r-dukhless.shtml.

Debord, Guy. *The Society of the Spectacle*. New York: Zone Books, 1994. http://www.antiworld.se/project/references/texts/The_Society%20_Of%20_The%20_Spectacle.pdf.

Derrida, Jacques. *Of Grammatology*. Baltimore: Johns Hopkins University Press, 2016.

———. "Structure, Sign and Play in the Discourse of the Human Sciences." In *Writing and Difference*, trans. Alan Bass, 278–93. Chicago: University of Chicago Press, 1978.

Descombes, Vincent. *Modern French Philosophy*. Translated by L. Scott-Fox and J. M. Harding. Cambridge: Cambridge University Press, 1998.

Dobrenko, Evgeny. "Socialist Realism." In *The Cambridge Companion to Twentieth-Century Russian Literature*, ed. Evgeny Dobrenko and Marina Balina, 97–113. Cambridge: Cambridge University Press, 2011.

Dobrynin, Sergey. "Nikolai Lebedev: *Legend No. 17* (*Legenda No. 17*, 2012)." *KinoKultura*, no. 42 (2013). http://www.kinokultura.com/2013/42r-legenda17.shtml.

Dolin, Anton. "Kak russkie rezhissery avtorskogo kino vyshli k massovomu zriteliu." *Daily.Afisha.ru*, 3 October 2016. https://daily.afisha.ru/cinema/3134-kruglyy-stol-kak-russkie-rezhissery-avtorskogo-kino-vyshli-k-massovomu-zritelyu/.

———. "Tri kita: *Leviafan*, rezhisser Andrei Zviagintsev." *Iskusstov kino*, no. 7 (2014). https://kinoart.ru/archive/2014/07/tri-kita-leviafan-rezhisser-andrej-zvyagintsev.

———. "Viking: Ne mir, a mech." *Afisha Daily*, 27 December 2016. https://daily.afisha.ru/cinema/4109-anton-dolin-o-filme-viking-ne-mir-no-mech/.

Dondurei, Daniil. "Bremia politiki." *Iskusstvo kino*, no. 1 (2013). https://www.kinoart.ru/archive/2013/01/bremya-politiki-reformy-v-kinoindustrii.

———. "Kinodelo: na puti k rynku." *Rossiiskoe kino: Paradoksy obnovleniia*. Edited by A. G. Dubrovin and M. E. Zak. Moscow: Materik, 1995.

———. "Kinopokaz: perezagruzka, chast' 1. Kinoteatr. Rossiiskim fil'mam otkazat'." *Iskusstvo kino*, no. 7 (2012). https://www.kinoart.ru/archive/2012/07/kinopokaz-perezagruzka-rossijskim-filmam-otkazat.

———. "Posle imperii: Kinorynok po-russki." *Iskusstvo kino*, no. 11 (1993): 3–9.

———. "Prodat' mozhno tol'ko sobytie." *Iskusstvo kino*, no. 2 (2014). https://kinoart.ru/archive/2014/02/daniil-dondurej-oleg-berezin-prodat-mozhno-tolko-sobytie.

Dostoevsky, Feodor. *Crime and Punishment*. Translated by Jessie Coulson. New York: W. W. Norton, 1989.

Douglas, Edward. "Exclusive: No Dusk Watch for Bekmambetov?" *Shock till You Drop*, 16 June 2008. http://www.shocktillyoudrop.com/news/6557-exclusive-no-dusk-watch-for-bekmambetov/.

Drake, Philip, and Michael Higgins. "The Political Celebrity and the Celebrity Politician." In *Framing Celebrity: New Directions in Celebrity Culture*, ed. Su Holmes and Sean Redmond, 87–100. New York: Routledge, 2006.

Draskoczy, Julie. "Dmitrii Mamuliia: *Drugoe nebo* (*Another Sky*, 2010)." *KinoKultura*, no. 30 (2010). http://www.kinokultura.com/2010/30r-drugoenebo.shtml.

Dubin, Boris. "Ideia 'klassiki' i ee sotsial'nye funktsii." In his *Ocherki po sotsiologii kul'tury: Izbrannoe*, 203–44. Moscow: NLO, 2017.

Dud', Iurii. "Chichvarkin #1—o Medvedeve, kontrabande i druzhbe s Surkovym/ vDud'." [Interview with Evgenii Chichvarkin], vDud', 25 July 2017. https://www.youtube.com/watch?v=QXijtvUOhX4.

Dumančić, Marko. Review of Feliks Mikhailov: *Jolly Fellows* [Vesel'chaki, 2009]. *KinoKultura*, no. 29 (2010). http://www.kinokultura.com/2010/29r-veselchaki.shtml.

Dyer, Richard. *Stars*. 2nd ed. London: BFI, 2002.

Dziewańska, Marta, Ekaterina Degot, and Ilya Budraitskis, eds. *Post-Post-Soviet? Art, Politics, and Society in Russia at the Turn of the Decade*. Warsaw: No. 7 (Museum of Modern Art in Warsaw), 2013.

Edelman, Robert. *Serious Fun: A History of Spectator Sports in the USSR*. New York: Oxford University Press, 1993.

Editors of *Cahiers du cinéma*. "Young Mr. Lincoln de John Ford." *Cahiers du cinéma*, no. 223 (1970): 29–47.

Eikhenbaum, Boris. "Kak sdelana *Shinel'* Gogolia." OPOiaZ. http://www.opojaz.ru/manifests/kaksdelana.html.

Eisenstadt, Shmuel Noah. "Multiple Modernities." *Daedalus* 129, no. 1 (2000): 1–29.

"Elki 1914: Rozhdestvenskaia komediia." *Elki* [official website]. See also Yolki. Bazelevs Studio. http://www.elki1914film.ru/game (15 July 2015).

Elsaesser, Thomas. "A Retrospect: The Film Director as *Auteur*—Artist, Brand Name, or Engineer?" Thomas-elsaesser.com. http://www.thomas-elsaesser.com/images/stories/pdf/elsaesser_the_author_a_retrospect.pdf.

Epshtein, Mikhail. "Slovo-2017: Verbal'nyi portret goda." *Snob*, 12 December 2017. https://snob.ru/profile/27356/blog/132227.

Esslin, Martin. "The Theatre of the Absurd." *The Tulane Drama Review* 4, no. 4 (May 1960): 3–15.

Etkind, Aleksandr. "Bremia britogo cheloveka, ili Vnutrenniaia kolonizatsiia Rossii." *Ab Imperio*, no. 1 (2002): 265–69.

———. *Vnutrenniaia kolonizatsiia*. Moscow: NLO, 2013.

Etkind, Alexander. *Internal Colonization: Russia's Imperial Experience*. Cambridge: Polity Press, 2011.

Fanailova, Elena. "'Brat' v 'russkom mire.'" *Radio Svoboda*, 3 May 2015. https://www.svoboda.org/a/26987757.html.

Faraday, George. *The Revolt of the Filmmakers: The Struggle for Autonomy and the Fall of the Soviet Film Industry*. University Park: Pennsylvania State University Press, 2000.

Faulkner, William. *Requiem for a Nun*. New York: Vintage, 2011.

Federal law of 22 August 1996 no. 126-FZ "On Government Support of the Cinema Industry of the Russian Federation" (with Changes and Additions) [Federal'nyi zakon ot 22 avgusta 1996 g. no. 126-FZ "O gosudarstevennoi podderzhke kinematografii Rossiiskoi Federatsii" (s izmeneniiami i dopolneniiami)]. http://base.garant.ru/10135918/#ixzz5TFxe4Yz9.

Fedorov, Aleksandr. "Zapadnyi mir na sovetskom i rossiiskom ekranakh (1946–2016)." *Mediaobrazovanie*, no. 4 (2016). http://www.kino-teatr.ru/kino/art/kino/4437/.

Filimonova, Tatiana. "Chinese Russia: Imperial Consciousness in Vladimir Sorokin's Writing." *Region: Regional Studies of Russia, Eastern Europe, and Central Asia* 3, no. 2 (2014): 219–44.

Fisher, William. "Gorbachev's Cinema." *Sight and Sound* (Autumn 1987): 238–43.

Flesch, Rudolf, comp. *The Book of Unusual Quotations*. New York: Harper and Brothers, 1957.

Fomin, Valerii. *Letopis' rossiiskogo kino 1981–1991*. Moscow: Reabilitatsiia, 2016.

Forster, E. M. *Maurice: A Novel*. New York: W. W. Norton, 2005.

Foucault, Michel. *Discipline and Punish: The Birth of the Prison*. Translated by Alan Sheridan. New York: Pantheon Books, 1977.

Franklin, Anna. "Torrents of Spring." *Screen International*, 30 May 1997: 13–14.

Freud, Sigmund. *The Uncanny*. Edited by James Strachey, Anna Freud and Carrie Lee Rothgeb. London: Hogarth Press, 1953.

Gai Germanika, Valeriia. "Vse umrut, a ia ostanus'?" *Razgovorchiki*. http://www.razgovorchiki.ru/arkhiv/germanika.htm.

Gaidar, Egor. "Veimarskii sindrom: Ob opasnostiakh postimperskoi nostal'gii." *Kommersant.ru*, 6 February 2006. https://www.kommersant.ru/doc/646878.

Gershenzon, M.O., and V. I. Ivanov. "A Correspondence between Two Corners." Translated by Norbert Guterman. *Partisan Review* 9 (September 1948): 951–1048.

Gogol, Nikolai Vasil'evich. *The Government Inspector*. London: Nick Hern Books, 1997.

———. *Taras Bul'ba* (1835 version). In *Mirgorod*, pt. 1. *Sobranie sochinenii N. V. Gogolia v semi tomakh.* Moscow: Khudozhestvennaia literatura, 1967. http://public-library.ru/Gogol.Nikolai/taras35.html

———. *Taras Bul'ba* (1842 version). In *Mirgorod*, pt. 1. *Sobranie sochinenii N. V. Gogolia v semi tomakh.* Moscow: Khudozhestvennaia literatura, 1967. http://public-library.ru/Gogol.Nikolai/taras.html.

Gordon, Dmitry. "GORDON: Liudmila Ulitskaia." 24 June 2018. https://www.youtube.com/watch?v=-XHayKyD5NM.

Gorky, Maxim. *My Universities*. New York: Penguin Classics, 1992.

Goscilo, Helena, ed. *Putin as Celebrity and Cultural Icon.* New York: Routledge, 2013.

———. "The Ultimate Celebrity: VVP as VIP *objet d'art*." In *Celebrity and Glamour in Contemporary Russia: Shocking Chic*, ed. Helena Goscilo and Vlad Strukov, 29–55. New York: Routledge, 2010.

Goscilo, Helena, and Yana Hashamova, eds. *Cinepaternity: Fathers and Sons in Soviet and Post-Soviet Film*. Bloomington: Indiana University Press, 2010.

Grachev, Sergei. "Daniil Kozlovskii: 'Aktery i sportsmeny v politike—eto smeshno i grustno.'"

Argumenty i fakty, 24 April 2013. http://www.aif.ru/culture/person/42764.

Gracheva, Elena. "Nedostoevskii podrostok." *Seans*, no. 8 (November 2006). http://seance.ru/blog/nedostoevskiy-podrostok/.

Graham, Seth. "*Chernukha* and Russian Film." *Studies in Slavic Cultures*, no. 1 (2000): 9–27. http://www.pitt.edu/~slavic/sisc/SISC1/docs/graham.pdf.

———. "Fedor Bondarchuk: *Stalingrad* (2013)." *KinoKultura*, no. 44 (2014). http://www.kinokultura.com/2014/44r-stalingrad.shtml.

———. "Models of Male Kinship in Perestroika Cinema." In *Cinepaternity: Fathers and Sons in Soviet and Post-Soviet Film*, ed. Helena Goscilo and Yana Hashamova, 70–88. Bloomington: Indiana University Press, 2010.

Grau, Lester W. "The Cossack Brotherhood Reborn: A Political/Military Force in a Realm of Chaos." https://web.archive.org/web/20150826055134/http://fmso.leavenworth.army.mil/documents/cossack/cossack.htm.

Gray, Beach. "Dmitrii Kiselev: *Six Degrees of Celebration 2*." *KinoKultura*, no. 36 (2012). http://www.kinokultura.com/2012/36r-elki2.shtml.

———. "Global Russian Cinema in the Digital Age: The Films of Timur Bekmambetov." PhD dissertation, University of Pittsburgh, 2016.

———. "Levan Gabriadze et al: *Yolki 3* (*Elki 3*, 2013)." *KinoKultura*, no. 45 (2014). http://www.kinokultura.com/2014/45r-elki3.shtml.

———. "Oxygen" (screening notes). Russian Film Symposium. 2010.

———. "Timur Bekmambetov, Iurii Bykov et al.: *Yolki 1914*." *KinoKultura*, no. 49 (2015). http://www.kinokultura.com/2015/49r-yolki1914.shtml.

———. "Timur Bekmambetov: *Six Degrees of Celebration*." *KinoKultura*, no. 28 (2011). http://www.kinokultura.com/2011/33r-elki.shtml.

"Greetings to Participants and Guests of the Celebration in Honour of the 65th Anniversary of Valery Kharlamov's Birth." Kremlin.ru, 16 February 2013. http://en.kremlin.ru/events/president/news/48108.

Grishakova, Marina, and Silvi Salupere. "A School in the Woods: Moscow-Tartu Semiotics." In *Theoretical Schools and Circles in the Twentieth-Century Humanities: Literary Theory, History, Philosophy*, ed. Marina Grishakova and Silvi Salupere, 173–95. New York: Routledge, 2015.

Grois, Boris [Boris Groys]. "Beseda Natal'i Nikitinoi i Borisa Groisa." *Dozor kak symptom*, ed. Boris Kupriianov and Maksim Surkov, 217–28. Moscow: Falanster, 2006.

———. *Utopiia i obmen*. Moscow: Znak, 1993.

Gusiatinskii, Evgenii. "Brat zhil, brat zhiv, brat budet zhiv." *Iskusstvo kino*, no. 3 (2001). http://kinoart.ru/archive/2001/03/n3-article7.

———. "Ni svoi, ni chuzhoi: *Zhivoi*, rezhisser Aleksandr Veledinskii." *Iskusstvo kino*, no. 8 (2006). https://kinoart.ru/archive/2006/08/n8-article5.

Hallenbeck, Bruce G. *Comedy-horror Films: A Chronological History, 1914–2008*. Jefferson: McFarland, 2009.

Hansen, Thomas Blom, and Finn Stepputat. *Sovereign Bodies: Citizens, Migrants, and States in the Postcolonial World*. Princeton: Princeton University Press, 2005.

Harding, Luce. "Nikita Mikhalkov's *Burnt by the Sun 2* Becomes Russia's Most Expensive Flop." *The Guardian*, 27 April 2010. https://www.theguardian.com/world/2010/apr/27/nikita-mikhalkov-russia-war-film.

Hashamova, Yana. "Two Visions of a Usable Past in (Op)position to the West: Mikhalkov's *The Barber of Siberia* and Sokurov's *Russian Ark*." *Russian Review* 65, no. 2 (2006): 250–57.

Hecht, Gabrielle. *Being Nuclear: Africans and the Global Uranium Trade*. Cambridge, MA: MIT Press, 2014.

Herring, Scott. *Another Country: Queer Anti-Urbanism*. New York: New York University Press, 2010.

Hobbes, Thomas. *Leviathan or the Matter, Forme, & Power of a Common-wealth Ecclesiasticall and Civill*. Hamilton: McMaster University Archive of the History of Economic Thought, 1998.

Hosking, Geoffrey Alan. *Empire and Nation in Russian History*. Waco: Baylor University Press, 1993.

Huntington, Samuel P. "The Clash of Civilizations?" *Foreign Affairs* 72, no. 3 (1993): 22–49.

Hurault-Paupe, Anne. "The Paradoxes of Cinematic Movement: Is the Road Movie a Static Genre?" *Miranda*, no. 10 (2014). https://journals.openedition.org/miranda/6257.

Hutton, Patrick H. "Historiographical Background to the Memory Phenomenon." In his *The Memory Phenomenon in Contemporary Historical Writing: How the Interest in Memory Has Influenced Our Understanding of History*, 1–27. New York: Palgrave Macmillan, 2016.

Huyssen, Andreas. "Authentic Ruins: Products of Modernity." In *Ruins of Modernity*, ed. Julia Hell and Andreas Schönle, 17–28. Durham: Duke University Press, 2010.

———. "Present Pasts: Media, Politics, Amnesia." *Public Culture* 12, no. 1 (2000): 21–38.

Iampolski, Mikhail [Mikhail Iampol'skii]. "Russia: The Cinema of Anti-modernity and Backward Progress." In *Theorizing National Cinema*, ed. Valentina Vitali and Paul Willemen, 72–87. London: Palgrave Macmillan, 2006.

Iampol'skii, Mikhail. *Muratova: Opyt kinoantropologii*. St. Petersburg: Seans, 2015.

"Ivanushka, the Little Fool." In *Russian Fairy Tales*, comp. Aleksandr Afanas'ev, trans. Norbert Guterman, 62–66. New York: Pantheon, 1973.

Jameson, Fredric. *The Political Unconscious*. Ithaca: Cornell University Press, 1981.

———. "Postmodernism, or the Cultural Logic of Late Capitalism." *New Left Review* 1, no. 146 (1984). https://newleftreview.org/I/146/fredric-jameson-postmodernism-or-the-cultural-logic-of-late-capitalism.

Jarzynska, Katarzyna. "Russian Nationalists on the Kremlin's Policy in Ukraine." *OSW Commentary*, Centre for Eastern Studies, no. 156 (24 December 2014). http://aei.pitt.edu/59228/1/commentary_156.pdf.

"Jordan Peele: The Art of the Social Thriller." BAM.org. http://www.bam.org/film/2017/jordan-peele.

Kaganovsky, Lilya. *How the Soviet Man Was Unmade: Cultural Fantasy and Male Subjectivity under Stalin*. Pittsburgh: University of Pittsburgh Press, 2008.

Karaganov, Sergei. "Evropa: Okonchit' kholodnuiu voinu." *Izvestiia*, 8 April 2014. https://iz.ru/news/568861.

Karakhan, Lev. "Cinema without Controls: Nostalgia for the State." Unpublished paper presented at the American Association for the Advancement of Slavic Studies. November 1996.

———. "Zhazhda novoi krovi: 'Nochnoi dozor'—tekhnologii kommercheskogo uspekha." *Iskusstvo kino*, no. 12 (2004). http://kinoart.ru/archive/2004/12/n12-article2.

Kas'ianova, Ol'ga. "Kinotavr-2015: Pioner, Topor, Kladbische." *Seans*, 13 May 2015. http://seance.ru/blog/kinotavr-2015-pioner-topor-kladbishche/.

———. "Kinotavr-2015: 'Strana Oz' Vasiliia Sigareva." *Seans*, 12 June 2015. http://seance.ru/blog/reviews/strana_oz/.

Kellner, Douglas. "Celebrity Diplomacy, Spectacle, and Barack Obama." *Celebrity Studies* 1, no. 1 (2010): 121–23.

Kendall, Joshua. *The Man Who Made Lists: Love, Death, Madness, and the Creation of Roget's Thesaurus*. New York: Berkley, 2009.

Keys, Barbara. *Globalizing Sport: National Rivalry and International Community in the 1930s*. Cambridge, MA: Harvard University Press, 2006.

———. "Soviet Sport and Transnational Mass Culture in the 1930s." *Journal of Contemporary History* 38, no. 3 (2003): 413–34.

Khodonova, Aleksandra, and Timur Bordiug. "Evgenii Chichvarkin budet nabliudat' za 'Evroset'iu.'" *Kommersant"*, 20 November 2008. http://www.kommersant.ru/doc/1075367.

Kichin, Valerii. "Pochtal'on Triapitsyn." *Rossiiskaia gazeta,* 21 August 2014. https://rg.ru/2014/08/14/tryapitsin-site.html.

Klekhovskii, Dariush. "'Taras Bul'ba': Pol'skii vzgliad." *Uroki istorii XX vek.* https://urokiistorii.ru/article/410.

Klochkova, Kseniia. "Ministr kul'tury Medinskii: Deneg na fil'my o 'Rashke-govniashke' bol'she ne dam." *Fontanka.* http://www.fontanka.ru/2014/12/09/202/.

Klyamkin, Igor. "Putin's War Patriotism." *Open Democracy,* 10 May 2013. https://www.opendemocracy.net/od-russia/igor-klyamkin/putin%E2%80%99s-war-patriotism.

Kokotiukha, Andrii. "Chomu zaboronennomu v Ukraiini 'Tarasu Bul'bi' neobkhidna reabilitatsiia." *Glavred.* http://glavred.info/avtorskie_kolonki/chomu-zaboronennomu-v-ukrayini-tarasu-bulbi-neobhidna-reabilitaciya-299068.html.

Komm, Dmitrii. "Kovcheg bez potopa." *Neprikosnovennyi zapas* 3, no. 29 (2003). *Zhurnal'nyi zal.* http://magazines.russ.ru/nz/2003/29/komm.html.

Koselleck, Reinhardt. "War Memorials: Identity Formations of the Survivors." In his *The Practice of Conceptual History: Timing History, Spacing Concepts.* Stanford: Stanford University Press, 2002.

Kott, Aleksandr. "Aleksandr Kott: Kino bez slov—eto moi parallel'nyi mir." Interview by Mariia Tokmasheva. *ProfiCinema,* 25 May 2014. http://www.proficinema.ru/questions-problems/interviews/detail.php?ID=159327.

Kovalov, Oleg. "Russkii kontekst: 'Russkii kovcheg,' rezhisser Aleksandr Sokurov." *Iskusstvo kino,* no. 7 (2003). http://kinoart.ru/archive/2003/07/n7-article3.

Kraliuk, Petro. *Taemnychyi agent Mykola Gogol abo pro schcho rozpovidae "Taras Bul'ba."* Lviv: Vydavnytstvo Staroho Leva, 2016.

Kristeva, Julia. *Powers of Horror: An Essay on Abjection.* New York: Columbia University Press, 2010.

Kudriavtsev, Sergei. *Svoe kino.* Moscow: Dubl'-D, 1998.

Kulinicheva, Ekaterina. "Kto sygraet L'va Iashina." *Gazeta.ru,* 1 July 2015. https://www.gazeta.ru/sport/2015/07/01/a_6863029.shtml.

Kupriianov, Boris, and Maksim Surkov, eds. *Dozor kak simptom.* Moscow: Falanster, 2006.

Kuvshinova, Mariia, Liubov' Arkus, and Konstantin Shavlovskii. *Balabanov.* St. Petersburg: Seans, 2015.

Laderman, David. *Driving Visions: Exploring the Road Movie.* Austin: University of Texas Press, 2002.

Landsberg, Alison. *Prosthetic Memory: The Transformation of American Remembrance in the Age of Mass Culture.* New York: Columbia University Press, 2004.

Lane, Christel. "Legitimacy and Power in the Soviet Union through Socialist Ritual." *British Journal of Political Science* 14, no. 2 (1984): 207–17.

Larina, Kseniia. "Seksual'naia revoliutsiia v rossiiskom kino." *Kul'turnyi shok,* Ekho Moskvy (Moscow), 7 September 2013.

Larsen, Susan. "In Search of an Audience: Russian Cinema of Reconciliation." In *Consuming Russia: Popular Culture, Sex, and Society since Gorbachev*, ed. Adele Barker, 192–216. Durham: Duke University Press, 1999.

Ledeneva, Alena. *How Russia Really Works: The Informal Practices That Shaped Post-Soviet Politics and Business.* Ithaca and London: Cornell UP, 2006.

Lermontov, Mikhail. "Son." In his *Sochineniia v shesti tomakh*, 197. Moscow: Izdatel'stvo Akademii nauk SSSR, 1954.

Levada Center. "Odobrenie organov vlasti." 10 July 2018. https://www.levada.ru/indikatory/odobrenie-organov-vlasti/.

Lévi-Strauss, Claude. *The Savage Mind*. London: Weidenfeld and Nicolson, 1962.

Leyda, Jay. *Kino: A History of the Russian and Soviet Film*. Princeton: Princeton University Press, 1983.

Lipovetsky, Mark. "Anything Goes: How the Russian News Became a Postmodern Game without Rules." *The Calvert Journal* 10 March 2015. https://www.calvertjournal.com/articles/show/3736/political-steampunk-postmodern-game-mark-lipovetsky.

———. "The Formal Is Political." *Slavic and East European Journal* 60, no. 2 (2016): 185–204.

———. "War as the Family Value: Failing Fathers and Monstrous Sons in *My Stepbrother Frankenstein*." In *Cinepaternity: Fathers and Sons in Soviet and Post-Soviet Film*, ed. Helena Goscilo and Yana Hashamova, 114-37. Bloomington: Indiana University Press, 2010.

Longworth, Philip. *The Cossacks*. London: Constable, 1969.

Lotman, Juri. "Primary and Secondary Communication-Modeling Systems." In *Soviet Semiotics: An Anthology*, ed. Daniel P. Lucid, 95–98. Baltimore: Johns Hopkins University Press, 1988.

Lowenstein, Adam. *Shocking Representation: Historical Trauma, National Cinema, and the Modern Horror Film*. New York: Columbia University Press, 2005.

Lübecker, Nikolaj. *The Feel-Bad Film*. Edinburgh: Edinburgh University Press, 2015.

Lukashuk, Zmiter. "Svetlana Alekseevich: Ia daiu znak, chto my soprotivliaemsia." EuroRadio.fm, 1 January 2017. https://euroradio.fm/ru/svetlana-aleksievich-ya-dayu-znak-chto-my-soprotivlyaemsya.

Lüthi, Max. *The European Folktale: Form and Nature.* Bloomington: Indiana University Press, 1986.

Maliukova, Larisa. "Pogovorim o strannostiakh liubvi." *Iskusstvo kino*, no. 8 (2012). http://kinoart.ru/archive/2012/08/pogovorim-o-strannostyakh-lyubvi-kokoko-rezhisser-avdotya-smirnova.

———. "Pontovaia vyskochka." *Novaia gazeta*, 15 May 2008. https://www.novayagazeta.ru/articles/2008/05/15/38064-pontovaya-vyskochka.

———. "*Viking* stal liderom rossiiskogo prokata v novogodnii uikend." *Radio Business FM*, 3 January 2017. https://www.bfm.ru/news/343061.

Mal'tseva, Anastasiia. "Svetskoe obshchestvo i klerikal'noe soznanie: 6 tsitat iz lektsii Iriny Prokhorovoi." *Snob.ru*, 16 October 2014. https://snob.ru/selected/entry/82396.

Martin, Terry. *The Affirmative Action Empire: Nations and Nationalism in the Soviet Union, 1923–1939*. Ithaca: Cornell University Press, 2001.

Maslova, Lidiia. "'Kinotavr poshel drugim putem." *Kommersant"*, 29 May 2006. https://www.kommersant.ru/doc/677203.

Massad, Joseph. *Desiring Arabs.* Chicago: University of Chicago Press, 2007.

Matizen, Viktor. "'Iskhodit' sleduet iz vysshei pravdy o cheloveke' 2009, 2012." Two interviews with Andrei Zviagintsev. In his *Kino i zhizn': 12 diuzhin interv'iu samogo skepticheskogo kinokritika*, 2: 653–74. Vinnitsa: Globus-Press, 2013.

———. "Iurii Arabov: Teper' po povodu patriotov." *Iskusstvo kino*, no. 12 (2013). https://www.kinoart.ru/archive/2013/12/yurij-arabov-teper-po-povodu-patriotov.

"Mat' Chichvarkina pered smert'iu byla izbita." *Lenta.ru*, 21 July 2010. http://lenta.ru/news/2010/06/21/nogood/.

McCannon, John. *Red Arctic: Polar Exploration and the Myth of the North in the Soviet Union, 1932–1939.* New York: Oxford University Press, 1998.

Medvedev, Sergei. "A General Theory of Russian Space: A Gay Science and a Rigorous Science." *Alternatives: Global, Local, Political* 22, no. 4 (1997): 523–53.

———. "Otkuda vzialsia 'Krymnash'?" *Radio Svoboda*, 22 July 2015. https://www.svoboda.org/a/27147455.html.

Merridale, Catherine. *Red Fortress: The Secret Heart of Russian History.* London: Penguin, 2014.

Miller, Cynthia J., and A. Bowdoin Van Riper. Introduction to *The Laughing Dead: The Horror-Comedy Film from Bride of Frankenstein to Zombieland*, ed. Cynthia J. Miller and A. Bowdoin Van Riper, xiii–xxiii. Lanham: Rowman & Littlefield, 2016.

Mitchell, W. J. T. "Imperial Landscape." In *Landscape and Power*, ed. W. J. T. Mitchell, 5–34. 2nd ed. Chicago: University of Chicago Press, 2002.

———. "Introduction." *Landscape and Power*, ed. W. J. T. Mitchell, 1–4. 2nd ed. Chicago: University of Chicago Press, 2002.

Molchanova, Maria. "Kinokratiia: 'Okno v Parizh' Iuriia Mamina." *Diletant*, 29 January 2017. http://diletant.media/articles/33711400/.

Moltke, Johannes von. "Ruin Cinema." In *Ruins of Modernity*, ed. Julie Hell and Andreas Schönle, 395–417. Durham: Duke University Press, 2010.

Muers, R. *Keeping God's Silence: Towards a Theological Ethics of Communication*. Malden: Blackwell, 2004.

Mulvey, Laura. "Visual Pleasure and Narrative Cinema." *Screen* 16, no. 3 (1975): 6–18.

Nair, Sheila. "Sovereignty, Security, and the Exception: Towards Situating Postcolonial homo sacer." In *Routledge International Handbook of Contemporary Social and Political Theory*, ed. Gerard Delanty and Stephen P. Turner, 386–94. Abingdon: Routledge, 2011.

Nationmaster. https://www.nationmaster.com/country-info/stats/Geography/Land-area/Square-miles.

Nekrasova, Elena. "Zakupki.ru: O mekhanizmakh gospodderzhki kinematografii." *Iskusstvo kino*, no. 3 (2014). https://www.kinoart.ru/archive/2014/03/zakupki-ru-o-mekhanizmakh-gospodderzhki-kinematografii.

Nigmatullin, Airat. "Petr Buslov: 'Dlia menia Stalin—chelovek, kotoryi vyigral voinu.'" *Biznes Online*. https://www.business-gazeta.ru/article/322559.

Noordenbos, Boris. "Ironic Imperialism: How Russian Patriots Are Reclaiming Postmodernism." *Studies in East European Thought* 63, no. 2 (2011): 147–58.

Norris, Stephen M. *Blockbuster History in the New Russia: Movies, Memory, and Patriotism*. Bloomington: Indiana University Press, 2012.

———. "Guiding Stars: The Comet-like Rise of the War Film in Putin's Russia: Recent World War II Films and Historical Memories." *Studies in Russian and Soviet Cinema* 1, no. 2 (2007): 163–89.

———. "Packaging the Past: Cinema and Nationhood in the Putin Era." *KinoKultura*, no. 21 (2008). http://www.kinokultura.com/2008/21-norris.shtml.

———. "Tsarist Russia, Lubok Style: Nikita Mikhalkov's *Barber of Siberia* (1999) and Post-Soviet National Identity." *Historical Journal of Film, Radio, and Television* 25, no. 1 (2005): 101–18.

North, Christopher. "Noctes Ambrosianae," Colloquy 42. *Blackwood's Magazine* 45 (April 1829): 527. https://babel.hathitrust.org/cgi/pt?id=iau.31858021710672;view=1up;seq=524.

O'Mahony, Mike. *Sergei Eisenstein*. London: Reaktion Books, 2008.

Olick, Jeffrey, and Joyce Robbins. "Social Memory Studies: From 'Collective Memory' to the Historical Sociology of Mnemonic Practices." *Annual Review of Sociology* 24 (1998): 105–40.

Østbø, Jardar. *The New Third Rome: Readings of a Russian Nationalist Myth*. Stuttgart: Ibidem, 2016.

Oushakine, Serguei. "Ivan Vyrypaev: *Oxygen*." *KinoKultura*, no. 26 (2009). http://www.kinokultura.com/2009/26r-kislorod.shtml.

Panou, Eirini G. "The Signum Harpocraticum in the 8th-century Christian Art of Nubia." In *Actual Problems of Art Theory and History*, 5: 246–62. St. Petersburg, 2015. https://www.academia.edu/9636716/The_Signum_Harpocraticum_in_the_8th-century_Christian_Art_of_Nubia_Actual_Problems_of_Art_Theory_and_History_Vol._5_2015_St_Petersburg_Russia.

Parfenov, Leonid. *Namedni*. 16 May 2004. https://www.youtube.com/watch?v=Y9V3b4Xfbjo.

Parfitt, Tom. "Russia Plants Flag on North Pole Seabed." *The Guardian*, 2 August 2007. https://www.theguardian.com/world/2007/aug/02/russia.arctic.

Paul, William. *Laughing, Screaming: Modern Hollywood Horror and Comedy*. New York: Columbia University Press, 1994.

Pippin, Robert B. *Hollywood Westerns and American Myth: The Importance of Howard Hawks and John Ford for Political Philosophy*. New Haven: Yale University Press, 2010.

Plakhov, Andrei. "Ballada o Tarase." *Kommersant"*, 6 April 2009. https://www.kommersant.ru/doc/1148011.

———. *Kino na grani nervnogo sryva*. Moscow: Seans, 2014.

———. "Konets postmodernizma? Vozvrashchenie modernisma?" In *Posle Tarkovskogo: Materialy IV Mezhdunarodnoi nauchnoi konferentsii, provedennoi v ramkakh IX Mezhdunarodnogo kinofestivalia im. Andreia Tarkovskogo "Zerkalo"*, comp. Aleksei Artamonov, ed. Vasilii Stepanov, 172–83. Moscow: Seans, 2016.

———. "'Russkii kovcheg' priplyl v Rossiiu." *Kommersant"*, 21 April 2003. https://www.kommersant.ru/doc/378102.

———. "V raskopkakh Stalingrada." *Kommersant"*, 9 October 2013. https://www.kommersant.ru/doc/2314393.

Plokhy, Serhii. *Unmaking Imperial Russia: Mykhailo Hrushevsky and the Writing of Ukrainian History*. Toronto: University of Toronto Press, 2005.

Posner, Dassia. *The Director's Prism: E. T. A. Hoffmann and the Russian Theatrical Avant-Garde*. Evanston: Northwestern University Press, 2016.

Prikaz 184 (22 December 2017). Federal'nyi fond sotsial'noi i ekonomicheskoi podderzhki otechestvennoi kinematografii (Fond Kino). http://www.fond-kino.ru/projects/otbor-liderov-otecestvennogo-kinoproizvodstva-v-2018-godu/.

Prilepin, Zakhar. "Kamuflirovannye bludni epokhi peremen." *Kommersant"*, 28 October 2007. https://www.kommersant.ru/doc/2299773.

Prokhorov, Alexander. "The Adolescent and the Child in the Cinema of the Thaw." *Studies in Russian and Soviet Cinema* 1, no. 2 (2007): 115–29.

———. "The Myth of the 'Great Family' in Marlen Khutsiev's *Lenin's Guard* and Mark Osep'ian's *Three Days of Viktor Chernyshev*. In *Cinepaternity: Fathers and Sons in Soviet and Post-Soviet Film*, ed. Helena Goscilo and Yana Hashamova, 29–50. Bloomington: Indiana University Press, 2010.

Prokhorova, Elena. Review of *Peculiarities of the National Hunt* (Osobennosti natsional'noi okhoty), dir. Aleksandr Rogozhkin. *KinoKultura*, no. 50 (2015). http://www.kinokultura.com/2015/50/fifty_osobennosti-okhoty.shtml.

Prokhorova, Irina. "'Bumera' smotriat ot istoshcheniia." *Gazeta.ru*, 14 August 2003. https://www.gazeta.ru/2003/08/14/zriteljlubit.shtml.

Propp, Vladimir. *The Morphology of the Folktale*. Austin: University of Texas Press, 1975.

Prozorov, Sergei. *The Ethics of Postcommunism: History and Social Praxis in Russia*. New York: Palgrave Macmillan, 2009.

———. "The Management of *Anomie*: The State of Exception in Postcommunist Russia." In *Agamben and Colonialism*, ed. Marcelo Svirsky and Simone Bignall, 32–51. Edinburgh: Edinburgh University Press, 2012.

"Putin otsenil fil'm 'Legenda No. 17' o Kharlamove i dal naputstvie iunym khokkeistam." *RIA Novosti*, 18 April 2013. https://ria.ru/tv_sport/20130418/933223162.html.

Quote Investigator. https://quoteinvestigator.com/2019/02/26/tired/#return-note-21833-2.

Raiter, Oliver. "Men'shinstva v khoroshem smysle." *Gazeta.ru*, 9 February 2004. https://www.gazeta.ru/2004/02/09/oa_111519.shtml,

Ram, Harsha. *The Imperial Sublime: A Russian Poetics of Empire*. Wisconsin: University of Wisconsin Press, 2003.

———. "Prisoners of the Caucasus: Literary Myths and Media Representations of the Chechen Conflict." *Berkeley Program in Soviet and Post-Soviet Studies Working Paper Series*, 1999.

Razlogov, Kirill. "Gosudarstvennyi komitet SSSR po kinematografii." *Kino: Entsiklopedicheskii slovar'*. Moscow: Sovetskaia entsiklopediia, 1986.

———. "Kinotavr: Caught in the Crossfire." *KinoKultura*, no. 18 (2007). http://www.kinokultura.com/2007/18-razlogov.shtml.

Reuters Staff. "Syria Air Strikes Push Putin's Rating to New High: Russian State Pollster." Reuters.com, 22 October 2015. https://www.reuters.com/article/us-russia-putin-idUSKCN0SG0SB20151022.

Rivette, Jacques. "Génie de Howard Hawks." *Cahiers du cinéma*, no. 23 (May 1953): 16–23.

Rodnianskii, Aleksandr. "Aleksandr Rodnianskii: Rossiiane ne khotiat videt' real'nost' na ekrane." *Vedomosti*, 22 March 2012. https://www.vedomosti.ru/opinion/articles/2012/03/22/obschestvennyj_autizm.

Rodnyansky, Alexander. "Yes, 'John Carter' Was a Hit in Russia. Here's Why." *IndieWire*, 27 April 2012. https://www.indiewire.com/2012/04/yes-john-carter-was-a-hit-in-russia-heres-why-47806/.

Rogatchevski, Andrei. "Aleksei Fedorchenko: *Celestial Wives of the Meadow Mari*." *KinoKultura*, no. 41 (2013). http://www.kinokultura.com/2013/41r-nebesnye-zheny.shtml.

Roget, P. M. "Explanation of an Optical Deception in the Appearance of the Spokes of a Wheel Seen through Vertical Apertures." *Philosophical Transactions of the Royal Society of London* 115 (1 January 1825): 131–40. https://archive.org/details/jstor-107736/page/n1.

Roget, Peter. *Thesaurus of English Language Words and Phrases Classified and Arranged so as to Facilitate the Expression of Ideas and Assist in Literary Composition*. London: Longman, Brown, Green, and Longmans, 1852.

Rojek, Chris. "Celebrity and Religion." *Stardom and Celebrity: A Reader*, ed. Sean Redmond and Su Holmes, 171–80. Los Angeles: Sage, 2007.

Romodanovskaia, Nina. "Alexei Uchitel': 'Ia ne snimaiu pro mentov—ia snimaiu pro liudei.'" *ProfiCinema*. http://www.proficinema.ru/questions-problems/interviews/detail.php?ID=158966.

Rostotskii, Stanislav F. "Seansu otvechaiut: *Sibirskii tsiriul'nik*." *Seans*, no. 17–18 (May 1999). http://seance.ru/n/17-18/rezhisser-film-kritik-2/sibirskiy-tsiryulnik/sibirskiy-tsiryulnik-2/.

Russell, P. "Ephraem the Syrian on the Utility of Language and the Place of Silence." *Journal of Early Christian Studies* 8, no. 1 (2000): 21–37.

Rutkovskii, Vadim. "Sigarev-geroi i pervye itogi 'Kinotavra-2015.'" *Snob*, 11 June 2015. https://snob.ru/selected/entry/93781.

Ryklin, Mikhail. "Dozor kak simptom." *Seans*, no. 29–30 (December 2006). http://seance.ru/n/29-30/portret-konstantin-ernst/dozor-kak-simptom/.

Said, Edward. *Culture and Imperialism*. New York: Vintage, 1994.

———. *Orientalism*. New York: Vintage, 1979.

Saprykin, Iurii. "Iurii Saprykin ob ekranizatsii romana Sergeia Minaeva 'Dukhless.'" *Afisha*, 5 October 2012. https://daily.afisha.ru/archive/vozduh/archive/sapr-on-duhless/.

Sarris, Andrew. "Toward a Theory of Film History." In his *The American Cinema: Directors and Directions, 1929–1968*, 19–37. New York: E. P. Dutton, 1968.

Satubaldina, Assel. "Bekmambetov's New Film *Search* Claims Award at Sundance Film Festival." *The Astana Times*, 4 February 2018. https://astanatimes.com/2018/02/bekmambetovs-new-film-search-claims-award-at-sundance-film-festival/.

Savel'ev, Dmitrii. "Interv'iu s Petrom Buslovym: "Bumer." Sed'maia seriia, pervyi klass." *Seagull Magazine*, 23 January 2004. https://www.chayka.org/node/323.

Schueller, Malini Johar. "Decolonizing Global Theories Today." *Interventions* 11, no. 2 (2009): 235–54.

Schulmann, Ekaterina. "Babushkas Rule." *Chatham House*, August–September 2017. https://www.chathamhouse.org/publications/twt/babushkas-rule.

Schwartz, Barry. "Rethinking the Concept of Collective Memory." In *Routledge International Handbook of Memory Studies*, ed. Anna Lisa Tota and Trevor Hagen, 9–21. London: Routledge, 2015.

Seaton, Albert. *The Horsemen of the Steppes: The Story of the Cossacks*. London: Bodley Head, 1985.

Seckler, Dawn. "What Does Zhanr Mean in Russian?" In *Directory of World Cinema: Russia*, ed. Birgit Beumers, 28–34. Bristol: Intellect, 2011.

Sedgwick, Eve Kosofsky. *Epistemology of the Closet*. Berkeley: University of California Press, 1990.

Segida, Miroslava. "Segida-info." *Iskusstvo kino*, no. 4 (1996): 73–76.

Segida, Miroslava, and Sergei Zemlianukhin, comp. *Domashniaia sinemateka: Otechestvennoe kino, 1918–1996*. Moscow Dubl'-D, 1996.

———. *Fil'my Rossii: Igrovoe kino (1995–2000)*. Moscow: Dubl'-D, 2001.

———. *Fil'my Rossii: Igrovoe kino/TV/video (1992–2003)*. Moscow: Dubl'-D, 2004.

Sellors, C. Paul. *Film Authorship: Auteurs and Other Myths*. London: Wallflower, 2010.

Serebrennikov, Kirill. "Foreword." In *Performing Violence: Literary and Theatrical Experiments of New Russian Drama*, ed. Birgit Beumers and Mark Lipovetsky, 9–11. Bristol: Intellect, 2009.

Shaw, Tony, and Denise J. Youngblood. "Cold War Sport, Film, and Propaganda: A Comparative Analysis of the Superpowers." *Journal of Cold War Studies* 19, no. 1 (2017): 160–92.

Shelukhin, Serhii. *Ukraiina—nazva nashoii zemli z naidavnishykh chasiv*. Prague: Beskid, 1936.

Sheveleva, Aleksandra. "Televidenie pri Putine: Ot nedoveriia k liubvi." *BBCRussian.com*, 26 February 2008. http://news.bbc.co.uk/hi/russian/russia/newsid_7264000/7264980.stm.

Shmyrov, Viacheslav. "Prazdnik gde-to riadom." *Seans*, 20 June 2011. http://seance.ru/blog/gena-sidorov/.

Shpagin, Aleksandr. Contribution during 2003 Russian Film Symposium (*Arrogance and Envy*), quoted in Natalia Sirivlia and Elena Stishova, "Solov'i na 17-oi ulitse: Antiamerikanism v sovetskom i rossiiskom kino," *Iskusstvo kino*, no. 10 (2003), http://kinoart.ru/archive/2003/10/n10-article2.

Simonov, Ruben. *Stanislavsky's Protégé: Eugene Vakhtangov*. Translated and edited by Miriam Goldina. New York: Drama Book Specialists, 1969.

Simpozium po strukturnomu izucheniiu znakovykh system: Tezisy dokladov. Moscow: Izdatel'stvo Akademii nauk SSSR, 1962.

Sirivlia, Natal'ia. "Liubit' po-russki: 'Starukhi,' rezhisser Gennadii Sidorov." *Iskusstvo kino*, no. 11 (2003). http://www.kinoart.ru/archive/2003/11/n11-article6.

Sirivlia, Natal'ia, and Elena Stishova. "Solov'i na 17-oi ulitse: Antiamerikanism v sovetskom i rossiiskom kino." *Iskusstvo kino*, no. 10 (2003). http://kinoart.ru/archive/2003/10/n10-article2.

"Six Degrees of Celebration (2010): Release Info." IMDb.com. https://www.imdb.com/title/tt1782568/releaseinfo?ref_=tt_dt_dt.

Skretcowicz, Viktor, Susan Rennie, William Aitken, Grant Cunningham, and Frances Phillips, comps. *Dictionary of the Scots Language* [Dictionar o the Scots Leid]. University of Dundee. http://www.dsl.ac.uk/.

Snyder, Timothy. "Vladimir Putin's Politics of Eternity." *The Guardian*, 16 March 2018. https://www.theguardian.com/news/2018/mar/16/vladimir-putin-russia-politics-of-eternity-timothy-snyder.

Soares, John. "East Beats West: Ice Hockey and the Cold War." In *Sport and the Transformation of Modern Europe: States, Media, and Markets, 1950–2010*, ed. Alan Tomlinson, Christopher Young, and Richard Holt, 35–49. New York: Routledge, 2011.

Sokolov, Mikhail. "Pod kliukvoi Stalingrada." *Radio Svoboda*, 18 October 2013. https://www.svoboda.org/a/25140727.html.

Souleimanov, Emil Aslan, and Huseyn Aliyev. "Blood Revenge and Violent Mobilization: Evidence from the Chechen Wars." *International Security* 40, no. 2 (2015): 158–80.

Ssorin-Chaikov, Nikolai. "On Heterochrony: Birthday Gifts to Stalin, 1949." *Journal of the Royal Anthropological Institute* 12, no. 2 (2006): 355–75.

"Stanislav Belkovskii: Na pike sobytii." *Radio Vesti*, 12 September 2014. https://radio.vesti-ukr.com/etherethemes/7243-na-pike-sobytij-12-sentjabrja.html.

"State Group Goskino Faces New Role in Shifting Soviet Film Industry." *Variety* 335, no. 12 (5–11 July 1989): 66.

Stepula, Nadiia. "Fil'm 'Taras Bul'ba': Mystetstvo na sluzhbi. . ." *Radio Svoboda*, 8 April 2009. https://www.radiosvoboda.org/a/1604982.html.

Stishova, Elena. "Adrenalin: *Legenda No. 17*, rezhisser Nikolai Lebedev." *Iskusstvo kino*, no. 5 (2013). http://kinoart.ru/archive/2013/05/adrenalin-legenda-17-rezhisser-nikolaj-lebedev.

———. "Melankholiia: Russkaia versiia. *Ispytanie,* rezhisser Aleksandr Kott." *Iskusstvo kino,* no. 8 (2014): 71–76. http://kinoart.ru/archive/2014/08/melankholiya-russkaya-versiya-ispytanie-rezhisser-aleksandr-kott.

———. "Mne ne bol'no." *Iskusstvo kino,* no. 10 (2013). http://kinoart.ru/blogs/mne-ne-bolno.

Stites, Richard. "Crowded on the Edge of Vastness: Observations on Russian Space and Place." In his *Passion and Perception: Essays on Russian Culture,* 47–58. Washington, DC: New Academia Publishing, 2010.

Street, John. "The Celebrity Politician: Political Style and Popular Culture." *Media and the Restyling of Politics: Consumerism, Celebrity and Cynicism,* ed. John Corner and Dick Pels, 85–98. London: Sage, 2003.

Strukov, Vlad. *Contemporary Russian Cinema: Symbols of a New Era.* Edinburgh: Edinburgh University Press, 2016.

Sul'kin, Oleg. "Vremia tantsora prishlo v Ameriku." Article and interview with Vadim Abdrashitov. *Novoe russkoe slovo,* 22 October 1997, 20.

Suny, Ronald Grigor. "The Empire Strikes Out: Imperial Russia, 'National' Identity, and Theories of Empire." In *A State of Nations: Empire and Nation-Making in the Age of Lenin and Stalin,* ed. Ronald Grigor Suny and Terry Martin, 23–66. Oxford: Oxford University Press, 2001.

"S''emki novogodnei komedii *Elki.*" *Gorodovoi,* 12 September 2013. http://www.kino.gorodovoy.spb.ru/news/784285.shtml.

Therborn, Göran. "Entangled Modernities." *European Journal of Social Theory* 6, no. 3 (2003): 293–305.

Thompson, Kristin. "Introduction: Sequel-itis." In her *The Frodo Franchise:* The Lord of the Rings *and Modern Hollywood,* 1–13. Berkeley: University of California Press, 2007.

Thunø, E. *Image and Relic: Mediating the Sacred in Early Mediaeval Rome.* Rome: L'Erma di Bretschneider, 2002.

Tikkanen J. J. *Zwei gebärden mit dem Zeigefinger.* Helsingfors: Druckerei der Finnischen Literaturgesellschaft, 1913.

Tlostanova, Madina. "The Postcolonial and the Postsocialist: A Deferred Coalition? Brothers Forever?" *Postcolonial Interventions: An Interdisciplinary Journal of Postcolonial Studies* 3, no. 1 (2018): 1–37.

Tolstunov, Igor'. "Igor' Tolstunov: U vas milliony, u nas—rynok." Interview with Andrei Plakhov. *Kommersant'',* 14 April 2010. https://www.kommersant.ru/doc/1353941.

Toumanoff, Cyril. "Moscow the Third Rome: Genesis and Significance of a Politico-Religious Idea." *Catholic Historical Review* 40, no. 4 (1955): 438.

Truffaut, François. "Une certaine tendance du cinéma français." *Cahiers du cinéma,* no. 31 (January 1954): 15–28.

Tsyrkun, Nina. "'Stalingrad' i nekanonicheskii kanon." *Iskusstvo kino,* no. 11 (2013). https://www.kinoart.ru/archive/2013/11/stalingrad-i-nekanonicheskij-kanon.

Uchitel', Aleksei. "Mne vse khochetsia poprobovat'." *KinoBusiness*, 18 June 2014. https://www.kinobusiness.com/interview/mne-vse-khochetsya-poprobovat/.

Uskov, Oleg. "Aleksandr Mitta blagoslovil 'ne remeik' svoego fil'ma 'Ekipazh'." rg.ru kinokratiia. 28 December 2015. https://rg.ru/2015/12/28/mitta-site-anons.html.

Uspenskii, Vladimir A. "Progulki s Lotmanom." *Lotmaniana Tartuensia: O Lotmane: Memuary*, http://www.ruthenia.ru/lotman/mem/vl_usp95.html.

———. "Progulki s Lotmanom i vtorichnoe modelirovanie." In *Lotmanskii sbornik 1*, ed. Evgenii Permiakov, 99–127. Moscow: IC-Garant, 1995.

Vainer, Arkadii, and Georgii Vainer. *Vizit k Minotavru*. Moscow: Molodaia gvardiia, 1972.

Veledinskii, Aleksandr. "Menia potrias fil'm *Strasti Khristovy*." Interview by Lidiia Andreeva. *Russkoe pole* (2004). http://moloko.ruspole.info/node/876.

Vertov, Dziga. "The Birth of Kino-Eye." In *Kino-Eye: The Writings of Dziga Vertov*, ed. Annette Michelson, 40–41. Berkeley: University of California Press, 1984.

———. "On the Significance of Nonacted Cinema." In *Kino-Eye: The Writings of Dziga Vertov*, ed. Annette Michelson, 35–37. Berkeley: University of California Press, 1984.

Vodolatskii, Viktor. "Proekt federal'nogo zakona 'O patrioticheskom vospitanii.'" Sozd.parlament.gov.ru, 16 November 2017. http://sozd.parlament.gov.ru/bill/315234-7.

Volkov, Denis. "Putin's Ratings: Anomaly or Trend?" Institute of Modern Russia, 23 December 2014. https://imrussia.org/en/nation/2135-putins-ratings-anomaly-or-trend.

VTsIOM (Russian Center for Public Opinion Research). "Putin's Performance Rating: New Record High," 22 October 2015. https://www.wciom.com/index.php?id=61&uid=1194.

Wakeham, Pauline. "Becoming Documentary: Edward Curtis's *In the Land of the Headhunters* and the Politics of Archival Reconstruction." *Canadian Review of American Studies* 36, no. 3 (2006): 294.

Walker, Shaun. "From One Vladimir to Another: Putin Unveils Huge Statue in Moscow." *The Guardian*, 4 November 2016. https://www.theguardian.com/world/2016/nov/04/vladimir-great-statue-unveiled-putin-moscow.

Wang, Yiman. "A Star Is Dead: A Legend Is Born: Practicing Leslie Cheung's Posthumous Fandom." In *Stardom and Celebrity: A Reader*, ed. Sean Redmond and Su Holmes, 326–40. Los Angeles: Sage, 2007.

Wardle, Ralph M. "The Authorship of the 'Noctes Ambrosianae.'" *Modern Philology* 42, no. 1 (1944): 9–17.

Werner, Cynthia, and Kathleen Purvis-Roberts. "Unraveling the Secrets of the Past: Contested Versions of Nuclear Testing in the Soviet Republic of Kazakhstan." In *Half-lives and Half-truths: Confronting the Radioactive Legacies of the Cold War*, ed. Barbara Rose Johnston, 277–98. Santa Fe: School for Advanced Research, 2007.

White, Hayden. "The Forms of Wildness: Archaeology of an Idea." In *The Wild Man Within: An Image in Western Thought from the Renaissance to Romanticism*, ed. Edward J. Dudley and Maximillian E. Novak, 3–38. Pittsburgh: University of Pittsburgh Press, 1973.

Widdis, Emma. "Viewed from Below: Subverting the Myths of the Soviet Landscape." In *Russia on Reels: The Russian Idea in Post-Soviet Cinema*, ed. Birgit Beumers, 66–75. London: I. B. Tauris, 1999.

Wilmes, Justin. "From *Tikhie* to *Gromkie*: The Discursive Strategies of the Putin-Era Auteurs." *Russian Literature* 96 (2018): 297–327.

Wixman, Ronald. *The Peoples of the USSR: An Ethnographic Handbook*. Armonk: M. E. Sharpe, 1984.

Woll, Josephine. "Exorcising the Devil: Russian Cinema and Horror." In *Horror International*, ed. Steven Jay Schneider and Tony Williams, 336–58. Detroit: Wayne State University Press, 2005.

World Bank: Data (Land Area). https://data.worldbank.org/indicator/AG.LND.TOTL.K2.

Yampolsky, Mikhail [Mikhail Iampol'skii]. "Cinema without Cinema." In *Russian Critics on the Cinema of Glasnost*, ed. Michael Brashinsky and Andrew Horton, 11–17. Cambridge: Cambridge University Press, 1994.

"Yolki 2 (2011): Release Info." IMDb.com, https://www.imdb.com/title/tt2124096/releaseinfo?ref_=tt_dt_dt.

"Yolki 3 (2013): Release Info." IMDb.com, https://www.imdb.com/title/tt3121434/releaseinfo?ref_=tt_dt_dt.

"Yolki 5 (2016): Release Info." IMDb.com, https://www.imdb.com/title/tt5840988/releaseinfo?ref_=tt_dt_dt.

"Yolki 1914 (2014): Release Info." IMDb.com, https://www.imdb.com/title/tt3877844/releaseinfo?ref_=tt_dt_dt.

"Yolki novye (2017): Release Info." IMDb.com, https://www.imdb.com/title/tt6907804/releaseinfo?ref_=tt_dt_dt.

Yoon, Saera. "Transformation of a Ukrainian Cossack into a Russian Warrior: Gogol's 1842 'Taras Bulba.'" *Slavic and East European Journal* 49, no. 3 (2005): 430–44.

Youngblood, Denise. "Andrei Kravchuk: *The Viking*." *KinoKultura*, no. 57 (2017). http://www.kinokultura.com/2017/57r-viking.shtml.

Yurchak, Alexei. *Everything Was Forever, until It Was No More: The Last Soviet Generation*. Princeton: Princeton University Press, 2005.

———. "Gagarin and the Rave Kids: Transforming Power, Identity, and Aesthetics in Post-Soviet Nightlife." In *Consuming Russia: Popular Culture, Sex, and Society since Gorbachev*, ed. Adele Marie Barker, 76–109. Durham, NC: Duke University Press, 2005.

Zabaluev, Iaroslav. "Eto brat'ia i sestry geroev 'Bumera.'" *Gazeta.ru*, 15 October 2015. https://www.gazeta.ru/culture/2015/10/15/a_7822199.shtml.

"Zakrytyi pokaz—Gruz 200." 29 December 2011. https://www.youtube.com/watch?v=ZFfqxRZRicI.

Zalizniak, A. A., Viach. Vs. Ivanov, and V. N. Toporov, eds. "O vozmozhnosti strukturno-tipologicheskogo izucheniia nekotorykh modeliruiushchikh semioticheskikh system." In their *Strukturno-tipologicheskie issledovaniia: Sbornik statei*, 134–43. Moscow: Izdatel'stvo Akademii nauk SSSR, 1962.

Zarubin, Pavel. "Legenda nomer 11: Putin vstretil svoi den' rozhdeniia na l'du." *Vesti.ru*, 7 October 2015. http://www.vesti.ru/doc.html?id=2672753#.

Zelizer, Barbie. "Reading the Past against the Grain: The Shape of Memory Studies." *Critical Studies in Mass Communication* 12, no. 2 (1995): 204–39.

Zhizhina, Nadezhda. "Eshche raz o teatral'nykh maskakh v gipsovom dekore bosforskikh dereviannykh sarkofagov I–II vekov." *Trudy istoricheskogo fakul'teta Sankt-Peterburgskogo universiteta* (2015). https://cyberleninka.ru/article/n/eschyo-raz-o-teatralnyh-maskah-v-gipsovom-dekore-bosporskih-derevyannyh-sarkofagov-i-ii-vekov.

Zverev, Aleksei. "Zakhar Prilepin: 'V Rossii proiskhodit to, o chem ia mechtaiu s 90-kh.'" *Kul'tura*, 1 October 2014. http://portal-kultura.ru/articles/books/63186-zakhar-prilepin-v-rossii-proiskhodit-to-o-chem-ya-mechtayu-s-90-kh/.

Zvonkine, Eugénie. "*Auteur* Cinema during the Thaw and Stagnation." In *A Companion to Russian Cinema*, ed. Birgit Beumers, 204–29. Malden: Wiley Blackwell, 2016.

INDEX

www.ingramcontent.com/pod-product-compliance
Lightning Source LLC
LaVergne TN
LVHW081250100826
845148LV00009B/1185

* 9 7 8 1 6 4 4 6 9 2 7 1 4 *